li by

offi

NSIGHT

y Jon Swain

THE SUNDAY TIMES
INVESTIGATES

• • • • • • •

Reporting that made history

Introduction by
Jonathan Calvert, Insight editor

Edited by
Madeleine Spence

Published by Times Books

An imprint of HarperCollins Publishers
Westerhill Road
Bishopbriggs
Glasgow G64 2QT
www.harpercollins.co.uk
times.books@harpercollins.co.uk

HarperCollins Publishers, 1st Floor,
Watermarque Building, Ringsend Road,
Dublin 4, Ireland

First edition 2021

The contents of this publication are
believed correct at the time of printing.
Nevertheless the publisher can accept no
responsibility for errors or omissions,
changes in the detail given or for any
expense or loss thereby caused.

A catalogue record for this book is
available from the British Library.

ISBN 978-0-00-846831-6

10 9 8 7 6 5 4 3 2 1

Typeset by Jouve, India

Cover graphic (background pattern)
© Milart/Shutterstock

Printed and bound in Great Britain by
CPI Group (UK) Ltd, Croydon, CR0 4YY

Our thanks and acknowledgements go
to Lily Carlton, Joanne Lovey and
Robin Ashton at News Syndication and,
in particular, at The Sunday Times,
Bob Tyrer, Madeleine Spence and
Jonathan Calvert and, at HarperCollins,
Jethro Lennox, Kevin Robbins and
Kerry Ferguson.

CONTENTS

INTRODUCTION

IT WAS the January of the big freeze, the Beatles were poised to release their second single and Cliff Richard's new film *Summer Holiday* was premiering at Leicester Square in London. Stepping out of the neatly polished vintage Bristol convertible into the ice-cold morning were three smartly dressed young men in their late twenties.

"We've been taken over by a bunch of Teddy boys," the newspaper's foreign editor was heard to remark haughtily as he peered from the window to see the three new recruits enter the multi-storey Thomson House building on Gray's Inn Road. The men were taken through the smoke-filled *Sunday Times* newsroom and shown their small "broom cupboard" office at the back of the editorial floor. They were there to break the mould and within months they would pioneer a new form of journalism, which would be so successful that it would inspire generations of investigative reporters for decades to come.

The date was Tuesday, January 8, 1963 and *The Sunday Times* was in a period of transformation and innovation under the editorship of Denis Hamilton, a former lieutenant-colonel who had won medals for bravery in the Second World War. The effects of post-war paper rationing were finally over and newspapers were fast gaining excess pages as they competed for new readers and advertisers. Many of the features that are so familiar in the modern-day *Sunday Times* were introduced at around that time. A new magazine colour supplement was added, followed by a stand-alone business section. But there was still plenty of space to fill as the newspaper expanded.

With this in mind, a few weeks earlier Hamilton had approached Clive Irving, the 29-year-old editor of *Topic* magazine, who had just returned from covering the Cuban missile crisis in New York. The magazine had been set up as a British version of *Newsweek* and Irving had been experimenting with a new style of long-form narrative journalism. But the project had been given no time to succeed because its publishers ran out of money and were forced to close down the magazine. After just ten weeks as editor, Irving was out of a job.

"We were sitting dejected in the office and I got this call from Denis Hamilton," he recounts. "And he said: 'I like what you have been doing, come here and do it for us and bring the two best people with you.' I did." So he turned up on that chilly Tuesday morning with his two colleagues from the ill-fated *Topic*: Jeremy Wallington and Ron Hall – then aged 27 and 28.

This was the first *Sunday Times* Insight team. The trio were a good fit, with complementary skills and attributes. Irving, an affable Londoner who had worked on the *Express* and *The Observer*, was a gifted writer who took charge as the team's editor. Hall, a Sheffield builder's son, who had studied maths at Cambridge University, added the intellectual ballast and rigour. He was a punctilious checker of Irving's copy and would pore over the typewritten script with his red pen, questioning minute details and assertions. The third member, Wallington, was a former grammar school boy from High Wycombe who was the owner of the Bristol convertible. Good-looking and personable with a sharp dress sense, Wallington would be dispatched to use his charm with interview subjects. One of their first tasks was to come up with a name for the team. "Insight" was their first idea but it was almost rejected. When Irving first suggested it, the newspaper's lawyer pointed out that there was already a medical specialist publication of that name. But the second suggestion "Scrutiny" was forcefully rejected by Hall because it reminded him of the word "scrotum". So, lacking any further inspiration, they persuaded the lawyer that it would be fine to use Insight. Such was the low-tech technology at the time, Irving actually hand-drew the first white-on-black Insight logo, which was then cut into a printer's block. The same hand-drawn logo went on to appear in the newspaper for four decades.

Initially, Insight wasn't really an investigation team at all. They were given two pages in the newspaper each week, which they were asked to fill with a narrative reconstruction of a major or little-appreciated event that had happened during the previous week. The intention was to add depth and analysis for readers who had more time to linger over the newspaper on a Sunday. The view was that Saturdays rarely produced the types of big breaking news stories that normally filled the daily newspapers so there needed to be a different way of telling the news on a Sunday. But Irving had greater ambitions for his team than to simply produce what he describes as the "analytic synoptic stuff". It would be their work on the unfolding scandal surrounding John Profumo, the Secretary of State for War, his affair with 19-year-old Christine Keeler and her links to a Russian spy that gave them the opportunity to adopt a more investigative style. They changed the way they worked and, in doing so, set up a template for the brand of journalism that will feature in this book.

*   *   *

In the early months of 1963 the Insight team had received a tip-off about the Profumo story from a well-connected socialite and they began amassing large amounts of information about the minister and his activities. Profumo was threatening to sue several European newspapers and the *Sunday Times* lawyer advised that the legal risks of running the story were too great. But the dam broke in early June, when Profumo confessed about his affair to the Cabinet Secretary and resigned. This gave the team the first real opportunity to show how an exposé could be written powerfully using their narrative story-telling techniques. Instead of just adding detail and analysis to the week's events, they were now breaking news. It was exactly the type of work that Irving had wanted to do when he first took the job and within weeks they moved on to produce their most famous early investigation. The slum landlord Peter Rachman had come to the team's attention as the protector of Mandy Rice-Davies, a showgirl who was also involved in the Profumo affair. Insight's investigations into Rachman revealed that he was using ruthless bullying tactics to oust tenants so he could subdivide the properties into smaller flats and rent them at higher prices. Many of the tenants were recent migrants from the West Indies on low wages. The story created waves. Not only did the name Rachman go down in history as a byword for a landlord exploiting tenants, but it also led to important reforms with the introduction of the 1965 Rent Act, which strengthened the protection given to tenants. That was the power of investigative journalism as a force for good.

It seems strange now looking back that other newspapers were not also doing this type of work. But investigations were generally viewed by broadsheet newspapers as a little grubby.

"The tabloids did basic muckraking – 'I made an excuse and left' stuff on brothels and naughty vicars – but it's important to realise that no quality broadsheet had ever practised investigative journalism," said Irving, now 88 years old and living in New York. "I soon realised we had a huge inherent advantage. The authority of the paper itself opened doors that would otherwise have been slammed shut. That helped in collecting really high-placed sources."

The success of Insight's early work led to a key change that would be crucial to the functioning of subsequent teams whose articles appear in this book. The team were given time to develop and research their own stories, free from what Irving once described as "the tyranny of the news cycle". They were no longer required to fill two pages a week and instead were given the space to investigate important stories over several months.

"An important part of this was that I said to Hamilton that I don't want any deadlines and I want to be left alone until I tell you that we have got the story. And I don't want to be forced to be doing news stories on it that actually weaken it, until we are sure we have got it all together and it is ready to run," Irving recalls. "And he astonishingly agreed to that." When occasionally Irving would be asked where Insight had got to with a particular investigation, he would reply: "It's in my secret box and it will come out when it is ready."

The team's news narrative style also required a different way of introducing their stories. Hard news had mostly been written in the same way. There would be a concise punchy first paragraph presenting the most gripping facts and then the rest of the information would unfold in descending order of importance. But Irving and Hall invented the classic Insight drop intro, which would become a regular and often-copied feature of the team's work over many years. Irving describes it pithily as "an oblique intro full of context and atmosphere, and length". The essence of the style is captured perfectly in an obituary of Hall by Magnus Linklater, a former senior editor at *The Sunday Times*.

According to Linklater, a typical Insight intro would run: "At 11.30 precisely, a steel-grey Mercedes 150 SL screeched to a halt outside the MI6 building in central London, and a small, squat figure emerged, a Havana cigar clenched between his teeth . . . ." He points out that Hall himself would mock the style and it was often parodied, particularly by the satirical magazine *Private Eye*, but it was nonetheless ground-breaking at the time. It is a style that still can be seen in many newspapers to this day.

Irving left Insight in 1964 when he was promoted to be the *Sunday Times*'s managing editor, news, and he took Wallington with him as his deputy. The pair would later move on to high-flying jobs in charge of current affairs at Granada and London Weekend Television. It was Hall who would be the standard-bearer for the style and ethos of the first team over the next 18 years – first as Insight editor and then as a senior editor on the newspaper. Such was the success of the team, that it spawned many imitators. Among the most notable was the *Boston Globe*'s similarly named Spotlight team, which was formed four years after Insight in 1967, and was made internationally famous by *Spotlight*, the 2015 Oscar-winning Hollywood film about its work exposing sexual abuse in the Catholic Church.

*   *   *

Over the years the Insight team has become unique in its longevity and has built a formidable reputation. It has now been producing award-winning stories for 58 years. No other newspaper or broadcaster has had a team of reporters consistently producing investigative stories over such a long time. It has remained at the core of *The Sunday Times* news section and it is an important and well-read brand for a newspaper that appreciates the vital role played by investigative journalism in a healthy functioning democracy. There are many awkward facts that the wealthy and the powerful would rather the newspaper's readers did not know. Power can be abused to hide crime, corruption, incompetence and moral hypocrisy. Investigative stories can nail the lies and bring the wrong-doing to the nation's attention in a way that corrects the wrongs, sparks political debate and opens the door to genuine change for the public good. It is time-consuming, expensive and painstaking work but it is a challenge the newspaper has never shirked. The stories in this book are a testament to this.

When reading this book, it should be noted that the dates given are when the articles first appeared, and some context has been added at the beginning of chapters and before some articles to explain the background to the events recounted. There is an index of people, places and events at the end of the book for quick reference. It is perhaps worth remembering that some of the articles were written 40 and 50 years ago, when views that might offend today were tolerated. The original language, style and format of the articles are as they appeared in the newspaper and have not been amended.

The book begins with the first major Insight story in the months after Harold Evans had become the editor of *The Sunday Times* in 1967: the unveiling of Kim Philby as a Soviet spy. Although there were no by-lines on articles of that era, much of the Philby work was done by two dogged young Australians, Bruce Page and Philip Knightley. They were given great encouragement by Evans, an editor who instantly understood the value of Insight's work and went on to rapidly expand the number of journalists working for the team. The staffing of Insight reached a peak of 17 reporters in the early seventies and some of their extraordinary work can be read in the pages that follow. It is fascinating to revisit the team's forensic dismantling of the official version of the 1972 Bloody Sunday massacre by British troops in Londonderry. More than 250 witnesses were interviewed in just a few weeks and the resulting account became the blueprint for the reinvestigation of Bloody Sunday by Lord Saville, whose findings led in 2010 to an apology by the British Government to the families of the dead. At the same time, the team were still working on its famous long-running campaign on behalf of victims of the thalidomide drug. The stories, which are reprinted here, are still held up in journalism colleges today as an object lesson in how the power of the press can be harnessed to fight injustice.

In the late seventies, the Insight team led by Paul Eddy spent two years researching the design flaw underlying the crash of a Turkish Airlines DC-10 outside Paris. It is remarkable now to look back on how they were able to reconstruct the tragedy with such detail, as well as uncovering fresh evidence that the accident could have been avoided. Moving on to the eighties, the foreign correspondent Jon Swain won Reporter of the Year for his work exposing the Libyan connection to the Miners' Strike in 1984 – the first big Insight story under the new editor Andrew Neil. This was followed by probably the most jaw-dropping of all Insight's investigations. In 1986, the Insight journalist Peter Hounam revealed photos and detailed diagrams of Israel's previously unconfirmed weapons programme. It was a story which highlighted the extraordinary risks sometimes taken by whistleblowers and their bravery in helping draw significant matters of concern to the public's attention. The whistleblower in this story paid a heavy price. He was an Israeli nuclear technician called Mordechai Vanunu and he was being protected by Insight journalists in the UK. But he left his safe house in the UK to join an attractive American woman in Italy, not knowing that she was a Mossad agent. When they reached their hotel room, he was drugged and captured by Mossad agents. He was then taken by boat to Israel, where he served 27 years in jail and to this day is forbidden from talking to journalists.

I was only too aware that I was walking in the footsteps of giants when I first joined the Insight team in late 1993. The team's work was awe-inspiring for a young journalist who avidly read *The Sunday*

Times while working on investigations on a much smaller scale for a regional newspaper. The team I joined actually bore some similarity to the original 1963 trio. Maurice Chittenden was the team's editor. He possessed a cheeky charm and wore pinstripe suits long after they had gone out of fashion but he was also, like Irving, a superb writer. He was more than ably assisted by his deputy Mark Skipworth who, like Hall, was the intellectual driving force – as well as being obsessively hard-working, full of ideas and always on top of the detail. The team also had a fourth member: Randeep Ramesh, a very able and super-bright young Cambridge graduate fresh out of university. I was given the Wallington role of going out and doing the legwork.

Our first major story proved to be one of the biggest of the decade. We had been asked by Neil, who was in his last weeks as editor, to look into allegations he had picked up over lunch with the Harrods owner Mohammed Fayed that members of parliament could be hired to ask questions in parliament. After a long period of research – during which John Witherow took over as editor – we decided to go undercover to find out whether the allegations were true. I bought a cream summer jacket and went to meet MPs, pretending to be an investor seeking commercial advantage by paying MPs £1,000 to ask a question in the House of Commons. The resulting "Cash for Questions" scandal caused an uproar far greater than we had ever imagined when we first wrote the story. It heavily damaged John Major's Conservative government, which became mired in "sleaze" allegations and ultimately led to the formation of the Nolan Committee, which laid down a new ethical code for all public officials that is still in force today. It also resulted in a job offer from *The Observer* to become its investigations editor, which I took. I returned to *The Sunday Times* just as Insight editor Stephen Grey and a long cast of talented reporters were painstakingly piecing together the events that led to the 9/11 attacks in 2001. Their long and detailed reports, published over several weeks, were one of the great examples of journalism being a first draft of history and have been reproduced in this book.

I finally became the Insight editor in 2005 and have been so ever since. It is simply one of the best jobs in journalism, in my opinion. When I spoke to Irving in preparation for this Introduction, I was struck by how the template they created all those years ago had survived the years. If anything, the narrative form has become even more important, especially as the internet is ideal for longer reads unfettered by the limited space in printed newspapers. One of the main differences, of course, is that we have instant access to vastly more information through computers. As a result, the modern Insight teams have been comparatively lean, with two permanent members – although we are often ably assisted by our colleagues in the newsroom. We have been given freedom and time to work on our stories by a succession of editors from Witherow to Martin Ivens and now Emma Tucker.

The people who have made it a success over the last 16 years are four of the most brilliant and talented journalists still writing today – all award winners many times over. Since 2005 I have worked alongside Claire Newell (until 2011) and Heidi Blake (until 2015), who both went on to head their own investigative teams. They produced many well-known stories while part of the Insight team during those years, including the two famous investigations into Fifa, world football's governing body, which can be read in the later chapters. Since 2015 the deputy Insight editor has been George Arbuthnott and we have become inseparable as work colleagues. For a while, we did have a team of three, when the newspaper's current northern editor, David Collins, was at Insight between 2015 and 2017. Together we did the Doping Scandal and the SAS war crimes investigations, which have also been included in this book.

The final selections are from our most recent work on the pandemic, which formed the basis of a book entitled *Failures of State*, which I wrote with George and which was published in March 2021 by HarperCollins. They were stories that proved that, 58 years on, the narrative exposé form is still a powerful draw for readers. Our first article in the series "38 days when Britain sleepwalked into disaster" was the most read online article in *The Sunday Times*'s and *Times*'s history.

Jonathan Calvert, Insight editor

THE SUNDAY TIMES INVESTIGATES: REPORTING THAT MADE HISTORY

1967
THE THIRD MAN: THE
TALE OF KIM PHILBY

In 1967, Insight revealed that Kim Philby, the former head of the Soviet Section of the British Secret Intelligence Services (SIS, now MI6), was himself a Soviet spy. It was one of the most catastrophic failures in the history of the Intelligence Services, and the British establishment had for years attempted to keep it a secret.

When British spies Guy Burgess and Donald Maclean defected to the Soviet Union in 1951, revealing themselves to be double agents, suspicion immediately fell on their colleague Kim Philby. It was clear the men had been tipped off by a third double agent within British intelligence, and Philby – as a contact of both – was the obvious choice. Yet, the establishment was quick to clear his name and keep him in its ranks.

Then, in 1963, Philby vanished, only to resurface in Moscow. Even after his defection, he was never officially acknowledged to have worked in SIS, let alone to have been a figure of such importance. Only a handful of politicians and intelligence insiders had been allowed to know the embarrassing truth: that the man put in charge of spying on the Soviets was actually working for them. That was until The Sunday Times began pulling at the Philby thread. Few could have expected the story that would eventually unravel.

Over the course of three articles, Insight chart for the first time the life story of Kim Philby: his arrival at Cambridge University in 1929, his recruitment by the Soviet Union in 1933, his penetration of SIS in 1940, and his rise to Soviet Section chief in 1944. They survey the damage Philby exacted on his colleagues in the intelligence community throughout his time as chief, and, finally, pick apart the story behind his eventual downfall and defection to the Soviet Union in 1963.

THE PHILBY CONSPIRACY

8 October 1967

PHILBY'S ACHIEVEMENT in becoming head of the Soviet section of the British Secret Intelligence Service, whilst himself being a Soviet agent, was surely the greatest professional coup in the twisted history of the espionage business.

It is true that Philby went on to higher things when he became the linkman between the Secret Intelligence Service and the American Central Intelligence Agency. In that position, he could give his Soviet spymasters thorough general knowledge of the operations of both the major Western intelligence organisations.

But there is a classic quality about the earlier achievement. The selection in 1944 of Philby, a Soviet agent of more than ten years' standing, as the right man to conceive, build up and control a new British operation against the Russians is an event embodying the purest essence of espionage.

Why was Philby able to do it? He was, of course, superbly equipped for the role of a spy: in fact, he deployed during his career a surprising number of the spectacular personal qualities which are usually attached to spies in fiction.

His pistol-shooting was excellent. His mind was swift and clear, and his nerves were extremely strong. Despite some powerful drinking, he remained physically very tough and resilient.

He was also extremely attractive to women. It might seem possible actually to pin the Bond image on him – but for such awkward facts as his noticeably inelegant dress, and his lack of interest in the glamorous ornaments of life. (Far from being the sort of man who calls imperiously for Tattinger *Blanc des Blancs*, he was well known for his readiness to drink anything from raki to cooking bitter.)

But far above all those qualities, he had a capacity to disguise his feelings and intentions. This is the crucial professional attribute of a spy, and Philby possessed it to an amazing degree. For thirty years he lived as a passionate Communist behind the facade of a middle-class Englishman with Liberal-to-Conservative opinions. And those years were spent in journalism and intelligence: work in which political discussion in some detail is a frequently unavoidable duty.

Even with hindsight, it is almost impossible to find chinks in the mask that Kim Philby put on when he was twenty-two. There are one or two clues to its existence: his writing, for instance, is careful and restrained, with little sign of pleasure or eloquence.

Another point is that people who knew Philby, interviewed separately, report a central impression about his character in strikingly similar terms. They describe an elusive sense of distance or remoteness: of not being able to quite engage with Philby's mind. "One had the sensation," says a wartime colleague, "of a set of very flexible but tough and quite tireless defences at work."

Those defences were possibly tiring during the last days in Beirut, just before his defection to Russia in 1963. He had then been, like John le Carré's hero, "out in the cold" for a long time. Philby's third wife, Eleanor, has told friends of moments when Kim would start up in the night and stammer the beginnings of what sounded like a cry for help. But apart from that there is scarcely a suggestion of the mask slipping, apart from a small wartime incident recounted by Hugh Trevor-Roper, now Regius Professor of Modern History at Oxford.

Trevor-Roper accidentally met Philby one day in the war and over a drink they began discussing historical analysis. The discussion was just warming up when Philby declared abruptly and with great force: "Of course, when it comes to historical analysis, there is nothing that compares for a moment with Marx's *Eighteenth Brumaire of Louis Napoleon.*"

For a moment, Trevor-Roper had a sense of being engaged with Philby's real "intellectual persona". But the guard returned at once.

It is, of course, a question whether Philby could have kept up his cover for thirty years had he been forced to spend more time in first-class intellectual company. But he did not have to: and that is the crucial point about his career.

It was the ineptitude of the British service then which made his career possible. The Buchanesque, clubman's Secret Intelligence Service which recruited Philby in the forties might have been designed to be brought down by a man like him. The only comfort to be extracted from the debacle is the fact that Philby's depredations were the essential cause of the massive reform of the service which took place in the late fifties and early sixties.

Because its decrepit bureaucracy was protected by layers of official mystery, the SIS was even less prepared than any other section of the British establishment for the rigours of mid-twentieth-century existence. The Service was a caricature of the establishment: which is why this story of espionage becomes a kind of social document. It is an account of a great breach that opened up in the defences of a class, and therefore of the defences of the nation whose interests that class conceived itself to be protecting.

How Philby's family was alienated

The circumstances of Philby's birth, on New Year's Day, 1912, are rich in ironies and allusions which resonate throughout his later years. He was born at Amballa in India, under the British Raj, whose administrators displayed in exceptionally pure form those British middle-class virtues which the adult Philby secretly despised.

But more important was the fact that India had then been for many years a vital area of British intelligence endeavour. This was aimed at charting the political currents moving through the vast mass of the Indian population, and at guarding against the "threat from the North" – from Tsarist Russia – which never came. Three decades later, the Indian connection, and the patronage of an ex-Indian Intelligence superior in the SIS, gave crucial impetus to the process by which Philby gained leadership of the anti-Soviet department.

Intelligence work is, of course, the central theme of one of Rudyard Kipling's most potent pieces of myth-making. His novel *Kim*, in which a brilliant half-English boy who grows up as an Indian is promoted by taciturn sahibs into a romantic conception of espionage.

"Even Lurgan's impassive face changed. He considered the years to come, when Kim would have been entered and made to the Great Game that never ceases day and night . . . He foresaw honour and credit in the mouths of the chosen few, coming to him from his pupil."

It seems an almost unbearable coincidence that Philby, named Harold Adrian Russell by his parents, should have played with Indian children and acquired, irremovably, the name Kim.

The father, Harry St John Bridger Philby, was at the time of Kim's birth an officer of the Indian Civil Service – but a distinctly eccentric one. It is not possible to understand the character of the Soviet super-spy without reference to the character of his father.

St John (or "Jack") Philby was one of those people like Thomas Doughty, T. E. Lawrence and – most recently – Wilfred Thesiger, who could scarcely be anything but products of middle-class England, but who rejected its ordered virtues for the passionate, egotistic culture of the Arabian deserts.

British Middle Eastern policy during the first world war sharply decreased St John's affection for his native land. As an Arabist, St John was caught up in the attempts to promote Arab revolution against Germany's Turkish allies. Sent on a mission to Ibn Saud, St John became a close friend of that courageous, intolerant, hospitable monarch: certainly he fell in with the Arab belief that Britain reneged on her promises once the war was won.

St John reacted more passionately than most of the British Arabists who believed that their country had behaved disgracefully. He more or less washed his hands of Britain, and withdrew to Saudi Arabia, where in the years between the wars he made his famous penetrations of the deadly and mysterious deserts of the Empty Quarter.

St John's remarkable capacity to assume the mantle of an alien culture culminated in his becoming a Muslim, and adding a Muslim wife to his English wife Dora. This was Umferhat, a former slave-girl by whom he had two sons.

He retained, however, numerous English links, such as membership of his London club (the Umferhat exploit led to his being labelled "the polygamous pillar of the Athenaeum"). And then, when he returned to Britain at the onset of the second world war, he was imprisoned under Regulation 18b, the famous mechanism for dealing with potential Nazi sympathisers.

The reason for St John's fairly brief detention was the fact that he had advised his old friend Ibn Saud that Britain was unlikely to do well in the coming war. The precise extent of his anti-British feeling is hard to chart: friends minimise it, but Alison Outhwaite, a journalistic colleague of Kim Philby's, recalls St John in wartime exulting over the prospect of the effete British being vanquished and sanitised by "the new Romans".

Certainly, St John cautioned Kim vigorously against accepting the values or trusting the good faith of the English establishment.

The relationship between Kim and St John was often stormy, but there is no doubt that a strong emotional bond existed. St John's most frequent advice to his son seems to have been "get your facts right and clear" and then to "always go through to the end with whatever you think right, no matter what it is".

Kim was at his father's bedside when the old man died in Beirut in 1961. St John's last words, worthy of any deathbed anthology, were: "God, I'm bored."

Cambridge: a hardening of resolve

In 1929 Kim Philby went up to Cambridge: like his father, to Trinity, the largest and most distinguished college in the University. He was seventeen, and an Exhibitioner from Westminster School. He was a well-knit, fair-haired youth, with something of a stammer. He was rather reserved, and upright to the point of being puritanical.

Guy Burgess, although a year older than Kim, did not arrive at Trinity from Eton until 1930. Donald Maclean arrived at his smaller, duller college, Trinity Hall, in 1931.

Philby did not start at Cambridge as a Communist. (When in the sixth form at Westminster, he went on holiday to Spain and returned with a strong romantic attachment to the Spanish Royalists.) But he swiftly moved leftwards. John Midgely, a Trinity contemporary, remembers campaigning with Kim Philby for the Labour Party in the 1931 General Election. "My friends," Philby used to begin his standard speech, "the heart of England does not beat in stately homes and castles. It beats in the factories and on the farms."

There was no question, though, of his being swept up in a public wave of Left-wing fervour. Philby went down in 1933, when Socialists and Communists were still a small, scattered underground in conservative Cambridge. It was, in fact, the watershed year. Burgess and Maclean both stayed on into that brief era of ideological commitment at the universities, which forms so big a part of the thirties legend. (There is Burgess using a car as a battering-ram during a vigorous brawl which accompanied an anti-war demonstration. There is Maclean defining reality in Cambridge Left as "the economic situation, the unemployed, vulgarity in the cinema, rubbish on the bookstalls, the public schools, snobbery in the suburbs, more battleships, lower wages . . . and the rising tide of opinion which is going to sweep away the whole crack-brained mess . . . ")

Philby's movement away from the moderate Socialism of 1931 was a more private operation, but (possibly accelerated by Ramsay MacDonald's "betrayal" after 1931) it was conducted with a dispatch which alarmed some people. A Westminster contemporary who went to Oxford recalls going over to the Cambridge Union to debate some such issue as "The Class War is Inevitable". Lunching in Kim's rooms, this man was startled by how vehemently Left-wing Philby had become. "Almost everyone was to some degree left. But Kim I would have said was a fellow-traveller at least."

Philby did not acquire a brilliant academic record: it took him four years to scrape a modest BA in history. But he did acquire a lifelong affection for Guy Burgess, who was also reading history, but to much more spectacular effect. Goronwy Rees, one of Burgess's closest friends, claims that there was some homosexual element in the Burgess/Philby friendship. If this was really so, it could scarcely have been crucial, because the friendship survived into years when Philby was most demonstrably heterosexual. And the platonic friendship between Rees himself and Burgess demonstrates Burgess did not always seduce his friends.

Philby was quiet, even obscure, but Burgess was "the most brilliant undergraduate of his generation" (Rees). Guy was a large, flamboyant fish in one of the larger social ponds. This also contained, at various times, people like Victor (now Lord) Rothschild and Anthony Blunt (now Sir Anthony, Keeper of the Queen's Pictures), later important denizens of the wartime "secret world"; the future diplomat F. E. Hovell-Thurlow-Cumming-Bruce, said by the *Trinity Magazine* to "sing the Red Flag in his bath"; James Klugman, a brilliant literary historian, wartime officer of Special Operations Executive, and long-standing Communist Party warhorse ("Hairy chest" is the *Trinity Magazine*'s cryptic comment on him); and John Cornford, the poet who died in the Spanish Civil War.

The temper of this Trinity-based society was Leftish, but by no means as earnestly so as might be thought. (Of those mentioned, only Burgess, Klugman and Cornford were Communists.) For instance, in the week the Hunger Marchers reached Cambridge in 1934, the university newspaper *Varsity* had as its main story an amusing interview with an all-in wrestler.

Before he left Cambridge, Philby was already acquiring knowledge of a harsher world: in vacations, he had begun travelling in Eastern and Central Europe. The journeys, often made by motorcycle, extended after he went down in summer 1933 into a stay of several months in Germany and Austria.

It was these journeys in the early days of the Nazi terror which hardened Philby's resolve, made him a determined Communist, and led eventually to his recruitment as an agent. A frequent companion of his was a Westminster school friend, Ian – later to figure importantly in the story. Ian, although he admired Philby enormously, avoided emulating his hero's conversion to Communism.

A few months after he left Cambridge, when he was still short of his twenty-third birthday, Philby was given his lifetime task: to penetrate British Intelligence. There can be virtually no doubt about the date: every piece of objective evidence available points to this period in late 1933. And it coincides with the accounts Philby has given to his children, visiting him in Moscow since the defection.

The façade of Philby and Burgess

On February 24, 1934, Philby married in Vienna an Austrian Jewish girl eighteen months older than himself. This was Alice Friedmann, already a divorcee, the daughter of a minor official named Israel Kohlman. "Litze", as she was usually known, was a dark, gypsy-like girl. She was a passionate Communist: today, married for the third time, she lives in East Berlin.

Shortly after his marriage, Philby was in London working at his first job in journalism, as a £4-a-week sub-editor on a dying liberal magazine named the *Review of Reviews*. From now on, both he and Litze scrupulously avoid betraying their Communist sympathies. The next five years of Philby's life are to be spent obscuring his left-wing past beneath a right-wing camouflage. Philby did not move precipitately, to judge by the impression his colleagues had of his politics. Both Alison Outhwaite, who also worked on the *Review*, and Sir Roger Chance, his editor, assumed he was a Labour Party man. Miss Outhwaite often wondered why Philby was prepared to stay in such a dead-end job. He seemed deeply reserved, but on one occasion when she pressed him about this subject, he replied: "What does it matter? I'll be in the trenches in a few years, anyway."

Obviously, an excellent way to insulate oneself against charges of Communism was to condone Adolf Hitler's National Socialist regime. A fairly convenient body existed through which this could be done: the Anglo-German Fellowship, which was used at various times by both Burgess and Philby.

Veterans of the Fellowship differ about the degree to which membership implied *approval* – if at all – of Hitler's rougher tactics. They also differ on the precise point in the unfolding of the European tragedy at which membership of the Fellowship became insupportable: although, of course, unanimity on this point was achieved in September 1939. However, there was never much doubt about the staunch anti-Communism of the organisation, which was reinforced in Philby's day on occasions like Ribbentrop's 1936 address on the need to keep down the "Komintern".

Burgess went about constructing a right-wing facade in roughly the same manner as Philby, but naturally brought markedly less discretion to the task. By the latter 1930s most of his acquaintances had heard vague whispers that he was a Communist agent: the whispers resulted from the rather incomplete secrecy in which Guy attempted to recruit people.

In 1937, he tried to persuade the writer Goronwy Rees to join up. They had known each other since undergraduate days (Rees at Oxford, Burgess at Cambridge) but had drifted apart. And then suddenly "Guy popped up once more". Today, Rees wonders whether Guy sought him out.

Their friendship became fairly close again, and one day Guy announced "with a good deal of weight and seriousness" that he was a Comintern agent. Burgess said Rees must not ask him questions, because he was "sworn to secrecy", but volunteered the fact that he was a political agent. He went on to say that his greatest coup had been to seduce and extract information from that bisexual M. Pfeiffer, an aide of the French war minister (later Premier) Daladier.

Rees declined to join Burgess in the work, and in fact became so agitated about the matter that he confided in the novelist Rosamond Lehmann. Various distorted echoes of this incident reverberated around London for years to come.

Presumably during his brief period as secretary to Captain J. R. J. Macnamara, the Tory MP for Chelmsford (with whom he attended the Berlin Olympics), Burgess got to know Sir Joseph Ball. Ball, an ex-MI5 man, and paymaster in the Zinoviev Letter scandal, was then Chamberlain's *éminence grise* in Tory Central Office: a hardened and ruthless intriguer.

Because of this connection, Burgess seems to have got into the thick of the pro-appeasement intrigues, which Ball launched on Chamberlain's behalf in the winter of 1937/38. But by that time Philby, in Spain, was already set for greater things.

Times job: toeing the Franco line

Going to the Franco side of the Spanish war was good for Philby's right-wing image. Getting a job as a *Times* correspondent was good preparation for penetrating British intelligence: between the wars, one or two *Times* correspondents had been recruited into the Secret Intelligence Service without the Editor's knowledge.

Philby arrived in February 1937 with an introduction from a D. F. L. Towers, of London General Press. This was a small-time agency which does not normally dispatch war correspondents. It seems that 25-year-old Philby was trying hard, because he was calling himself "*Times* correspondent", which he didn't become until May, after getting a "spec" article accepted.

In later years in Moscow, Philby said: "I wouldn't have lasted a week in Spain without behaving like a Fascist." One of the first things he did in the hot summer of 1937 was to acquire a Royalist mistress ten years older than himself. This was Lady (Frances) Lindsay-Hogg, a divorcée, formerly a middling-bright star of the London stage under the name "Bunny" Doble.

She says that Kim was "of middle height, more fair than dark, with wide-open blue eyes and a dreadful stammer". It is intriguing that the fairly mild stammer of Trinity days should have worsened: something that can readily be seen as the result of increased inner tension with Philby's cover coming under test.

It was, she says, Kim's "sincerity" that she found most appealing. They rarely discussed politics, but Frances seems to have assumed that his ideas at least did not clash with hers – which were romantic and far to the Right. She says he spoke little of himself, but often and with deep affection of his father.

Kim and Frances remained "liado", as the Spanish say, until the end of the war in 1939, when they parted painlessly and on good terms. Frances knew of the marriage to Litze: Kim gave her to understand it had drifted apart.

The Kim-Frances relationship had an odd sequel in the early fifties. Frances visited the Philby family in London not long after the Burgess and Maclean scandal, and Philby's withdrawal from Washington. Despite the fact that Frances was quite uninterested, and had scarcely read the newspapers, Kim insisted on telling her all about his "shock and surprise" at the news that Burgess had fled to Moscow.

Frances is puzzled in retrospect now that Philby himself is in Moscow. "It seems to show the most extraordinary duplicity," she says. But somehow, her basic view of his character remains unaltered.

Franco's Press officers, conservative and Catholic Spaniards, remember Philby as "objective" and "a gentleman". They all liked him – except for an unorthodox officer named Manuel Lambarri, who says that Philby "built a wall between himself and everybody else".

The reports which the young man sent to *The Times* were meticulous, but not hugely exciting, and they never gave Franco's men the slightest cause for complaint. Here is a sample from August 26, 1937:

"Santander fell to the Nationalists today, and troops of the Legionary Division of the Twentieth of March entered the city in triumph. . . . Part of the column was formed of captured militiamen, who added a Roman flavour to the triumph. The enthusiasm of the populace lining the streets was unmistakably genuine. . . . "

On occasion, his reporting went further than this down the Franco line. Indeed, early in 1939 the Spanish Republican office in London complained bitterly to *The Times* that Philby was writing Franco propaganda. The suggestion that Philby "overcorrected" from time to time is strengthened by the claim of Karl Robson, then of the *Daily Telegraph*, that Kim was "more pro-Fascist than he needed to be".

A narrow escape – and a medal

The recollections of most of the Englishmen who met Philby in Spain would jibe fairly well with that of his Trinity contemporary Peter Kemp, a volunteer officer in Franco's army. Kemp recalls an agreeable but slightly distant companion, who generally restricted his conversation about the war to technical military considerations.

But to Karl Robson, who shared a room with him for some time, Philby set out a view of politics in some detail – one which amounts to a mirror-reversal of what must have been his genuine views.

Philby complained that the British understood neither the Spaniards' point of view nor their mentality, and that this was one of their difficulties in dealing with the Spanish situation. He argued that Communism was the coming world power, and that all that mattered was to resist it. China, he said, would turn Communist and join with Russia to become the most important single political factor in the world.

One curious point is that many people who knew the man thirty years ago declare at first that he was a quiet and entirely unmemorable person. But questioned, they remember in surprising detail. Lord St Oswald (Rowland Winn), who was another journalist in Spain, believes there was "a certain power in Philby's personality which was not apparent at the time".

A second oddity was noted by Enrique Marsans, a Spanish conducting officer who worked with Kim. Marsans found him rather uncompetitive. "He never fought for his own way, or resorted to ruses to obtain good copy, like the others," says Marsans. It is worth remembering that the secret agent, once he has taken his place in the secret world, is largely relieved of the need to compete in the open world. Already, he has "honour and respect in the mouths of the chosen few".

On New Year's Eve 1937 the war put Philby's physical courage sharply to test. In a freezing dawn, several cars left the Grand Hotel, Saragossa, to take reporters to the important battle for Teruel. Nearing the lines, the convoy drew up in the bleak main square of a village named Caude, and waited for news of the best vantage-point.

In one car, Philby sat talking with Dick Sheepshanks, a brilliant young Etonian from Reuters, and two Americans, Ed Neil and Bradish Johnson. A shell had just fallen, almost unnoticed, half a mile away.

Suddenly, there was a violent explosion: Philby's car had caught the full impact of a shell. When rescuers forced the door open, Johnson fell out dead with a gaping wound in his back. Sheepshanks, unconscious, was dying of wounds in his face and head. Neil's leg was broken in two places: he had numerous shrapnel wounds, which caused his death two days later from gangrene.

Philby was stunned. After slight head and wrist wounds had been dressed, he rejoined the convoy: he was, says Ignacio Lamadrid, "sad but serene". Frances has a vivid memory of Philby's return to the base-town with his head in bandages, wearing sandals and a blue, mangy woman's coat reaching down to his knees. "His hands were shaking," she says, "but his mind was absolutely clear."

On January 2, when Neil died, Philby sent a cool dispatch about the death of his companions. "Your Correspondent," he wrote, "who was in the car, escaped with light wounds and has recovered." The shell, it turned out, was from a Russian gun, a 12.40cm, known in the war as a "quarter to one". The fact that his Soviet friends had nearly killed him may well have moved his sense of humour: he was certainly moved in some way on March 2 when Franco personally awarded him the Red Cross of Military Merit. (There were posthumous medals for the dead reporters.) According to Frances, Philby returned from the ceremony "exhausted with emotion", which she puts down to his being "sensible of the high honour done him".

When the war ended, Philby had completed two years as an under-cover Communist in Franco's camp. Was he already spying? There are two bits of evidence: one is that an officer named Pedro Giro recalls that in a cafe in Salamanca a German agent passed a note to Giro with a warning against two men then in the cafe. According to the German, these men were British agents. Twice subsequently Giro saw Philby locked in conversation with the same two men.

Another point was noticed by Sam Pope Brewer, an American journalist (whose wife, Eleanor, Philby was to acquire twenty years later in Beirut). At Press conferences, Kim was always the last questioner: the man who wanted to know *just* which regiment had made *just* which move. It was detail that could hardly be retailed to the readers, even of a newspaper of record. However, it was detail of the sort that might fairly easily be retailed to intelligence men.

The likeliest thing at this point would be that Philby, anxious to ingratiate himself with British intelligence men, was collecting and passing on any titbits that he could get.

The initial penetration into SIS

When the British Expeditionary Force left for France to commence the war on Hitler, Kim Philby went with them as *The Times*'s No. 1 war correspondent. He was now a moderately distinguished young man, although not popular with all his colleagues. It was one period of his life when the famous Philby charm did not quite come off.

The Times's No. 2, Bob Cooper, thought Philby a wild, slightly drunken and rather brutal young man. Kim, it seems, was addicted to a curious bar game which involved busting people's knuckles. Also, as in Spain, he was rather conspicuously "liado" with a girl, this time Lady Margaret Vane-Tempest-Stewart; somehow, once again, the other correspondents couldn't find time for such diversions.

William Forrest, the Daily Mail correspondent (then a recent ex-Communist who had covered the Spanish war from the Republican side) merely thought Philby was unpleasantly pro-Fascist. He was wearing the Franco decoration on his war-correspondent's uniform.

Philby spent most of his time in the less potentially demanding company of Bernard "Potato" Grey, a tough, amiable and apolitical Daily Mirror man. They put in a lot of serious drinking, in between trying to "stand up" entirely insupportable stories of the true Phoney War stamp (the classic was a rumour about a girl masquerading as a squaddie after volunteering out of patriotism). One of Kim's dispatches begins, in weariest cable-ese: "TIDE-WAR ONROLLS. . . . "

Summer 1940, and the Dunkirk disaster brought Philby back to London. And at last, the conditions were ready for his crucial penetration of British intelligence.

These conditions were rather well illustrated by the circumstances of the house at No. 5 Bentinck Street, where old friend Guy Burgess was living (with his collection of whips), and where Philby spent a good many nights over the next nine months or so. The place was, says Kenneth Younger, who was then in MI5, "a bit of a joke in intelligence circles".

This appears to have been quite an understatement. The house accommodated, in various ways, a remarkable sample of the staffs of the two major British secret departments. The house also accommodated regularly, or received at parties, an assortment of hangers-on of the people engaged in secret work. Some of this coterie were homosexuals, and one or two at least were mighty drinkers. Burgess had by now thrown aside his pro-Fascist cover and was again talking a pyrotechnic streak of Marxism, as was a regular visitor, the Swiss journalist Eric Kessler.

The house was once occupied by Victor Rothschild, then in MI5. He still came occasionally to dinner but the most regular inhabitant was Burgess, who since early 1939 had, rather amazingly, been a member of one of the sub-departments of SIS.

Anthony Blunt, the art historian, who had left the Warburg Institute to join MI5, was a resident. Teresa Mayor, Rothschild's present wife, and his assistant in secret counter-sabotage work, stayed from time to time. Guy Liddell, one of the most brilliant operators in MI5, was a visitor, and so was Desmond Vesey, another MI5 official. Two of Guy Burgess's intimate friends, Jack Hewitt and Peter Pollock, spent time at Bentinck Street. Both were used from time to time to do odd jobs for the security service.

What would J. Edgar Hoover have made of it all? Presumably no damage was done to the crusade against Hitler, but the Bentinck Street set-up seems a remarkable off-duty rendezvous for so many members of the secret departments. In retrospect, it seems that the passage through the Bentinck Street establishment of the Communist super-spy, Philby, was almost the least remarkable event to occur there in the early forties.

Philby's accession to secret work did something to countervail the rather strong MI5 bias of the Bentinck Street establishment. Almost immediately after his return from France, he was taken into the same part of the SIS as Guy Burgess: Department D. This department was concerned with sabotage, subversion and propaganda, as against information-getting. Philby's particular job was lecturing on propaganda-leaflet technique.

At the beginning of 1941 Department D was liquidated, and its function taken over by the new Special Operations Executive. Philby was taken into SOE to be trained as an agent: but abortively. He performed brilliantly in training for unarmed combat, small arms, demolition and survival. But in the end, it was decided that because of his stammer, and the fact that his work in Spain had made him known to a great many German military people, it would be suicidal to send him into Occupied Europe as an SOE agent.

And so, in the summer of 1941, after a year in these peripheral departments of the "secret world", Philby was recruited for work in the Secret Intelligence Service itself. He was asked to join Section V of the SIS: it was the real penetration.

The bizarre set-up of Colonel Menzies

What was the nature of the world which Kim Philby was now on the brink of entering? To understand how he, a committed Communist of eight years' standing, managed to penetrate MI6, it is essential to understand the particular quality of that organisation's susceptibility then: its improbable leaders, its bizarre recruiting policies, its uneasy relations with the rest of the intelligence community.

MI5, or the Security Service, was and is responsible for counter-espionage in Britain and the colonies, with the Special Branch under it. MI6, otherwise known as the Secret Intelligence Service (SIS), was and is concerned with espionage and counter-espionage in foreign countries.

Since the palmy days of the first world war they had both suffered a severe contraction. Their most durable attribute – apart from their unbroken tradition of strong military leadership – had proved to be the powerful spirit of mutual rivalry which had attended their creation.

The director of MI5 was still, remarkably, Colonel Sir Vernon Kell. Kell, an Army veteran of the Boxer Uprising, had set up and run MI5 since 1909. In the early years he had fended off a bid for control from the Navy, and it was this tussle which led directly to the creation of SIS half-way through the 1914–18 war.

This was when foreign operations were discerned to be different in nature from internal security. They were handed over to the Navy's candidate for Kell's job, Captain Mansfield Cumming.

Something of the flavour of those Buchanesque days, when the directors handled the big operations personally, is captured in the story of a visit which Kell and Cumming paid to Paris. The head of the deuxième bureau had informed them that he had found a man from Schleswig who had full details on the German answer to the *Dreadnought*.

A hotel rendezvous was fixed, and Cumming, searching the foyer for his contact, found a very agitated fellow who produced the password. He pushed him into the room where Kell was waiting, where the informant promptly dropped dead before being able to give his news. On seeing Kell, he had been seized with a heart attack, brought on by sheer terror at the mask which the director of MI5, in his mania for security, had put over his face.

By 1939, Kell was a very old man running an outfit whose principal occupation for the past twenty years had been spasmodic tracking-down of the Bolshevik menace.

His men were better suited for this than for the looming European war. They had been recruited almost exclusively from the Indian Police. As such, they had several strong attractions for a department with a minute budget and limited work. Since the subcontinent was, with the Bolsheviks, the main focus of British security work, they had that rare advantage, experience in the field. They were also pensioned, reliable and unlikely to disturb the calm of the organisation.

SIS was scarcely less moribund. Just before the war, the incumbent "C", Admiral Sir Hugh Sinclair, died and there was a reshuffle at the top, but this did not alter the prevailing atmosphere.

The new C was Colonel Stewart Menzies, an Old Etonian who had served in action with the Guards during the first world war and then gone into secret work. The immediate effect of his promotion was a redoubling of an internal feud, mainly between his two chief lieutenants, Colonel Claud Dansey and Colonel Valentine Vivian. Dansey had virtually run the secret service during Sinclair's declining years and confidently expected to succeed him. But Menzies fobbed him off with the new title of Vice-Chief of the service, somewhat below the new Deputy Chief, Vivian.

Vivian, who was to feature more prominently than anyone else in Philby's rise to power, was another effective officer and politician, well-loved by at least some of his staff who knew him affectionately as Vee-Vee. He is the original of "Colonel V" in Compton Mackenzie's novel *Water on the Brain* – a portrayal for which Mackenzie was successfully sued.

In the wartime history of SIS what really mattered was that it escaped any basic reconstruction. By the end of 1940, after the comfortable self-deceptions of the phoney war, two great reforms had been imposed on the rest of the intelligence community. In SIS, thanks partly to Menzies's political agility, partly to the self-generating mystique of the operation, nothing seriously changed.

The first reform, the construction of SOE, impinged on SIS but did not damage it. Special Operations Executive for sabotage in occupied Europe and help to the Resistance, was forged from the morass of competing and overlapping intelligence departments spawned in the previous three years. Chief among these was Department D, originally a creature of C's and the result of a sudden awareness that the impending war was likely to demand sabotage and propaganda as well as information-gathering. D now lost its residual parental connection.

It had assumed a weird variety of functions. At one expropriated Hertfordshire mansion it set up a training school for saboteurs, at another it dabbled in propaganda. It was in charge of the short-lived "leave-behind" operation, set up when invasion seemed imminent, to plant caches of guns in remote farmhouses for use by a putative peasant *maquis*.

Sub-groups proliferated, including MI(R), which quickly rivalled its parent, and a separate propaganda apparatus known as "the Electra House crowd". The atmosphere of Department D seems to be well represented by a famous interlude in a tangled meeting when Guy Burgess, an early recruit on the propaganda side, almost persuaded everyone that it would be a brilliant idea to starve the Germans out by setting fire balloons loose over the cornfields of the Hungarian *posta*.

By the end of 1940 this ragbag of warring bureaucracies was taken in hand, under Dalton's Ministry of Economic Warfare. SOE was established in Baker Street, after a draconian weeding-out of the more grotesque adventurers and misfits naturally attracted to work there. The main executioner was Gladwyn Jebb, then a rising young man seconded from the Foreign Office. Philby was one of the lucky "D's" taken into SOE. But Burgess, who had been recalled from half-way point in a trip to Moscow, was regarded by Jebb – to his fury – as unsuitable, and forced to return to the BBC.

This discovery that war was too serious to be left to the amateurs and the superannuated hit MI5 at roughly the same time.

They, too, had begun by giving work to any friends of friends who arrived on the doorstep. An extreme example of the sort of unlikely catches they made was Brian Howard, homosexual, poet and Gargoyle intimate of Burgess and Maclean.

Howard's best epigrammist was Evelyn Waugh: "mad, bad and dangerous to know". Another judge has described him as "the leading arrogant swine of his generation". Nevertheless, to the horror of even his friends, he was given an MI5 job, wining and dining as many people as possible and reporting back to MI5. For this, his usual way of life anyway, he was paid generous expenses in lieu of salary.

He quickly became redundant, having told all he knew. He became ludicrously indiscreet, and his biographer describes his habit of approaching strangers in bars, telling them he worked for a very secret organisation and accusing them of being Fascist spies.

This preposterous kind of recruit was checked only by the firing of Kell and almost all his Indian henchmen in the autumn of 1940. This summary decision, perhaps the most swingeing departmental clean-out of the entire war, was taken by the Security Executive, then chaired by Lord Swinton.

The team which now took over represented the first victory for civilian professionalism in the history of the British intelligence services. It was led by Sir David Petrie, a solid Scotsman with long intelligence experience.

Under Petrie the two men who virtually ran MI5 were the first of the new breed of trained specialists: Guy Liddell and another man who plays a crucial part in the history. We do not name him because in an unprecedented switch of immense significance he was later to become director of the Secret Service (though his identity is certainly known to the Russians, there are other considerations).

This man will be referred to by his code name "C". He was the first young graduate to enter the service, in 1936, as a potential lifetime employee. At this time early in the war, he was already perhaps the most able single man there, and a future director of MI5.

The young "C" and Liddell quickly set about reshaping MI5, to put the emphasis on brain-power before long service. The bulk of MI5's work was and is essentially file-pushing, carried out by a vast army of bureaucrats.

But for the higher counter-espionage, brains were needed. They were provided, notably, by Anthony Blunt, now Keeper of the Queen's Pictures, and Victor Rothschild, a clever physics don who had been an Apostle (along with Blunt and Guy Burgess) at Cambridge.

Two lawyers made up the quartet which soon established an ascendancy. They were Herbert Hart, now Professor of Jurisprudence at Oxford, and Helenus "Buster" Milmo, now a High Court judge.

The Security Executive, which had ordained these reforms, had a very able secretariat, including, for example, the young William Armstrong, now Permanent Secretary at the Treasury. But there was one organisation which it almost completely failed to touch: SIS.

If the SIS was not already well enough protected by its own impenetrable mystique, its survival was probably guaranteed by an inspection made into it just before war began by Gladwyn Jebb and Maurice Hankey. They passed the outfit fit for service.

SIS during the thirties had recruited, in the tradition of the Great Game, partly from the same dependable source as MI5, the Indian Police, and partly among rich, upper-class young men from the City, a source much favoured by Colonel Dansey. It was rather a pleasant catch, because the money was untaxed and most people did not bother to work too hard.

Dansey used to attract the young men by telling them that the compensation for their anonymity was membership of a very select elite. However, this had little in common with the sort of elitism to be enjoyed in the Foreign Office. The secret agents, being rarely either very intelligent or very energetic, were most unlikely to have got a proper diplomatic posting. As a result, they did little beyond wandering round Europe, collecting what amounted, for the most part, to gun-room information.

It was these men, often known generically as "The Stockbrokers", who gave the service its connection with White's Club in St James's. This notorious liaison stands fully at the centre of any picture of the wartime secret service. And it epitomises the roguish, dilettante quality of SIS, of which the rest of Whitehall, and especially the embryonic professionals of MI5, were to become increasingly contemptuous over the next decade.

Most of the top brass of the SIS belonged there. Menzies himself spent much of the war in White's bar, closeted with his personal assistant, Peter Koch de Gooreynd, who in civilian life was his stockbroker. It was, they thought, one of the more secure places in London. The etiquette in the club at the time was to leave them alone when they were together, since it was understood that they were "running the secret service or something".

White's provided, too, a fertile source for emergency wartime recruits, on the basic English principle that if you could not trust your club, who could you trust? Obviously Evelyn Waugh's *Put Out More Flags* is not so much a novel as a piece of accurate reportage. This is nicely shown in a snatch of dialogue between a *Sunday Times* reporter on the Insight inquiry and a veteran of the period.

Reporter: Rather a lot of crooks seem to have got into SIS, SOE, etc., during the war.

Veteran: Well, you have to take what you can get in wartime, don't you?

Reporter: They seem to have got most of them out of the bar at White's.

Veteran: Well, you wouldn't find anything except crooks there, would you?

Reporter: Where were you recruited?

Veteran: Boodles'.

The service was divided into five functional sections. Section I was Political under David Footman, a first world war veteran who had entered SIS from the Levant Consular Service. Sections II, III and IV covered the three armed services, of which the Navy, with overall responsibility of code-breaking, was much the most important. Section V handled counter-espionage, or, more exactly, "intelligence espionage" – spying on the German networks.

By 1941, when Kim Philby joined Section V, the fortunes of the secret service were at a very low ebb. The Venlo Incident and its aftermath had robbed them of all their European agents, and Churchill was getting annoyed at the shortage of information coming from the continent (even – the ultimate indignity – asking SOE, which was essentially a sabotage outfit, to provide some).

The one brilliant coup which sustained Menzies's reputation, in fact, was the code and cypher operation run by the naval captain, Edward Hastings, at Bletchley.

This was unquestionably a stunning triumph. The Germans, remembering the facility with which the British had cracked their manual codes in the first world war, had developed a machine cypher which they believed not even the British could penetrate. Breaking it would involve not merely analytical de-coding but a de-cyphering operation which was virtually impossible without possession of the same machine as the one used to transmit.

Perhaps the most important of all the machine codes was the one used in U-Boat communications. These were confidently used by U-Boat captains, each of them equipped with a machine called an "Enigma", to report their daily positions to Admiral Doenitz. If they had not been cracked, the carnage of the Atlantic convoys would have lasted far longer than it did.

On August 27, 1941, much earlier than has yet been commonly appreciated, the British Navy captured a U-boat and its Enigma machine intact. It was the U-270, and its unfortunate – or possibly co-operative – captain was called Hans Joachim Rahmlow.

The boat was rapidly converted into a research vessel, and renamed the HMS *Graph*. Possession of an Enigma meant a great leap forward for the code-breakers, and before the end of the year they had a working model of how the machine codes worked. Remarkable though this feat was, it was matched by the Navy's astuteness in concealing their success from the Germans for the entire length of the war. Even when the Bismarck was located by code intercepts, RAF reconnaissance planes were sent over the prize battleship to divert the Germans from the truth about its discovery.

This triumph would not have been possible without the skill of the regular Navy. And the remarkable code-smashing which resulted came only fortuitously under Menzies's control, since Hastings's General Code and Cypher School was for all practical purposes an independent operation.

But Menzies ensured that he personally delivered the code intercepts to Churchill. This, the raw material, of the "Most Secret Sources" whose decisive value Churchill himself has amply chronicled, was what principally shored up SIS's failing reputation.

When Philby entered the service, the busting of the machine codes was still beyond the horizon. What little there was to sustain the flagging morale of the men he was about to join still came mainly from the code school, with the steady stream of manual code-breaking taken up from the first world war.

To this was added the personal *réclame* of Menzies himself. Throughout the war, his inexplicably magnetic aura and his knowledge of the back doors of Whitehall could never be underrated by SIS's enemies.

Yet the retrospective judgements on him seem to vary only in the degree of their disenchantment. Three, perhaps, typify the assorted opinions of those who ran into him:

"He was terrifying to work with because he acted entirely on instinct. He rarely read a single case right through, yet he often came up with the answer."

"He was honest and brave, but he only lasted because he was a high-class schemer."

"He was a good second-class man, who should never have had the job."

Burgess gets a job for Philby

The circumstances of Kim Philby's arrival on this lamentable scene can now be charted with some certainty.

Failing membership of White's, the *sine qua non* was a personal introduction. It seems highly probable that this was supplied in the first instance by his recent colleague in D Department, Guy Burgess.

Apart from Burgess's own claim, on one occasion, to this distinction, there is the evidence of one of their colleagues in D, who states categorically: "Philby just did not have the contacts to get that sort of job on his own. I know it was Burgess who rang up someone and got him in."

Burgess had at least one notably good contact in SIS, David Footman, the head of the political section. They had known each other for several years. Although this was not enough to satisfy Burgess's own intense ambition to continue in secret work, it happened that Footman had known Philby's family since Kim was a child. The connection seems to have smoothed Philby's path towards his chosen slot.

The responsibility for actually inserting him there was taken by Colonel Vivian. Again, Kim's family background was a strong factor in his favour. "I'm getting in the son of old St John Philby," Vivian told a senior colleague. "Knew him in India. Son's been a war correspondent for *The Times*. Seems a bright chap."

To be fair to the Colonel, it must be said that no one else cast the slightest doubt on the wisdom of this. Far from it. Philby's arrival, once promised, was eagerly awaited. The word down at Prae Wood, Section V's Hertfordshire headquarters, was: "It will all be different when Philby gets here."

It is not hard to find the roots of this expectancy. Apart from the general tribulations of the service, Section V was languishing under a cloud peculiarly its own, in the shape of its chief, Major Felix Cowgill. Newly-recruited dons, viewing this man with rising desperation, looked hopefully for some sort of improvement.

Cowgill ran Prae wood, in the words of an inmate, like a bad private school. But his quality is best exemplified by the argument he is said to have produced against suggestions that Section V should set up a German sub-section.

He insisted that it was customary always to attach SIS field staff in a foreign country to some more permanent British presence there: if an embassy, the embassy; if an army, the GHQ. But in Germany we had neither army nor embassy: there could therefore be no possibility of placing SIS men there.

Compared with such Indianism, Philby had useful credentials. He had made a name for himself as a reporter. Fresh from Spain and the BEF he had even seen active service. In fact he had some of the qualities of the messiah which SIS certainly needed. It was thought a stroke of luck that Vivian had got him to take the job.

The true measure of his status was the willingness of SIS to overlook his Communist past. One source actually claims that this had already been enough to disqualify him from SOE, although this suggestive detail cannot be firmly established.

In days when personal recommendation had yet to be superseded by a consistent process of positive vetting, it may be a moot point whether SIS even knew about the Thirties phase.

The kind of anti-Communist sensitivity of which the secret departments were capable is illustrated by the fact that an academic of lifelong Tory views was barred. The "trace" showed an alleged Communist connection: it later emerged that this was a mistake over the title of a medical friendly society. Perhaps the most significant story is Peter Kemp's about his vetting for SOE. When they heard he had fought in the Spanish Civil War, there were some very anxious looks – but once it was realised that he had fought on Franco's side, there were gasps of relief.

The question of Philby's political stance is also raised by the nature of the man who preceded him to Prae Wood – his old Westminster school friend and travelling companion of before the war, Ian, who had been recruited from S. H. Benson's advertising agency.

When Ian arrived, he added his praises to the swelling antiphon for his close friend Kim. But, after listening to him, at least one man thought it surprising, though praiseworthy, that Philby had been taken on. For in the early thirties, Ian had explained at boring length to Oxford friends that his hero Kim Philby was a Communist.

When Philby arrived, he took over the Iberian subsection of Section V, with Ian as his deputy. The Section had been spitefully designated by the deposed Colonel Dansey "the red-flannel bloomers brigade". But, dealing entirely with counter-espionage, it was the one most exactly suited to Philby's real *métier*.

The essence of this particular facet of the Great Game is to discover and nullify the operations of the enemy's own intelligence organisations. CE is in fact the heart of the spying business, and the basis of the charge – easily justifiable in the light of history – that opposing networks exist principally to give employment to each other.

The front-line weapon of counter-espionage is the double agent, planted inside the enemy operation. It is a vulnerable but highly potent occupation. To evaluate the potency of an agent, already planted as a double, who is then replanted by his new employers as a supposed double agent with his real masters, involves a bewildering series of multiplications.

This, of course, had not yet happened to Philby. The Russians, useful as they would have found any information he could give them about the code-breaking side of SIS, were about to launch into the same war as the British. But from now, well into the critical years of the Cold War, Section V and counter-espionage was to be Philby's ladder to the top.

For Vivian, their master, Philby and Ian were "my two little intellectuals", and, by comparison with the stockbrokers with whom he was used to working, that was no doubt an apt description.

But only in the most relative sense could Kim Philby be described as an intellectual. His life shows little sign of his ever having been interested in abstract ideas.

"Intellectual" was precisely what he was not. But the key to his instant success at Prae Wood is unquestionably provided by the affectionate, possessive respect with which Vivian regarded him as one.

By the real intellectuals there he was welcomed as a refreshing breath of oxygen – "the first able man to get a powerful job," said one of them. What was far more important was that he did not refrigerate the climate for the Indians.

He was able to "handle" the intellectuals without himself displaying any of the attributes of an intellectual which "the White's" element found so distasteful: i.e. talking about incomprehensible ideas, making incomprehensible jokes, or humiliating the Indians by referring to works of literature.

He made a big difference to the Iberian section, whose theatre was a vital one in the intelligence battle. Spain was a neutral, friendly to Germany, and provided the perfect base for operations against the keystone of British communications, Gibraltar.

Portugal was friendly to Britain, but Portuguese Mozambique, which also came under Section V, was the centre of German espionage operations in Southern Africa. It was in this connection that Philby sent Malcolm Muggeridge to be our man in Lourenço Marques (and Graham Greene to Sierra Leone), with a brief to counter German attempts to spy on British shipping movements.

As a boss, Philby was a quick success. He possessed both grasp and human sympathy, faculties which evidently won him intense personal loyalty. This was to be a feature of his entire career, and it is with an almost unspeakable sense of irony that associates recall the word which they always felt summed him up: "Integrity".

"You didn't just like him, admire him, agree with him," says one man who saw him often from the war to his defection. "You worshipped him." A worshipper put it graphically: "If he had told me to shoot at the chief of police I would have done it. I believed in him."

His toughest office reprimand used to be: "I say, you shouldn't really have done that, you know." His capacity to produce a report in decent English without a draft also seems to have wonderfully impressed his colleagues.

It is the immediate, somewhat superficial, characteristics which made the deepest impression. Charm, universal acceptability, an ordered mind, these, together with the pathetic stutter, were the hallmarks of his devastating success. And the greater this success became, the more surely it obliterated any possibility of suspicion against him.

Another trait he rapidly displayed at Prae Wood was his capacity for alcohol. When he drank he drank hard, but he never lost control. A man under pressure might be expected to lay off completely or to drop his guard on the occasional, all-releasing binge. It is more proof of the inner strength against which perhaps no interrogator could have found a counter that Philby did neither.

Besides, he was a far from regular social drinker. He would often give the pick-up cricket games and the pub a miss, and go straight off home to his wife, Aileen. The match, his second, had been an unlikely one, since Aileen Furse's family was strongly "county" (Somerset) and bristled with colonels and admirals, who Philby despised. But during this period at least, he was a devoted husband and father.

By 1943, two years after coming in, he was firmly established as one of Menzies's very best men. Someone has described him at this period as a "passenger in the racketeering upper-class world". But it would be truer to say that the passenger was cutting a steady tread towards the driver's seat.

In terms of notable coups pulled off by his section, his body of achievement was probably not much more substantial than that of anyone else involved in Section V's efforts to grapple with the Abwehr. He himself once claimed to his family that he had a leading role in the famous deceit of The Man Who Never Was, but this is hotly disputed by those who ran that operation.

Much more relevant was the talent he had shown for diplomacy within SIS, and his toughness in defending it against its bureaucratic enemies. The re-formed MI5, which had little time for the incompetents who abounded in the traditionally more prestigious outfit, had proved to require as much defensive attention in SIS as the Germans.

Graham Greene was almost fired after he bungled the task of getting an SIS man into the Azores. The agent had only been able to communicate, after some days, with the help of MI5. The top people at SIS were furious, but Philby, Greene's boss, defended him impressively.

The blind respect for Philby

But by early 1944 Philby was getting bored by the limitations of the Iberian subsection. Around this time, Section V moved back to London, to a house in Ryder Street, and Kim could not have been happier. "I'll just be glad to get away from this damn green," he told a colleague. Shortly after the move, Philby set out to get rid of his immediate obstacle to promotion, the luckless Cowgill. His ally in this was his acolyte, Ian. Philby seems to have persuaded Col. Vivian that Cowgill was not up to the job. Cowgill was later dispatched to Germany and less testing police work. He retired as Services Liaison Officer in München-Gladbach, a sad decline. Col. Vivian is reported to have been much affected by the necessity for this, and to have wailed to Philby: "Just think, Kim, only the other day I was recommending him for the OBE." Anyway, the Major got his order in the end.

Philby's intention was evidently to take over the leadership of Section V himself. But his plan depended on Ian getting the Iberian section, with Graham Greene, in turn, taking Ian's spot at number two. Greene, suffering an attack of Jansenist morality, is reported to have resigned in disgust at this office-jobbing, and the scheme collapsed.

This left Philby temporarily in a vacuum, a fact to which someone seems to have alerted his old employers, *The Times*. They wrote to him at the end of January, 1944, and offered him a job as a correspondent with the invasion forces then being assembled for D-Day.

They lunched him at the Reform, where he expressed polite interest but said that it was up to the Foreign Office to say whether or not he could leave his present work.

After an interval of some weeks, the Foreign Office, through Frank Roberts (later Ambassador to Russia and West Germany), replied, saying that this was not possible. Philby, they said delicately, was not on the Foreign Office staff, but his work was of particular interest to them and they would, if asked, "recommend most strongly against his removal from his present job".

Naturally the British were not going to let a top counter-espionage controller go anywhere near where the Germans might capture him. But the episode shows one interesting point, which is that Philby could have gone back into journalism had he wished. There was a market for him.

The fact that he did not do so can now be explained with painful clarity.

What he was offered, perhaps in the interval between *The Times*'s approach and the Foreign Office's deflection of it, was something which must have made the failure of the Section V office conspiracy seem a very fortunate interruption.

The main body of the Section was in any case losing its relevance. There was only one front now where counter-espionage mattered in winning the war – Western Europe. And this work had been effectively taken over from SIS's moulting empire by a special group in the Cabinet War Room run by, of all things, an MI5 man. Although SIS had a representative on this group, he seems to have been an infrequent and incapable attender.

At this distance, Philby's selection by Menzies and Vivian, a few months before D-Day, to revive the defunct counter-espionage operation against the Soviet Union can surely be said to have had a more telling impact on history than any other single event in the secret service.

To Philby, the new job must have had a flawless perfection, a marvellous interlocking symmetry, which would be the envy of any spy in history, past or future. It must also have seemed to represent the ultimate folly of the defenceless men above him.

It was on every count an astonishing decision. The creation of the Soviet section came, we should remember, at a time when not only were the Russians a vital part of the anti-German alliance but the Americans had adopted as their policy Roosevelt's belief that an accommodation with Moscow would be an essential prop of the post-war world. This, at that time, was the understanding, however tenuous and ill-conceived, in both Moscow and Washington.

It is not hard to imagine with what dazed fascination Moscow must have received the new intelligence from their man in London: that Britain had already identified the Soviet Union as the new enemy, and was launching a major espionage operation against her. This chilling awareness of Britain's real and secret purposes can have been only partly mitigated by the confidence that, in their execution, they were unlikely to elude Moscow's own control.

Philby's appointment to the job is a measure of the respect, the blind, unwavering, total respect, in which he was held by his superiors. Was he not the brightest young man in the service? Had he not virtually saved SIS from splitting apart, and salvaged for Menzies and Vivian their reputations and their jobs? Was he not simply a dedicated professional, set on staying with the service, whose only political feeling consisted of mild bored Socialism?

All this might have been understandably persuasive but for one inescapable fact. It is at this point, much more than at the time of his arrival in 1941, that Philby's once overt commitment to Communism and his employers' knowledge of it, becomes critical.

It is very difficult to believe that, had they then been conscious of it, they would still have given him the Soviet job. Had they, then, forgotten it? Had it been obliterated from the record by his excellent performance? Or was it, just conceivably, noted, and in a moment of supreme political naiveté ignored?

For almost any other job in the Service, a Communist past might still, at the moment, have been plausibly ignored. For this particular job, it was surely something which not even Philby's dazzled admirers, if they had addressed themselves seriously to the question, could have overlooked.

But they did so. The ageing colonel, who was the sole incumbent of the inactive Soviet section, was pensioned off, and Philby moved in to build an empire which, within eighteen months, occupied an entire floor in Ryder Street and employed over 100 people.

It was not long before the old charm began to work.

He was once again a hard-working, easy-going boss. "At nine or ten at night," one of his team said, "Kim would be sweating over his papers. You always had the feeling he was burning the midnight oil. I remember thinking to myself at the time, there's a young man who's going places."

Within two years, the section had accumulated a vast store of information on Communists in western countries, front organisations and the other now familiar stuff of Cold War counter-espionage. And Kim Philby had acquired, to a riveting extent, the confidence of his staff.

"He could get them to do anything for him," one of them has recalled. This witness remembers that everyone there came from a strict security background, where the rigid tradition was that office desks should be locked at night. But Kim broke that tradition as he broke so many others. "Don't worry about that," he said. "I'll lock them up later."

"I didn't like to do it," this witness now says, "but he was so charming that I couldn't refuse anything he asked."

The extent to which the members of the SIS failed to understand the nature of the alien they had nurtured is shown by the comment Insight received when we wrote to Menzies (now General Sir Stewart) for his comments. In reply, he wrote: "What a blackguard Kim Philby was."

PHILBY AND MACLEAN: THE YEARS OF DAMAGE

―――――●―――――

15 October 1967

FEELINGS about Kim Philby vary sharply among his old colleagues in the British Secret Intelligence Service. Some preserve a degree of affection, and ruminate upon the "misplaced idealism" which led him to work for the Russians. Some see his career largely as a technical feat. "He was an agent who really lived his cover," they say.

Others take a more impassioned view, like the man who said to us: "Philby was a copper-bottomed bastard, and he killed a lot of people."

Espionage and counter-espionage can seem so much like civilised office-games that the blood can get forgotten. But in this account of Philby's career from 1945 to 1951 there are two crucial episodes which luridly illuminate the realities of the game.

The first case is a man alone: a Soviet intelligence officer caught in the act of trying to defect to the West. That story ends with a bandaged figure being hustled aboard a Russian plane in Istanbul.

In the second case, there are some 300 men in armed parties, slipping across the Iron Curtain border from Greece into Albania. This was a scheme designed to test the feasibility of breaking Communist control of Eastern Europe by subversion: the story ends in a crackle of small-arms fire on bleak hillsides, and the total discrediting of a policy which might have caused the Soviet Government a lot of trouble.

Behind each case is the shadow of Kim Philby – the Soviet penetration agent at the heart of the Secret Intelligence Service, the man whose loyalty went unquestioned for so long. Indeed, it might never have been questioned, but for the fact that Philby was caught up in the complex aftermath of Donald Maclean's espionage for the Russians.

Maclean's own espionage work was essentially different in character and its precise effect can only be presumed. The Western intelligence community probably still does not know exactly how much information Maclean actually got through to the Russians out of the material that was available to him. This would explain the fact – confirmed to us independently by ex-CIA man Robert Amory and verified by a State Department official – that in 1956 the CIA and SIS were working on plans to snatch Maclean back from Moscow. As he has never been interrogated in the West, even such questions as the nature of his contacts must still be mysterious.

What can be closely mapped in this article is the scope of his information – most vividly illustrated by the amazing "non-escort" pass, which allowed him free access to the greatest storehouse of American weapons secrets, the Atomic Energy Commission HQ in Washington. (That pass was used often, and late at night.) Philby, of course, knew that it was worth some risk to get Maclean away before he could be questioned. He never guessed that the accident of Burgess's flight with Maclean in 1951 would begin the destruction of Philby's own unique position.

The Volkov affair: Philby sends a defector to his death

The last days of the second world war, and the first days of the peace, were marked by urgent discussions among young Englishmen who had been caught up in the military machine on how to re-assemble their broken careers. Most had one urgent impulse: to do something which had nothing to do with their war work. It was an impulse from which Kim Philby seemed to be immune.

He showed no desire to revive his excellent pre-war prospects in journalism. To friends who did not know what his wartime "civil service" job had been, he said: "I've decided to join the bureaucrats. The future belongs to them." To war-weary colleagues in the Secret Intelligence Service, like Malcolm Muggeridge, he evinced a willingness to work on against Russian instead of German antagonists which they found simply baffling.

Muggeridge recalls a drunken evening in Paris in 1945, when at Philby's insistence, the two of them lurched round to take a look at the Russian Embassy. Philby marched up and down, shaking his fist at the silent building, and demanding: "How are we going to penetrate them?"

Philby's zeal, of course, is highly explicable in retrospect: a long-term Soviet agent who had succeeded in early 1944 in becoming head of the British counter-Soviet espionage operation would hardly be ready to get out of the business. His war was just beginning, and the cavorting outside the Russian Embassy was no more of an indiscretion than the action of a racing-driver who cuts one corner extra-close to revel in his control.

Around this time, however, Philby was involved in a serious and peculiar incident. The way it was handled raises strange questions about the philosophy on which the Secret Intelligence Service was working in those days: if only because when the incident, years later, came to the attention of Britain's other main secret department, MI5, it was taken as virtually conclusive evidence that Philby was working for the Russians.

Early in August 1945 an unexpected visitor with a heavy Russian accent called at the British Consulate in the Beyoglu district of Istanbul in Turkey. The man, obviously very nervous, demanded an interview with a certain high-ranking British diplomat. He wanted no one else present but himself and this diplomat – not even an interpreter.

The officer was found and the man was ushered into a quiet room. There, he spelt out the reason for his visit. He gave his name as Volkov. Ostensibly, he was a newly-appointed Russian consul in Istanbul. Actually, he said, he had been appointed head of Soviet Intelligence for Turkey.

He had arrived only two months earlier from the Moscow headquarters of the NKVD (then initials of the Russian secret service), and he had a proposition to make. In return for £27,500 (an odd amount, but probably converted from a round sum in roubles), plus a laissez-passer to Cyprus, Volkov was prepared to offer certain valuable counter-espionage information. Were the British interested?

The British diplomat was not one of the resident SIS men operating under diplomatic cover – although the Russian, it seems, assumed that he was. Nevertheless, the diplomat expressed cautious interest. What was the information for sale? Naturally, said Volkov, he was not prepared to give details until there was a deal. But – and here he handed over a batch of handwritten notes and sketches – this was an outline of what he had to sell.

The British official read rapidly, and with mounting excitement, through the headings: addresses and descriptions of NKVD buildings in Moscow with details of burglar-alarm systems, key impressions and guard schedules; numbers of all NKVD cars; a list, of Soviet agents in Turkey, together with their means of communication; and finally – almost as a throwaway – names of Russian agents operating in Government departments in London." It all looked as though Comrade Volkov, before taking up his post in Istanbul, had spent some time in Moscow acquiring material which could take him into the Western world with a golden one-way ticket.

The British official went straight to his Ambassador, Sir Maurice Peterson. But the reaction from the Ambassador was one of straight horror: he had for some time been trying to prevent what he regarded as an "invasion" of the Embassy by SIS men under cover, and he saw the Volkov business as a step in the same direction. "No one is going to turn my Embassy into a nest of spies," he said. "If you must go ahead with this business, do it through London."

The official returned to the waiting Russian. London would have to have time to make a decision on the proposition, he said.

Volkov agreed to wait, but he made two conditions. Firstly, any outline of his documents must be handwritten by the man he was speaking to, and not typed. There was a Russian agent operating in the British Embassy in Turkey, he said, so he could not risk anyone typing copies of his material. Secondly, there must be a decision within twenty-one days. If he had not heard by the evening of the twenty-first day, he would assume the deal was off. He departed after making complex arrangements for getting in touch.

The British diplomat spent a long night preparing a hand-written brief addressed to the SIS in London, and it went away with the courier next day. After a week, there had been no response, and a cable was sent from the Embassy in Turkey asking for a reply. After another week, there was still no reply; and on the twentieth day the diplomat who had interviewed Volkov had still heard nothing, and was almost frantic.

Then, at last, on the morning of the twenty-first day, an agent arrived from London and announced he had come to take personal charge of the Volkov affair. He was a calm, unhurried figure wearing a cutaway collar with a flowing Byronesque cravat. It was Kim Philby.

The diplomat who had interviewed Volkov, with nerves understandably taut, pointed out that the delay had probably ruined the whole deal – and asked why the hell couldn't someone have come out sooner. Philby produced casually an almost incredible excuse. "Sorry, old man," he said. "It would have interfered with leave arrangements."

They tried to contact Volkov, and waited for word to come back. Nothing happened. In the end they sent men out to look for "Consul Volkov" – but he could not be found. Throughout the afternoon, the interviewing officer could get no further explanation of the delay from Philby. "I finally made up my mind," he told friends later, "that either Philby was criminally incompetent, or he was a Soviet agent himself."

When it was clear that Volkov was not coming, Philby returned to London. And then a few days later, something occurred which revived the whole unhappy affair in the mind of the interviewing officer. A Russian military aircraft made an unscheduled, and quite irregular landing at Istanbul airport.

While the control tower was still trying to think of something to do, a car raced out across the tarmac to the aircraft. A heavily bandaged figure on a stretcher was lifted from the car and put into the aircraft – which immediately took off.

It seemed to be an urgent Russian removal in the bravura style which was more common then, although still to be seen on occasion. And it seemed a fair assumption that the man being removed was the unfortunate Volkov: on which the interviewing officer decided to pass on his doubts about Kim Philby to someone else.

He contacted a British SIS officer, and reported his version of the Volkov incident. But nothing seems to have happened. If there was an inquiry, it was kept strictly inside the SIS family circle. And clearly the incident, although later thought so damaging, did not stunt Philby's immediate career nor his rise from London directorship of anti-Soviet operations, through an important field command to the position of CIA liaison in Washington.

Philby survives an inspection

Since the disclosure that Kim Philby became a Soviet penetration agent in 1933, several attempts have been made to pretend that Philby was some kind of wartime undesirable, who was accidentally left behind in the peacetime SIS. This argument is badly weakened by the fact that there was a vigorous shakeout of the SIS in 1946, which was intended precisely to remove any unsuitable people who had slipped in during the confused days of the war.

Many wartime recruits were asked to leave the Service as a result of this. It is not quite clear whether the operation was a part of the general inspection of the Foreign Office carried out that year under the present Lord Caccia – that inspection did touch on SIS and MI5 – or whether it was really a separate affair. What is quite clear is that Philby survived it.

The year 1946 began on a good note for him, because he received an OBE in the New Year's honours (the list gave no specific reason for the award and merely said he was employed "in a department of the Foreign Office"). Philby's colleagues and subordinates thought it was well deserved: he was an immensely hard-working officer – more often than not the last man in the office at night, and the one who took on the chore of locking up.

The only thing which seemed even slightly likely to impede his rise to the top of the Service was a slight neglect of the social obligations of departmental life. At that time, the SIS was devoted enough to the idea of togetherness to maintain a country house, with swimming pool, for the weekend entertainment of the staff. (The philosophy, perhaps more typical of the CIA these days, was to keep the secret world as self-sufficient as possible, even at the risk of inbreeding.) Philby, though, did not spend much time with his colleagues after hours: seemingly, he preferred to spend the time with his second wife Aileen and his growing family.

A good reason for Philby to limit the time spent with his colleagues would have been the fact that it would lessen the strain of perpetually dissembling his political feelings. Most of the people in the SIS at this time seem to have held right-wing views, sometimes extremely pronounced.

One woman who worked in Philby's department recalls an occasion when she was discussing the forthcoming 1945 General Election with another woman colleague. "I was just saying: 'Wouldn't it be awful if the dreadful Socialists got in,' when I got that feeling one does that there was someone standing behind me. I looked round – and there was Mr Philby giving me a look of such malevolence."

But no harsh words accompanied this baleful look. And in fact Philby seems to have got through his career as an SIS executive with scarcely a harsh word to anyone, whether about politics or simple office inefficiency. It was one of the major reasons, naturally, for his success: he was noted for his heavy stammer and his even, controlled temperament.

Malcolm Muggeridge, however, claims to have detected in Philby at this time a quality of "suppressed violence" – and this is an intriguing insight in the light of current psychiatric thought about stammering. Stammering is thought to arise from inhibited rage in early childhood: later, it is often found as part of an enormously powerful inhibition against expressing aggression towards other people.

The strange role in Turkey

In early summer 1946, Philby relinquished his London department, and took up an important new post "in the field". He went to Turkey under diplomatic cover. Ostensibly he was a "temporary First Secretary" stationed in Istanbul for passport-control work. In fact, of course, his work was espionage.

The year of this appointment was to be significantly highlighted 17 years later in the British Government's rueful admission that they at last knew the truth about Philby's loyalties. The Government, said Edward Heath, was "now aware . . . that he worked for the Soviet authorities before 1946".

But when Philby arrived, with a wife and four children, he looked exactly like a perfectly ordinary diplomat.

Sir Michael Cresswell, a pre-war acquaintance of Philby's, called in on Philby and found it hard to believe he was in intelligence work. "It didn't seem like his line."

Istanbul had been an important neutral centre in the war against Germany. Now, the East-West confrontation gave it even greater importance. It was at the centre of a cold war which seemed likely to go hot at the drop of an ultimatum. Turkey has a long border with the Soviet Union, and another border with Communist Bulgaria. In the forties, Stalin was loudly claiming a big slice of Eastern Turkey, plus the right to put Russian bases on the Bosphorus and the Dardanelles. The Turks, in reply, were clamouring for Western military aid. A civil war was raging in nearby Greece, which looked as though it could easily go Communist also.

The city of Istanbul has numerous advantages for espionage. Much Communist shipping passes through the Bosphorus. The city has flourishing communities of Armenians, Georgians, Bulgarians and Albanians with direct links to their home communities behind the Curtain. And in the dark, winding alleys of old Stamboul, there are innumerable bars and coffee-houses where clandestine meetings are easy.

Philby worked from the British Consulate-General, a vast barracks-like building standing in a walled compound in Beyoglu, the "new" part of the city. He established the family in a beachside house on the Asiatic shore of the Bosphorus. Life was far from austere, but Philby clearly found the society boring. He wrote to a friend in London: "I wonder why they don't hire the same bus to take the same people to all the same parties . . . "

Things were enlivened by visits from Guy Burgess on holiday from the Foreign Office in London. Guy's most spectacular exploit was a dive into the Bosphorus from the upper floor of the Philby residence: presumably only the inspiration of *raki* guided his body between the rocks.

But the intricacies of his job should have saved Philby from any threat of boredom. The first curiosity about it was that *he* should be doing it: why would the head of a department go out to do a field job, even in such a crucial area as Turkey?

In this context, it is worth mentioning the only reference to Philby which seems to occur in Turkish intelligence files: a reference to his meetings with a group of Bulgarian and other East European "students" whom the Turks were inclined to think were spies. Such contacts seem humble work for a man who had just been a departmental head.

The more one investigates the nature of Philby's work in Turkey, the more curious it looks. In the middle of the period, he was brought back to England for a "James Bond" course at a spy-school near Gosport: shooting, unarmed combat, sabotage. A fellow-student says that Philby topped the course.

He spent a good deal of time in Turkey travelling around the Lake Van district, close to the Soviet border. He kept a curious souvenir of the period, which in later years he displayed in his Beirut apartment: a large photograph of Mount Ararat, which stands on the Turkish-Soviet border. Most people who recognised the double-humped shape of Ararat would puzzle over that picture, and when some of them asked whether the negative was reversed, it used to amuse Philby enormously.

Presenting people with this tangible evidence of his own duplicity gave him a perverse thrill. He would usually imply that he had taken the picture himself, though another version of the story suggests it was really the work of a brilliant Armenian named "Bill" Ekserdjian, reputed to have been one of Philby's most effective agents.

The picture seems to have been an ironic symbol of Philby's enigmatic status. Clearly, throughout his Turkish period he was closely in touch with the Soviet intelligence network, and equally clearly his superiors in London knew this. But like a detective, a counter-espionage agent in the field can only get results by mixing with the "criminals" he is trying to catch.

The technique had been elaborated by men under Philby's own command in the war: gaining contact through intermediaries with German agents, and feeding them a skilful blend of true and false information about British operations.

The vital question is how far Philby's superiors had given him permission to venture into this moral twilight? Had they actually given him permission to play a "double-agent" game with the Russians – to pretend to them that he was a British agent willing to work for them: which, unknown to London, was exactly what he was?

It would explain several puzzling points: most importantly, it would explain the passionate defence of Philby by his colleagues in the SIS when the security officers in MI5 were convinced that he was a traitor. The actions of a man in Philby's job can be virtually indistinguishable from treachery. Unless his friends stand by him, he has no defence when something goes wrong. Very shortly after the Turkish tour, things began to go wrong for Philby, and when they did the SIS stood by him with an extraordinary, apparently inexplicable determination.

Maclean learns atom secrets

Meanwhile, Donald Maclean's diplomatic – and espionage – careers had been developing in Washington, where he stayed as a First Secretary until September, 1948. He had arrived there in Spring 1944, a golden boy of the foreign service, and at 31 still unusually young for his rank.

Behind him were four successful wartime years in London, where he had displayed his talent for swift, meticulous disposal of paperwork. His efficiency was made only more palatable by his casual doziness of manner.

The war years, in fact, were the best of his diplomatic life. An eminent colleague of the time says that they were the peak of the momentum which guaranteed Maclean's subsequent promotions, even in the face of an obviously declining performance.

It is not hard to see why he declined. Unlike Kim Philby, Maclean shows every sign of having been deeply troubled by his duplicity and subject to traumatic fits of doubt. Genuine ambivalence was always a feature of his brand of Communism.

For any Marxist of this particular disposition the alliances of the war were a blessed relief from anguish. In Maclean's case, those years provided no foretaste of the lurid personality break-up to come; they were years when he could serve both his country and his ideology without betraying either.

Marriage, as the bombs were falling on Paris, had tempered the gregarious, impressionable youth of the Left Bank cafés. He and Melinda, despite bad patches, were close. Their life in Washington was unexceptional, and he was widely regarded as worthy rather than brilliant. His main recreation was tennis, which he often played with George Middleton, later head of the Foreign Office Personnel Department. The two also developed a mixture of water and cigarette butts to keep the insects off their roses in the humid summers.

The only flaw in this picture of the rising young diplomat was on the social side. Melinda was an unenthusiastic hostess, and Maclean had a strong distaste for the after-hours obligations of Embassy life. On the cocktail circuit, the couple were noted principally for the extraordinary solecism of persistently standing apart, holding hands.

As a common First Secretary, it is doubtful how much information of real value Maclean would ever have been in a position to supply to Moscow. But half way through his tour in Washington, he got a job of far greater significance. The new ambassador, Sir Archibald Clark-Kerr (Lord Inverchapel), himself a political eccentric by FO standards, found in Maclean an especially appealing subordinate. When the post of British Secretary to the Combined Policy Committee on atomic affairs fell vacant, Maclean was the man designated to fill it.

This committee was the result of the secret Quebec Agreement between the United States, Britain and Canada; its main function was to control the exchange of atomic information between the three Governments.

Maclean became secretary in February, 1947, six months after the passage of the MacMahon Act which severely restricted US participation in this exchange. At first sight this appears to indicate that Maclean can have had access to nothing significant – the impression sedulously conveyed in all British Government statements from the moment Maclean defected.

But startling new evidence has now come to light which entirely contradicts this view. It consists of the only known documentary assessment of the matter made by either the British or American Governments: a letter written in 1956 by the State Department to Senator James Eastland, chairman of the Senate Internal Security sub-committee, which was then proposing to hold its own investigation into the damage done to the US by Burgess and Maclean.

Dated February 21, 1956, and written after discussion with the intelligence agencies, the letter makes clear exactly what were the sensitive categories of information Maclean had access to. In paragraph 10, it states:

"He had an opportunity to have access to information shared by the three participating countries in the fields of patents, declassification matters and research and development relating to the programme of procurement of raw material from foreign sources by the Combined Development Agency, including estimates of supplies and requirements."

The CDA was the creature of Maclean's CPC. Its essential task was the *pre-emptive* purchase (mostly from the Belgian Congo) of uranium, which was still thought to be in exceedingly short supply, ahead of the Russians. As well as being able to foment political trouble in Belgium over the CDA's secret deals with Union Minière du Haut Katanga, the Russians would have valued anything Maclean could tell them about where the West was buying its uranium, in what quantities and at what price.

It goes on to illustrate how little the MacMahon Act had in practice cut off. It took until January 1948 to negotiate a *modus vivendi* for operating the act, and in that period "Maclean in his official capacity had access to information relating to the estimates made at that time of ore supply available to the three governments' requirement of uranium for the atomic energy programmes of the three governments for the period from 1948 to 1952, and the definition of scientific areas in which the three governments deemed technical co-operation could be accomplished with mutual benefit."

Apart from this final reference to what amounts to the entire early blueprint for the peacetime atomic energy programme, General Leslie Groves, father of the American atomic programme, has elucidated particulars in the reference to ore supply. In 1946, the United States perfected a new method for converting low-grade ore into high-grade uranium by processing the waste from South African gold mines. This increased the supply and reduced the cost in equal measure. The mere knowledge that it could be done would have been of critical value to Moscow's physicists, just as the mere knowledge of the practical workings of the MacMahon Act would have been a rare, rational guide to her intelligence planners.

But Maclean's "official capacity" stretched beyond these committees into the AEC building itself. This has been disclosed by Admiral Lewis Strauss, the former AEC chairman.

Admiral Strauss has described how he "learned that an alien was the holder of a permanent pass to the Commission's headquarters, a pass, moreover, which was of a character that did not require him to be accompanied within the building". The holder of this pass was Donald Maclean.

Maclean was able to get his pass because the AEC was split over the exchange of atomic information into pro- and anti-British groups. The general manager of the AEC at that time, Prof. Carroll L. Wilson, now of the Massachusetts Institute of Technology, was in the pro-British group (Strauss was anti). When Maclean's boss, the British representative on CDA, Sir Gordon Munro, approached Wilson for a pass for Maclean, Wilson was quite ready to grant it. Wilson recently admitted to *The Sunday Times*: " Yes, I gave the order for a non-escort pass to be issued . . . I saw no reason why I shouldn't. If I had had any suspicions I would not have done so. But I thought Maclean to be safe."

The pass was in fact a badge, to be picked up at the desk of the AEC lobby. When Strauss discovered it had been issued, he also discovered that the guards' record showed that Maclean "was a frequent visitor in the evenings and after usual work hours". Brian La Plante, then a security officer in the building, recalls that Maclean was using his pass "so often and at night" that he eventually reported him, and the pass was withdrawn. No inquiry, however, was held.

When security access to a building is tightly controlled, security inside tends to be limited. It is clear, from the evidence of former employees, that Maclean could have had access to virtually any rooms and files he chose. It is clear from the regularity of his late-night visits that his intentions were fully satisfied.

In particular, this meant that whatever restrictive effect the MacMahon Act did have on Maclean's access to current information was nullified by the previous records, kept in great detail, which he could freely plunder.

This work constitutes sound evidence for describing Maclean as an atomic spy of much higher significance than has hitherto been recognised. Even so, it was only the first of his two periods of espionage on the grand scale.

Cairo – the strain is too much

By now, however, there were signs of Maclean's incipient crack-up. He never found treason an easy matter; his successes seem to have borne heavily on him. He had begun to drink more freely; life with Melinda was becoming more difficult.

These dormant traumas came vividly into the open at his next post, Cairo, to which he was sent from Washington to be Head of Chancery, after what in FO jargon is called "an accelerated promotion".

Melinda, with four servants, adored the British Raj element still left in Cairo society (many officials had been transferred from India and had brought their pretensions with them). She even found a new interest in the social round. Her apogee as a hostess was a party for the Duke of Edinburgh. Deciding HRH would like a break from protocol, she organised noisy, adolescent games like "Murder". The royal guest was enchanted.

In Donald the change brought out all his latent aggressions. His occasionally overt anti-Americanism had aroused little concern in Washington; it was shared anyway by many of his embassy colleagues. But in Cairo he soon made himself unpopular for "Bolshie" views. He found the corrupt Farouk regime nauseous and the time-hallowed British policy of ostentatiously doing nothing about it even more so.

Instead of getting drunk like a gentleman, he now embarked on a series of epic, Dylanesque binges. He was arrested by the Egyptian police, dead drunk and without shoes. His hangovers reached such proportions that he was often absent from the office. Eventually the Embassy Security Officer, Major "Sammy" Sansom, took notice.

"He was a brilliant chap but highly unreliable," Sansom recalls. "I reported his drinking to Carey Foster (Head of Security in the FO) direct via the diplomatic bag." Normally such reports would have passed through the Ambassador, but as Maclean was Head of Chancery he would have had to see them first.

Sansom, a regular ranker unendowed with diplomatic gifts – "I was the most hated man in the Embassy" – had already clashed with Maclean. To his fury he had been refused permission to initiate spot searches on Embassy staff. Sansom also blamed Maclean for losing the fifth copy of a top secret telegram from London.

As Cairo was a "Grade A" Embassy they received copies of important cables from all over the world. Maclean, as Head of Chancery, had access to even more than the Ambassador. Sansom's security role gave him the power to have several typists sent home for indiscreet affairs with Egyptians. But Maclean was sacrosanct – he had too many important friends.

In later years wild rumours circulated about Maclean's Cairo peccadilloes. A senior diplomat was even asked by MI5 whether he had attended a (completely mythical) party in Gizera where Maclean was supposed to have entertained the guests by publicly seducing an Arab boy. But the truth was lurid enough, without embroidery.

By Spring 1949 his alcoholism had reached grotesque proportions. One Embassy wife tells how Maclean would call round for a drink in the evenings. Instead of ringing the bell he liked to clamber over the garden-wall and bark like a dog outside, pawing at the window to attract attention.

Early in March the Macleans hired a wide-sailed barge and set off up the Nile to have dinner with friends at Helouan, 15 miles from Cairo. Harriet, Melinda's sister, was with them on holiday; their idea was to spend a picturesque couple of hours having a kind of floating cocktail party before dinner.

But the wind dropped and the voyage took nearly eight hours. By then everyone was very drunk; so was their host. Irked at being wakened at 2 a.m. he refused to let them in.

Melinda was the first casualty. In a drunken fury on the boat Maclean tried to throttle her. The second was an American who fell over as soon as they landed and cracked his skull. An Egyptian watchman, attracted by the noise, challenged the party with his ancient rifle. Maclean disarmed him and started to swing the gun round his head. A fellow member of the Embassy tried to take it away and slipped down the bank with six feet four of Maclean on top of him. He finished up with a broken leg.

By this time the reluctant host was prevailed on to unlock his door. The injured American was carried into a bedroom, and out again when they found their hostess was there, unconscious from drink and wearing only a pair of slacks. Maclean had by now terrified the Egyptian servant into unlocking the drinks cabinet and he took his colleague with the broken leg a bottle of gin as an anaesthetic.

For a while he was maudlin and contrite. Then a taxi arrived and he refused to ride in it on the eccentric grounds that the driver was an abortionist. The battle-stained party got back to Cairo the following afternoon.

Miraculously the escapade was hushed up but a second, two months later, got into the Egyptian Press. A writer friend of Maclean's arrived in town and got off to a bad start by meeting an Ambassador's wife without his trousers on (they were being dried after a mishap with a whisky decanter). Later he embarked on a two-day blind with Maclean and they finished by forcing their way into a flat belonging to the US ambassador's secretary. They smashed the furniture, dumped a lot of her clothes in the lavatory, and smashed the bath with a marble shelf.

"It was marvellous to see it go up in smithereens," the writer enthused. Maclean's orgy was less a matter for aesthetic pleasure. He disliked the girl because she was American.

But even during Maclean's Cairo crack-up, the occasions for treason seem not to have eluded him. For in July, 1948, two months before Maclean left Washington, a new field of maximum interest to Soviet intelligence had been opened to him. This was the top secret negotiation of the North Atlantic Pact, the seminal Western initiative in the developing Cold War.

Again Maclean's continuing proximity to this is more than a hypothesis. The State Department letter, in one of its most pointed passages, states categorically that "Maclean is known to have had knowledge" of the exchanges. But, more than this, the letter suggests that he was familiar with everything which "led up to" signature of the Pact in April, 1949.

This gives a fresh perspective to the British Government's consistent insinuations that Maclean's postings after Washington provided him with no opportunity for important espionage. Being a "Grade A" embassy, Cairo was kept informed on British diplomacy across the board. Maclean, as head of Chancery, was excellently placed to monitor the continuing Washington talks.

The death of a secret army

While MacLean was still in Cairo, Philby had moved into a new job in Washington. He arrived there in October, 1949, and promptly began the most savagely destructive phase of his career.

Washington must have seemed to Philby to be his redemption after the purgatory of Istanbul. He went to America as liaison man between Britain's SIS and the American CIA. Now he was at the heart of western intelligence – at a time when, as a top CIA man of the period said, "relations were closer than they have been between any two services at any time". "You must remember," he said, "that at this time the CIA regarded themselves almost as novices." And Philby was acknowledged as perhaps Britain's most brilliant operative.

Philby had particular value to the CIA at this time. Being the western expert on the subject, he virtually set up the CIA's anti-Soviet espionage operation.

The damage Philby did during his two years in Washington is almost impossible to assess without considerably greater access to secret information than any newspaper could hope to obtain. But we have pieced together an account of the worst disaster that was ultimately charged to Philby's account, the Albanian debacle.

The Volkov incident in 1945 had been a piece of surgery, swift and casually brutal. The Albanian debacle five years later was altogether a more considered and a bloodier affair. What Philby betrayed was an attempt by Britain and America, at the height of the Cold War, to overthrow Russian influence in Albania by means of guerrilla-fomented uprisings.

For 17 years this has remained one of the most extraordinary secrets of the Cold War. It has suited both sides to leave it that way.

For the West, the Albanian affair was a disaster costing 150 lives. For Russia it was a nasty preview of what could happen in other parts of her uneasy empire.

In 1949, the weakest sector of the Russian empire was the Balkans. The Communist rebels in Greece were on the point of collapse. Jugoslavia was Communist but had broken with Russia. Even Albania was unsteady. The Jugoslav Communists had run Albania since the war; now Tito's cooling had forced Russia to move her own "technicians" and "advisers" into Albania.

At this point the Foreign Office and the American State Department had the same idea: could Albanian nationalism be harnessed to overthrow Russian influence? Perhaps the process of disaffection might even be helped along a bit?

Ernest Bevin, the Foreign Secretary, was adamantly opposed to the idea. But the Foreign Office contained a vocal faction in favour of establishing "resistance movements" in virtually every country of occupied eastern Europe. This was enthusiastically supported by the hairier denizens of SIS, particularly the old SOE operators who firmly believed the dictum that "politics is war carried on by other means" – or as it might be, the same means.

But, over Albania, Bevin seems to have reckoned without American pressure. So far as the story can be pieced together the factions in the Foreign Office and the SIS appear to have joined forces with the hawks of the State Department.

Bevin was persuaded to sanction a "pilot experiment" in subversion: a clandestine operation, to be organised jointly by the SIS and the CIA, to infiltrate guerilla bands into Albania to foment anti-Russian uprisings.

The man responsible for co-ordinating the British and American halves of the joint operation was, naturally, the British liaison man in Washington, Kim Philby. His experience as ex-controller of the Turkish station – the biggest and most active in that part of the world – made his advice on clandestine operations particularly valuable.

Certainly, the operation was well planned. One of the first steps was the formation, around the summer of 1949 of a "Committee of Free Albanians", based in Italy, and apparently a front organisation for recruiting guerrillas.

In the spring of 1950, the guerrillas were ready to go. First in small groups, then in larger bands, they slipped up into the mountains and over the border into Albania. The plan is said to have been that the groups were to make for their old homes and try to stir up trouble there – taking to the mountains if things got too hot.

It was a disaster. *The Russians just seemed to know they were coming.*

The reception was brisk and bloody. Within a month, 150 or so guerrillas – about half the total force – were either killed or captured, along with a number of Albanians at home who had been unwise enough to welcome the warriors.

The 150 survivors struggled back into Greece – to the embarrassment of the Greek Government. The SIS in London had hastily to bully the bewildered Home Office into allowing 150 mysterious Albanians into Britain (where a weird "welcome back" party was thrown for them at the Caxton Hall in London). It is unclear whether the Home Office was told the truth about these refugees – according to one source the Albanians were improbably described as "good friends of ours in Greece".

The Ministry of Labour then had the task of finding work for the crew. In the end, the Forestry Commission turned numbers of them into lumberjacks, and jobs were invented for most of the others at an ordnance factory.

The post-mortem on the debacle was prolonged. After a year opinion was still split. The Americans were uneasily convinced of treachery. And what few indications there were pointed to Philby, they thought. But in Britain the SIS appear not to have accepted even the evidence of treachery. Without the advantage of hindsight, the evidence at the time must certainly have seemed far from conclusive.

But knowing what is now known of Philby, it is clear that the Albanian expedition – and, indeed, many other aspects of the information flow between British and American intelligence – must have been leaked to the Russians. The effect was totally to discredit in British eyes the policy of "positive interventions" in Communist Europe, and to weaken it for some years in America.

Philby would, no doubt, have gone on holding this crucial liaison job for some more years, if it had not been for developments in Maclean's crumbling career at the Foreign Office.

Maclean cracks – and is promoted

On May 11, 1950, Maclean boarded a London-bound plane from Farouk field. Melinda, now totally unable to cope with him, had gone to the ambassador, Sir Ronald Campbell, pleading for him to be sent home from Egypt. The official verdict, probably accurate enough, was that he was suffering from a nervous breakdown.

After a medical board, the Foreign Office gave him six months leave in London on condition that he underwent a psychiatric course. They had treated him generously largely because senior FO officials felt he was archetypically one of their own. He looked so right, unlike Burgess, of whom one senior official said after an interview: "His qualifications are adequate but what about his fingernails?"

The six-month break was of very dubious benefit. He was helped through it mainly by an experienced, aristocratic woman friend, one of the few women who ever seems to have understood him. His appointed analyst, a forbidding Viennese lady he called "Dr Rosie", was less helpful. Following her advice to accept his homosexuality without guilt, he fell in love with a Black porter at a Soho club – he repaid Maclean's dogged devotion by beating him up.

Melinda returned from Cairo only reluctantly, after an extended affair with a relative of King Farouk noted for his virility. Soon she was talking of leaving again.

His intelligent woman friend was Maclean's only prop. She met him "recovering from DTs" in the country garden of Lady Henderson, mother of "Nikko" Henderson, now British Minister in Madrid. He confided to her his sexual problems with Melinda and his absurd, unrequited passion for the porter.

And at her house he christened his alter ego "Gordon" – a reference to the tusky boar illustrated on an export gin bottle. He had borrowed the idea from a rumbustious writer friend who had acquired the habit of referring to his own alter ego as "Charlie Parsley".

He himself was drunk, often, and combatively. He looked like a wreck. Cyril Connolly was appalled at the decline, which he described with his usual precision: "His face was usually a livid yellow, his hands would tremble. . . . In conversation a kind of shutter would fall as if he had returned to some basic and incommunicable anxiety."

At this period Maclean sent a desperate letter from a temporary address in Oxford where he said his diet consisted of "sedatives and pints of bitter". His normally inhibited handwriting lurched down the page as he wrote: "There are two men in a car waiting outside. They've been there for four hours."

Are they after me? he asked. And then with the obsessional self-questioning of a man undergoing analysis he went on to wonder whether he had invented the strangers in the car as a projection of his own guilt.

His friends told him it was all paranoiac nonsense. They did not, of course, realise that the remorse went deeper than mere anxiety about the bouts of drunkenness and homosexuality.

Maclean's real worry was that the security men were on him. The Eumenides with blood on their paws, as he once called them, were out to avenge his treachery in Washington. The other guilt was an invention so he could tell his friends how he felt, though not why.

On the Soho circuit, there were few people who did not see him fighting (usually unsuccessfully). And on one farcical occasion at a club in Carnaby Street he had dived at the painter Rodrigo Moynihan and bitten him painfully in the knee. The *doppelgänger* Gordon was thoroughly in command.

He was also behaving with mounting indiscretion. Mark Culme-Seymour, a friend from pre-war Paris days, remembers an evening at the Gargoyle Club in Dean Street when Maclean lurched about, red-faced accosting other patrons. "Buy me a drink," he said. "I am the English Hiss."

But neither these well-known escapades, nor the Cairo debacle, were enough for the Foreign Office to jettison him. By the end of his six months, he was passed fit not merely for employment but for promotion, as if his career had never been interrupted. On November 8, 1951, he became Head of the FO American Department.

Since then, various attempts have been made to downgrade the importance of this post, notably by Harold Macmillan, in the 1955 debate, who said that it dealt mainly with Latin-American affairs: "The US questions which are dealt with . . . are largely routine, welfare of forces, visitors and the like."

As a description of the department's executive powers, this was true enough. But the best comment on it is nevertheless Senator Eastland's scrawled in the margin of the State Department letter which quoted it: "*Nuts.*"

Power of action is one thing, access to information another. In the Foreign Office what matters as much as writing policy advice, is being on the top "distribution lists" for other departmental material. This was the strength of the Head of the American Department.

For a period after starting his new job, Maclean seemed much improved. Every evening he caught the 5.19 from Charing Cross to Tatsfield in Kent, where he and Melinda had bought an ugly house called Beaconshaw.

But in the new year, 1951, he started drinking heavily once again. One night in Mark Culme-Seymour's flat he said, a propos of nothing: "What would you do if I said I was working for Uncle Joe?"

Later he added that everything he did in the American Department was designed to assist Communism. Culme-Seymour wondered whether he should report this conversation, but decided that Maclean was probably just drunk. Anyway, he thought if there was anything in it, MI5 would surely know already.

The particular help which Uncle Joe was getting is clearly indicated from the State Department's account. It was in two areas: the Japanese Peace Treaty negotiations and – what American officials regarded as the most specific item of destructive activity – the Korean War strategy.

The State Department account says that Maclean had full knowledge of the critical American decision to "localise" the Korean conflict. In November, 1950, just after Maclean had started his new job, President Truman instructed General MacArthur not to carry the war across the Manchurian border or to blockade the Chinese coast, even in the event of a Chinese invasion of Korea.

MacArthur, backed by his intelligence chief General Charles Willoughby, was always convinced that this priceless information had reached the Chinese via the Russians. He went to his grave certain not only of this, which meant that the Chinese could invade with impunity, but of the enemy's foreknowledge "of all our strategic troop movements".

His belief was that the leaky security of the British was the main culprit, something which the State Department document, with specific reference to Maclean, does nothing to refute and much to confirm. It establishes just how badly Washington judged itself to have been burned by Maclean's tenure of the allegedly insignificant American Department.

The net now begins to close

But it was not only Maclean's personal crack-up which made his appointment remarkable. Even as he took his seat at the American desk, his loyalty had begun to be doubted. For two years, British security men had been on the trail of alarming atomic leakages, and for at least six months Maclean himself had been a principal suspect. The net was now beginning to close. It was a secret: known only to the tightest circle in London and Washington. But among those kept informed of every move was the resident SIS man in America, Kim Philby.

Now, for the first time, the careers of Maclean and Philby became critically intertwined. For both men it was the fatal encounter.

SECRET TRIAL OF KIM PHILBY

———————•———————

22 October 1967

AT 9.30 a.m. on his last day in England, May 25, 1951, Donald Maclean was walking decorously from Charing Cross Station to his room in the Foreign Office. Guy Burgess, never a devotee of early rising, had only just got out of bed in his New Bond Street flat by Asprey's. He was reading *The Times* and drinking tea made by his friend Jack Hewit. Everything was relaxed and unhurried.

By 10.30 everything had changed irrevocably. Burgess, warned through Kim Philby in Washington that Donald Maclean was about to be interrogated, made a vital decision. By that evening Maclean had gone, in a cloud of mystery – and Burgess had gone with him.

But for Burgess's excited and unnecessary flight, things might have been very different for Kim Philby. Conceivably, the most remarkable Soviet spy ever to penetrate the Western intelligence community might have remained undetected for another ten years. Certainly it is now clear that it was only his almost fortuitous double link – with both Burgess and Maclean – which turned suspicion on him.

Had the cool, untrusting Philby been finally betrayed in 1951 by the bonds of Burgess's impulsive friendship, it would have been an ironic finale. But the damage Burgess did to him was more than compensated by the inflexible loyalty of his friends in the Secret Intelligence Service. Insight's inquiries have now established, in detail, that Philby, publicly sacked from the Foreign Service in 1951, was in fact secretly employed as a British agent by the SIS – even during the shadowy period before he became an *Observer* foreign correspondent at the request of the Foreign Office.

This did not merely mean that Philby, the Soviet spy, had a second chance to penetrate British intelligence. It meant that the impression gained from Parliamentary statements on two occasions was false.

The story of how all this happened is in part the story of a clandestine battle between the two principal secret departments of the British Administration: the Secret Intelligence Service (MI6) and the Security Service (MI5). A major turning-point in this struggle was a strange "secret trial" in which Philby successfully defended himself against the charge that he was a Communist agent. The result of the struggle was victory for MI5: the discrediting of the SIS eventually became so acute that Sir Dick White was promoted from being head of MI5 to take over as head of the rival SIS, which he remains today.

That radical break with Secret Service tradition is generally reckoned to have been a great success. Under Sir Dick, an urbane civilian with considerably more administrative ability than the soldiers and sailors who went before him, the SIS works smoothly and is reckoned – especially by Americans – to have regained the high reputation that it had begun to lose.

The career of Kim Philby went through two major phases. The first phase, described in our two previous articles, was one of penetration into British Intelligence and of steady rise through its ranks. The landmarks can be swiftly noted: 1940 joins a branch of SIS; 1941 becomes a sub-section chief; 1944 put in charge of counter-Soviet operations; 1946 goes to Turkey to organise operations against the Russians; 1949 goes to Washington as link-man between SIS and the Central Intelligence Agency.

The second phase, despite a stubborn rearguard action by Philby, is essentially one of decline, detection and ultimate defeat: the destruction of the unique position Philby had built up at the heart of the Western intelligence-system.

The dividing point between the two phases was the day of the Burgess-Maclean defection. The events of May 25, 1951, can be reconstructed in detail.

Burgess's relaxed mood that morning was understandable. He did not have to go to the office because he was under suspension. He had just been ordered back from a minor post in the information department of the Washington Embassy for a complex of indiscretions involving homosexuality, drink, driving offences and inattention to duties. Burgess's FO career was clearly over at the age of forty.

Maclean, outwardly, looked in much better shape. Only thirty-seven, he had been Head of Chancery in Cairo. A set of drunken escapades in Cairo had been a setback but now, after time off for psycho-analytical treatment, he was in charge of the American Department of the Foreign Office in London, where work was not onerous, but information was always available. He was, however, in worse trouble than Burgess: he had been passing massive amounts of information to the Russians, and the two discreet men who followed him along Whitehall were MI5 men.

About an hour after Maclean reached his desk, a brief and important meeting took place in the same building – in the spacious elegance of the Foreign Secretary's room. The head of the FO Security Branch and a high official of MI5, met the Foreign Secretary, Herbert Morrison. Morrison gave them authority to interrogate Donald Maclean about the leakages of information to the Russians which the British security men had been investigating for more than a year.

This brief, high-level exchange was the result of a longer and more agonised session the day before at lower level. Two officials each from the three departments involved – SIS, MI5 and the Foreign Office – had met to discuss whether the time was ripe to interrogate Maclean. The SIS and MI5 men argued for a little more delay, but the FO men said that the time had come to "jump" Maclean. They said that Maclean, who had been aware for some time that he was being followed and was being cut off from top-secret telegrams, was jumpy and ready to crack.

This was the last lap of an investigation which had begun early in 1949, when the American Central Intelligence Agency discovered that certain British atomic information had reached the Russians. The source was established as the British Embassy in Washington, and the nature of the case involved both MI5 (responsible for British counter-espionage generally) and SIS (responsible for counter-espionage on foreign soil, apart from its own espionage, and for liaison with the CIA). Towards the end of 1949, Kim Philby took over as SIS man in Washington, and so he was swiftly embroiled in the spy-hunt.

The crucial fact before the half-dozen officials was that exhaustive analysis of the Washington embassy files made Maclean the best prospect as a Russian spy – but that there was no way to get legal evidence unless Maclean could be persuaded to confess. Everything, therefore, hung on a successful interrogation. The conviction of the FO men that Maclean was "ripe" carried the meeting.

Philby would have known of the interrogation decision within hours: he would have known from his own part in the SIS investigation how important a Soviet spy Maclean was. And now the time for a getaway had been sharply reduced.

There was, however, still time: because the decision did not mean immediate interrogation. May 25, when the officials' decision was ratified by Morrison, was a Friday, and this meant that the interrogation would not begin until Monday morning. It would almost certainly have nailed Maclean. MI5 had prepared their best man, William Skardon: the relentless, courteous ex-Murder Squad detective who had cracked the atom-spy Klaus Fuchs. Maclean, haunted by guilt about both espionage and homosexuality, was just out of psycho-analysis, and should have been a helpless target.

But Skardon never got to his man. Just about the time that Morrison was giving his assent on Friday morning, Guy Burgess was taking the first concrete step towards getting Donald Maclean out of the country.

By chance, Burgess had two tickets for the steamer Falaise, leaving Southampton that night for Brittany. They had been intended for a holiday with a young American man whom Burgess had met earlier in the month on the Queen Mary. Now Burgess went to Green Park to meet the young man and tell him the trip might have to be called off.

He explained he would not know for sure until later in the day. Burgess did volunteer an explanation – "a young friend in the Foreign Office is in terrible trouble, and I am the only one who can help him" – which sounded like an improvised fantasy. But on this occasion, Burgess was telling the literal truth.

Burgess's mood had changed sharply, suddenly. At nine a.m. he had been relaxed in bed, hearing a cheery farewell from his friend Hewit: "Don't do anything I wouldn't do." After that, he had made several leisurely phone calls in connection with his holiday trip with the American.

But from the time that jaunt was cancelled, Burgess scarcely stopped moving. He made more phone calls, hired a car "for about ten days", bought a new suitcase and clothes, went home to pack, had some drinks in the Reform Club and finally drove off through the rush-hour traffic to Donald Maclean's house at Tatsfield in Kent.

Meanwhile, Maclean had enjoyed a leisurely birthday lunch with friends in London. (He was thirty-eight on May 25.) Maclean was wearing his hat with the brim turned up all round, his personal symbol of good spirits. He was pleased about the child his wife Melinda was expecting, and about the fact that he had overcome his absurd infatuation for a night-club porter. His MI5 "tails", whose instructions were to follow him only during the day, saw him off on his usual 5.19 train from Charing Cross.

Late that night, after dining at Tatsfield, Burgess and Maclean drove in the hired car down to Southampton. At midnight, they boarded the Falaise with a minute to spare. They were so late that Burgess left the car parked illegally on the quay. A sailor asked what they were doing, and Burgess bellowed: "Back on Monday."

A feud breaks out in the secret world

For a spy, as for a politician, the essential requisite is the simplest; luck. And it seems that Philby's luck ran out when Burgess, for reasons that he could never quite explain to people in Moscow, chose to go all the way with Maclean.

He was inevitably involved with the mechanism of the escape; after the decision to expedite Maclean's interrogation, it became a rush job. And Burgess had a priceless asset: two steamer tickets ready booked.

But there was no real reason for Burgess himself to defect: he was going to have to leave the Foreign Office, but he was not going to be charged with any offence. And it was only the fact that Burgess disappeared which drew attention, suddenly, to Kim Philby.

Had Maclean alone vanished, Philby would merely have been one of the "outer ring" of suspects. He knew that Maclean was to be grilled: but so did a great many other people who would have been likelier suspects. But Burgess had been living in Philby's house in Washington just before he was recalled, and on top of that he was a long-standing friend of Philby's.

Irresistibly, Philby was promoted to being one of the top half-dozen suspects: if only because if one drew up a list of Maclean suspects and a list of Burgess suspects, he was the only man who figured on both lists. Also, Philby became the target of a ferocious blitz by the Americans, who began complaining bitterly that they had given a man free run of the CIA for 18 months, whom they now found had shared his house with a notoriously and obviously insecure man who had capped all his indiscretions by decamping to Russia.

The weekend after the defection, a four-man team led by G. A. Carey Foster, the head of Q-Branch in the FO, flew to Washington and questioned Philby. Almost immediately afterwards Philby was withdrawn from his post as CIA/SIS liaison officer: apart from any suspicions the British had, the Americans were no longer prepared to deal with him.

In a sense, it was a cool piece of nerve on Philby's part to come back to London and face the music, rather than defect himself at the earliest opportunity. But there was one thing strongly in his favour. MI5, of course, were inevitably in charge of the investigation of the "third man" affair. But once MI5 began to investigate an SIS officer like himself, two entirely different philosophies of security were bound to come into headlong collision.

The MI5 philosophy was one of meticulous examination of files and records: the department was a group of spycatchers, trained in building up cases against suspects. The SIS philosophy, essentially, was based on personal trust.

Immediately and predictably, the two departments split on how to handle the Philby case. MI5 wanted to make a long, detailed investigation of him: SIS of course opposed this. They offered an alternative, which was that General Sir Stewart Menzies, the chief of the SIS throughout Philby's meteoric rise, should spend a day talking things over with Philby to see if anything had gone wrong. This, inevitably, was rejected.

The Philby dispute was sharpened by the antagonism already existing between SIS and MI5 officers. (In a discussion with an eminent MI5 man of the period, we mentioned the Whitehall tradition by which SIS men are known as "the Friends". He said, bleakly: "I used to refer to them as 'the Enemies'.")

War had left the two departments with entirely different legacies. MI5 had been totally reconstructed at the beginning of the war, and its operations placed firmly in the hands of civilian, professional intelligence-men. In 1946, the gang-busting policeman, Sir Percy Sillitoe, was made Director of MI5: its driving-force was a man named

Dick White, who had joined the service as a bright young graduate in 1936. MI5 began to chalk up some notable Cold War spy-captures, like Nunn May and Fuchs.

SIS, fortuitously, had avoided wartime reconstruction: its leadership remained ex-military, with a strong hangover of Indian Police influence. At the time of the Burgess-Maclean defection, the Service was still being run by Stewart Menzies, and the days when his henchman Colonel Claud Dansey could say that he would "never knowingly use a university man" were not far away.

But the SIS was clearly having trouble matching-up to the massive and powerful Soviet KGB – which would have been hard enough even without the fact that the SIS's best man was secretly working for the Russians. "In those days," says an ex-SIS desk man, "we just didn't get any high-grade information out of Russia, and we never did until Penkovsky came along in the sixties." If anything, this feeling of being under pressure probably strengthened the SIS determination not to lose their best "pro" because of the prejudices of Sillitoe and White in MI5.

Philby has to resign from his Foreign Office cover-job, inevitably. And it is this "resignation" with which both Harold Macmillan in 1955, and Edward Heath in 1963, made great play in their statements to the House of Commons. Heath, whose task was to admit that Philby's loyalties had at last been finally proved by his defection to Russia, was particularly energetic.

Heath said that Philby was asked to resign from the Foreign Service in July, 1951 ("which he did"). He then explained how Philby had had a period of "some employment, presumably arranged by himself", before the Foreign Office suggested in 1956 that *The Observer* might like to give him a job. It was, of course, the *Observer* job, as correspondent in Beirut, that Philby held at the time of his defection in January, 1963; even after reading between the lines an MP would probably have got the impression that Philby had been dismissed from all Government service in 1951.

What Philby did lose was his very prestigious job in America: and presumably his chances of going to the top of the Service. There may have been some debate within the SIS about how to use Kim's talents: but by the end of the year he was back, hard at work, as a very important kind of agent in the field.

But it looks, from the evidence, as though they used him for an intricate and dangerous game: trying to penetrate Russia and get some better information out. And as Philby started out on his new job, the MI5 men under Dick White began, despite SIS displeasure, to make a long, thorough investigation of Philby's career – which he knew would result sooner or later in a new assault on his position.

Strange encounter in Turkey

In a small gossipy community like Cyprus it is difficult for a newcomer to remain a stranger for long. So when Philby arrived there in October, 1951, three months after his "resignation", he was soon swept into the island social round.

Gradually, the impression crept around that Philby was "something to do with, the British BMEO" – the British Middle East Office.

Philby's office was in a collection of huts in the middle of an agricultural research station near Athalassa known locally as "the stud farm". Unusually for a research station, it had radio masts, underground tunnels, and a heavy security guard.

Philby was seldom there. His real job, of course, was still with the SIS. Instead of running a network of agents, Kim Philby had become one himself. Kicked out of his office in Washington, he had been sent out into the field.

As well as his charm and his heavy drinking, there were two other things about Philby during this period which stood out – his sudden interest in Armenian folk music, and his frequent spells away from Cyprus.

Soon after he arrived on the island Philby began to attend the Melkonian Institute, a centre frequented by Armenians from all over the Levant but mainly by refugees from Soviet Armenia. It was an interesting place. Armenians are, perhaps, the world's most tightly-knit community and when it comes to keeping in touch allow no consideration of political borders to interfere. At the Melkonian Institute, it was said in Cyprus, it was possible to send a message to Soviet Armenia in four days.

Philby, a competent piano player, could have claimed a passion for music as an explanation for his interest in the Melkonian Institute.

His absences were a little harder to explain – especially after a bizarre encounter which occurred in Eastern Turkey in the winter of 1952.

A group of 12 British Council scientists on a field expedition in Greenmantle country near the border between Turkey and Soviet Armenia drove into a mountain outpost called Dogubayazit and stopped for petrol. The attendant told them that there was another Englishman in town, a man carrying a rucksack and travelling on foot.

The scientists found this hard to believe. It had been snowing heavily and they had passed no one on the one road that leads into Dogubayazit from the north. In any case, what would a lone Englishman be doing in an area under such tight military control that it was almost impossible to get a pass? But on the chance that the petrol attendant might be right they trudged through the snow to the local tea room, a shanty of tin and tent poles. Kim Philby was inside sipping tea and smoking a cigarette, holding court in Turkish with the locals.

One of the scientists who knew Philby well said hello to him and then asked him what on earth he was doing there. Philby, who had taken the unexpected meeting with considerable calm, said simply: "Collecting geological samples. I'm on a holiday." The scientist, who had suspected Philby's SIS connections in Cyprus nodded and did not press the matter. But after they had given Philby a lift to Erzurum, the British Council group began to discuss how he could have got to Dogubayazit.

They had not passed him on the road from Kars. He could not have come north from Van because the road was blocked by snow, and no one at checkpoints on the Erzurum road recognised him as having passed that way. At least two of them became convinced that Philby could have reached Dogubayazit only on the 60 mile road around Mount Ararat from Erivan in Soviet Armenia. Had Philby crossed the border?

At that time the Turkish side of the border was only loosely patrolled. But the Soviet side was lined with two rows of barbed wire and fortified with watch towers half a mile apart. If Philby had crossed to Turkey from Russia then he had either taken an incredible risk or else had been permitted to pass.

The implications of this were so startling that the scientists, who were not unaccustomed to meeting SIS officers, decided that it would be best to forget the incident.

It is easy to understand their reasoning. It is less easy to understand that of the SIS. Why put Philby, an agent under suspicion of working for the Soviet Union, into an area where he is bound to come into contact with Russians?

Only two theories can explain this. Either the SIS thought that Philby had been fully cleared or else they were playing one of those labyrinthine games which make up the more esoteric extensions of espionage. Their reasoning would go like this: if Philby has been working for the Russians then his demotion to the field will hurt. They will be trying to work him back again. What better way to do this than to feed Philby a selection of perfectly genuine items. In any case, since the essence of espionage is to make contact with your opposition, what have we to lose?

Philby's secret trial

Meanwhile, MI5 had completed their mammoth investigation of Philby, and wanted to put the results to test. The method finally chosen was a full-scale mock trial, in which only the absence of an authentic judge would detract from the purpose of the exercise: to discover, by simulation of the proceedings, whether a criminal prosecution of Philby was likely to succeed. In July, 1952, learned counsel were briefed. What, exactly, would they be able to bring in evidence?

Although something must by now have been discovered about Philby's political past, it seems clear that the probe did not stretch very far: three separate witnesses to the Vienna period of burgeoning and unconcealed Communist conviction recall, with some surprise, that they were never approached by British investigators.

But this had evidently not come to light in 1952. The two basic items available to the mock prosecutors were the operational catastrophes – the Volkov affair and the sinister collapse of the Albanian subversion mission.

Despite the fact that Philby stood badly compromised in both cases, the trial was an embarrassing disaster for the authorities. It lasted three days, and on none of them did the accused offer the slightest chink of an admission.

Leading for the prosecution was an old MI5 hand, Helenus "Buster" Milmo, QC (now a High Court judge). The room was filled with lawyers who were also chosen for their wartime security clearance. One of them, summing up the ensuing dialectical joust, said: "It was as if the cleverest man in the world were being cross-examined by the stupidest man in the world" – a harsh judgment on Milmo, who did no worse than anyone else might have done in the face of such finely tuned defences.

Philby's technique was in fact relatively simple: to deny everything, and to spin out his answers to the most straightforward questions. "I know it looks strange," he would say, "but I didn't do it. That's not the way it was." And lacking a scintilla of hard evidence, beyond the bare association with Burgess in Washington, the prosecution could get no further.

"Was it a fine day?" Milmo would ask. "I think it was 57 degrees, a slight north-westerly wind, some cloud," Philby would reply: "Yes, you could say it was a fine day." Even without a stutter, a few hours of this treatment can undermine any inquisitor, Milmo's line of questioning got angrier.

In the eyes of most SIS men, who thought Philby should never have been interrogated, their view was completely vindicated. But in the eyes of MI5, the pseudo-judicial farce had merely preserved him from the sort of handling which had been so fruitful in the past – the soft-touched, long-drawn-out encounter with the most frightening interrogator in the security business, William Skardon. Skardon appears to have been contemptuous of the mock trial crudities, and the fact that it was all over in days not weeks. Philby might not have cracked under the slow strain; but at least he would not have seen his interrogator off quite so drastically.

But Philby's wanderings in Turkey and his four years out in the cold went for nothing – because of a grotesque piece of bad luck. In October, 1955, Col. Marcus Lipton, MP, electrified the House of Commons by naming Philby as the "third man" behind the defection.

Even now, the people involved are unclear what happened. They merely share an uneasy – and, as it happens, justified – suspicion that they were pawns in some subtler gambit. Col. Lipton himself seems to favour the idea that the CIA planted the information on him, presumably to embarrass the British Government into taking action against Philby. A more Machiavellian interpretation holds that Philby's old friends arranged it, knowing that the lack of proof would leave the Government no choice but to clear Philby.

The truth is more prosaic. The whole thing was planted by Mr Jack Fishman, the resourceful news editor of the *Empire News*, a Sunday paper now defunct. Lipton's direct informant was the *Empire News* crime reporter, Johnny Hunt-Crowley.

It was a textbook example of an ancient journalistic device to evade the laws of libel, which hinges upon the privilege a newspaper has of reporting what is said in Parliament with no fear of a libel action.

Fishman was a connoisseur of this technique and he decided to prime two Labour MPs – both noted for the catholicity of their parliamentary questions – Col. Marcus Lipton and the late Norman Dodds.

But how had the *Empire News* heard about Philby in the first place? Fishman is reticent: he murmurs of "East German contacts". But another man who worked on the story has a rather different recollection. Henry Maul, the London editor of the *New York Sunday News*, used to work for the *Empire News* one day a week, and he says: "The details came from a man Johnny Hunt-Crowley met on the train up from East Grinstead."

In retrospect, it looks as if Hunt-Crowley's man was an MI5 contact who had been on the fringe of the inquiry into the defection. In retrospect, too, it is remarkable how the details he adduced jumble highly-secret accuracy and ignorant gossip.

Dodds got cold feet about asking a question, after consulting Col. George Wigg, his spy-minded back-bench colleague. Wigg was against so blunt an instrument as a Parliamentary question.

But Lipton pressed on, fortified at the last minute by a cutting Hunt-Crowley produced from the *New York Sunday News*. This set out, in great detail, what Lipton took to be the CIA case against Philby. Lipton was not to know that the journalist Maul had written it in the *Empire News*'s office in London.

Nobody behind this exercise, however, could have foreseen the consequences the question would have. In public, the only response it drew was a categorical assurance from the Foreign Secretary, Harold Macmillan: "I have no reason to conclude that Mr Philby has at any time betrayed the interests of this country, or to identify him with the so-called 'third man', if indeed there was one."

To the jubilant Philby, dispatching the subsequent Press conference with ruthless ease, it looked like the final rehabilitation.

How Harold Macmillan decided

MacMillan's attitude to the secret services was patrician to a degree. "I do not expect the gamekeeper to come and tell me every time he catches a fox," he once said. He adhered to the code that politicians should know little and inquire less about their intelligence networks. Indeed, civil servants affirm that Macmillan – unlike, say, Wilson – had no very high regard for intelligence gleanings, except on what he called "nuts and bolts" (technical information about missiles and such). One of Macmillan's closest colleagues expressed the attitude pithily: "Good thing if the Russians did see our Cabinet minutes twice a week. Stop all that bloody dangerous guesswork."

So the brief on Philby that thudded on Macmillan's desk at the Foreign Office in the latter half of October, 1955, propelled Macmillan into a ruling situation. The Philby affair, he declared, was a domestic squabble which the feuding services should have resolved among themselves. Instead, it had blown up into a major embarrassment to the Government. And now he had to arbitrate.

Nor did the brief presented to him help much. It had been compiled by the Permanent Under-Secretary at the FO, Sir Ivone Kirkpatrick, and the FO Adviser to SIS at the time, Sir Patrick Dean (now Ambassador in Washington). And it was, according to one excellently-placed source, a document remarkable for what it did *not* say.

At this political level, the reconstruction of events is naturally a delicate matter. But the FO apparently felt that its job was to play safe. The brief therefore detailed only what little was proved against Philby: a Communist past and an "imprudent association", as the jargon had it, with Burgess.

At this time there was certainly some powerful lobbying for Philby, headed by the influential Conservative MP and former SIS man, Richard Brooman-White, but there is no evidence that this decided Macmillan.

Macmillan found a compromise. Publicly, what weighed with him was his familiar preoccupation with the relation between the liberty of the individual and the power of the State. He was therefore prepared to go into the Commons and clear Philby – because there was no proof.

But privately his verdict was blunt. Philby must go. To questions about liberty in this context, Macmillan said: "I'm not shooting him, just firing him." The SIS view at this time was in line with Macmillan's public statement. If mere suspicion of disloyalty was sufficient to wreck an SIS career from now on, were any of them safe?

What happened next can only be explained by one almost incredible assumption: the SIS rebelled. *They hired Philby yet again.*

Three facts are indisputable. Philby was fired in October, 1955. For at least six months he was without a regular job. But when Philby went to Beirut in September 1956 as correspondent for *The Observer* and *The Economist*, he was secretly employed as an SIS field agent. And the introduction to *The Observer* – his journalistic cover – had come from a Senior Foreign Office official.

A surprising new C is appointed

The parliamentary debate in November had provided a rare opportunity for dutiful hosannas to the secret service. But even then time was running out not only on the incumbent C, the reluctant "Sinbad" Sinclair, but on the traditional intelligence philosophy his appointment represented. His retirement in Spring 1956 was the end of a 40-year epoch: he was the last of the soldier-spymasters.

Some reform had already been imposed by the revival, in 1953, of the wartime post of FOA (Foreign Office Adviser) to SIS. And the first holder of the job, Sir George Clutton, later ambassador in Warsaw, brought a greater measure of FO supervision over SIS's activities.

Ironically, however, Clutton's successor as FOA, Michael Williams (now Minister to the Holy See), was directly involved in the debacle which finally swept away the old order. This was the notorious escapade of Commander Crabb in April 1956, who failed to return from an underwater mission against the Ordzhonikidze, the ship which brought Bulganin and Krushchev on a visit to this country.

As the swan song of the old guard, this struck a pathetically appropriate note. It was a hare-brained scheme from the start, with not the slightest discernible advantage to offset the unimaginable political risks involved.

That it should ever have been conceived is an apt measure of Sinclair's insensitivity to the perils of his job. The instinctive political poise of a Menzies would have saved him. So would firmer control over subordinates with whom, admittedly, Sinclair was poorly endowed.

The Crabb affair's only dividend was that it at last enraged the politicians, enough to conduct a radical SIS reform. The Prime Minister,

Anthony Eden, even confided that he took the whole operation as "a personal affront".

Sinclair promptly retired, and Williams, the unfortunate FOA, was moved to another job. Even though Sinclair's successor was already virtually decided, a three-month interval elapsed before his formal appointment.

The name which emerged astounded the secret world – not least the CIA. The name of the new C had been the priority target for the CIA's top man in London for weeks, but it was not surprising that in this particular mission he failed.

Sir Dick White, civilian and professional, had succeeded Sillitoe at MI5 three years earlier. For one man to switch as director from one side to the other was barely thinkable, least of all in the bastion of SIS, White's Club. But the decision was forced through, mainly by Harold Macmillan, then Foreign Secretary, and Lord Normanbrook, secretary to the Cabinet, on the interesting grounds that Sir Dick, in the words of a contemporary, was "the only man we could trust".

One of the first discoveries to strike Sir Dick when he arrived in July must have been the fact that his old bogey, Kim Philby, was still on the books.

White was said to have been extremely angry. But Macmillan's response was possibly the more interesting: he did not care much. He set so little store by political intelligence that it did not seem to him Philby could do any harm at all sitting in Beirut.

In April, Philby had begun negotiations to establish a new cover, as a correspondent in Beirut. A senior Foreign Office man had made an official approach to *The Observer* on Philby's behalf, and roughly simultaneously, Philby himself approached *The Economist* through a third party. It has always been a sore point with Donald Tyerman, then editor of *The Economist*, that, although he checked on Philby with Harold Caccia at the FO, he was never told either by the Office or by *The Observer* that Philby's initial entrée had been strictly an official one.

There is considerable evidence that the FO was interested specifically in placing Philby in Beirut. He had family qualifications, and the posting, an important espionage centre, had special attractions for the FO and SIS.

When Sir Dick took over, negotiations were virtually complete. This had a single, decisive impact on the status of Philby's relations with SIS thereafter. However uncertain the degree of suspicion may have been in April, in September, when he left for the Middle East, it was absolutely firm in the eyes of C himself. For practical purposes he was at last definitely "blown".

Philby cracks – and disappears

Kim Philby was easily the most popular man in the British-American community in Beirut. The English speakers there are a gossipy little village, racked like all exile groups by feuds and quarrels. Kim was drunk a lot of the time, often passed out at parties or behaved outrageously if he managed to stay on his feet. And he had begun his social career in Beirut by stealing another man's wife.

Yet, even in the last months when he finally began to crack up under an intolerable burden of deceit, he was always invited back. Drunk or sober – more often drunk – Philby was one of those men who make women feel protective while keeping the respect and liking of men. He did not have an enemy in Lebanon.

There had, briefly, been some reserve when he arrived in Beirut in September, 1956, with a slight taint of the Third Man debate still clinging to him. But this soon melted away. Philby was so obviously a man down on his luck, gamely trying to re-establish himself in the tough competitive trade of a foreign correspondent after nearly 17 years away from journalism; a man who had made mistakes (and admitted them), the worst, so his Beirut friends thought, being an ill-advised but not discreditable friendship with the appalling Burgess. What they did not know, or failed to notice at first, was the amount of time spent with the British SIS station officer and his frequent trips to Cyprus.

As far as his work – or cover – as a journalist was concerned he began with certain advantages. He knew some Arabic, he had a compendious knowledge of the Middle East and, of course, he was the son of the eminent Arabist St John (few people have read St John's books – "just one damn wadi after another," one weary reader said) but St John's fame gave Kim an impeccable parentage in Arab eyes. He soon had friends everywhere.

Philby and Eleanor used to share Thanksgiving turkey with John H. Fistere, a former *Fortune* magazine writer more recently running a travel agency in Beirut, and his equally American wife – self-inflicted punishment, one would think, for someone as reportedly against the

American way of life as Philby. After Philby left Beirut, Fistere, like all of Philby's Beirut friends, combed his recollection for clues which might have indicated that Philby was concealing strong Left-wing political views. He could recall only two – very slight straws in the wind indeed!

One night Fistere was arguing with a group of Arab nationalists on a well-worn theme: were the fundamental aims of American democracy and Russian Communism the same? Yes, said the Arabs. Of course not, said Fistere. The aim of Soviet Communism was to enslave free men. Fistere appealed to Philby, who managed to stammer out that he thought the fundamental aims were the same. "I always assumed Kim was for the Free World," Fistere recalled recently. "I could not understand how he could equate Communism and the American Way."

Meanwhile Philby continued to expand his official contacts. He spent a great deal of time, more than any other correspondent, with people from the British and American Embassies. He was a constant caller on the SIS station chief, an old friend, and very friendly with Miles Copeland, well known to be a retired CIA man.

In fact, Philby was the best informed man in Beirut. In 1958, for example, he predicted positively that the American Marines were going to land in Lebanon three days before they did in fact arrive.

Five years passed in Beirut. As far as a journalist can have a routine, Philby had one. He rose around ten a.m., as often as not with a hangover; drank a prairie oyster to his own recipe; and walked some five hundred yards downhill to the Normandy Bar. Here he checked his mail and had his first drink of the day. Most afternoons he held court at the Normandy, and many evenings he dined out with his wide circle of friends and contacts.

Then in 1961 it all changed. George Blake, the Russian spy, was arrested and Philby, with his agent's inbuilt danger detector, knew that he was no longer safe. When the interrogation of Blake was complete an SIS man, a close friend of Philby's, arrived from London and in a brief but embarrassing interview told him that there was now irrefutable evidence that Philby had been working for the Russians. Philby took the challenge gracefully, admitted it, and then shrugged it off with a tantalising remark he has since repeated several times: "Knowing what I did I couldn't have done anything else."

Now Philby began to crack. He seemed to be undergoing the same collapse under strain that Maclean had suffered in Cairo more than a decade before; but this was happening to a man with considerably more self-discipline than Maclean had ever possessed.

His work for his two papers dried almost to a trickle. His drinking began to embarrass even his most tolerant friends. After a few cocktails he would be incoherently drunk and social evenings often lasted only long enough to get Kim into a taxi.

Why did the British Government do nothing about him? It seems that Sir Dick White was allowed four choices. Philby could be eliminated. (Sir Dick immediately rejected this choice as abhorrent.) The Lebanese Security Police could be taken at their word ("There is no reason why we should interfere with the removal of a wanted British subject to his homeland.") and Philby brought forcibly back to Britain and justice. The SIS could try to persuade Philby to return and face charges. Or there could be an attempt to "frighten Philby into defecting".

To Harold Macmillan, now Prime Minister, it was a matter of small importance – it was not then thought Philby was doing damage as he was under such suspicion by "C".

But to the SIS Philby's gaily Bohemian survival in Beirut after betrayal was more than they could bear. If Philby could not be brought back to England, for unproductive questioning by uniformed police, he could at least be sent into exile. For the sake of the SIS morale, it was therefore finally decided to confront him with the evidence and break him down – break him down in a way which could never be done in England.

This was acceptable also to Macmillan since Philby's return to Britain under any circumstances would result in a messy trial and demands for an enquiry into the running of the Security Services. Philby had already damaged SIS morale enough. Far better if he left the West for good.

The CIA, less worried about public opinion, wanted more direct action and at one point were considering a swift attempt to snatch Philby. When he disappeared on his way to keep a dinner engagement at the house of Hugh Balfour Paul, first secretary at the British Embassy, they became so Third Man conscious themselves that they grilled Balfour Paul at length to try to find out if he had given the warning.

After the disappearance came the pattern of cryptic letters now so familiar from the Burgess-Maclean case. Even then none of his friends had the slightest suspicion that he was going to Russia. Indeed, even after reports that he had arrived in Moscow most of Philby's

Beirut friends remained unconvinced until one of them, an Indian journalist called Godfrey Jensen, wrote to Philby addressing the letter "Kim Philby, Esq., Ministry of Foreign Affairs, Moscow".

In two weeks he got a reply. The letter consisted mostly of vague generalities but one phrase stood out: "My tongue is looser now." But did this mean that free from the tensions of a lifetime his stammer had gone? Or that he could more freely express the political views that had been his main motivation for thirty years. It is typical of Harold Adrian Russell Philby that he did not say.

1968–76
THE THALIDOMIDE
SCANDAL

Between 1958 and 1961, thalidomide was marketed in the UK by Distillers Biochemicals as a panacea for morning sickness in pregnant mothers. The drug, however, was the stuff of nightmares, causing severe birth defects. As a wave of "thalidomide babies" emerged in the early 1960s, the true nature of the drug suddenly became apparent.

Sixty-two families, outraged that Distillers had given them a remedy that would mean their children would now need specially adapted cars, clothes, homes and care for life, went to the civil courts seeking compensation.

Simultaneously, Insight began investigating the disturbing history of thalidomide. They found that Distillers had licensed the drug from a German manufacturer, Chemie Grünenthal, which had failed to do adequate research on the impact of thalidomide on unborn babies. It also became clear that Distillers had neglected to do its own independent research on the subject. Yet both were actively marketing the drug as safe to be taken during pregnancy.

British law at the time dictated that The Sunday Times could not report freely on the scandal, nor the inadequate compensation – a trust fund of £3.25m – being offered to the families by Distillers. Yet the tenacious editor, Harry Evans, risked heavy fines and the threat of jail to publish a continued campaign pressuring the company into offering an amount sufficient for justice to be done. It was a risk which would take The Sunday Times to both the High Court and the European Court of Justice.

Eventually this dogged determination succeeded in forcing Distillers to revise the offer to a £28.4m settlement. It also led to a change in UK law, enabling the press to report on an ongoing court case when it is deemed in the interest of the public to do so.

In the first extract, published eight years before Insight were able to tell the story of thalidomide in the UK in full, the team forensically outline the initial development and marketing of thalidomide in Germany by Chemie Grünenthal. At the time, nine men were set to stand trial in the German city of Aachen. They were accused of failing to properly test the drug's impact on pregnant mothers during its development, yet marketing it as safe nonetheless.

In the second extract, seven years later, Insight finally tell the full story of thalidomide in the UK, the impact it had on so many families, and the long road to the truth finally emerging.

THE THALIDOMIDE FILE

•

19 May 1968

NEXT WEEK in a converted canteen near Aachen, nine men will go on trial before a German court charged with intent to commit bodily harm and with involuntary manslaughter.

The trial is expected to last two years. There will be fourteen judges. The prosecution alone will produce 352 witnesses. The evidence that has been taken already runs to 70,000 pages. There has been nothing remotely comparable in Germany, in scale or in emotional intensity, since Nuremberg.

The defendants are the owner, six present employees and two former employees of a firm called Chemie Grünenthal.

Few, if any, of the victims will be present in court. There are thousands of them in Germany alone, at least one thousand adults suffering from severe nerve damage, and perhaps five thousand babies born with appalling deformities. Some of them died. Some of them were killed at birth. Some, tragically handicapped, are still alive. The drug was sold under many names. It became notorious as thalidomide.

This is what the prosecution case amounts to:

- that in 1958 the nine men in the dock put on sale a drug which, even when taken according to instructions, caused an unacceptable degree of bodily harm.

- that they failed to test it properly.

- that they went out of their way to advertise it as safe when they could give no guarantee that it was.

- that in fact it was so very far from safe that it caused those who took it to itch, shake, sweat, vomit, and even to lose the power to stand upright.

- that when these reactions were reported to them they first systematically brushed them aside; that some of them lied to doctors who questioned them; then – when the reports became too insistent to be ignored – did all they could to suppress them and, with money, to induce other doctors to write favourable reports.

- and that this same drug, which the sales department called "the apple of our eye" because it was so profitable, caused an epidemic of monstrously deformed babies.

All this the nine defendants will deny. As far as the nerve damage to adults is concerned, they will maintain that they acted promptly and responsibly when the danger was first brought to their attention. As for the deformities, they will claim that there is still no proof that thalidomide was the cause.

Ever since the news of the disaster became known to the public in November, 1961, there has been intense interest in the story of thalidomide. Hundreds of journalists are now converging on the trial, and hundreds of newspapers will be rewriting the human story of the thalidomide victims. It is a terrible story, of children born to lifelong pain and humiliation, and of brave people struggling under every kind of disadvantage to make the best of their own, their children's or their patients' broken lives.

That tragic story has often been told, and each learns what he can from it. But are there other, more practical lessons to be learned? How could educated men, doctors and scientists, make such a mistake, and, having made it, refuse to admit it? Was it blind, unavoidable tragedy, or was it that avoidable kind of tragedy which men call crime? These and many other matters are questions for the court; here at least, from authentic documents, is the full story of what happened.

The firm of Chemie Grünenthal has its headquarters in the little town of Stolberg, near the Belgian border, in a sturdy three-storey building which started life as a copper foundry in the eighteenth century. The onion-domed roofs and walls of rough masonry overlook a courtyard lined with laurels and Mercedes.

Grünenthal was set up after the Second World War. It was an offshoot of an old family firm called Dalli-Werke, Maurer & Wirtz, which makes soaps, detergents, and cosmetics in Aachen. The head of the new firm was Hermann Wirtz, a member of the family. Their first pharmaceutical products were antibiotics: first foreign ones made under licence, and later two new drugs discovered in their own laboratories, called xanthocillin and tyrothricin.

In July, 1946, the company took on, as head of its research lab, a thirty-two-year-old called Dr Heinrich Mückter. Mückter had qualified both as a chemist and as a doctor before the war. During the war he was a senior doctor (*Chefarzt*), at the Institute for Typhus and Virus Research at Cracow (Krakow), in Poland, which came under the German Army High Command.

According to evidence presented at the Nuremberg Nazi doctors' trial, this Institute provided Weigl serum out of the intestines of lice, which was used to inoculate thirty-one human guinea pigs taken from among the prisoners at the infamous Buchenwald concentration camp. Ten of the prisoners died as a result of being given the virus. Mückter's precise role at the Institute is not clear. The Polish authorities merely say: "Mückter was loyal to his German superiors but committed no criminal acts against the Polish population."

Apart from Wirtz and Mückter, the most important of the other executives at Grünenthal were self-made men: Jacob Chauvistre, who had started with Dalli-Werke straight from school and worked his way up to joint managing director; Hermann Leufgens, the other joint managing director, who had also worked his way up from a commercial apprenticeship, and Klaus Winandi, the sales manager, who had worked for Dalli-Werke before the war, and had been a prisoner of war. All six are among the nine who will be in the dock next week.

Chemie Grünenthal, in fact, was a small firm typical of the many such firms which brought about the post-war economic miracle in Germany. It was run by ambitious, competent men, who thought in terms of "my company, right or wrong". Certainly none of them could see far beyond the company's interests.

The first tests on drug K17

Thalidomide was discovered by accident. In the spring of 1954 Mückter was looking for an effective diuretic, working with a substance called carbonic anhydrase. (A diuretic is a drug that reduces body fluids and therefore obesity. Since obesity and associated heart disease was becoming a big medical problem in the West it was expected to be a good seller.)

To arrive at the final chemical, Mückter and his two assistants, Dr Herbert Keller and Dr Wilhelm Kunz, had to go through a number of different stages, each of which yielded a by-product. As a matter of routine they tested the by-products for pharmacological action. One of them looked promising. It was a piperidine compound of glutamine. Its chemical name was phthalimido glutarimide. It was white and tasteless and it crystallised into fine needles. They labelled it K17. It became known internationally as thalidomide.

Mückter was a good enough chemist to suspect from its molecular structure that K17 could have a sedative action, because of its similarity to glutethimide, already in use as a sedative. He was also a shrewd businessman; shrewd enough to have a contract which gave him 1 per cent of Grünenthal's turnover as a bonus over and above his salary, and shrewd enough to see that in K17 Grünenthal could be on to a good thing.

The sleeping pill boom that has been a phenomenon of modern western civilisation was already well under way – in Britain alone it was estimated that one million people took some sort of pill every night. There was a huge market for a new sedative, especially one free from barbiturates with their unpleasant side effects and danger of suicide.

Mückter's work changed gear. K17 became the focus of his research programme. In the first weeks of 1955 his team began pharmacological and toxicological tests on animals, mainly on rodents. The results of the tests on animals were summarised in a paper by Kunz, Keller and Mückter, published in 1956.

The extraordinary thing about their findings was not that K17 had a sedative action – they had suspected this – but that it apparently had no *dos toxalis* 50, the fatal dose that kills half the laboratory animals in an experiment. In other words it appeared that thalidomide was incredibly harmless, even when taken in large doses. It could not kill. *This was a vital finding.* It was to be the basis of Grünenthal's advertising for the next five or six years, and was one of the main reasons why the use of thalidomide became so widespread. But how good were the tests employed by Mückter and his colleagues to decide that thalidomide had "extremely low toxicity"?

In 1965 scientists at the University of Stockholm were asked to analyse the German report. They made the following points:

"The number of animal experiments in the toxicity tests was far too small; that because of this, a low frequency of side effects could not be detected, though these are important for a sedative like thalidomide and very necessary if the substance is to be declared unpoisonous. The conventional toxicological and pharmacological tests are most unsatisfactory. Kunz, Keller and Mückter openly tried to hoodwink the reader by creating a false impression of the scope of their tests."

The prosecutor puts it like this: "this sales talk ignored the fact – universally recognised in pharmacology . . . that no amount of experiments conducted on any amount of animals . . . can entitle a manufacturer to speak of 'guaranteed non-toxicity' and 'harmlessness' for human beings."

Grünenthal had no qualms. They went ahead with clinical trials. The preliminary results of the effect of thalidomide on human beings were given at a "Thalidomide Symposium" held in the Grünenthal factory on December 16, 1955. The nine doctors Grünenthal had recruited for the tests included dermatologists, psychiatrists and neurologists. Their verdict was hardly overwhelmingly favourable. Four were in favour of the drug, four had mixed reactions and one was decisively against it.

The main report in favour was by Dr Hermann Jung, a part-time Grünenthal employee earning about 200 DM a month (about £17) as a routine tester. Early in 1955 in a clinic in Cologne he gave K17 to 20 patients, mostly tubercular, for four weeks. On the basis of these trials he reported at the beginning of June that the drug was ready to be marketed. He went on experimenting however and in later tests found that K17 produced dizziness, constipation and a drop in temperature, shivering and a buzzing in the ears. But, undeterred, Jung told the thalidomide symposium in December:

"We have in K17 a substance which at the correct dose level has no undesirable side effects. I believe that K17 is a satisfactory drug, and that with the necessary propaganda it will succeed in the pharmaceutical market."

So further trials followed. Again K17 was sent out to specialists. Two replied favourably but any satisfaction this might have given Grünenthal was shattered by a critical report from Dr Ferdinand Piacenza, the doctor in charge of the Wasach Sanatorium near

Oberstdorf. Dr Piacenza said he had been forced to break off tests with thalidomide because of "absolute non-toleration". He described various side effects including, significantly, symptoms of what he considered to be allergic reaction.

Mückter replied on behalf of Grünenthal: "We have never had such a negative report as yours." He blamed too high a dose for the reactions in Piacenza's patients – "K17 is such a strong sedative that in general small doses are sufficient" – and dismissed Piacenza's suggestion that K17 was an allergy-producing substance. "The only explanation left is that [the reactions] are a disturbance in the nervous system, following too high a dosage over a long period of time."

This remark of Mückter's is significant on two counts – it shows that he was aware that K17 could affect the nervous system and that there was a point at which dosage became too high. It is odd, therefore, that when K17 went on the market, the company's instructions should include the vaguely worded phrase, "In case of sleeplessness Contergan can be taken in higher doses without any danger."

Thalidomide's prospects at this stage were not good. In the three years since the drug had been discovered, testing had been sporadic. The numbers and controls had been inadequate, not all the possible trials on animals had been carried out, the trials on humans had left many questions unanswered and had given rise to misgivings about toleration and side effects. Yet, on September 2, 1957, at a meeting between Mückter, Winandi and managing director Chauvistré, it was decided to put thalidomide on the market.

The great publicity campaign

Thalidomide went on sale on Tuesday, October 1, 1957. After some deliberation Grünenthal had chosen the word CONTERGAN as a brand name. Thalidomide was exported to about 11 European, 7 African, 17 Asiatic and 11 American countries. In addition it was produced by a number of firms under licence, under a total of 51 names such as Softenon, Softenil, Distaval, Babysitter (a version specially for children), and Neurosedyn. There were a few imitations of the drug in Italy and Japan, for which Grünenthal were not responsible.

Once they had decided to launch the drug they decided to do it properly. They spent money copiously. They bought 50 advertisements in the major medical journals and sent out 200,000 letters to doctors.

The theme was set out in a circular dated September 26, 1957, issued by Mückter's scientific research department, and addressed to all associates. The idea was to emphasise "sure to work and completely non-poisonous". The circular continued: "The atoxicity proved in animal experiments makes Contergan completely safe and this gives the preparation its special opportunity."

A claim of safety in pregnancy

The next stage in Grünenthal's sales campaign proved to be the decisive step in the tragedy. They began promoting it for use by pregnant and nursing women.

On May 2, 1958, Dr Augustin Peter Blasiu, who was retained by the company, published an article in *Medizinische Klinik*: "Experiences Gained with Contergan in Gynaecological Practice", based on tests in his own private nursing home in Munich.

The article said that he had used Contergan on 370 patients, of whom 160 were nursing mothers, since 1956. "Side effects were not observed, either with mother or babies," he reported. The general tone of his article was entirely favourable to Contergan – except for one major flaw, it did not mention *pregnant* women.

As Dr Blasiu said later: "This drug was never prescribed for pregnant women. It is my basic rule never to give sleeping pills or tranquillisers to mothers-to-be. In my article I say that I gave Contergan only to nursing mothers and operation cases."

In view of this Grünenthal's next action is inexplicable. They sent 40,245 general practitioners a leaflet containing extracts from Dr Blasiu's report with a carefully-worded letter implying that thalidomide could be taken safely during pregnancy.

The letter reads [italics ours]:

"Dear Doctors,

In pregnancy and during birth the feminine organism is under great strain. Sleeplessness, unrest and tension are constant complaints. The prescription of a sedative and hypnotic that *will hurt neither mother nor child* is therefore often necessary. Blasiu has given many patients in his gynaecological department and in his obstetrical practice Contergan and Contergan forte. Depth and length of sleep were good and patients could be easily awakened from deep sleep. Contergan had no effect on the nursing baby."

In a statement to the German authorities in 1964, Blasiu stated that he knew nothing of this letter, and that if he had known, he would have taken steps to have it stopped. "I would most emphatically have resisted the circulation of such a letter using my name and referring to my report. I consider that this letter from the firm to the medical profession is unfair, misleading and irresponsible ... "

That thalidomide was safe, even for expectant and nursing mothers, was now one of the main themes of the company's advertising and was to remain so until it withdrew the drug from the market. Yet the claim continued to be based on dubious premises. As late as 1961, Grünenthal was approving claims in sales leaflets such as the following sent to doctors in Canada:

"OB/GYN patient – No side effects in pregnancy or lactation. When 100 mg. of Kevadon was administered for insomnia to expectant mothers (16) and nursing mothers (12) all of the babies were born or nursed without any abnormalities or harmful effects from the medication."

Reference 16 is a report by Dr Ray Nulsen, called "Treatment of Insomnia in the Third Trimester of Pregnancy", which was published in the *American Journal of Obstetrics and Gynaecology*. Dr Nulsen, an American, was examined for a deposition on April 14, 1966. (Merrell, a large American pharmaceutical concern, was associated with Grünenthal in trying to get the authorities in the United States to accept thalidomide for sale there.) Part of the examination goes as follows:

Q. Now, did you know, sir, that an article was published in the *American Journal of Obstetrics and Gynaecology* entitled "Trial of Thalidomide in Insomnia Associated with the Third Trimester"?

A. Yes.

Q. And does it bear your name?

A. Yes.

Q. Now, sir, did you physically write the article?

A. No.

Q. Who wrote it?

A. Dr – or someone at the Merrell company.

Q. Did you supply for this article any of the information with respect to the chemical facts contained in this article?

A. No.

So Grünenthal were quoting, as support for their claim that thalidomide was safe to use on pregnant mothers, first, a doctor who had not tested the drug on pregnant women at all, and second, a doctor whose report had been written for him by an employee of a pharmaceutical company closely linked with Grünenthal itself.

The first complaint about Contergan from an independent source reached Grünenthal in July, 1958. Professor Gustav Schmaltz, in Frankfurt, had not been testing the drug, merely giving it to his patients as Grünenthal prescribed. He reported that thalidomide caused giddiness and slight disturbance of balance in the elderly. Grünenthal replied: "We feel obliged to say that this is the first time such side effects have been reported to us . . . "

This was simply not true. All through the early clinical trials, from 1955–7, criticism had been raised on just these points – dizziness and disturbance of balance – by three of the nine doctors whose tests had been quoted at the original Thalidomide Symposium back in 1955.

The year 1959 was "Breakthrough Year" for Contergan. The publicity campaign was having its effect. Sales figures increased *dramatically*; they went up fourfold from May to December.

But 1959 was also the year that complaints from well-known members of the German medical profession about side effects grew from a trickle to an indignant and persistent flow. Grünenthal's reception of these complaints shows how committed the company had become to the success of Contergan.

Did it harm the nerves?

The first major signs of trouble were nothing to do with malformed babies, for which thalidomide was eventually to become so notorious. Because of the nine-month delay of pregnancy, it was some time before the medical profession began to catch on to the tragic effect on the unborn child. What they did start to notice early in 1959 was the emergence in adults of a worrying nervous disorder called peripheral neuritis. It is with this illness that much of the story is concerned.

The company files show exactly when the salesmen, in their reports to headquarters, began to hear of the problem.

In March that year Dr Heinzmann of the Koblenz sales office reported that a dispensing chemist complained of abnormally cold hands and feet after taking Contergan forte. In April Dr Frenkel, working in the clinic run by Professor Amelung in Königstein, told a Grünenthal representative that he had noticed side effects following the use of Contergan.

Then, in July, a blistering letter about thalidomide arrived from Pharmakolor AG of Basle, Switzerland, who worked in close association with Grünenthal:

"To date twenty well-known doctors have told our representatives that when they themselves or their patients took one tablet of thalidomide they found themselves still under its effect the next morning, suffering from considerable sickness, involuntary trembling of the hands, etc. Professor Ludwig, head of the second medical department Burgers hospital, Basle, told us yesterday that he gave his wife a tablet of Softenon Forte. He adds: 'Once and never again. This is a terrible drug.'"

Yet, when Dr Ralf Voss, a well-known nerve specialist in Düsseldorf, wrote to Grünenthal in October, citing a case and asking: "Is anything known about whether Contergan can lead to the damage of the peripheral nervous system?" Dr Sievers and Dr Mückter replied:

"Happily we can tell you that such disadvantageous effects have not been brought to our notice."

In other words they flatly denied any knowledge of the letter from Pharmakolor, Dr Piazenca's report in 1956 and the growing number of reports from salesmen.

Dr Voss did not give up. At the end of November he again reported to Grünenthal that he had now diagnosed peripheral neuritis in three more of his patients and believed there was a definite connection with Contergan, which each had been taking for at least a year.

Dr Sievers replied:

"We have no idea how these cases of polyneuritis could have been caused by Contergan. We shall pay appropriate attention to this matter in the course of further clinical studies."

This appears to have been pure flannel; no clinical testing programme was in fact initiated. Dr Voss decided to take matters into his own hands. He began to collect cases of peripheral neuritis. By the following April, 1960, he had five of them, and he was ready to read a paper on them at a conference for neurologists in Düsseldorf.

Grünenthal moved rapidly on learning of Voss's plan. Dr Sievers visited Dr Voss. He then reported on all five cases in detail to Leufgens, Mückter, Werner and Kelling.

Dr Voss's lecture went unnoticed by the Press but not by the medical world. On April 8 Dr Paul Ervenich of Duisburg's St Anna Hospital, complained that patients for whom he had prescribed Contergan had reported nerve damage "of the most severe kind". He had sent one of his patients to Professor Laubenthal of the Neurological Clinic in Essen, who had said it was very probable that Contergan forte was the fundamental cause. And from Essen on May 10 came still another complaint: "All our medical representatives have sent in reports from doctors who have confirmed peripheral neuritis."

Keeping it 'over the counter'

There was now a real possibility that the hostility brewing among doctors would force the authorities to place Contergan on prescription (in Germany it was being sold over the chemist's counter). The Grünenthal defence became even fiercer. Winandi, the sales director, wrote sharply on May 13 to Herr Langohr, sales manager in Essen:

"We must realise before all else that such a quick rise in the turnover of a sedative must lead to certain apprehensions in the minds of doctors and chemists. Not all members of this clientele can keep their ethical attitudes within 'the limits of the market economy'. There will certainly be doctors conscious of their responsibility who, in view of this trend, will start speaking about addiction."

Winandi suggested that a good way to stop the demands of doctors and chemists for thalidomide to be put on prescription would be to spell out how much the trade stood to lose if that happened. "Furthermore during such talks it will be advisable to bring economic aspects into the conversation . . . and a hint can be dropped that the consumption of these drugs will also boost the chemists' sales, which would certainly drop if compulsory prescription were to be introduced."

"Economic aspects," in fact, weighed at least as heavily on Grünenthal as on the chemists. They were a small company. Thalidomide had succeeded so well that they were on the way to turning into a one-product company.

The sales department reported in April, 1960:

"Unfortunately we are now receiving increasingly strong reports on the side effects of this preparation, as well as letters from doctors and chemists who want to put it on prescription. From our side everything must be done to avoid putting it on prescription, since already a *substantial amount of our turnover comes from over-the-counter sales.*"

A note of desperation began to creep into the firm's efforts to get favourable reports on the drug. On March 30, 1960, a representative reported to Stolberg that initial approaches to a doctor in Iran had been unsuccessful. "However, since the Iranian doctor is very materialistic in his outlook concrete details should be forthcoming soon."

And a letter to the Portuguese licensees, Firma Paracélsia, was even franker:

"To be quite clear about it: A quick publication, perhaps in three months, with the reports of 15–20 successful cases who have tolerated the drug well, is more important to us than a broadly founded, large work, that will not appear for eight to twelve months. From this you can see what kind of testers we have in mind."

Sometimes methods were even more direct. A Frankfurt neurologist, Horst Frenkel, had first complained to the firm in 1959 that the drug produced side effects, and had been gathering evidence ever since. Now, he intended to publish. On October 29 Dr Sievers and Dr Heinz Kelling, the company's liaison chief, paid him a visit. They asked Frenkel to collaborate with their firm and withdraw the article he had already sent to the *Medizinische Welt*. Frenkel refused.

But the publication of Dr Frenkel's report *was* delayed. Instead a *favourable* article appeared in *Medizinische Welt* by a woman doctor who had done work for Grünenthal. It was some time before the reasons for the delay in publishing Dr Frenkel's article emerged. The liaison chief, Dr Kelling, in his annual report noted: "The friendly connection with Dr Matis has positively contributed to a delay in the treatment of the submitted manuscript." Dr Paul Matis was the editor of *Medizinische Welt*.

With tactics like this Grünenthal were able to hold back some of the swelling professional criticism of thalidomide. But not all. In December, 1960, one of the foreign companies already marketing thalidomide under licence put the basic drug into a sucrose suspension and tested this new form on animals before sending it out for clinical trials. The results were clear. It killed them. The lethal dose for thalidomide had been found.

Dr Nowel's delicate mission

On October 21, 1960, Mückter wrote a memo in which he conceded that something had to be done about the advertising of Contergan. A new qualifying paragraph was duly included in the instructions of use. It ran: "As with almost all drugs, patients with special dispositions may become hypersensitive after longer or shorter periods of use. Trembling and irritation of the hands and feet may occur suddenly, but as soon as the use is discontinued, such allergic reactions will subside."

However, there was no letting up in the battle to avoid compulsory prescriptions. At the end of 1960 another internal memo came from the firm's "political department" outlining a delicate fact-finding assignment:

"In the first phase Dr Nowel should visit all the health departments in the Ministries and the framework for these visits should be:

1. A general discussion about our most recent products.

2. Taking up of contacts with reference to our work together in the field of civil insurance schemes.

3. Only after these introductory themes may the subject of Contergan be brought up carefully, and there might be no impression given that this subject is the main reason for the visit.

"In the process of this discussion he must find out the personal view of the chief chemist, the state of competition against Contergan, and the current efforts being made on the question of compulsory prescription."

Dr Nowel said later of his own level of information about side-effects: "As far as I can recall Doctors Mückter, Sievers and Leufgens and Winandi so played down the side-effects problems that I could form no proper opinion on the matter. At no time was the matter discussed at any meeting at which I was present."

Communication about side-effects of Contergan was mostly confined to the executives of Grünenthal, and very little filtered down to the salesmen actually dealing with doctors and chemists. However some representatives were obviously instructed to allay fears about Contergan wherever they could. The firm's representative in Bonn, for example, reported to headquarters that he had accomplished this: "My happy laughter and appropriate references to the completely harmless properties of this preparation were successful in putting the often worried pharmacists' hearts at rest."

Sales were now booming. By January 1961, the sale of thalidomide accounted for 50 per cent of Grünenthal's total turnover. (Dr Mückter, whose salary was geared to sales, was now earning about £600 a week.) Considering this, the sales department was probably expressing the general feeling in Grünenthal when they wrote late in 1960 that, because of the "tiny number of side effects" of Contergan, rival companies had started to exploit and exaggerate them. "However," the sales department went on reassuringly, "everything is being done to protect this apple of our eye."

Mückter himself was not unduly worried. He wrote to a colleague in an overseas firm:

"As you probably know the preparation Contergan has now surpassed all other hypnotics in Germany and is far and away above the others. From the sales return we estimate that at the present time *more than 1,000,000 people in West Germany alone take Contergan every day* . . . This high consumption has resulted in occasional cases of reaction being observed and these have been judged by specialists to be Contergan allergies. The reactions are partly dermal, with rashes, and partly neural, either central or peripheral. Both varieties of reaction disappear after ceasing the preparation."

By now, however, at least one key man at Grünenthal was beginning to recognise that the peripheral neuritis statistics could not so easily be dismissed. Dr Hans Werner von Schrader-Beielstein, a young physician who had joined the firm in 1957 wrote in an internal memo that the company knew of 150 cases "in which polyneuritis allegedly occurred after the use of Contergan". About the same time Dr Voss returned to the attack.

On February 15, 1961, Voss stepped before his fellow neurologists at the Medical Academy in Düsseldorf and began:

"I have come to tell you about a new illness that I first came across in October, 1959. I have since found out that some of you have come across it too. It is about a picture of toxic polyneuritis after the long use of Contergan. I have diagnosed 14 cases in my practice. The illness begins with a numbness in the toes that usually is not noticed by the patient. This numbness spreads to the ball of the foot, then to the ankles and finally to the calves, maximally up to the knee. Many months later, hardly ever at the same time, numbness begins in the tips of the fingers."

To date, Dr Voss noted, there was not a single case of recovery after the drug had been stopped.

Voss's lecture rocked Grünenthal. Some executives were for putting the drug on to prescription immediately. Others were for making light of the side effects. The second group seems to have won.

Grünenthal was now fighting on the defensive. The sales department's monthly report for April seemed to be preparing the staff for a rearguard action:

"We will have to reckon with more intensive problems as those unfavourable publications already known to us, and some still to come, are published. Measures to control the situation have been taken. Preparations for the application to put Contergan under prescription were made . . . It is necessary to employ several first-class doctors in customer relations. Steps toward this have been taken under the motto: 'It must succeed, whatever the cost.'"

But the number of cases of peripheral neuritis attributed to Contergan continued to rise. By the end of May they had reached 1,300. In that month Mückter's salary just failed to touch its January peak: it was still almost £600 a week. From May, 1961, complaints began to take their toll. Sales began to fall.

During the month, one of the company's medical salesmen estimated to headquarters that the introduction of compulsory prescription would cause a drop of at least 50 per cent in Contergan's turnover:

"For me, as a businessman – such as I always remain besides my medical activity – this is sufficient reason for selling Contergan . . . as much as possible. In my opinion, the Central Office should allow a further discount of 10–15 per cent for large orders of Contergan. In such cases, I always make sure that the chemist will remain absolutely silent. If the matter is handled carefully, this can be fixed. It is only in such cases that I will then take orders."

But other employees were deeply troubled. Grünenthal's clinical-research director, Dr Michael, bared his heart to management on May 10:

"I personally maintain the point of view that there is now no longer any doubt that, under certain circumstances, which I am unable at the present moment to understand or explain, Contergan can cause the nervous injuries described. I am convinced that all those who are in the firm with us must also subscribe to this view. . . . I consider it to be simply impossible that the firm should officially adopt the standpoint that these reports are exclusively a matter of unqualified polemics . . . "

The health department gets tough

Now the attitude of Government departments began to change. At the end of May the firm's representatives, Dr Nowel among them, had visited the health department of the Ministry of the Interior in Düsseldorf. To Dr Hans Tombergs, a senior civil servant, they had explained that they might like to see Contergan put on prescription, lest sales of the drug get out of hand. Dr Tombergs had been cordial and receptive. Now, on June 8, Dr Nowel called on Dr Tombergs again. This time, Nowel could feel the chill. Grünenthal had withheld information from him, Dr Tombergs said. The company had been informed in December, 1959, by Dr Voss that thalidomide produced side effects, but had never reported this. Furthermore, the company's circulars were in direct contradiction to the reports of doctors.

For an hour, Nowel tried to soothe Tombergs. He steered the talk to other matters, some of them even private. Finally, gingerly, he returned to the subject. Grünenthal, he assured Tombergs, had received no correspondence from Dr Voss until autumn, 1960.

Nowel was badly upset by the conversation. Like all but a handful of senior men in the firm, he had been kept in the dark. He returned to Grünenthal and made a surreptitious inspection of the records. Then, shaken, he sat down and wrote an angry letter to his superiors:

"Regrettable result: In fact correspondence regarding thalidomide has taken place during October–December 1959. The first letter of Dr Voss points out that nerve damage has been observed in patients after the use of thalidomide during a longer period. Result: Such an incomplete direction to co-workers who are responsible for the negotiations with the ministry led not only to the undermining of the good name of the firm but also the co-workers."

Finally, Nowel made an entry on his filing cards: "We are more than to blame."

By now there were those, even inside the firm, who were coming to accept that it was indeed to blame; that thalidomide could indeed cause moderately serious nerve damage. What had not yet dawned on anyone's mind at Stolberg was that on one category of users – pregnant women and their unborn children – the damage could be catastrophic.

All this time, because of Grünenthal's assurances that thalidomide was absolutely safe even for pregnant women, it had been used extensively by expectant mothers. Now some doctors began to question the wisdom of this.

A doctor in Heilbronn asked whether Contergan could be used safely in preparation for a Caesarean. Werner and Sievers replied: "On the grounds of our discoveries so far, we would like to say that there is no evidence that Contergan reaches the foetus through the placenta."

Another inquiry about Contergan and pregnancy came from Finland – this one from the company's representative informed Stolberg that she had been asked three questions by a Finnish doctor:

1. When the thalidomide is given to women patients, does it pass to the placenta?
2. Can the preparation have a harmful effect on the child in the event of it getting to the embryo via the placenta?
3. In what part of the organism is thalidomide broken down?

Mückter scrawled underneath each question:

1. Not known.
2. Unlikely.
3. Probably in the liver.

Now the legal department sent a long and gloomy memo to company officials: "We must reckon that sympathy will not be with a huge firm with a turnover of millions, but, rather, with a relatively helpless, harmed patient." The legal department then recommended that Grünenthal attempt to settle all claims out of court.

A mood of defeatism seized Dr Mückter. On July 14, he startled his colleagues with a dire warning: "If I was a physician, I would not prescribe thalidomide now. Gentlemen, I warn you. I won't repeat what has already been said beforehand. I see a very great danger."

Others at Grünenthal remained convinced that salvation lay in the acquisition of professional endorsements. On August 1, Dr Michael tried to obtain one from Dr Max Engelmeier, a lecturer on nervous disorders at the University of Münster. Dr Engelmeier refused. He had already had experience with peripheral neuritis caused by Contergan, he said. Discouraged, Michael reported to his superior: "It's obvious that money alone will get us nowhere."

Towards the end of summer Contergan was put on prescription by health authorities in a number of German provinces. Surprisingly, perhaps, salesmen reported a positive reaction by doctors to this step. As autumn began, a feeling grew at Chemie Grünenthal that perhaps the worst had passed.

THE STORY THEY SUPPRESSED

27 June 1976

THE WOMEN'S HOSPITAL, Sydney, known locally as Crown Street, is a rambling late Victorian building set in the middle of one of the city's inner suburbs, surrounded by streets of terraced houses, pubs and factories. It is a busy, efficient hospital, handling each year some 4,000 pregnancies referred from all over Sydney, which makes it the biggest obstetrics hospital in Australia and probably in the southern hemisphere.

In August 1960 a woman was admitted to Crown Street as an emergency case. She had been vomiting for several days. All standard methods of stopping this had failed and the physical effort of the vomiting was threatening to bring on a miscarriage. Thinking about what to do next, Dr William McBride, one of Australia's leading obstetricians, a consultant at Crown Street, remembered a drug which Walter Hodgetts, the senior NSW representative for Distillers Company Biochemicals (Australia) Ltd. (DCBAL) had persuaded him to try. The drug was thalidomide, known in Australia as Distaval. The hospital pharmacy filled the prescription and after the second dose the vomiting stopped. (The patient gave birth to a normal child in April 1961.) McBride was impressed and began to prescribe Distaval for pregnant women who complained of morning sickness, nervousness, or inability to sleep.

On May 4, 1961, McBride attended the birth of a baby called Wilson. Mrs Wilson had been going to Crown Street from early in her pregnancy and there had been no reason to expect that the birth would be other than a normal one. But the delivery team was upset to see that the baby was malformed. It had upper limb abnormalities.

The radius bone was absent in each forearm. In addition there was a bowel atresia – the bowel had no opening. McBride transferred the baby to the Royal Alexandra Hospital for Children for an emergency operation for the atresia but this was unsuccessful and the baby died a week later.

Baby Wilson's death disturbed McBride but he was also puzzled by the nature of the child's malformations. Although the average malformation rate in live births is some two per cent, which means that two to three malformed babies are born at Crown Street each week, McBride had not seen a baby with this particular combination of malformations in his seven years at the hospital. Still, there was no reason to think that this was anything other than a cruel statistic.

On May 9, the week after the Wilson case, McBride had no hesitation therefore, in writing for DCBAL a testimonial letter for Distaval.

"I have used your Distaval tablets for an extensive period, both in the treatment of morning sickness and Hyperemesis Gravidarum, and I have found it is extremely efficient in controlling these conditions. I have also used 100 mg tablets as a sedative during labour and I am most impressed with this drug in this condition and I would be only too pleased to support any application to have this drug put on the NHS [National Health Service]."

The key to why DCBAL were keen to have this letter is in the last sentence. The company hoped to have Distaval "free-listed," so that it could be prescribed without cost to the patient, a move that would greatly increase sales. To this end, salesmen had been collecting letters of recommendation from doctors who had been given the drug to try and DCBAL executives had been doing their best to get something about Distaval published in the Australian medical Press.

But in March, Distaval was refused free listing. No reason was given, but one refusal did not preclude a second application, so DCBAL had stepped up its efforts to get doctors to write letters of support. The need to get Distaval free-listed was given added urgency by the news that Chemie Grünenthal (also referred to as Grünenthal, the German company that first developed thalidomide in 1954, licensing it in 1956), which had sold DCBAL only "non-exclusive" rights for Australia, was now planning to launch its own thalidomide, Contergan, in opposition to Distaval.

While DCBAL was concentrating on this campaign, Baby Wilson's death had not been forgotten. Like all good hospitals, Crown Street had a mortality committee, a group of senior medical men who met regularly to consider the hospital's mortality figures and to discuss ways of reducing them. Baby Wilson now became a statistic, and then a tiny coloured pin on a map of Sydney which the medical superintendent, Dr John Newlinds, had been examining with concern since the beginning of the year. The fact was that Crown Street's congenital malformation rate had been running at about five times that of Australia's second largest women's hospital, in Melbourne, and at about three times the national average.

So it was with considerable concern that on May 24, Dr McBride attended the birth at Crown Street of another malformed child, Baby Wood, especially since its malformations were strinkingly similar to those of Baby Wilson, even including bowel atresia. Baby Wood was also transferred to the Royal Alexandra Hospital and it too died after an operation.

It sometimes occurs in obstetrics that a doctor goes for years without seeing a bad case of a malformed child and then sees several in a short period. McBride now tried to convince himself that this was what had happened to him. But on Thursday, June 8, 15 days after Baby Wood, McBride delivered a third malformed child, Baby Tait. Again this child had limb deformities similar to the two earlier cases and again an atresia of the bowel was present. Since the two earlier operations had proved unsuccessful it was decided to keep this baby at Crown Street and it died soon after in the hospital nurseries.

McBride was now a very worried doctor. The medical superintendent, Dr Newlinds, who met him in the hospital corridor after Baby Tait's birth, asked him if he had any idea of what was going wrong. McBride was non-committal but said he would consider the matter over the coming holiday week-end, the Queen's birthday, and would see Newlinds the following Tuesday. Over Saturday, Sunday, and Monday June 10, 11, and 12, 1961, McBride read up bowel atresia malformations and, because of a growing suspicion, on drug-induced abnormalities.

"There was not much available on this last one. The Ciba symposium of 1960 seemed to sum it all up. But I had, of course, all the hospital records of the three mothers. None of them had taken anything during pregnancy except Distaval. By Monday night I was certain in my own mind, even though I couldn't prove it, that Distaval was responsible for the malformations. That was all it could be."

On Tuesday morning, June 13, McBride went to Newlinds's office and told him this. Newlinds was shocked, but it did not cross his mind to question McBride's conclusion. McBride had been supervisor of students at Crown Street when Newlinds had been a student. McBride, a former medical superintendent at Crown Street himself, had urged Newlinds to apply for the position when it became vacant. Newlinds says, "Everything I know about obstetrics and gynaecology I learnt from Bill McBride."

So if McBride said he considered Distaval responsible for the deformed births at Crown Street, then that was enough for Newlinds.

He telephoned the hospital pharmacist and told her to withdraw Distaval from use in Crown Street. "It may have seemed a hasty step, but look at this way. I believed Bill. Distaval wasn't a life-saving drug. It wasn't penicillin I was withdrawing. It was a sedative and we had lots of others in the pharmacy." So the pharmacist put her bottle of Distaval tablets carefully to one side and Newlinds and McBride agreed that it would be McBride who would tell DCBAL of the decision to withdraw their drug, and the reasons for doing so.

McBride's warning is ignored

All this occurred 15 years ago [in 1961] and since no one at that time realised that the exact sequence of events and their chronology would be so important, no one made comprehensive notes, kept a diary, or recorded their actions. In compiling this account it has been necessary, therefore, to fall back on memory – which is fallible – but confirmed where possible by independent testimony, and reference to other events which can be more easily dated.

Dr McBride is certain that he telephoned the office of DCBAL that very week in June, 1961, asked to speak to the manager, and passed on his suspicions of Distaval. McBride says he even remembers the substance of the conversation.

"I said, 'Look. I know that there is no real proof against Distaval. But why not cease promoting it while we try to find out what is happening?'."

McBride says that DCBAL told him that Distaval had been widely used in Britain for more than two years and that surely if the drug were causing malformations these would have shown up long before then. (Although it is about two years after a drug has been on the market that any dangerous side-effects are likely to show up.)

But McBride says that DCBAL did promise to pass on McBride's suspicions to London and in return asked McBride not to spread his suspicions because the evidence was very circumstantial. McBride says DCBAL at no time mentioned that the drug was a German discovery and McBride came away from the telephone with the firm impression that thalidomide was a British development, probably DCBL's own.

McBride's recollection of the conversation and his dating is supported by other actions that week which are firmly dated. On the same day that he spoke with DCBAL, McBride wrote a paper for *The Lancet* – it was never published – setting out his theory about thalidomide-induced malformations and he started tests at Crown Street to try to reproduce in animals the malformations he had seen in humans.

McBride becomes certain thalidomide is a threat

The laboratory animals at Crown Street, mice and guinea pigs normally used for pregnancy testing, were fed 100 mg tablets of Distaval in their food. Since McBride was working in the dark there was no regulated dosage. "We just stuffed it into them." The white mice were allowed to go to term, the guinea pigs were sacrificed after four weeks. None of the offspring of these animals showed any abnormality. But because the hospital's supply of animals was not large there was no control group, which meant that there was no way of perceiving any sudden drop in the litter rate of animals fed thalidomide.

McBride consulted a pharmacologist who dismissed his suspicions but McBride remained convinced that he was right. When the DCBAL salesman Walter Hodgetts called on him on July 6, McBride told him that he had had three deformed births and that he believed Distaval was responsible. Hodgetts felt that this was sufficiently important for him to write a special report for his office.

There is disagreement over what occurred next. The managing director of DCBAL, William Poole, has sworn that he discovered only after thalidomide had been withdrawn that Hodgetts gave this report to the NSW sales manager, Frederick Strobl and that neither Strobl nor Hodgetts informed him (Poole) or any other senior officer of the company about McBride's suspicions, at that time. Poole says he knew nothing of McBride's suspicions until three months later. Hodgetts says that he made his special report to Strobl *and* to Poole and that in his presence Poole telephoned Ernest Gross, the chairman of DCBAL to relay the report. Strobl agrees. He says "Hodgetts came into my office and said McBride had had three cases of deformed births. I went into Poole's office and told him."

So early in July, 1961, at least two DCBAL employees, Hodgetts and Strobl – and possibly two more, Poole and Gross – knew that McBride suspected thalidomide of causing deformed births. Yet apparently no indication of this reached the head office in London until November 21, four months later. In the meantime DCBAL continued to sell the drug in Australia as vigorously as it had always done, and it remained on sale in Britain, Germany, and elsewhere. Many mothers who produced deformed babies ingested thalidomide in this period.

We can only surmise that, on reflection, DCBAL had decided that McBride must be wrong – a view that by early September McBride himself was almost prepared to share. Between June and September, 23 mothers who had been prescribed Distaval during pregnancy gave birth at Crown Street and not one had a malformed baby.

We now know that thalidomide can cause malformations only if taken between the fifth and eighth weeks of pregnancy. But in Sydney in 1961 the fact that 23 mothers who had taken Distaval had normal babies could only mean that McBride had been totally wrong. As well, early in September, the paper McBride had sent to *The Lancet* was returned – by surface mail!

A covering letter dated July 13 and signed by the assistant editor said that although McBride's theory about thalidomide was interesting, pressure to publish important papers was such that there was no space for this contribution – a fairly standard rejection if more polite than most.

Then, on September 13, 1961, another baby with what is now recognised as typical thalidomide malformations, was born at Crown Street, and thirteen days later yet another. In both cases the hospital records showed that the mothers had taken Distaval during early pregnancy. McBride was now absolutely certain that he was right – Distaval *must* be the cause of these malformed births. Again he telephoned DCBAL and this time adopted a tougher attitude.

"I told them that I was going to write letters to several medical journals both in Australia and England to raise my fears about the drug."

DCBAL assured McBride that this information would be passed to London and urged him to delay his letters until this was done. McBride agreed but as the weeks passed nothing seemed to happen: Distaval was still on the market.

What was happening, although McBride did not know it, was that Hodgetts began checking McBride's statement that the mothers of the malformed children at Crown Street Hospital had all taken Distaval. Hodgetts was given access to the hospital records and he even called on the mothers themselves to make certain that there had been no mistake. He reported to DCBAL that his check confirmed everything that McBride claimed, and that he accepted McBride's view about Distaval.

Poole now sent H. Woodhouse, the assistant sales manager, to see McBride in his Macquarie Street surgery to get from him an official report on the malformed births and to ask him to delay writing to any medical journal until the report could be studied by DCBAL's medical advisers in London. Woodhouse and McBride met on November 16, and five months almost to the day after McBride's first telephone call to DCBAL warning of the possible dangers of thalidomide, the company took its first detailed statement from him.

Woodhouse wrote a report and got it into the following day's post. It arrived in London on 21 November and was passed on to Grünenthal for their comments.

The truth about thalidomide begins to surface

Six months before McBride's conclusions reached Germany, a young lawyer called Karl Schulte-Hillen went to see Professor Widukind Lenz, head of the University Clinic for Children, Hamburg. Schulte-Hillen was both the father and the uncle of deformed children and he was convinced that the reason for the deformities was due to some local factor. Lenz was sceptical but three months later he found time to drive to Münster, where Schulte-Hillen lived, to talk to his opposite number at the local children's clinic, Professor Kosenow, and to Professor Degenhardt, a well-known human genetics expert.

They told him that reports of similar deformities had been coming in from other towns in the region, that they had already set up a working group to look for an explanation, and that they so far had no idea of the cause.

One of the reasons was that the type of deformity was so rare. Known as phocomelia (from the Greek: *phokos*, a seal and *melos*, a limb), it is a condition in which the hands or feet, or both, start immediately from the main joint, like the flippers of a seal. Pictures of it were almost unavailable, medical school textbooks carried only Goya's drawing of a phocomelic baby in the arms of a Spanish peasant woman, and Dr Gruber, of the University of Göttingen, who had devoted his life to studying malformation in human beings, said that before 1961 he had seen more babies born with two heads than with phocomelia.

Puzzled, Lenz began to ask colleagues back in Hamburg whether they had heard of any phocomelia cases and simply by word of mouth learnt of 16 within a matter of days. He checked the statistics. In the 25 years from 1930 to 1955 out of 212,000 births in Hamburg there had been only one case of phocomelia. Yet a quick check of two big Hamburg hospitals showed that in the 13 months up to October, 1961, out of 6,220 births, there had been eight cases. This rare and terrible human catastrophe appeared to have suddenly become an epidemic.

So Lenz began the painstaking task of interviewing the mothers of the deformed children. At first only two mentioned thalidomide. Then suddenly, on November 12, 1961, four more mothers who had taken thalidomide turned up.

By November 14 Lenz knew of 14 cases in which the mothers of deformed babies had either definitely or probably taken thalidomide in pregnancy. Lenz immediately telephoned Grünenthal, spoke to Dr Heinrich Mückter, told him what he had discovered, and said that he felt thalidomide should be withdrawn immediately.

Lenz said later that Mückter seemed unconcerned, replied that it was the first he had heard of any such suggestion, and offered to send a representative to see Lenz "in a few days". After the conversation, Lenz wrote to Grünenthal formally putting his conclusions and saying he considered it "indefensible" to wait for strict scientific proof before withdrawing thalidomide.

Grünenthal got the letter on November 16 and asked Lenz whether the following Monday, November 20, would be a convenient day for the

Grünenthal man to come to see him. Lenz agreed but was surprised on the Monday to find not one representative from Grünenthal but three, including the company's legal adviser.

Lenz was unwilling to talk without a witness on his side so postponed the meeting until that afternoon when he had arranged anyway to see the Hamburg health authorities. This proved a wise precaution because the Grünenthal men adopted what one of the health officials described as "an aggressive manner".

Lenz said later, "I had the impression that the Grünenthal people showed no interest in the facts or arguments that pointed towards thalidomide being the cause of the deformities. Quite the reverse. Instead they showed a lively interest in every detail which showed up the quality of my research in an unfavourable light." According to Lenz the Grünenthal men even threatened him with legal action for such an "unjustified attack" on their product.

The health authorities sided with Lenz. They asked Grünenthal to withdraw thalidomide. The Grünenthal men said no. At the next meeting, at the state Ministry of the Interior in Düsseldorf, on the following Friday, the health men tried again to persuade Grünenthal. Once more they refused.

During a lunch break the Grünenthal men spent the time telephoning their office, and when the meeting resumed put up a proposal which they said was as far as they would go: they would attach stickers to all thalidomide packets saying "Not to be taken by pregnant women", and they would warn chemists and doctors not to prescribe or sell the drug to pregnant women. (In fact that very day Grünenthal put in the mail a circular describing thalidomide once again as "a safe medicine".)

The meeting grew heated, the Grünenthal men threatening legal action against nearly everyone. While Lenz was out of the room the Grünenthal men again attacked the quality of his evidence. Lenz overheard and burst back into the meeting in a rage. He said it was absolutely wrong for his evidence to be discussed in his absence. Finally the Ministry officials told Grünenthal that to withdraw the drug would be the best solution. When the Grünenthal men still hesitated the ministry issued an ultimatum: withdraw the drug of your own free will or we will ban its sale.

The next day, Saturday, Grünenthal's top executives met at their Stolberg offices. Those who had attended the meeting with the State

Ministry of the Interior officials reported on what had happened and said they had concluded, reluctantly, that Grünenthal had no alternative but to withdraw thalidomide from the German market.

Mückter refused to agree, but then, to the amazement of his colleagues, produced a letter he had received the day before from Distillers in London, relaying the substance of Dr McBride's conviction that thalidomide had caused deformed births in Australia.

The letter read:

"Dear Dr Mückter,

We have had a rather disturbing report from a Consultant Obstetrician of deformities in children which could be associated with the taking of thalidomide by mothers in early pregnancy for morning sickness...In six cases thalidomide was the common factor."

The others thought this was a clinching argument, but Mückter still refused to take thalidomide off the market, saying he would take full responsibility for the decision. In the end, all that was decided was to send out a circular letter to doctors and chemists reporting Lenz's suspicions.

The next morning, Sunday, November 26, 1961, the German newspaper *Welt am Sonntag* came out with a well-displayed story reporting Lenz's suspicion that the epidemic of deformed babies was due to thalidomide. The paper had got the story from a doctor who had heard Lenz's theory discussed informally at a paediatricians' conference in Dusseldorf a week earlier.

The paper cited most of the arguments which Lenz had put to Grünenthal in his letter of November 16, including this:

"Every month's delay in clarification means that 50 to 100 horribly mutilated children will be born."

It was strong stuff but it was effective where the Ministry and Lenz had failed. There was a meeting at Stolberg that afternoon and Grünenthal agreed to withdraw thalidomide immediately. A circular the following morning announced the withdrawal. "Publicity," it said, "has removed the basis for scientific discussion."

Grünenthal telephoned their licensees, including Distillers in London, assuring them that it was taking immediate steps to investigate the evidence. DCBL withdrew the drug the same day, Monday, November 27. Letters announcing this decision went off to the *British Medical Journal* and *The Lancet* and were published on Friday, December 1, and Saturday, December 2.

The most crucial scientific question was the one Mückter had been asked by the Finnish doctor back in July: did thalidomide pass the placenta so that it could affect an unborn child? Mückter had replied "not known", and had done absolutely nothing to find out.

Now, when it was too late, Grünenthal put its researchers to work to look at this crucial area. It did not prove difficult. They used a radioactive version of thalidomide to track its passage in the bloodstream of mice to see whether it crossed the placenta. Four weeks after the decision to withdraw thalidomide they had an answer. It did.

But this was still not enough for Grünenthal. They insisted that there was no evidence that thalidomide was responsible for deformed births and they began a campaign to discredit Lenz and "influence the Press for our purposes".

Lenz was made out to be an irresponsible fanatic. Grünenthal's line of attack can be judged from a report written by an American drug company executive after being briefed by Grünenthal. "Dr Lenz has been interested in genetics for a long time. His father was a famous and popular geneticist in Nazi times, since he had 'proven' the validity of the master race concept on genetic grounds. He first broached his suspicions to Grünenthal on November 16 but was unwilling to give any details. He simply wanted them to take the drug off the market immediately and is supposed to have told Grünenthal that he had a 'vision' indicating thalidomide as the cause of all these deformities."

A journalist specialising in medical questions was engaged by Grünenthal to write articles for newspapers and technical journals putting Grünenthal in the "best possible light". A memorandum of a Grünenthal meeting set out the approach for doctors: "It was decided that all doctors – especially those in a position to influence public opinion – who make critical statements must be persuaded by the strongest possible means to change their minds or at least must be neutralised."

But there was little Grünenthal could do when in Britain, Dr George Somers, the Distillers pharmacologist, succeeded in producing in rabbits the same malformations thalidomide produced in human beings. He gave four white rabbits thalidomide from their eighth to sixteenth day of pregnancy. Of 18 baby rabbits born,

13 bore the horrible and characteristic deformities now associated with the drug.

Grünenthal pressed Distillers not to publish Somers's paper but Somers took his own decision and with a scientist's respect for the truth, wrote immediately to *The Lancet*. His letter was published on April 28, 1962. By then McBride and Lenz had also published, and reports of the damage caused by thalidomide began to pour in from all over the world.

Britain's Health Minister, Enoch Powell, fails to pursue justice

The emerging medical disaster of thalidomide was shocking enough, but there was now set in train a course of political and legal events to match the misery. The deformities, it became clear, were due to a drug prescribed on the National Health Service, but the parents who might reasonably have expected the Ministry of Health to be their protector, adviser and friend found themselves deserted. More than that: the Ministry of Health very rapidly took the side of Distillers. It not only abandoned the parents to seek what redress they could through a legal system whose inadequacy and perversity can now be traced in some detail. It also heavily discouraged them from seeking any redress at all.

The Minister who must accept responsibility for the decisions was Mr Enoch Powell. We have been able to discover his attitude and the way he was briefed, but the reasons for the decisions or the way he let things happen are obscure. Mr Powell himself refused to meet us to discuss the matter. It may be that at the time the Ministry was anxious that it might find itself sued for compensation; indeed Gerald Gardiner QC considered this a possibility when he came to examine the parents' case.

Whatever the reason, Mr Powell's Ministry by omission and commission was remarkably unhelpful to the parents. Firstly, it failed to co-ordinate the information on the incidence of deformed births due to thalidomide so that the parents remained a scattered, desperate group without any central advisory service – pitted against one of Britain's largest and most powerful companies. The degree of ignorance and isolation in which they were left is dramatically indicated by what happened when – five years later – compensation was agreed in 62 cases. More than 300 other parents then realised that they, too, had worthwhile claims – and they were too late to sue. Special permission had to be sought to sue "out of time".

Secondly, Mr Powell refused an official public inquiry of the kind set up after most disasters such as Aberfan or, more recently, the Summerlands fire, or automatically with an air disaster. An inquiry of this kind can elicit information which even experienced lawyers find difficult to obtain in a vigorously fought lawsuit; and very soon after Mr Powell's ruling the other engine of investigation, the Press, became barred from publication by rules of sub judice that were lifted only last Wednesday, 14 years later.

But more extraordinary than either of these failings, serious though they were for the parents and for society's understanding of a complex drug disaster, was the way the Ministry blandly accepted and propagated the reassurances put out by Distillers to convince everyone that thalidomide was an Act of God. We have come across an exchange of correspondence in 1962 between a parent and the Ministry of Health which illuminates Mr Powell's peremptory acceptance of the improbably definitive judgments of his civil servants.

Mrs Pat Lane, a Bristol schoolteacher who had taken Distaval, had given birth in November, 1961, to an injured daughter Julie. Like many other mothers, she spent the early months in a state of shock, grieving and depressed, but in July, 1962, when she returned from hospital where Julie had undergone her first operation, she was overwhelmed by anger. At 1 am she sat down to write to Mr Powell in the hope that he could somehow help – Mrs Lane did not realise then, of course, that she was one among 400 victims. She wrote:

"I am the mother of a malformed baby and took Distaval tablets when I was five weeks pregnant. These tablets were prescribed for me by my doctor after I had an asthma attack. Within a short while (same day) of taking Distaval my hands and legs were affected – they were completely numb. This in itself was frightening enough, but was negligible against the horror which lay in store for me at the birth of my baby, when my doctor had to tell me that my baby had only one ear and that was very tiny and deformed and again two days later when a Child Specialist told me she had growths on each of her eyes ...

"Before you cast this letter aside, just try to imagine how you or your wife would have felt at hearing such news, the heartbreak of talking to a baby when all the time you are afraid to admit to yourself whether she can hear or not ...

"We pay our National Health contributions in full confidence that the treatment we shall receive will help, if not cure our illnesses – NOT CREATE deformities. Why should my child and the others, some much worse off, have to spend probably a lifetime of pain and embarrassment, just because a company were allowed to market a product which could not have been properly tested.

"I want to know what you intend to do about compensating these children. If you or your family suffered such disabilities as a result of negligence, I feel sure you would also expect compensation for the unnecessary suffering involved. As I have watched my seven-month-old baby girl lying in her hospital cot recovering from an operation on both eyes during the past week I have felt compelled to write this letter to you as my duty to her . . . "

Four weeks later Mrs Lane had still not heard from Mr Powell so she contacted her local paper the *Bristol Evening Post* and it reported "Drug Mother is Planning Court Test Case". The same day, as it happened there was a letter in the post from the Ministry signed by Mr B. H. Betts, a civil servant in the supplies department, with apology for delay. Had it arrived earlier, Mrs Lane might well have been crushed for it asserted with authority that the manufacturers of thalidomide could not be held responsible for the tragedy.

The letter expressed the Minister's "deep concern" but indicated that thalidomide was "properly tested according to the state of knowledge at that time." It continued:

'The Minister is advised that it was subjected to the usual laboratory trials, that is, tests on animals followed by tests on the people developing the drug, and then given to doctors wholly independent of the firm for controlled clinical trials on selected patients. In this particular case there was not the slightest reason to suspect that the drug could have the side-effects it has and subsequent experimentation has shown that only in one of the several animal species investigated, the rabbit, was it able to produce congenital deformities in the young. You will see, therefore, that even negative results on animals would still not guarantee absolute safety when a drug comes to be used for human beings."

The same day as Mr Betts wrote the Ministry's letter to Mrs Lane, an even more comprehensive exoneration of Distillers was being written for *The Times* newspaper by "A Special Correspondent". It set out for the first time Distillers' legal defence (it was to remain essentially unchanged) and it was remarkable for its detailed knowledge of what seemed to be the facts of the case. Headlined *THALIDOMIDE TESTS SHOW NO SIGN OF DANGER*, the article began in much the same vein as the Ministry's letter:

"It seems established beyond doubt that before being put on the British market the drug was subjected in Britain with great thoroughness to all the tests which any pharmacologist would have applied in the circumstances at that time, and was given extensive clinical tests with no sign of danger."

The writer went on to say that the drug was tested "extensively" by Chemie Grünenthal, that Distillers had made their own pharmacological investigations and provided quantities of the drug for outside clinical tests so that was being given "a second independent scrutiny". They had conducted a long series of tests "which is right and normal with new drugs – on rats, mice, guinea pigs, cats and rabbits, all leading to the conclusion that the drug was virtually non-toxic."

The "Special Correspondent" dealt with the question why no tests were made to see if the drug produced birth malformations (teratogenic effects):

"The answer quite simply is that the need for such tests in such circumstances has never been made evident before. Testing new drugs is an evolving science and grows progressively more complex and more costly. The need to test for teratogenic effects has been irrevocably established . . . but it would be entirely wrong to say it should have been recognised earlier . . . This is not a matter in which a commercial firm has omitted tests which professional pharmacologists with no commercial interests would infallibly have carried out. They would infallibly not have carried them out . . . There is no reason to suppose that any pharmacologists would, unless by accident, have discovered this form of toxicity. . . ."

The close resemblance between the Ministry's letter to Mrs Lane and the extended argument which appeared in *The Times* and indeed a number of other newspapers and journals was no coincidence. The primary source material for *The Times* article and the Ministry's letter was provided by Distillers.

The Times article had curiously not been written by the paper's medical correspondent but by Duncan Burn, their industrial correspondent until the day before the article appeared (when he left the paper). Mr Burn told us that he, rather than the medical correspondent, wrote the article because his speciality was innovation and innovation is involved in the risks in launching new products. In preparing his article, Burn agrees he spoke with executives of Distillers "frankly and openly" and he also had access to what was "relevant" of Distillers' files, (After a short spell as an adviser at the Central Electricity Generating Board, Mr Burn went to work for Distillers.)

What happened at the Ministry of Health in 1962 has been related to us by Dr E. Conybeare. He had succeeded Dr Walter Kennedy, a senior medical officer at the Ministry who had gone to work for Distillers as their chief medical adviser. In July 1962 Dr Conybeare was approached by Distillers – not by Kennedy but by Dr D. M. Burley, another medical adviser.

Conybeare had a lengthy discussion with Burley on thalidomide and later talked to Powell before he answered questions on TV. (He remembers Powell asking later if he got it right.) It was not, he says, a particularly formal briefing of the Minister as he was not directly concerned with drugs like thalidomide: this was the concern of the Supplies Division which had to arrange that the Health Service had drugs and equipment the doctors and hospitals needed.

Conybeare says he told Powell that at the time thalidomide was marketed no one had had the least idea of its "potency" and that no animal tests existed at the time to test for the properties it had. "Distillers had taken thalidomide on trust from Chemie Grünenthal."

Conybeare had also been impressed with two other points: an acquaintance in the industry – someone not in Distillers – told him that if he had been faced with the drug he would not have questioned its credentials. And Conybeare says he was persuaded that thalidomide had been a valuable drug for old people as it could provide them with a good night's sleep without any of the dangers of the barbiturates. It was, he thought, "impossible to kill anyone," and what side-effects it has – peripheral neuritis – were not very serious, particularly when compared to the dangers of the barbiturates.

Dr Conybeare concedes that he – not unlike many others who spoke or wrote on thalidomide – had never seen any of the research. It was based "on hearsay . . . I knew nothing directly. But others were satisfied. It was only when used for pregnant women that this phenomenon appeared."

The event produced one sequel in terms of Government action: Mr Powell announced the formation of a new Committee for the Safety of Drugs, chaired by Professor Sir Derrick Dunlop.

The parents' fight for justice

In August 1962 the parents were therefore left to the law. It was, in the 15-year thalidomide story, to prove a disastrous experience for two reasons. First, the laws of contempt, prohibiting public discussion from the start of a lawsuit, worked to the advantage of Distillers until the public outcry in 1972–3. Secondly, the solicitors and barristers representing the children soon became persuaded that the case had small chance of success and a consensus view developed along these lines within the legal establishment.

The random nature of legal unlucky dip that was about to begin is best illustrated by the way Kimber Bull became the solicitors for the families in a case of formidable complexity and astronomical cost.

Pat Lane's story in the Bristol paper picked up by the national Press produced three other parents and they met at the Dorset Hotel in Southampton: Peter Carter, a municipal employee from Reading, Michael Carr Jones, owner of a small London furniture business and Edward Satherley, a travelling librarian from the Isle of Wight. They decided to fight and out of the four at the meeting, Edward Satherley's provided the best case. Satherley's doctor admitted prescribing the drug to Mrs Satherley in early pregnancy, and Richard Satherley's deformities were "typical of the middle bracket thalidomide cases: he was missing both arms".

Only one of the families, Carr Jones, had regular contact with a solicitor – mainly for the purposes of minor commercial transactions – and the families agreed to contact this firm.

It was Kimber Bull, a small Cheapside firm, in the early 1960s with four partners (one of whom, Charles White, moved to thalidomide full time).

None of the families seems to have appreciated that the case was classically the kind for highly experienced personal injury specialists.

Charles White came to represent the vast bulk of thalidomide litigants mainly because legal aid was needed to mount the case and the Law Society, which administers the scheme, encouraged other applicants to use Kimber Bull as principal or agent solicitors on the grounds that one firm could do the job more cheaply than many.

This was no doubt sound financial sense – the Law Society is conscious that it is spending public money – and the Law Society also shared the defeatism about the parents' case common to all except the victims themselves. Mr David Napley, one-time chairman of the Society's Contentious Business Committee, said: "We have known virtually from the beginning that there was no case."

This gloomy view was certainly assisted by the laws of contempt which are enforced by imprisonment or fine. The Press, it has to be said, had shown singularly little investigative energy after the disaster (mainly being content to publish Distillers' defence) but after the issue of the Satherley writ in November, 1962, the case went into a legal cocoon which allowed the development of a seemingly unchallengeable version of events. The parents and their legal advisers obeyed the sub judice rules with a fastidiousness which went considerably beyond that observed by Distillers.

Their view of the disaster was propagated in the scientific and medical press and when in 1972 The Sunday Times was banned from writing about the manufacture of the drug (while being free to campaign on moral issues), statements about the manufacture favourable to Distillers were nonetheless made with impunity in editorials and news reports in the Daily Telegraph, The Times, The Law Society Gazette and the Daily Express.

Sir James Marjoribanks, a Director of Distillers said: "Thalidomide went through all the necessary tests at the time" (Express, January 8, 1973) and Kenneth Fleet, the City Editor of the Daily Telegraph, approvingly quoted the view that "at the time it was standard medical dogma that the foetus was effectively isolated". The evidence that The Sunday Times had gathered which put such statements at least into question remained banned by the High Court and later the House of Lords.

The first legal opinion was given to Charles White in November, 1962, by Gerald Gardiner QC, one of the most respected silks in the country. Gardiner believed a case should be mounted, but among the difficulties which impressed him was the likely unwillingness of experts to give evidence against their colleagues. This makes the next development the more puzzling for it clearly suggested the need for an expert witness of impeccable credentials to act as ambassador to the medical profession and pharmaceutical industry.

Instead they accepted the first expert to offer assistance in the case, a man whose wife, because of thalidomide, suffered from peripheral neuritis. No one could question the devotion or energy of Dr Montagu A. Philips but his scientific reputation was not high (not, certainly, by comparison with Distillers' man George Somers). He was known to be associated with a cut-price drug firm an association certain to antagonise the pharmaceutical industry. Yet until the very last stages prior to settlement, Phillips remained Kimber Bull's only continuous scientific adviser.

To succeed in this first action against a drug manufacturer, the parents had to show that when thalidomide was being developed and sold a drug manufacturer ought to have known that drugs administered during pregnancy could damage the foetus. They ought therefore to have tested the drug on pregnant animals.

Distillers' defence would be the one it had rehearsed in the press – thalidomide was a valuable drug that had been submitted to all "the standard tests", that at the time tests were not done on pregnant animals because no one thought drugs might be dangerous to the developing foetus, and that it was anyway universally thought that if a drug did little or no damage to a mother it would do correspondingly little or no damage to the embryo. Even if they had done the tests, they would say, these would not have given warning of thalidomide's potential to damage the unborn child.

Evidence to challenge every one of these propositions could have been discovered, much of it from published scientific literature, but little of it was ever discovered by Kimber Bull and their advisers, so that Distillers' defence, formulated early in 1962, remained undented.

Two explanations are possible for this failure. Both solicitors and barristers appeared to be seeking simple, where possible single-word, answers to simply formulated questions. This explains the course of a so-called "aminopterin" argument which became unhelpful to the parents' case.

Both aminopterin and thalidomide were derivatives of glutamic acid. It had been shown in a paper by Thiersch published in 1951 that aminopterin caused foetal deformities. Phillips maintained that Distillers should have come across Thiersch's paper with its signal of danger. This however could never have been a knock-down point:

the bulk of biochemical opinion is that since there are thousands of glutamic acid derivatives, the vast majority of which are not teratogenic, there was no predictive value in the relationship between aminopterin and thalidomide.

In the absence of any other evidence the seductiveness of the aminopterin argument, first mooted by Phillips before Gardiner had even delivered his opinion, was all too understandable. What is more curious is why six years later the parents' case against Distillers collapsed when the aminopterin argument was deflated.

The failure of the parents' lawyers to gather the evidence had something to do also with the shortcomings of the Legal Aid system. The underlying principle is that a man on Legal Aid must have no advantages over an unaided man. David Napley says: "You have no absolute right because you are poor to be put in the same position as someone who has money. As far as possible the Legal Aid scheme applies the test of how a person of reasonable, if not excessive means, would spend his money."

Kimber Bull often felt that before they could approach an expert witness they must ask the Legal Aid Committee for permission to seek counsel's advice. This having been obtained, the Legal Aid Committee would then be asked to sanction consulting the potential witness. It was an intolerable constraint, particularly when combating a rich and powerful adversary (though a more experienced firm might have exercised greater initiative).

In the first year of the case Phillips and Charles White of Kimber Bull made approaches to a number of potential expert witnesses. Following Gardiner's advice, White approached Dr. J. A. Black, a senior lecturer in Child Health, at Great Ormond Street Hospital for Sick Children.

In July 1962, Dr Black had written an article which appeared in *The Practitioner*, surveying the literature on drugs which affected the foetus. Almost all of it predated thalidomide. Dr Black who was about to leave his London post, was reluctant to get involved in what was likely to be time-consuming litigation and also told Kimber Bull that there were others far better qualified than himself to give evidence. He had only surveyed the literature, not done any of the original research himself, and suggested they contact some of those whose work was cited.

Kimber Bull accepted Dr Black's refusal and never approached him again. Dr Black recalls the approach to him as being exploratory and says he did not get the impression of any great urgency. Had he understood their difficulties there is no question in his mind but that he would have been willing to give evidence. "After all," he says, "I had written the article to bring people's attention to the problem in general. My feeling was one of general principle. If you are going to market a drug used in pregnancy, you are morally – even if not legally – obliged to test it on a number of pregnant animals. And not just of one species. Had they done so it might have ended up as a nice drug for keeping horses quiet. It would not have been used on humans."

Had Dr Black been asked if it was common knowledge that drugs could damage the foetus, he would have replied "I wasn't even working in the field, but I would certainly have known." And he would have expected others to do so as well. But he was never asked.

Another potential witness, Dr A. L. Speirs, a paediatrician at the Sterling Royal Infirmary, was approached by Kimber Bull in January 1963. Dr Speirs replied, three days after receiving the letter, to say "I would prefer not to become involved in legal proceedings, *if at all possible.*" The solicitors interpreted this as a refusal to give evidence, and never approached Dr Speirs again.

The most important witness could have been Dr McBride, the Sydney obstetrician who had reported his suspicion that thalidomide caused deformed births to the Sydney office of DCBAL in June, 1961 – five months before the drug was withdrawn. A substantial number of the mothers who had thalidomide children in Britain took the drug after June so Dr McBride's evidence could have been vital to their case.

Kimber Bull wrote to Dr McBride in October, 1963, and asked him about his warning to DCBAL. But when there was no answer, Kimber Bull dropped the matter until after the 40 per cent compromise on liability was made in 1968.

Gerald Gardiner advised that a second line of attack should be constructed. He said in his opinion that from 1960 Distillers knew that thalidomide caused peripheral neuritis, with serious and in some cases permanent injury. Yet they failed to withdraw the drug or to give warning as early as they should have done. Gardiner always felt that the strongest hope for what he saw as a difficult case lay here. He had personal reasons for disquiet. A friend who was a tennis coach developed peripheral neuritis. When thalidomide was identified as the cause, he was taken off the drug; while his condition did not deteriorate, it did not improve and in desperation the man eventually committed suicide.

But Gardiner's view about the peripheral neuritis evidence was based also on the effect he thought would be created by revelation of the company's general ethics. Despite their knowledge of thalidomide's neurotic effects by at the latest September, 1960, company salesmen, he says, were told only in November, 1960, and then Distillers wrote only to a certain number of doctors in December when, said Gardiner, "they clearly played down the effects".

Gardiner believed the best test case would not be Satherley but a later one where the mother had proof of having taken thalidomide after evidence of peripheral neuritis had emerged and after Distillers had actually advertised the drug as safe for pregnant women. His advice was not taken.

After the October election in 1964, Gardiner left the case to become Lord Chancellor. He had written only one opinion after nearly two years in the slow-moving case.

The discovery of documents certainly took a long time: this is the process by which the defence and plaintiff have to exchange all documents they have relevant to the case. The process was begun in 1964 and was not completed until mid-1966 (not much less time than ICI and the trade unions took to complete the whole of the litigation over bladder cancer).

Despite repeated requests, Dr Phillips was not allowed to read the Distillers documents as they came in and he did not begin work on them until 1966, when the Law Society finally agreed to pay for him to do so. Not until 1967 did Distillers admit that thalidomide was the cause of the deformities.

Gardiner's place as Counsel was taken by Desmond Ackner QC, one-time chairman of the Bar Council and fresh from representing the parents after Aberfan.

He became convinced that the chances of winning the case were significantly less than evens. He believed they could not get the help of a jury trial. He was more depressed than Gardiner by the fact that this was the first case in which a child had claimed damages for injuries sustained before birth. And he thought the negligence case inadequate. "It would," he said, "involve establishing that prudent drug manufacturers in 1968 tested this kind of drug on pregnant animals throughout pregnancy . . . and if such tests had been carried out the embryopathic character of the drug would have been revealed." He advised that a settlement should be sought out of court, and negotiated with Distillers an undertaking to pay 40% of what the parents would have won in a successful action in return for a withdrawal of the allegation of negligence.

It came as a great shock to the parents, when they were summoned to a meeting in London, to hear Mr Ackner say that Distillers had done all that was humanly possible to check the drug, they had not been negligent, and that the 40% settlement was an "all or nothing deal". If any one of them refused the offer would collapse and they might all end up with nothing.

Mrs Christine Clark, a mother of one of the most severely damaged girls, vividly remembers the meeting, the first time many of the parents had met the solicitors representing them. She herself told Mr Ackner "that to accept on these terms was to succumb to moral blackmail" and she wanted to see Distillers men in court. Ackner replied that if they went ahead with the case there was a possibility of having nothing and of losing their legal aid.

What the parents did not and could not have known is that there was a certain truth in the advice their legal team gave them. Had they fought the case in February 1968, they would almost certainly have lost everything. But the reasons for this did not lie where the lawyers suggested. They would have lost all because their legal representatives had failed to put up the best case.

The campaign and settlement

The rest of the story is well known. Following *The Sunday Times* campaign in 1972, the parliamentary battle led by Jack Ashley, and expression of concern by large shareholders, a charitable trust worth £20 million was offered by Distillers. Only four cases remain unsettled and several others, including one of the original 62 families, have not yet agreed with Distillers on the individual cash payments. (The settlement reached provided for cash payments to the families as well as the creation of the Trust to secure the life-time needs of the children.)

The Trust, administered by Group Captain Ron Gardiner, is working remarkably well. Substantial sums are being speedily paid out as need arises. More than 120 specially adapted cars have been bought for the parents by the Trust and, soon, the children themselves will be provided with cars of their choice.

Later this year the Trust will appoint a doctor to study how advances in medical science throughout the world can be used to benefit thalidomide-damaged children. Many of the families feel that the most difficult years still lie ahead but the financial security which has at last been provided has eased their fears about the future.

1972
BLOODY SUNDAY

On a bright January day in 1972 in Londonderry, Northern Ireland, 13 Catholics participating in a protest march were shot dead by a company of British Army paratroopers tasked with policing the march. Fourteen more were wounded. It all happened in the space of just 20 minutes. The day would come to be known as "Bloody Sunday".

A tribunal shortly after the killings, led by Lord Chief Justice John Widgery, was widely condemned as a whitewash, designed to vindicate the paratroopers' actions, leaving the families of the deceased deprived of justice.

In search of the truth, Insight went to Londonderry and interviewed 250 witnesses, including civilians, soldiers, and those in the IRA. They studied the evidence from the Army records revealed in the Widgery tribunal and worked from 500 photographs taken on the day.

The investigation served as a blueprint for a later review of what happened on the protest march known as the Saville Inquiry. This led the British government, 38 years later in 2010, to apologise to the families of those who were killed by the British paratroopers.

This extract demonstrates the precision with which Insight scrutinised interviews, photographs, and military evidence in order to understand exactly how events unfolded on Bloody Sunday. The map shown on the facing page appeared alongside the original article.

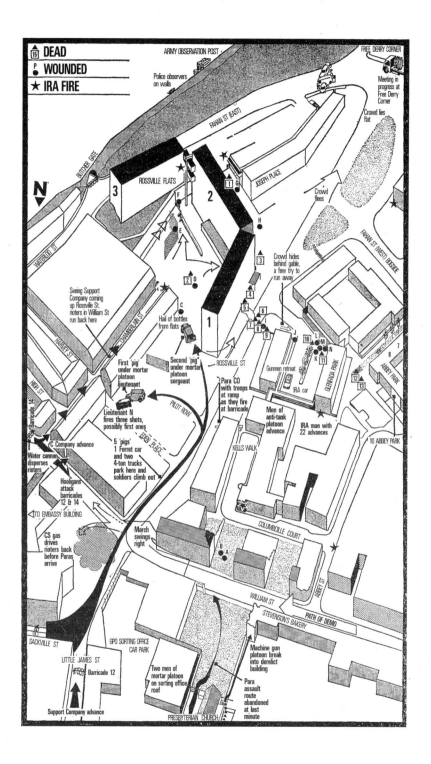

DEAD
WOUNDED
IRA FIRE

THE DECISION TO PUT CIVILIANS AT RISK

23 April 1972

SUNDAY, JANUARY 30 was a lovely sunny afternoon in Londonderry. The demonstration began assembling in Bishops Field in the Creggan after Sunday lunch. There was a carnival air about the proceedings. Many people had brought young children along with them, anticipating a well-disciplined though illegal march to the city centre.

They moved off around 2.30, behind a lorry carrying civil rights leaders, picking up increasing numbers of people. The column wound, in an orderly and good humoured way, through the streets of the Creggan and the Bogside.

The first hint of trouble came when the march, swollen by now to 5,000 (on the Army estimate) and 30,000 (on the marchers') reached the top of William Street. It became obvious that the procession would shortly arrive at an Army barrier blocking the other end of William Street. About 100 youths had forced their way to the front of the marchers; now some moved on ahead, clearly intent on a confrontation.

The organisers had decided to swing the lorry right into Rossville Street (see map) and hold a meeting at Free Derry Corner. They hoped the bulk of the marchers would follow. Many did, but a large section of the crowd simply did not realise the plans had been changed, and pressed on towards the Army barrier. Stone-throwing began.

Stewards made strenuous efforts to stop this, and also to persuade people to move over to Free Derry Corner for the meeting. At about 4pm they were succeeding; most peaceful marchers had left the confrontation area and were drifting towards the meeting. That left only the hard-core of 200–300 rioters in the immediate vicinity of the William Street barrier.

Plans to deal with this predictable confrontation had been laid in advance, after much consultation between politicians, soldiers and policemen.

Ever since Brigadier Andrew MacLellan arrived at Ebrington Barracks in Derry on October 27, 1971, to take command of 8 Brigade – the Army forces in the city – he had been labouring under the irksome but unavoidable problem of not actually carrying out his orders. The Commander Land Forces in Northern Ireland, Major General Robert Ford, issued them the day before MacLellan arrived. MacLellan was "so far as possible, to recreate the state of law in the Creggan and Bogside as and when he could".

But the truth was, as everyone knew, that invading the Catholic "no go" areas of the Bogside and Creggan would, as the GOC in Northern Ireland, General Sir Harry Tuzo, put it, lead to "fairly bloody" civilian casualties.

The second problem was, how could the Army hold down the enclave once they had overrun it? The police chief in Derry, Chief Superintendent Frank Lagan, said: "It was a military matter, and at certain levels the operation could have been carried out but, as I understand it, there weren't the levels available." The Army, in fact, reckoned they would need at least 5,000 men to garrison the area.

All he could do was to try to contain the violence along William Street, the rough demarcation line between the Bogside ghetto and the more prosperous commercial district to the north. He did not succeed. Through the first three months after internment on August 9 last year, the Security Forces faced on average about 50 shots a week. But during MacLellan's tour of duty – that is, from the end of October to Bloody Sunday on January 30 – the rate had risen to about 150 shots a week. And there had been a steady increase in nail bombings – up to about 40 a week.

Nor could MacLellan set against this relative powerlessness any success in arresting rioters. On average, only about 10–15 of the stone-throwers were being "snatched" every month. The hooligans were fast-moving and knew the alleys of the area since they could toddle; the soldiers were older, laden with rifle and flak jacket and quite often shield and visored helmet too. They did not stand a chance. The insertion of gunmen into these stone-throwing crowds cut the arrest rate in January even further: the soldiers could now not venture from the cover of their armoured carriers, or "pigs".

We have good reason to think that there was in consequence much pressure upon MacLellan. This came from the Joint Security Committee, chaired by the Prime Minister, Brian Faulkner. The JSC – on which the Army and police commanders sat with senior Stormont ministers – was the main forum for discussion of the military situation in the province. And, not unnaturally, the politicians wanted action in Derry.

How the men on the spot were ignored

The illegal march through the Creggan and Bogside, announced for Sunday, January 30, by the Northern Ireland Civil Rights Association (NICRA) was MacLellan's opportunity to show that, given a chance, Derry was as good as Belfast at handling trouble.

It is to MacLellan's credit that on the afternoon of Monday, January 24, he was persuaded that, once again, a cautious response would be the best policy. That afternoon the police chief, Frank Lagan, went to MacLellan's office to discuss the march. The two men got on well – both had a shrewd assessment of the limitations of force as an instrument of policy in a situation like Derry. Lagan said later that until Bloody Sunday, he and the Army had not been at variance on what course to follow in any given situation.

The meeting seems to have been Lagan's idea. He wanted them to present a joint front in their recommendations to their respective superiors, as the men on the spot, on the best policy in relation to the march.

As the pair saw the situation, they had four choices: stop the march before it started; stop it as it began; stop it, perhaps later on, but at a point of the Army's own choosing; or let it proceed.

The first two were impractical, requiring an invasion of the Creggan. MacLellan's view was that the march should still be stopped, but at the periphery of the Bogside, just before it reached the city centre. Lagan pointed out the possible consequences.

Sunday was likely to bring, as MacLellan said, "a very large march indeed". And Lagan had heard that the marchers were planning to disperse as they came to the edge of the Bogside to leave through all the possible exit roads and re-assemble in the city centre. Stopping this would lead to multiple confrontations.

Lagan also had enough experience of Derry to know that marches start in the city "at the drop of hat". He foresaw as the aftermath of such confrontations, violence lasting perhaps three days, during which such "informal marches" would go all over the city – even into Protestant areas. Those in turn might spark what Lagan called "confrontation between religious factions", adding ominously, "and this would be much more serious than the confrontation in the Bogside". It would, MacLellan remembered him saying, lead to "intense violence" – by which he meant gunfire.

In the end, on a balance of calculations, Lagan's view prevailed.

The march should proceed. But the Security Forces would uphold the law by photographing the marchers – the pictures being used as the basis for later prosecution of the ring-leaders. MacLellan told Lagan that he would recommend this to Ford.

It was already too late. That day, the 24th at his Lisburn brigade headquarters, the 39 Brigade commander, Brigadier Frank Kitson, had already summoned the commander of the First Battalion, the Parachute Regiment, Lieutenant Colonel Derek Wilford – and told him to prepare for service in Derry on January 29–30. Kitson was speaking on orders from Ford.

At this point, the first mystery of Bloody Sunday begins. For it is quite apparent that by the afternoon of Monday, January 24, a decision had been taken not only that the march was to be stopped whatever the expert opinion on the ground – but that a military operation to arrest a large number of people should be mounted at the same time. Who made this fateful decision?

The body supposedly running security matters in Northern Ireland – the Joint Security Committee – had not yet met to discuss the strategy.

The evidence that Ford had already selected the paras specifically for an arrest operation comes from MacLellan. Ford told him of the paratrooper decision on Tuesday, January 25.

"He allotted them to me for that purpose," MacLellan told the Widgery tribunal. And Ford went further: he impressed upon Widgery that the operation was carefully considered "for a fortnight or more before" – i.e. it was no last-minute change of plan.

So who planned the arrest operation? Lord Balniel, deputy to Lord Carrington, the Defence Secretary, said in the House of Commons on February 1 that "the arrest operation was discussed by the Joint Security Council. *Further decisions had been taken by Ministers here.*"

The decisions – the first one being, presumably, to stop the march; the second, to go further and mount an arrest operation – had already, by January 24, been taken in London by "ministers". Last Wednesday, on television, Geoffrey Johnson Smith, Minister for the Army, was even more explicit. The ministers, he said, "included" the Secretary of State for Defence, Lord Carrington.

But only two groups of ministers dealing with Northern Ireland include Lord Carrington. One is purely routine meetings of Carrington and his juniors at the Ministry of Defence – which is not what the careful phraseology of Balniel and Johnson Smith implies. The other group is the Northern Ireland Committee of the Cabinet.

But why did authority for the arrest operation have to come right from the top? Outside the tribunal, Army officers and Stormont civil servants have told us that any major operation in the Derry "enclave" had to be a political decision. Under questioning at the tribunal, Ford indicated the reason: essentially, because of the likelihood of combat with the IRA, and consequent risk to civilians. He was asked –

"Was the risk, if there was any form of confrontation with the IRA to those people (civilians in the area) considered by you?"

Ford: "It was, yes."

Stocker: "When you say it was considered, was it considered small enough to be acceptable, or was it considered and then the importance of the operation was such that the risk was accepted?"

Ford: "It was considered and considered small enough to be acceptable . . ."

Ford seemed then to feel the need to add something, for he went on: "Every operation of this type has an element of calculated risk in it."

That, presumably, was why Whitehall Cabinet ministers had to clear the arrest operation. Only ministers could take the "calculated risk" with civilian lives inherent to the plan.

At noon, in his office at Victoria Barracks, the RUC station in the centre of Derry, Lagan got a message from Shillington's office. "The message I got," he recalled later, "was that my views had been considered and the consensus of opinion was against me, and the barricades would go up."

The paratroops expand a limited concept

On the afternoon of Wednesday, January 26, the Derry Brigade commander, Brigadier Andrew MacLellan, discussed with the Commander Land Forces, Major General Robert Ford, his plans for January 30, including the arrest operation. The Army have since produced only two contemporary documents to indicate what the arrest operation was meant to be. The first is MacLellan's "8 Infantry Brigade Operation Order No 2/72". (The other is the Para commander's notes.)

Paragraph nine of MacLellan's order reads:

"1 PARA. (I) Maintain a Brigade Arrest Force to conduct a scoop-up operation of as many hooligans and rioters as possible.

"(a) This operation will be launched either in whole or in part on the orders of the Brigade Commander. (b) . . . (c) The scoop-up operation is likely to be launched on two axes, one directed towards hooligan activity in the area of William St/Little Diamond and one towards the area of William St/Little James St (d) It is expected that the arrest operation will be conducted on foot."

Sub-paragraph c is critical: the area it describes is confined wholly to the line of William Street – specifying the crossroads by the Catholic cathedral at one end and the wasteground at the other, the two local "aggro" spots.

Two days later, on Friday, January 28, MacLellan held an "Order Group conference" at his Derry headquarters to detail the proposed January 30 operations to all the commanding officers involved, including the paras' CO, Lt-Col. Derek Wilford.

Wilford found his order "quite clear". He merely under-estimated the difficulty of the task. As the map shows, he had to block off the escape routes from William Street. But the only route he could find for the bulk of his troops was over the back wall of the Presbyterian Church. An approach down Little James Street was not feasible because that would be a frontal assault on the rioters – which would simply drive them down Rossville Street towards the flats.

The troops Wilford had selected to be the "assault pioneers" in the scoop-up were his Support Company, under Major Ted Loden. But Loden did not see the church wall route until lunchtime on Sunday, January 30. He promptly told Wilford that it would not work.

With only two hours to go before he had to mount the biggest operation of its kind yet attempted, Wilford was without a plan. Not until the last minute, however, did Wilford abandon the flank approach to the rioters, which he knew was necessary, and settle for a frontal assault down Little James Street. Yet because it was a last-minute decision, the troops at the barricade were not expecting the paras. For up to three minutes, Loden and his men waited in full view of the crowd while the barricade was cleared. The rioters had ample time to retreat down Rossville Street. And the paras followed them – despite an explicit order from MacLellan: "No running battle down Rossville Street".

They did so because, in the process of briefing, all thoughts of the geographically limited operation which MacLellan had carefully defined became lost. When Wilford had briefed his own men on Saturday, January 29, he had left the details of how the scoop-up was to be conducted on the ground to Loden. But he never pointed out to Loden the meaning of MacLellan's plan. Loden told Widgery: "Whatever ground the operation had to take place on, it was true to say that it would be left to my discretion, but I was not particularly told that I would go down Rossville Street. That was the way it happened."

What the paras could expect down Rossville Street was distorted too. Ford and MacLellan both considered Rossville Flats of no danger as a sniper point. The Para platoon commanders were told the flats were particularly dangerous. And their approach to the whole operation is captured by the last line of Wilford's notes of his "battle concept": "Move, Move, Move!"

The question whether any or all of the paras were ordered to go in by MacLellan is meaningless, because a similar confusion existed there. There has been an understandable solidarity among the officers involved on this point. But the Brigade log, the para log, and the minute by minute transcript of the Army's radio messages that afternoon all agree that what MacLellan ordered the paras to do was to send a single company over the William Street barricade.

But the ability to order a limited arrest operation, involving only a few troops, had disappeared with the steady devolution of responsibility for the actual conduct of the scoop-up. Loden knew that he was in charge of that. Therefore he went in. Not for about 35 minutes did MacLellan have any idea where Support Company had got to. By then, it was all over.

Widgery finds that MacLellan did order the entire operation. The message in the Brigade log showing the contrary was a mistake by the log-keeper, he says. He ignores the fact that MacLellan's chief assistant – who actually transmitted the order to the paras – told the tribunal that the log-keeper, so far from making a mistake, had written down precisely what the assistant had told him. And in reproducing MacLellan's Brigade order, Widgery omits sub-paragraph c, which spells out its geographical confines.

Just before ten minutes past four, the 10 Armoured personnel carriers of Support Company moved through barrier 12 on Little James Street. They accelerated hard across William Street and up Rossville Street.

The leading APC ("pig" in Army slang) was commanded by Lt N, in charge of the mortar platoon. Behind came a pig commanded by Sgt O of mortar platoon, and then the pig carrying Major Ted Loden, the Support Company commander.

There was panic among the crowd of about 300–400 standing on the wasteground. The bulk of them were innocent bystanders, but they were rapidly joined by rioters who had fled up Chamberlain Street and through Eden Place.

All began to flee towards Free Derry Corner, most of them through the car park of Rossville Flats.

This crowd now split into four groups fleeing through the car park to Free Derry Corner. The biggest group ran roughly straight across the car park for the narrow passage between blocks 1 and 2.

The soldiers in the wasteground began a straightforward, albeit rough, arrest operation. The moment the paras appeared from the second pig stones and bottles started flying. Several soldiers were hit.

We agree with Widgery that it was "within a minute or two" of this arrest operation beginning that firing opened up. In the next ten minutes, soldiers from the mortar platoon fired 32 shots around the wasteground and the car park. They killed a 17-year-old weaver, Jack Duddy, and wounded at least four other people.

The Army say their shooting in the car park began only *after* troops engaged in the arrest operation were fired on from the direction of Rossville Flats. But there are inconsistencies. From Lieutenant N's lead pig, Soldier S said that he came under "immediate" fire as it halted and he jumped out. It was, he said, repetition shots from a single rifleman in the area of the flats – but he later said it might have been the sound of bombs.

Soldier V said that, while still inside the pig, he heard two bombs; as he jumped out and was moving to cover a snatch squad he heard single rifle shots – certainly high-velocity – from the area of the passageway between blocks 1 and 2 of the flats. Soldier Q, in the same pig, did not hear the two bombs go off: he and another soldier with a rubber bullet gun ran towards the car-park but had to take cover behind the northern end of block 1 from heavy stoning. Only then did he hear four or five shots.

The second pig, commanded by the mortar platoon sergeant, skidded to a halt seconds after soldiers from the lead pig had gone into action. Sergeant O jumped out to cover his men, had a bottle thrown at him, chased and arrested the culprit. Then came the first shots he heard, coming, he said, from four or five positions in the flats, "low-velocity and high-velocity being fired". But according to Soldier R, the first incidents in the car park were two explosions, after which he heard high- and low-velocity fire and pistol shots, all coming from the flats. Finally, Soldier T said that firing began virtually immediately after he jumped out – probably from a single rifleman in the centre of the flats.

It is understandable that impressions should differ like this. More difficulties for the official account of what happened follow from the account given by Lt N, as the commander of mortar platoon was the only officer in the area.

N was among the first out of his lead pig. He had varied success arresting people for several minutes until he came face to face with a stone-throwing crowd in Eden Place – between 75–100 people perhaps, he thought, about to surge out and attack his platoon from behind. "I paused for a moment; then I fired two aimed shots into the wall above their heads," he said.

These two shots from N's SLR are vital in the sequence of events. They were at the time the first shots of any sort reported by the Army when the paras moved in. The brigade log notes that at 4.15pm a unit of the Coldstream Guards positioned west of the wasteground reported hearing two high-velocity shots from the Rossville Flats area.

Civilian witnesses – notably two photographers, Jeff Morris of the *Daily Mail*, and Gilles Peress – were certain that N's two opening shots were the first. The most significant evidence, however, came from N himself. Having admitted to Widgery that he had lied when claiming on television to have seen a gunman, N was asked: "But any soldiers who did not see you fire would only have heard two high-velocity shots?"

N: "That is correct, sir."

Q: "Prior to you firing those shots, you heard no other shots?"

N: "I heard no shots which I was aware of."

Widgery was clearly alive to the danger that one group of soldiers might think fire from another group was coming from IRA gunmen. He made the point when trying to elucidate the sequence of fire between the car park and the barricade. Yet he was not prepared to mention the possibility that the soldiers in the car park could have mistaken N's warning shots on the wasteground for hostile fire. It is an omission which shakes confidence in the firmness of Widgery's conclusion that soldiers were fired on first.

The mother of thirteen shot at close range

The seven soldiers who fired those 32 shots in the car park claimed to have hit at least three gunmen and three nail or petrol bombers in the car park or the flats above it. All but one of the men they hit were, they said, dragged away by other civilians before the firing ceased.

There is, however, no argument that only five casualties from the courtyard have ever been identified. Duddy was killed by a bullet which entered his right shoulder. Michael Bradley, Michael Bridge, Patrick McDaid and Mrs Margaret Deery were wounded in circumstances which, on their own and other accounts, are at variance with the soldiers' versions.

To take a couple of examples: Soldier Q shot at, and saw fall, a dark-haired man throwing nail bombs. At least one exploded, according to Q, fairly close to Soldier S and Lieutenant N.

But Soldier S, like Lieutenant N, mentions no nail bomb blast. Instead, S fired 12 shots at a man with a carbine in the crowded passageway between blocks 1 and 2, hitting him with his last round.

Sergeant O claims that his first target, a pistol man, was tended by a Knights of Malta man. O then saw a man with a carbine on a walkway high up in block 3 of the flats. The man opened fire and O returned 3 shots, felling the gunman. Another man with a carbine appeared from the passageway between blocks 2 and 3 and opened fire towards O, who returned the shots.

There is, then, discrepancy between the known casualties and those the soldiers claim to have inflicted. Widgery suggested that the wounded might have been "spirited away over the border into the Republic". We have checked with Letterkenny hospital – which, 20 miles west of Derry, is the standard refuge of fleeing gunshot cases. They did not receive a single gunshot casualty on Bloody Sunday or in the week after, to their surprise.

Of the car-park casualties, Widgery acquits the one killed, Duddy, of having carried a gun or bomb. But the other casualties he virtually ignores. Michael Bridge is the only one of the four car-park wounded even to be named by Widgery – and it is accepted that, whatever the circumstances, he was shot not by the troops in the car park but by Lieutenant N. Michael Bradley, Patrick McDaid and Mrs Deery appear only in the list of wounded printed as an appendix to the Widgery report. Yet all of them raise serious questions.

Mrs Margaret Deery is a 37-year-old mother of 13. She told Insight she was standing on the edge of the car park just round the corner of the Chamberlain Street gable, when she saw a para jump from the pig nearest her – it was the platoon sergeant's pig – and aim in her direction. "I thought he was going to shoot at me or the chap standing next to me," Mrs Deery said. "I shouted to the chap near me: 'Look out, he's going to fire' and I sort of moved towards him, for protection, like." She felt a "thump" in the back of her leg, but never heard the bang. The soldier who fired was, she reckons, no more than 25 yards away.

Two men were at either side of her. Neither knows the other; both confirmed her story. One of them, a young boxer called Neil McLaughlin, even provides a plausible cause for the para firing. McLaughlin and several friends, among them Jack Duddy, had surged up Chamberlain Street and, rounding the gable into the car park, gave tongue when they saw the pig drawn up. They surged towards it – on their way, most if not all of them, to the back of the car park.

Did the para think he was being attacked – as indeed he may have been by some of the group? And, firing at his attackers, miss and hit Mrs Deery?

Mrs Deery is a small, dumpy woman who that day was wearing a dress and black stockings. It is inconceivable that the soldier whose bullet carried away the back of her thigh was not aware whom he had hit. Yet none of those seven soldiers of mortar platoon describes any target resembling Mrs Deery.

Widgery, who was aware that Mrs Deery had been shot in the car park, did not attempt to match the incident against the soldiers' claims – or even to comment upon the impossibility of doing so. He does not mention the problem, or the questions it poses. Essentially, in the car park, Widgery sets aside the civilian evidence that he heard.

So what do the civilians caught in the area say? The key witnesses were either scrambling to escape or were looking down from the flats.

Father Edward Daly, for instance, was running towards the passage between blocks 1 and 2 – to the rear of the crowd. He managed a respectable turn of speed which took him past a young lad running in the same direction. "As I passed he gave a bit of a laugh," Daly recalls. "I imagine he was amused by the sight of a priest in a dog collar running flat-out." I knew he was Jack Duddy, who had run up Chamberlain Street.

A second or two later, Daly heard a single shot from behind and, almost simultaneously, a gasping grunt. He looked back and saw Duddy falling forward on his face, hitting the tarmac hard. Daly ran on, assuming Duddy had been hit by a rubber bullet. Then there was a "fusillade of shots" and he dived for cover behind a small wall.

From there, he saw Duddy's body lying, to his puzzlement, on its back rather than face down as he had first seen it.

Simon Winchester, the *Guardian* reporter, was also running through that car park. He heard shots, he thinks fewer than 10, which seemed to come from behind him; they sounded to him like Army self-loading rifles. Winchester did not see or hear any shots coming from any direction other than the pigs, and he neither saw nor heard any nail or petrol bombs.

Up in block 2 of the flats, the centre block, residents gazed down in horror. Derrick Tucker, an Englishman with 14 years' military service, had seen the pigs pull up and the paras pile out. There was, he thinks, an interval of between 30 seconds and two minutes before they opened fire: the first shooting he saw was one para firing upwards towards block 1. (A para confirms he fired there.)

Tucker also saw Duddy crash down and watched Daly and others move out to him. Then he saw Michael Bridge dash towards the soldiers, get shot, and hobble away. Next, he watched a man – who was, in fact, Michael Bradley – run out from a small wall just below his window. Bradley was gesticulating and shouting towards the soldiers; he suddenly doubled up with his hands clutched to his stomach.

From the same block as Tucker, Mary Bonner is equally certain that she heard no shooting until the shot that she saw hit Duddy.

One, possibly two, IRA gunmen were in fact operating in the car park. But the Army never saw the first gunman – none of the soldier's accounts mentions any target corresponding to him. In fact, Widgery only heard of him when two civilian witnesses volunteered the information.

Father Daly, crouched over the dying Duddy, looked up to see a man in a brown jacket suddenly appear and move along the gable wall of the end house in Chamberlain Street. "I thought his movements were a bit strange and then suddenly I saw him produce a revolver in his right hand and he began firing at the soldiers, two or three shots at the soldiers just around the corner from him. I screamed at him, actually what I said was: 'For Christ's sake, go away or you'll get us all killed.' He glanced over at us and then moved back, just faded out of sight . . ."

The photographer, Fulvio Grimaldi, also saw this gunman, and took a picture of the gunman. He is also certain that the gunman did not appear until after the Army had killed Duddy and wounded others.

We know who this gunman was: a member of the Creggan section of the Official IRA. As with most of the IRA men we spoke to, we had to agree not to disclose his name.

We have not, obviously, been able to question all the several thousand people who live in Rossville Flats about the presence of other IRA gunmen or nail bombers.

But one civilian, whose name we agreed to withhold, told us that he did see someone with a carbine firing at the soldiers from the 5th floor of the flats. The man fired seven shots and three were returned at him. This gunman corresponds exactly with the man at whom Soldier O said he fired three shots and hit.

The timing of this incident is clearly important: O had already been firing at another target before that. This gunman cannot have been the first to open fire in the car park.

Returning fire out of all proportion

The shooting in Rossville Street itself probably began simultaneously with the firing in the flats' car park. Thirty-six men from the anti-tank and composite platoons of Support Company – the rear half of the convoy into Rossville Street – ran up the street and along the front of Kells Walk.

In the next 10–15 minutes, six civilians were shot dead within the space of ten yards square between the three-foot rubble barricade and the main entrance to block 1 of the flats.

The events are so fragmentary that it seems sensible to unify them by giving our conclusions first. These are that the Army shot – and killed one man – when a group of stone throwers ran out from the barricade to rescue one of their number caught by a para.

There had been no firing from the barricade at this point.

There is persuasive, though not conclusive, evidence that a pistol then appeared at the barricade and was used. The Army then returned the heavy fire killing at least three, probably five people in a single fusillade.

Our general conclusion is that the Army did not shoot a fleeing crowd. But their return fire was out of all proportion to what they were facing. And, with a gathering of 500 people in direct line of fire only 300 yards away, the firing was reckless in the extreme.

The sequence began when a youth – who had, with insane bravado, run up to the nearest pig – was grabbed by a para. Some of the 30-strong group behind the barricade surged forward. The rescue party fairly hastily turned back: "I am not so foolish as to try and frighten soldiers with guns," one of them observed.

But as they ran back through the gap in the barricade, a single shot was fired from Kells Walk. It hit Michael Kelly, an 18-year-old apprentice electrician, in the abdomen. He died almost at once, as four men hastily carried him from the barricade round the corner into Glenfada Park.

Soldier F of the anti-tank platoon, who killed Kelly, says that he heard two nail bombs at the barricade and then saw a man rise to throw another. He fired. Every civilian witness – and there are several of repute including a local businessman and the dean of humanities at the University of Ulster – denies that Kelly had anything in his hands when shot.

For a moment, the men at the barricade froze. Then they began diving for cover – as the sustained firing began. At this point, the sequence becomes a matter of split seconds – and unfortunately, evidence becomes scarcer, because people were keeping their heads down.

The Army's case is straightforward. Besides F's single shot to kill Kelly, eight other soldiers around Kells Walk fired 16 shots at the barricade. The four main soldiers who fired at men actually at the barricade say they saw a variety of pistols, nail bombs and rifles.

The nail bombs are the most difficult to accept. No independent witnesses, by which we mean witnesses near the barricade whose lives and careers do not hinge upon one verdict or another, heard nail bombs in the area of the barricade at that time.

The identification of riflemen depends on one soldier. G – who said he spotted a rifleman while lying prone on a ramp in Kells Walk. In order to do so, he would have to have been able to see through several inches of brick.

But there is a consistent thread in the soldiers' accounts of seeing a pistol at the barricade. Soldier U saw five or six men come out from Glenfada Park, and saw one of them fire twice with a pistol. U shot him and saw him fall.

Soldier P also saw a pistol fired, and returned four shots. The man went down, then two men dashed from Glenfada Park, stooped as if picking up something and ran on into the doorway opposite.

U says that while he watched an old man on the barricade cradling a wounded youth, a hand holding a pistol emerged from the doorway of the flats. He saw the pistol fire twice. The first shot ricocheted off the barricade and hit the old man in the left arm: the next shot, U thought, hit the wounded youth in the head.

This incident can, we believe, be explained by examining civilian evidence about the three men whose bodies fell on the barricade itself.

These were William Nash, a 19-year-old docker; John Young, 17, a shop salesman; and Michael McDaid, a 21-year-old barman. The evidence of civilians – though contradictory and lazy in parts – is unanimous in rejecting the Army's claim that there were gunmen and bombers around the barricade.

Matthew Connolly was standing next to a youth wearing a brown suit and light shirt who, he says, had no weapon. The youth went down hard, and Connolly saw a neat bullet hole in the right side of the chest (it was Willie Nash). Dennis McLaughlin saw the same youth running back over the barricade just before Kelly was shot, which suggests he was in the "rescue party". McLaughlin says Nash turned towards the soldiers; there were shots, he fell backwards and then rolled onto his face. Nash was shot in the right chest, the bullet passing through the lung, heart and abdominal cavity.

John Young's death was witnessed by James Begley, who knew him quite well. Begley dived for cover behind the barricade; as he looked up, he saw John Young crawling towards him from the direction of Glenfada. Young reached down to give Begley a hand up: "I was looking right up at him and his face was just suddenly smashed in . . . " Young was shot through the left cheek just below the eye; the bullet travelled downwards and tore its way out through his back.

Michael McDaid died almost immediately after Young. A moment earlier a local photographer had snapped McDaid strolling casually through the gap in the barricade, apparently unaware that the body of Kelly was lying a few feet away. He must have turned to face the Army again: Dennis McLaughlin, lying behind the barricade, saw one man falling forward (probably Young): "Then I saw a person's head bursting open with blood gushing out . . . I never saw where he came from, all I saw was red."

Mclaughlin says this man was wearing a lightish green jacket, which McDaid was. The head wound also fits: McDaid was killed instantly by a bullet which entered his left cheek just in front of the ear.

After the three men were shot, the shooting died away. Horrified spectators then saw an elderly man walk with an unsteady gait, from behind the Glenfada Park gable up to the barricade in full view of the Army. It was Alex Nash, father of Willie: "When I heard the big burst of firing, I went to look at the barricade and I saw that my boy Willie was down on it . . . I didn't think or anything, I just ran out to him. Then I thought they might shoot me too so I raised my hand with the fingers out to show I was unarmed."

Nash had one hand on his son's back, his left arm in the air. It was at this point that U's "mystery point" appeared. Alex Nash was shot through the left arm from the direction of the doorway, the bullet passing straight through from right to left. Medical evidence suggests the bullet was low-velocity, which fits a pistol. The balance of probability, as Widgery agreed, suggests that somebody poked a pistol round the doors of the flats and – it being clearly imprudent to step out into full view – fired blindly at the nearest soldiers.

It is not possible to say who killed Willie Nash, Young and McDaid; any soldiers firing towards the barricades might have done so. The three bodies were subsequently collected from the barricade by one of the pigs.

The Army's evidence included at least one nail bomber shot on the barricade. But tests showed that neither Young, McDaid nor Nash had handled gelignite. Paraffin tests on their hands indicated that all three could have fired a gun. But they could all have been contaminated accidentally: fragmenting bullets, heavy gunfire in the area and handling by soldiers whose own hands could have done this. Widgery concluded that there was a "very strong suspicion" that one or more of the three had used a weapon.

Two 17-year-old boys died in the immediate vicinity of the barricade. Sean McDermot and Frank Mellan saw Hugh Gilmour standing on the barricade facing the Army. Someone shouted "Christ, they're firing real ammo" and they ducked instinctively.

Looking up they saw Gilmour jump in the air, clutch his stomach and scream "I'm hit. I'm hit."

Geraldine Richmond heard Gilmour scream and start running. She ran beside him trying to help him along. Gilmour staggered past the Rossville Flats door, turned the corner at the end of the flats and collapsed.

Gilmour was shot through the left elbow, the bullet passing straight through to exit through the right chest. It is impossible to say who killed him. Widgery concluded that there is no evidence that he used a weapon.

Kevin McElhinney was killed by a single shot from behind as he crawled from the barricade area towards the Rossville doorway. Alex Morrison saw him throwing stones from the barricade, then turn and run when shooting started.

People across the road in Glenfada Park had an excellent view of McElhinney. Father O'Keefe saw a youth dragging himself along the pavement: "People around me were yelling, 'come on, lad, you're nearly there' and also shouting for those in the flats doorway to help him in. As he reached the first pole supporting the canopy over the doors he seemed to reach up for it, I imagined to haul himself inside. His body then jerked once and half-fell into the entrance."

Jim Norris, a Knight of Malta volunteer arrived to find McElhinney dying: "One leg was twitching violently and his eyes were rolling in his head ... his face was yellowish-white ... in a matter of seconds the floor was covered with his blood and the area around his heart was turning black."

Although McElhinney's paraffin test was positive, the forensic expert considered it inconclusive since the bullet which killed him had fragmented badly. He could, like all but one of those shot in this area, have been killed by any of the soldiers firing from Kells Walk. Widgery however, concluded that K, a sergeant using a telescopic sight, had probably fired the killing shot. He does not mention any of the unusually precise and corroborative evidence to the effect that McElhinney was crawling alone – all the soldiers talk of seeing two crawling men – and that all civilian witnesses say there was no weapon near him.

The mystery of the three bodies of Glenfada

We now come to the third killing ground, the courtyard of Glenfada Park and the cobbled precinct of Abbey Park into which Glenfada leads, where Lord Widgery said the Army firing "bordered upon the reckless". Four men were killed: James Wray, aged 22, Gerald McKinney, 35, Gerald Donaghy, 17 and William McKinney, 26. Five other men were wounded. They were: Joseph Friel, 20, Michael Quinn, 17, Joseph Mahon, 16, Paddy O'Donnell, 41 and Danny Gillespie, aged 31.

There are great problems about deciding what happened in Glenfada Park. One of these Lord Widgery mentions – the inability of the Army to account satisfactorily for 19 bullets fired apparently by one soldier. Lord Widgery however does not discuss the central dilemma: that none of the soldiers admits to having fired at a target in the area where Gerry McKinney and Gerald Donaghy were killed. This is because the inquiry never attempted to complete the identification of the bodies. We have done this with the help of photographs publicly available, and we have also discovered that the IRA was present in Glenfada Park and have plotted their movements.

The killings began with a small group, about 20 people, taking refuge around the northern gable of Glenfada Park, a few feet from the Rossville Street barricade. The shootings at the barricade had happened. Some of those sheltering had already brought the body of Michael Kelly, killed at the barricade, into the refuge of the Glenfada courtyard and were giving him futile first aid. They were photographed there. Bending over the body were Gerald McKinney and his brother-in-law John O'Kane. A priest, Father Denis Bradley, was giving the last rites. Gerald McKinney's employer, John Mclaughlin, the director of a local building firm, joined the group.

Also standing in that group was William McKinney, no relation of Gerry. He was a compositor at the local Catholic newspaper, the *Derry Journal* and a keen photographer: he had been on the whole march filming as it wound down into the Bogside.

Another priest was there too: a lecturer in humanities at the New University of Ulster at Coleraine, Terence O'Keefe. He recalls: "There must have been about 25 of us huddled behind the gable wall. There were at least two women. Several of them were debating whether to get clear of the area by cutting through the alleyway into Abbey Park."

The group round Kelly's body had already decided to carry him that way. They set out across the courtyard. Among them was James Wray, a six feet one inch dark-haired man, who had been soaked with the blue dye from the water cannon when he sat down in front of the stone throwers at barricade 14 in William Street.

Watching them and debating whether to make a dash for the alleyway leading into Abbey Park was Michael Quinn. He had taken temporary cover at the rear entrance of a house on the eastern side (Rossville Street) of the Glenfada courtyard.

At this precise moment, paras from Support Company's anti-tank platoon who, deployed along the ramp leading into Kells Walk, had been, they said in evidence, engaging nail bombers and gunmen at the Rossville Street barricade, moved into Glenfada Park. Their aim was to cut off the retreat of those at the barricade.

The northern side of the Glenfada quadrangle is a row of garages. At each end of the row an entrance leads into a corner of the Glenfada courtyard. It was in the north-eastern corner that the advancing soldiers were first spotted by a 14-year-old schoolboy, Gregory Wild. He yelled: "Look out there's a limey."

Two things happened at that moment. Wild remembers two shots ringing out. They came, he says, from the direction of the soldier he was looking at. Just in front of Wild, making for the alley leading into Abbey Park, was Joseph Friel, an Inland Revenue employee. He recalls: "One of the soldiers was standing a few yards ahead of the others: he had his rifle tucked in just under his shoulder, sort of held in tight with his right arm and it was aimed in my direction."

The fatal rush for safety from the paras

"I heard three shots, bang, bang, bang, and I felt a thump in my chest. I couldn't believe I was really hit. I imagined that a proper bullet felt like red-hot wire boring into you or something. I thought this was a rubber bullet. Then I looked down and saw the gash in my jacket and the blood started coming through."

Friel never stopped moving forward. As blood started from his mouth, he ran into the alley and two or three men grabbed him. Wild remembers that Friel became hysterical, shouting: "I'm hit, I'm hit." One of those helping him was Leo Young, who was at that moment searching the crowd for his younger brother, John. John was, in fact, lying dead or dying on the barricade in Rossville Street.

Leo Young remembers: "With some others I helped to carry Joe Friel over to the Murrays' house in Lisfannon Park." Friel was conscious and very scared: "There was so much blood coming out of me that I thought I was surely dying." He was treated in the house by Evelyn Lafferty – an 18-year-old student and a volunteer with the Derry branch of the Knights of Malta – and shortly afterwards taken to Altnagelvin hospital in a private car.

Friel's wound was across the front of his chest. The bullet had entered on the right side, cracked the breast bone and emerged on the left side. "If I had not turned round when Gregory Wild shouted the warning, the bullet would probably have hit me in the back," he says now.

At the precise moment that Wild shouted his warning of the oncoming soldiers, Michael Quinn had finally decided to make his dash for the alley. "I was running doubled over," he says, "when I was hit in the right upper cheek." Quinn staggered through the passage where he was helped to safety by a school friend.

Moving in the entrance to the alley was a 31-year-old unemployed man, Danny Gillespie. He says he saw the soldiers come into that opening at the north-east corner: one dropped to his knee and fired two or three shots. Gillespie felt a bang on his head; he started to bleed. He ran a few steps, stumbled in the alley itself, recovered and began to walk home unaided. He was seen, in a state of deep shock, with blood streaming down his face.

Also standing in that alley was a 17-year-old Creggan painter, Don Dunne. He remembers that when the crowd had cleared he saw, "a dark-haired youth lying partly on the pavement, partly on the road". At the other side of the courtyard, the horrified watchers could see three bodies. From the gable wall near the barricade, Father O'Keefe remembers: "Three people had dashed out from the gable and headed for the alley into Abbey Park. They went down almost simultaneously – two before they reached the pavement opposite and the third half on, half off."

The firing had terrified those who had thought themselves safe from the Rossville Street shooting. Some had rushed into the open doors of houses; others were hugging the walls – one was Paddy O'Donnell, a foreman at the Northwest Asphalt Company in Derry. He was beside the wooden fence along the eastern, Rossville Street, side of the courtyard. "There was a woman there trying to take cover beside this wooden fence," he says. "I got down, sort of on top of her back and pushed the two of us down to the pavement."

He did not know her, but she was, we discovered, Winifred O'Brien, who lives in the Creggan. She remembers: "This man sort of threw himself on top of me to protect me and I can't remember how it happened but he suddenly said he was hit in the right shoulder. He was going to put his own hankie on the wound but I had a brand new one and I opened his coat and put the folded hankie inside his shirt against the wound."

O'Donnell's memory is that: "The fence was hardly providing any cover, but it was the best we could get at the time. The next thing I knew there was a sharp crack and a bullet hit the wall beside me and sprayed me with chippings from the brick. Another bullet smacked into the wooden fence." (We examined this area in the week following that Sunday. There was a bullet hole in the brick. And the fence was split at one point as though a bullet had passed through.)

Just as Mrs O'Brien was putting the handkerchief on his wound – which was, in fact, only a flesh wound – O'Donnell looked up to find a soldier standing over them with a rifle. "He told us all to get up."

Fr Bradley remembers: "I would say it was no more than a minute after the shooting had stopped that we became aware of the soldier. He was obviously surprised by our presence. He told us to get our hands above our heads and stay still. Two or three other soldiers joined him. One fired between four and eight shots out of the park across Rossville Street in the direction of Free Derry Corner.

Bradley and the 20 or so other people at that gable end, including Father O'Keefe, were arrested by the soldiers and driven off in a truck. Glenfada Park was now deserted, except for the three bodies, two on the pavement, one half on the road – and the soldiers. The only civilian witnesses to what happened next were a handful clustered behind walls, or peering through windows, in Abbey Park. They could see back through the alley down which everyone had run towards them from Glenfada.

Sheltering in the doorway of 8 Abbey Park was John William Porter, a quartermaster sergeant in the Irish army. Porter had seen a man fall to the ground in Glenfada after several people had come through the alley – he lay half on, half off the pavement. Then Porter says: "He raised his head up off the ground and looked towards where I was standing at the door of No. 8. As he did so, I noticed that there was blood coming from the left corner of his eye. I also noticed that he held his arm limp and he was trying to press himself up with his right hand. He started to lift his head up off the park and as he did so I saw his jacket jump up in the air, twice, four or five inches. At the same instance I realised that this man had been hit twice in the small of the back."

We identified this man from photographs as James Wray. The autopsy later showed that Wray had, as Porter said, been shot twice in the back.

That was how James Wray died. Beside him were two still unidentified bodies. But there was more killing to come.

After the rush out of Glenfada into Abbey Park, people took shelter behind the buildings running along the line of Abbey Park – the backs of the Glenfada houses, in fact. John O'Kane had run through the alleyway with Gerry McKinney: "We dived for cover, and stood wondering how we could reach the boy who had fallen just as we entered the alley. Another youth, later known to me as Gerald Donaghy, said he would be able to get him if he lay on his stomach and crawled. We told him it was too dangerous. And as he started to crawl, we pulled him in."

O'Kane says that the firing was continuing, and they realised they would have to get out of the area. They started from cover – but to escape they had to cross the mouth of the alley back into Glenfada. "I heard people shouting 'Get back, get back' and I turned to go back to the wall. But my brother-in-law Gerald McKinney and Gerald Donaghy were still standing in the open. I shouted to them: 'Come back, it's not worth it.'"

"Gerry McKinney was standing with his left side to the alley into Glenfada, Young Donaghy was standing just next to him on his right. Gerry's arms were outstretched across the boy's chest. He said to Donaghy: 'Just a minute, son, till we see if it's clear.' As he turned his head towards the opening to see if it was safe to cross, his arms shot up in the air and he shouted: 'No, no.' As he did so a shot rang out and Donaghy fell to the ground holding his stomach and squealing."

O'Kane was petrified. "I could not move. People were telling me to come back into cover. Eventually some of them pulled me back."

The same incident was witnessed by a former RUC policeman, Charles Meehan. He knew Gerald McKinney personally, and he too saw him fling his arms in the air and shout: "No, no." He also saw Donaghy fall. Neither he nor O'Kane appeared at the Widgery tribunal.

Those witnesses who did appear – Mr William O'Reilly and a 12-year-old schoolboy, John Carr – both gave the same version of the shooting. O'Reilly was looking from the front ground floor window of his house, 7 Abbey Park. John Carr was looking from the first floor front window of his family's house next door, 8 Abbey Park.

If those witnesses are to be believed, there must have been a soldier who fired from the alleyway into Abbey Park. Both John Carr and O'Reilly said they saw one. And the first of the rescuers who tried to get to the bodies of McKinney and Donaghy claim they were fired on from the alley – among them was Leo Young, who, after carrying away the wounded Friel returned to the area.

"The bullet hit the cobblestones directly behind my heels and I fell down to one knee," he said. Young then went over to Donaghy's body, which was lying a few feet from Gerry McKinney's.

But as the crowd began gingerly to emerge from the houses in Glenfada and Abbey Park, the three bodies still lay in Glenfada courtyard. One, as we have said, was Wray. Who were the other two? Again, with the help of a series of photographs of the removal of these bodies, taken by two *Daily Mirror* men, Trevor McBride and Stanley Matchet, we have identified them. They were the *Derry Journal* compositor, William McKinney, and a 16-year-old Creggan boy, Joseph Mahon.

Both were alive when they were lifted up. Dr Maclean, who treated William McKinney, remembers him saying: "I'm going to die, aren't I?" Maclean replied: "Well, you've been fairly badly hit; but if we get you to a hospital in a hurry you'll probably be ok." He knew that he was not telling McKinney the truth; and McKinney did die before the ambulance arrived.

Mahon was less seriously injured and survived: "I was just walking along the south wall inside the car park when I saw a soldier come into Glenfada. Everyone started running towards the alleyway. Two others in front of me were hit and fell and then I was hit. I thought it was a rubber bullet."

After he had been hit he lay quite still face down on the footpath pretending to be dead. The other two bodies were quite close to him. He says he saw a group of six soldiers against the east wall of the courtyard. He also remembers seeing a soldier on the other, Abbey Park side, of the courtyard looking towards the alley; firing two or three shots and then shouting: "I've got another one of them, Dave." Mahon says the soldier then pulled back.

What do the soldiers say happened in Glenfada Park? One officer, the commander of Support Company's anti-tank platoon, Lieutenant 119, and five of his soldiers, E, F, G, H and J, were involved in or witnessed the action. According to their evidence, E, F, G, H and J fired 31 shots in the area. Eleven of these were, they say, at six gunmen and/or nail bombers. (There were, as we have shown, four people killed and five wounded in the area.) Soldier H accounts for the remaining 19 shots in a curious fashion.

But confusion begins over the precise nature of the soldiers' targets. Soldier F's version is that he and G fired on two men, one of whom was a bomber and the other a rifleman. G's version is that they shot two men, both were riflemen. And J's version is that he saw F and G shoot at two men and both were bombers. All targets were along the south wall of the car park leading to the alley to Abbey Park.

We have tried to match the soldiers' accounts with our findings from questioning IRA men – with some success. For the IRA officials were in Glenfada that day, and G's account of what he shot at can be matched in two instances with what the IRA admit happened.

One of the leaders of the Bogside official IRA section told us that one of their cars was parked in the Glenfada courtyard that afternoon and inside was a Sten gun, a carbine, two 303's and a .22 rifle. When Support Company roared down Rossville Street, he ordered the car out immediately – he thought they would be caught red-handed. But his men – about half a dozen – couldn't get the car out in time so he says they hurriedly unloaded it there. He shouted to them to retreat. And they did – through the alley into Abbey Park.

Entering the car park at the northern end, soldier G says he looked over the far side and saw two gunmen standing in the southwest corner – in other words, at the entrance to the alley into Abbey Park. They were holding short rifles of the M1 carbine type. He fired three aimed shots, from the kneeling position and saw both men fall to the ground. He says he knew he hit one and thought that he might have hit the other.

G had arrived in the courtyard believing that he had just survived a brush with another IRA gunman. As he was moving down towards the entrance to the courtyard, Soldier G says that he was warned by another soldier on the eastern side of Rossville Street that there was a gunman up the alley between Glenfada Park and Columbcille Court. He saw someone running in a half-crouched position and he got down into a kneeling position ready to fire.

"I could not do anything because there was nothing at the time that I could see, only that he was acting a bit strange," he said.

"I stayed in the kneeling position and as the man went into Glenfada Park I could see he had something in his hand, which after being warned, and which I got a glimpse of, was a weapon of some description. He turned left and started dodging back round the wall and looking back towards us." G took aim and, he says, fired two shots up the alleyway. He says he observed both shots strike the wall and that was the last he saw of the man.

Who was this man?

We can confirm there *was* an IRA gunman in that vicinity. As the IRA men in the courtyard unloaded the weapons, one of them disobeyed the order to retreat and ran up out of the north-west corner of the courtyard towards the advancing soldiers. He was armed with a .22 rifle, and he fired two or three shots. He could have fired at any of the advancing soldiers. It is possible that Soldier G saw him at some stage but Soldier G does not say he was fired on.

In fact, it seems more likely that the man seen by Soldier G was Jimmy O'Donnell, an apprentice mechanic at the Dupont factory in Derry. O'Donnell said he was "moving away from the area of the firing in Rossville Street when I saw the soldier come in through the alley between Columbcille Court and Glenfada Park. I ran. Suddenly, three bullets hit the wall above my head." O'Donnell, a serious, quiet man, was shattered. He dived for cover.

O'Donnell later showed us the bullet marks. There are three at about head height spaced along a distance of about 10ft. All are in the wall towards which G said he fired his two shots. Was he equally unlucky in his choice of target when he got to Glenfada? Certainly the wounds of all those shot in the courtyard are consistent with the civilian stories of running away.

The unexplained 19 bullets of Soldier H

All entry wounds were on the right of the bodies – except that of Wray, who was shot squarely in the back. The escape route through the alley meant, of course, that they were presenting their right sides to the soldiers. The two who were shot through the front – McKinney and Donaghy – were, on overwhelming eye-witness evidence, not shot in the courtyard.

Moreover, the results of the paraffin tests – to give some indication of whether any of the lead had at least been in proximity to a firearm – were negative for both McKinneys. The tests on Donaghy were positive in one expert's view, and negative in another's. Both experts agreed, however, that the tests on Wray were consistent with his having used a firearm.

Yet Wray is the best identified of all the dead in the photographs we have assembled. (With his height and his black woollen cap on his head he was, of course, one of the most conspicuous.)

He was first photographed among the stone throwers at barricade 14 in William Street – where he got soaked in blue dye from the water cannon. He was photographed again carrying a civil rights banner in front of troops at barrier 12 at Great James Street. Finally an *Irish Times* photographer caught him in the group carrying Kelly's body. In none of these pictures can he been seen with a gun, and the last moments of his life appear to have been entirely pacific. Whatever "aggro" he may have indulged in, Wray did not seem to be acting like a gunman.

But the most mysterious of the Glenfada killings are the shootings of Gerry McKinney and Gerald Donaghy through the alley into Abbey Park.

What happened? The ballistics evidence is clear. The bullet removed from Gerry Donaghy was fired from Soldier G's rifle. And in his evidence on Day 14 of the tribunal, Soldier G agreed that he had moved across the courtyard to the bodies of what he says were lying in the courtyards Soldier F had shot at. The bodies were lying in the courtyard's southwest corner by the alley. G says he wanted to see if he could pick up their weapons. He found none.

But examined by the counsel for the Army, Brien Gibbens, G was asked: "Before you got the recall (to quit the Glenfada area) did you fire through that alleyway in the direction of Abbey Park . . . ?"

G replied: "Yes, sir." Gibbens's next question was not: "What did you fire at?" it was merely, "Did you see any bodies . . . ?" G: "No, sir."

Gibbens did not pursue the matter. (Nor did the counsel for the families.) The exchange made so little impression upon the tribunal, in fact, that in his closing speech, Stocker, the counsel for the tribunal, said: "According to the military witnesses, no soldier fired a shot in the area between Glenfada and Abbey Park, or through the alleyway into Abbey Park."

This mistake is the more extraordinary because, before admitting having fired this unknown number of rounds at unknown targets in Abbey Park, G had already accounted for all the six shots he claims to have fired. Where did the extra bullets come from – assuming that the Army's grand total of 108 rounds fired is correct? G's companion in the anti-tank platoon, Soldier H, may provide the answer to much of the Glenfada mystery.

He said he saw a rifleman firing from a window of a flat on the south side of the Glenfada courtyard. He said he fired one aimed shot at the man – who withdrew, but bobbed up again a few seconds later. H fired again. According to H, the gunman duly bobbed up 18 times and he duly put 18 shots through the window. On the 19th shot, the gunman was "seen to fall". H, incidentally, had to change magazines before the final shot.

No bullet holes were found in the window through which H said he had fired. There was, however, one through an adjacent window. Widgery's conclusions are precise. Referring to the 19 shots he says: "It is highly improbable that this cycle of events should repeat itself 19 times; and indeed it did not. I accepted evidence subsequently given, supported by photographs, which showed that no shot at all had been fired through the window in question. So 19 of the 22 shots fired by Soldier H were wholly unaccounted for."

Widgery's conclusions on the general Glenfada evidence are that: "In the face of such confused and conflicting testimony, it is difficult to reach firm conclusions but it seems to me more probable that the civilians in Glenfada were running away than that they were seeking a battle with the soldiers in such a confined space."

Even after examining the forensic evidence of the paraffin tests, Widgery concludes: "The balance of probability suggests that at the time when these four men were shot (dead) the group of civilians was not acting aggressively and that the shots were fired without justification." The firing, he said, "bordered on the reckless".

But on the basis of "confused and conflicting testimony", Widgery makes no effort to work out the circumstances of each death. Nor does he even work out that Gerry McKinney and Gerald Donaghy were killed, not in Glenfada, but in Abbey Park. The main reason for this is that, although Mahon is listed by Widgery among the wounded, Widgery never called him to give evidence. The fact that Mahon was one of the three bodies in Glenfada was thus never suspected by the tribunal.

Yet Widgery could have resolved at least some of the confusion had he made full use of the photographs. But introducing the section on Glenfada and Abbey in his report, he says: "One important respect in which the shooting in Glenfada Park differs from that of the Rossville Street barricade and in the forecourt of the Rossville Flats is that there is no photographic evidence."

This, as we have shown, is incorrect. We could not possibly have unravelled the sequence of events in the area without the use of the pictures taken on the day, most by newspaper photographers, and all available to the tribunal. Indeed, in the case of the invaluable *Daily Mirror* pictures, the tribunal had a full set. They did not use them.

The shooting in Joseph Place – the area running up from the southern end of block 1 to the passageway between blocks 2 and 3 – came very soon after the main engagements around the barricade and in Glenfada Park. It was all over very fast. Yet two men were killed and another two wounded in an engagement in which the Army insists that it fired only two shots. The soldier who fired these two, moreover, did not mention the fact until making his *third* official statement almost three weeks after Bloody Sunday. Widgery makes no comment on these disturbing facts, simply examining the two deaths as individual cases.

Patrick Doherty, a 30-year-old plumber's mate, was the man in a series of pictures that *The Sunday Times* printed the week after Bloody Sunday. Taken by Gilles Peress, they were interpreted by us as showing Doherty at the moment of being hit while crawling towards the passageway between blocks 2 and 3 from the car park. We were wrong. The overwhelming evidence, accepted by Widgery, is that Doherty was shot the other side of the passageway.

Charles McLaughlin saw Doherty, a workmate at Du Pont, crawling out from under the front room of his flat in block 2. McLaughlin opened his window and shouted down: "For God's sake don't cross into the open or they'll shoot you." Doherty, however, continued to move slowly across, crawling almost on his stomach. "At that stage they shot at him."

Doherty was killed by a bullet which entered his right buttock and travelled virtually parallel with his spine, causing massive internal damage, before tearing out through the left chest. The only direction from which he could have been shot was to his right, down towards the mouth of Glenfada Park.

It was from here, as we have heard, that Father Bradley saw Soldier F firing towards Joseph Place. Soldier F says that he shot twice at a man with a pistol crouched exactly where Doherty was killed. The gunman turned slightly to his left when he saw Soldier F, who did not notice where the other round, which missed, had struck. He explained to the tribunal that this entire incident had "slipped my mind" when he made his first two statements; he had originally attributed the two rounds to another incident when he fired several shots.

"Doherty's reaction to the paraffin test was negative," says Widgery. "In the light of all the evidence I conclude he was not carrying a weapon. If Soldier F shot Doherty in the belief that he had a pistol that belief was mistaken."

Soldier F's fatal "mistake" may have extended further than Doherty. Although F denies having seen anyone between him and the alleged pistol man when he fired, there are good grounds for believing that his other shot killed Barney McGuigan, a 41-year-old painter.

McGuigan had been in the group around Jack Duddy, dying just round the corner from the Flats door. He tried to comfort Geraldine Richmond, badly shaken, and drew her away towards the telephone box a little further up. There was more shooting and then people heard a voice "squealing" in pain and fear. Richmond says McGuigan got very distressed and decided, against her pleas, to go to this unknown man. Several witnesses saw him step out waving a white hankie in his left hand, his other hand empty: through the letterbox of a house in Joseph Place, Joe Doherty saw McGuigan step out, get shot and crash to the ground: "the soldier who shot him was in the alleyway leading to Glenfada Park . . . he fired two rounds in the direction of McGuigan."

Doherty was the first to reach McGuigan's body. It was a horrific sight. The bullet had entered the left side of his head, shattering it and then exiting through the right eye. McGuigan lay in a huge pool of blood with his brains spattered on the pavement.

Although every witness is certain McGuigan was not armed, he was positive on the paraffin test. A scarf thrown over McGuigan to cover his shattered head was so heavily contaminated that it had clearly been used to wrap a recently fired gun; McGuigan also had lead particles on a hand. But Widgery accepted evidence that it was not McGuigan's scarf, and supposed that he had simply been in close proximity to someone who had fired.

If Soldier F did, in fact, kill McGuigan with his second shot, there are still two more shootings in Joseph Place to be accounted for – and no soldiers to claim the rounds. Daniel McGowan and Patrick Campbell were both wounded in a direct line of fire from where Soldier F was standing. Campbell was hit at the base of the spine as he ran from the phone-box area towards Joseph Place and was shot in the leg. Apart from mentioning them in the index of wounded, Widgery makes no comment on their importance in deciding the disturbing question of how four men were hit when only two shots were officially fired.

Why the IRA was late for battle

Lord Widgery – especially as translated by the Press – appears to lay much stress upon the question of "who fired first?" And he has been reported as pinning the blame firmly upon the IRA.

In reality, the question of who fired first has not been satisfactorily resolved. And it may be a less important question than it seems, because what matters is whether or not the military response was appropriate, considering the real nature of the threat against the soldiers.

It can be argued that the level of Army firing could only have been appropriate had the soldiers been faced with a serious and co-ordinated attack from the IRA. Is there evidence of such an attack?

No independent evidence of any such attack was adduced before Lord Widgery.

What can be discovered about the plans and intentions of the IRA on Sunday, January 30? While Lord Widgery was naturally not able to take evidence from IRA members, we have been able to interview both Provisionals and Officials.

There is, of course, no reason to take their evidence as gospel, or anything like it. But the stories that they do tell fit reasonably well with the other evidence.

The IRA does, of course, nightly try to kill British soldiers, but the march brought inhibiting political complications; if people got shot as a result of IRA initiative, it was argued, they would lose popular support. They also decided to concentrate that day on guarding the Creggan, which they thought the Army would raid while the crowds were away marching.

So both wings of the IRA had special orders for the day designed to avoid a confrontation with the Army. Both held staff orders meetings on the Saturday. The Officials decreed there were to be no weapons in the Bogside except those held by the Bogside Official Unit – and these were to be held in several safe dumps. All other weapons were to be held in two cars on patrol in the Creggan.

The second order was that no-one was to initiate firing on the Army. Existing orders on "defensive" fire were reinforced. During the Army firing the Officials' report lists one "defensive" shot – across William Street – and seven "unauthorised", fired by men out of anger and frustration. Two of those men we have already pinpointed – one around Glenfada and the other in the Flats car park.

The Provisionals' orders were more simple. As a result of an appeal by local MPs, all their arms were withdrawn from the Bogside – except for those acting as stewards on the march.

When the firing became heavy both wings admit they ordered the recall of their guns to the Bogside. One Official car and two Provos cars, all containing armed men, sped down from the Creggan. Both wings insist, however, that they did not arrive until after the army shooting had stopped. There are several eye-witness accounts which agree with this.

From an analysis of the shots that is true. The Provisionals admit to a burst of machine gun fire from the area of the Bogside Inn, which is recorded by the Army after 4.40. It is certain that they fired other shots. Eyewitness accounts vary from none to 50, but witnesses agree all shots were fired after 4.30.

Confusion, panic and uncertainty was the general condition of most of the people who were between William Street and Free Derry

Corner on January 30. This applied as much to the IRA as it did to most of the unarmed, if sometimes obstreperous, Bogsiders in the area.

And also it applied to officers and soldiers of the First Battalion, the Parachute Regiment. But the paratroopers, unhappily, were armed for a full-scale battle rather than an arrest operation. It was their disproportionate fire power which made the catastrophic possible, and the circumstances of their mission which made it inevitable.

1976
THE TURKISH AIRLINES
DISASTER

On March 3, 1974, Turkish Airlines flight 981 left Paris's Orly airport heading for London Heathrow, packed with passengers. Just minutes after take off, a cargo hold door blew open, ripping a gaping hole in the side of the plane. Six passengers, still strapped to their seats, were instantly sucked into the sky, while the plane dived into the forest below. Of the 346 people on board, none survived. It was, at the time, the worst air disaster in history. As Insight would later discover, it was also entirely preventable.

The crash was caused by a fault with the cargo door of the DC-10 aircraft. It was an issue with all DC-10s, which manufacturer McDonnell Douglas had promised to fix after another plane almost crashed in similar circumstances, two years earlier. But it was a promise it had failed to keep, instead simply falsifying the paperwork to suggest that the plane was fit to fly when it was not.

The fatal error and resultant cover up by McDonnell Douglas came spilling out as the Insight team set to work. This three-part series begins with a dramatic foreshadowing, when in 1972, a DC-10 was forced to make a crash-landing minutes after take-off, when its cargo door blew out. The survivors, interviewed by Insight, were able to provide some idea of what happened in the skies above Paris two years later, when nobody survived to tell the tale.

THE PLANE THAT FELL OUT OF THE SKY

———————•———————

17 October 1976

AT ABOUT 7.20 in the evening of June 12, 1972, American Airlines Flight Number 96 took off from Detroit, bound for Buffalo and New York. The plane, a DC-10, was lightly loaded with only fifty-six passengers, a little freight, and a corpse, travelling in a coffin in the aft baggage compartment, located under the floor of the rear passenger cabin.

First Officer Peter Paige Whitney, aged 34, flew the take-off. The Captain, 52-year-old Bryce McCormick, handled the radio communications. When he reached 6,000 feet, Whitney switched on his autopilot, but the plane was still flying through clouds and out of habit he kept his hands on the control column.

Back in the passenger cabin, the "fasten seat belt" and "no smoking" signs had been turned off. In the first-class compartment Al Kaminsky and his friend Hyman Scheff left their wives to play gin rummy in the forward lounge. With so few passengers on board, the eight flight attendants were in no hurry to begin their chores. Cydya Smith, the chief flight attendant (whom American Airlines likes to entitle the "First Lady"), started to make the coffee, but the others remained in their seats, chatting or reading.

At about 11,500 feet, five minutes after takeoff, the DC-10 finally broke through the last of the clouds. Captain McCormick could see a Boeing 747 far above them and said: "There goes a big one up there". Whitney leaned forward, close to the windshield, to get a better view. At that moment, two miles above Windsor Ontario, the plane revealed a basic design flaw that had been built into every DC-10.

McCormick heard a loud bang. To Whitney it sounded like a book being brought down on a table very solidly. The rudder pedals under

McCormick's feet jerked in opposite directions – the left pedal down to the floor and the right upwards, jamming McCormick's knee against his chest. Simultaneously a cloud of dust particles from every crack and crevice in the cockpit sprayed into McCormick's face, temporarily blinding him. The earphones were torn from the back of his head.

Whitney, leaning forward to see the high-flying 747, was spared the worst effects of the dust storm. But the three throttle levers – one for each of the DC-10's engines – had moved back, unaided, to an almost idle position and, robbed of its power, the huge aircraft decelerated.

The door leading from the flight deck burst open, releasing the dust storm and with it the crew's hats, which were blown through the first-class compartment in head-height procession. All of the passenger cabin was filled with a damp, white rolling fog which seemed to pour from the ceiling and from the galley deck below. It enveloped everything.

Two metal hatches in the cabin floor, normally concealed by carpet, were thrown into the air and one of them struck Mrs Kaminsky in the face. The wound began to bleed profusely. Parts of the cabin ceiling fell down and one section hung suspended from an electric cable.

In the rear passenger compartment, empty on this flight except for two flight attendants, the cabin floor partially collapsed into the cargo hold below. A circular cocktail bar at the back of the plane fell into the cavity. So, briefly unconscious, did one of the flight attendants, Beatrice Copeland.

The other woman, Sandra McConnell, found herself fighting for balance on a section of the floor that was progressively giving way. She felt as though she were slipping down into the baggage compartment and towards a great tear where the rear cargo door had been in the side of the fuselage. The coffin and the corpse it contained had already fallen through that hole and were tumbling two miles to earth. Sandra could see the clouds rushing by beneath her feet.

The wounded Mrs Kaminsky and her friend Mrs Scheff were hysterical, both convinced that they were going to die. Mrs Scheff screamed repeatedly that she would never see her children again.

Unaware of these particular dramas – and of the hole in the fuselage – the flight crew fought to regain control of their machine, which had yawed savagely to the right. The autopilot had disengaged itself. As McCormick's vision returned he yelled: "Let me have it," and took over the controls from Whitney. The DC-10's nose fell steadily towards the horizon.

Bryce McCormick is, both by habit and inclination, a conservative man. He is cautious, a stickler for crew discipline, and he flies, unwaveringly, by the book.

It was this conservatism which led McCormick initially to regard the DC-10 with some caution when he was chosen to fly one by American Airlines early in 1972.

The DC-10 was obviously radically different from the other planes that McCormick had flown for the airline during his 28-year career. But it was not the huge difference in size and engine power which concerned him so much as the total absence in the DC-10 of any mechanical means of operating the control surfaces. In smaller jets, like the 707 and DC-8, there is a reversion system standing by to operate the flaps, rudder, and elevators by hand if the hydraulic systems should fail. But the wide-body jets – the DC-10, the Boeing 747 and Lockheed Tristar – rely exclusively on hydraulics. What would happen, McCormick asked, if all systems were knocked out?

He found the answers through experimentation on a DC-10 flight-deck simulator at American Airlines training school in Fort Worth, Texas. Most airline pilots now do the bulk of their training on simulators that can reproduce flight – and almost every kind of hazard – with amazing accuracy and realism.

On the Fort Worth simulator McCormick was able to test his alarming hypothesis of total hydraulic failure and, with the help of an instructor, he gradually learned how to exploit the DC-10's exceptional ability to "fly on its engines." Without assistance from the rudder or the ailerons, the plane can, for example, be turned to port by increasing the thrust of the starboard-wing engine. If the thrust of both wing engines is increased, or the thrust of the tail engine decreased, the nose of the DC-10 will rise, while the reverse procedure will cause the nose to drop.

McCormick became so adept at the technique that, he claims, he was eventually able to "fly" the Fort Worth simulator from climb-out to the approach phase without touching any of the controls, save for the throttles. On June 12, 1972, two miles above Windsor, Ontario, the lives of the 67 people depended on McCormick's ability to perform much the same trick, this time for real.

The rudder was worse than useless. The pedals in the cockpit were immovable and the rudder itself trailed to starboard, causing the plane to yaw continuously to the right. The elevators – the flaps on the back edge of the horizontal tail which control pitch – were sluggish and it took considerable force from the pilots to move them up and down. The stabilisers – the front parts of the horizontal tail which "trim" the aircraft into the correct altitude – did riot appear to work, and the lever came away in McCormick's hand. The tail engine's control cable had snapped leaving the pilots' throttle lever slack and impotent.

All of the wing surfaces were working properly but the ailerons – which allow a plane to bank – need very delicate handling. Overly vigorous use of the starboard ailerons coupled with the trailing rudder that was forcing the DC-10 to yaw to the right would have sent the plane into a spin.

McCormick's first act, after he had recovered from the dust storm, was to arrest the DC-10's dive. The nose was dropping toward the horizon, and McCormick knew that if it went down too far there could be no recovery from the dive. Not a moment too soon, he pushed the wing-engine throttles fully forward. Without hesitation, or surge, the two engines delivered a burst of power and the DC-10's nose pitched up.

With the immediate danger passed, there was a temptation to make a controlled emergency descent. Indeed, this is the procedure laid down in most flight manuals for the victims of mid-air collisions, which is what the crew of Flight 967 thought they were. But, in the past, too many pilots have taken that option before fully diagnosing the extent of the damage, with disastrous results. At any altitude less than 14,000 feet there is ample oxygen for humans to breathe and anyway, McCormick is a firm believer in the cautionary maxim which says that pilots who hesitate will probably survive. He rejected an emergency descent with a sharp "negative", and instead began to experiment, very gingerly, with the controls.

He discovered that he could counteract the starboard bias of the rudder by setting the ailerons to port at an angle of forty-five degrees. And by cutting out the idle tail engine altogether (by switching off the fuel boost pump) he lightened the loads on the elevators, making them marginally more responsive.

But the DC-10 could not be banked in either direction by more than a very gentle 15 degrees without risking a spin and to steer the aircraft McCormick had to use the differential engine power technique that he had so diligently rehearsed on the simulator at Fort Worth. Very slowly he turned the aircraft around and headed back towards Detroit. As he began a gentle descent he pondered the problem of how to land.

When Beatrice Copeland recovered consciousness she was lying on top of the wreckage of those sections of the cabin floor which had partially collapsed into the baggage compartment. Ceiling panels had fallen down on top of her and one of her feet was trapped by the twisted metal, preventing escape. She began calling for help.

Sandra McConnell, the other flight attendant stationed at the back of the DC-10, had managed to prevent herself from falling all the way into the cavity and had climbed into one of the rear lavatories to await rescue.

One of the women's colleagues telephoned the flight deck to ask for help, but flight engineer Clayton Burke, mindful of American Airlines regulations, was reluctant to appear in the passenger cabin without his hat. While he searched in vain for his departed hat, Beatrice wriggled her foot out of the trapped shoe and she and Sandra saved themselves. One of them called the flight deck and told Burke not to bother.

However, Captain McCormick was able to find time to reassure his passengers. Over the public address system, he said that there was a mechanical problem, and they were returning to Detroit where he was sure American Airlines would provide another plane with the minimum of delay. He apologised for the inconvenience. It all sounded so routine that even Mrs Kaminsky took comfort.

Cydya Smith took over the PA system to prepare the passengers for an emergency landing. She couldn't find the script, written for just such an eventuality, so she ad-libbed and described the "brace position" – head down, hands clasped under knees – which is reckoned to reduce the physical shock of a heavy landing. The other women, armed with plastic bags, collected the passengers' spectacles, pens, combs and jewellery, which can become dangerous missiles at the moment of impact. They also collected the passengers' shoes which can cause foot and ankle injuries. One man, not fully understanding the procedure, offered his socks.

About twenty minutes after leaving Detroit, Flight 96 was back on the airport controller's radar screen. The DC-10 was approaching the runway at 160 knots (184 mph) – 30 knots faster than the normal landing speed – but McCormick found he could not reduce power without an alarming increase of the sink rate.

The DC-10 touched down at 186 miles per hour. Immediately, under the influence of the wayward rudder, it veered to the right, departed from the runway, and headed off across the grass toward the airport buildings.

As the 150-ton aircraft bounced over the rough ground and across taxiways, McCormick began to have doubts – for the first time since the drama had begun – of his ability to save the plane. He had put both wing engines into reverse thrust, but they showed no sign of being able to stop the DC-10 in time.

It was the first officer, Whitney, who provided the solution. Without waiting for orders, he pushed the throttle lever of the port-wing engine into the full reverse thrust position and beyond – getting 10-per cent more power than the permitted maximum – while taking the starboard wing engine out of reverse. With the influence of the rudder thus overwhelmed, the DC-10 abandoned its collision course, and headed back for the runway. It came to rest half on the concrete, half on the grass, a mile and a half from the runway threshold.

The passengers slid down the emergency chutes, only to be detained for a while by an army of FBI agents who suspected that Flight 96 may have been the victim of sabotage. But explosives experts who examined the plane could find no trace of a bomb and everybody was eventually released.

That night, McCormick, Whitney, and Burke, not inveterate drinkers, had no trouble killing a quart bottle of Scotch.

The formal investigation into the cause of the near disaster began the next morning. American Airlines set up an inquiry panel, headed by its Director of Safety Mark Eastburn, to hear evidence from the crew and the ground staff at Detroit. The key evidence came from William Eggert, who worked as a cargo loader for the airline. He described the trouble he had encountered in closing the aft cargo door of the-DC-10 just before takeoff.

Doors have always been a problem, and a potential hazard, in pressurised aircraft. The simplest solution, the "plug" door – larger than its frame and opening *inwards* – has the disadvantage of consuming cargo space. Also, the bath-plug principle by which it works (the greater the pressure, the tighter the fit) demands that both the door and frame should be solid and inflexible, with consequent weight problems.

So a lighter but more complicated alternative was developed, initially by Boeing: the "tension-latch" door. This is hinged *outward* at the top and swings down against a rubber seal. It is then pulled shut by a hydraulic or electrical power unit.

The design of the Boeing 747 door includes fail-safe characteristics that have managed to alert the crew in time on the 17 recorded cases (up to 1974) of door-latch failure. The DC-10 design on the face of it looked equally foolproof, but in reality was almost absurdly unreliable.

As the DC-10 door is lowered onto its rubber-seal, latches, somewhat like the leg and talons of a bird, grip hold of spools on the door and pull it home. If these talons are "over-centre" on the spools, they cannot creep open. As a "make-sure" device the external door handle is linked to locking pins which in theory can be driven home only when the talons are properly in place.

But in practice the linkages between the handle and the locking pins were far too weak and flexible. A baggage handler of normal strength could push the handle fully down, thinking he was driving the pins home, when all he had done was bend the linkage rods out of shape.

There was an additional supposed line of defence. Until the external handle was properly pressed home, a small vent door within the larger door remained open. In fact the design was such that if a door handle was falsely pressed home – by bending the linkage – the vent would close with it. In such a case, it would merely be giving an extra false indication of the large door's status.

The inquiry established that these faults had displayed themselves devastatingly on Flight 96. At first everything had worked normally. The cargo loader Eggert had closed the door electrically and then held the button while he counted to ten and kept his ear pressed against the door listening, to the latches being driven into place. He was quite sure that the four latches had fully closed, although there was no means for him to make a visual check.

However, he was unable to pull down the external handle which was supposed to drive home the locking pins. He checked for obstructions but, finding nothing, pulled on the handle again – this time adding weight with his knee – and succeeded in moving it into the fully locked position. But although the vent door closed Eggert noticed that it was slightly crooked. Not satisfied, he unlocked the handle and repeated the process with the same result.

Eggert consulted an American Airlines supervisor and a mechanic, who were standing near the plane, and was told not to worry, crooked vent doors were apparently a regular problem.

The door itself was found shortly after the inquiry in a field about twenty miles from the airport. Examination showed that the four-latches had failed to go over by one third of an inch. In theory, of course, that discrepancy should have been sufficient to prevent the locking pins from moving and the handle closing. In fact the locking pin bar had simply broken.

McDonnell Douglass, the makers, of the DC-10 afterwards conducted a series of tests which showed that the force required to overcome the system was 120 pounds – no great feat of strength for a full-grown man. Other tests by General Dynamics, the sub-contractors who had built the door, showed that as little as 80 pounds of force was sufficient.

Yet another fault was shown up at the inquiry. Burke, the flight engineer, testified that the cockpit warning light, which is supposed to show any incorrect latching of the door, had switched off normally. Tests made later by the National Transportation Safety Board showed that misalignment in the door mechanism could make the operation of the switches controlling the warning light useless. The crew was thus misled into taking off with a hazard as lethal as a largish bomb.

The aviation industry does not normally receive such manifest warnings of basic design flaws in an aircraft without cost to human life. The Lockheed Electra, the British Comet and the Boeing 707 – to mention just three – all claimed many lives before their respective "bugs" were identified and ironed out. Windsor deserved to be celebrated as an exceptional case when every life was saved through a combination of crew skill and the sheer luck that the plane was so lightly loaded.

It was not the only fortuitous warning that McDonnell Douglas had. As early as May, 1970, the very first DC-10 (Ship 1) was being pressure-tested on the ground some months before the maiden flight. Suddenly the forward cargo door blew open (this was blamed on the "human failure" of a mechanic). And as was the case later it caused the collapse of a large section of the cabin floor.

The fact that the 3,000-square-foot expanse of a wide-body jet floor would be vulnerable to the explosive decompression of the cargo compartment beneath – introducing a sudden massive differential in air pressure equivalent to many tons weight – is perhaps predictable. But the May, 1970 incident provided the first graphic demonstration.

The result of the near-disaster was a demand by the US Federal Aviation Authority (the FAA) for McDonnell Douglas to provide safety modifications to the cargo doors on all DC-10s. The two struck a "Gentlemen's Agreement": no official FAA directive would be issued as long as McDonnell Douglas promised to make the fix on all of their DC-10s. As the next article shows, it was a promise not kept.

---◆---

FAT, DUMB AND HAPPY

---●---

24 October 1976

ON JUNE 13 1972, the day after a DC-10 crash-landed at Windsor, Ontario, engineers from the Federal Aviation Administration contacted McDonnell Douglas to find out if there had been any previous problems with the plane's cargo doors, or if the failure over Windsor had come out of the blue.

The company had little to say. It admitted there had been a few "minor problems" but Douglas failed to hand over to the engineers operating reports which airlines using DC-10s would have filed as a matter of routine.

Richard Sliff, then the most senior engineer in the FAA's Western Region office in Los Angeles (which had been responsible for certificating the DC-10), was "disturbed" by Douglas's attitude. He is a highly experienced test pilot, well acquainted with the fact that airplane systems nearly always give some kind of warning before they fail. He was sure that the airlines' reports would give some clue as to the degree of the cargo door problem. And so, in his words; he "raised a fuss" with Douglas until he got them.

On examining the records Sliff realised, perhaps for the first time, the extent of the danger: although there were fewer than 40 DC-10s in service, and although the plane had been in service for only 10 months, there had already been about 100 reports of cargo doors failing to close properly.

The trouble was that the electric actuators on the doors were not always succeeding in driving the latches, shaped somewhat like the talons of a bird, over the spools on the door sill. They were sticking part way.

In the 100 or so previous incidents the danger had been discovered before take-off through the manual locking mechanism fitted to every door to verify that the latches were fully closed. But, as Windsor had demonstrated, the so called "make-sure" system was absurdly unreliable because it could be overcome if the man closing the door were to apply between 80 and 120 pounds of force.

Obviously something was going to have to be done to make it physically impossible for a door to be improperly closed. But in the immediate aftermath of the Windsor incident, neither the FAA's Western Region office nor anyone at the Douglas plant could see any neat and immediate engineering answer to the problem. And there were DC-10s taking off virtually every hour.

If the plane was not to be grounded – a step with serious economic consequences in the middle of the summer air-travel season – there would have to be an interim "fix": something which could be agreed upon and installed rapidly and which would ameliorate the situation until a proper redesign could be accomplished.

The problem was simple enough to define: The "make sure" mechanism was supposed to drive locking pins over the latches inside the door to confirm that they were fully closed. The trouble was the man closing the door could not really be sure the locking pins had actually gone home.

Why not, therefore, place a small peephole made of toughened glass in the middle of the metal door skin over one locking pin? Then the man closing the door would be able to see whether the pins were safely home.

Nobody in the Western Region office thought this was a complete solution, for the door sill of a DC-10 stands some 15 feet above the ground, and each locking pin is less than 2 inches long. To make a proper inspection, each baggage handler would have to wait for the door to come down, and then move his mobile platform along to peer into the 1-inch peephole. At night, he would need a flashlight, and it might in any case be difficult to see through glass streaked with oil, dirt and water.

Still, if in addition the wiring to the electric actuators was "beefed up" to reduce the chance of the latches sticking, and if ground crews could be suitably alerted to the danger, the peephole would make the DC-10 reasonably safe until something better could be worked out.

The one thing that no one in the Western Region office doubted was that these and any future modifications would have to be enforced by a series of Airworthiness Directives from the FAA. As the name implies, ADs as they are known for short, are only issued when airworthiness – and therefore safety – is directly concerned and they carry the full force of federal law.

By June 16, four days after the Windsor incident, the Western Region office was well advanced in its preparations to issue an AD against the DC-10. But although the day had begun with the assumption that everybody in the FAA recognised the danger and the need for urgency it soon became clear that something rather strange had happened.

In 1972 the head of the Western Region was a career public servant named Arvin O. Basnight. On June 16 he had started his day early, for the case of the DC-10 door was a considerable crisis on his beat and he wanted to make sure that the text of the proposed AD was completed and approved by the Washington headquarters as soon as possible.

But at 8.50 that morning he received an unexpected phone call from Jackson McGowen, president of the Douglas division of McDonnell Douglas. Late the night before, said McGowen, he had spoken on the phone with John Shaffer, head of the FAA in Washington and, of course, Basnight's boss.

They had "reviewed" the work Douglas had already done on devising "fixes" for the DC-10 door. According to McGowen, Shaffer had been pleased to hear that this work had been going on in co-operation with the Western Region office – so much so that Shaffer now saw no need for any Airworthiness Directives. Instead, "the corrective measures could be undertaken as a product of a gentlemen's agreement".

Recovering from his surprise, Basnight called in Dick Sliff who said that work on an AD was already far advanced. Furthermore, so far from Douglas having co-operated in a handsome manner with the FAA, Sliff pointed out that he had been forced to raise a considerable fuss before the company had been ready even to disclose that a serious problem had been identified.

Even more worrying was the fact that Douglas appeared to believe that rewiring the power supply to the electric actuators was the only "corrective measure" needed.

With Sliff present, Basnight telephoned Washington and spoke to James Rudolph, effectively number three in the FAA hierarchy under Shaffer and Deputy Administrator Ken Smith, to ask him, albeit politely, what the hell was going on.

Rudolph knew nothing about any gentlemen's agreement and he said that while he looked into it the preparation of an AD should continue. Later in the morning Smith called Basnight from Washington and said much the same thing.

Throughout the afternoon the Western Region staff continued working on the text of the AD. But no word came from Washington about issuing it. Uneasily aware that Washington's day ends three hours earlier than California's, Basnight and Sliff placed another call, fairly late in the afternoon, to Rudolph. They were told that John Shaffer was not in the office and could not be found – from which they gathered that there could be no question of rescinding Shaffer's decision against issuing an AD.

Almost immediately Smith came on the line with Rudolph, and the two of them explained to Basnight and Sliff that they were trying to set up a telephone conference between Washington, the Douglas plant, and the four airlines then flying DC-10s. The aim would be to obtain all-around agreement on effecting the changes that would have been demanded in an AD.

By this time Basnight must have recognised that he was being decisively cut out of the executive process. And if confirmation of this was needed, it came when, after waiting for some time without information, he and Sliff heard from the Douglas plant that the telecon had taken place.

Basnight called Rudolph yet again, to try to find out what exactly had been agreed with the airlines. Had the airlines, then, been asked to make all the changes that would have been in the AD, and in particular to install the peepholes?

The answer was no. All that the airlines and Douglas had specifically agreed to do was beef up the electric wiring and install a placard on each cargo door warning baggage handlers not to use more than 50 pounds of force: precisely how a baggage handler was supposed to measure his muscle power was not explained.

The peephole idea had not been discussed in detail because, of course, at the time of the telecon the semantics were still being worked out at the Western Region office. Well then, could the specification for the peephole now be sent to the airlines? Again the answer was no.

Rudolph explained that a telegram confirming the agreement reached over the phone had already been sent to the airlines, signed by the Deputy Administrator Smith. Smith had now left the office (it was late on Friday evening in Washington) and it was too late to modify or add to the telegram. "Mr Rudolph . . . suggested we work the problem on Monday, but indicated he agreed with our proposed amendment," said Basnight.

On Monday, June 19, Basnight did indeed have further dealings with his Washington HQ, but none that produced any more substantial guidance for the airlines using DC-10s.

Early in the morning he received a call from Joe Ferrarese, one of Rudolph's senior colleagues, who said that he was instructed to ask Basnight to destroy all but one copy of the teletype messages to airlines that the Deputy Administrator had signed for transmission on Friday night. Basnight replied – no doubt rather drily – that he had not yet received any copies of his message, but on doing so he would act as required.

Shortly afterwards, three copies of Smith's message arrived in a sealed envelope. It consisted of a briefly stated request to all airlines operating DC-10s to accomplish the wiring modification and install the warning placards. It made no mention of inspection holes. Basnight called in Sliff, handed him one copy of the message for his records, and destroyed the other two. Next day, feeling no doubt that he was a little exposed, he sat down and wrote a 1,500-word Memorandum to File recording the events of the previous few days. That was something he had never felt moved to do before in all of his 30-year career.

Given that the FAA has a prime duty to protect public safety how could it have happened? We believe that the answer lies in the schizoid nature of the FAA administrator's job and particularly in the character of the man who President Richard Nixon chose to fill it.

When the FAA was established by Act of Congress in 1958 it was given responsibility not only to regulate the safety standards of American aviation but also to promote its commercial success. In theory there should be no conflict between these ambitions so long as the FAA's administrator, who is always a political appointee, is able to cope with a dual role – part policeman, part promoter.

He must be able to identify with the industry's viewpoint while standing slightly apart. The trouble with John Hixon Shaffer was that he identified totally with the industry. Indeed he was an embodiment of it.

Shaffer served with the US Air Force from 1946 to 1953 and spent most of that time working with aircraft manufacturers developing new bombers such as the Boeing B-47. When he resigned from the Air Force, with the rank of lieutenant-colonel, he deliberately took a job outside the aviation industry with the Ford Motor Company to avoid, he says, accusations that he had been "feathering my own nest". But after three years with Ford, he deemed it proper, in his own words, "to go home" and he became an executive – and, eventually, a vice-president and small stockholder – of TRW, one of the largest engineering sub-contractors in the aerospace industry.

Shaffer is a muscular, outgoing man who graduated from West Point during the Second World War and survived a tour of duty on the horrendous B-26, an aeroplane widely thought to have inflicted more damage on the US forces than those of the enemy. From an examination of the DC-10 affair, he emerges as an honest man, but one very unwilling to perceive any faults in the industry that had made him prosperous and successful.

He arrived at the FAA through the introduction of Melvin Laird, then Secretary of Defense, and from the beginning he saw his chief task not in terms of safety administration, but as one of defending the aviation industry against the depredations of the increasingly active environmentalist lobby. Therefore, to Shaffer, the sad failure over the DC-10 appears as a relatively minor incident in his tenure at the FAA.

The major achievement, he feels, is that during that time "to the everlasting credit of the U.S.A., we didn't fall for the misbelief that aircraft noise is really so bad". As he points out: "Only 7m people are affected by airport noise in this country!"

Shaffer does mildly regret his period as Administrator – which ended in March, 1973 – in that it cost him, he estimates, some $400,000 in salary and "missed opportunities" generally. However, it was worth the financial sacrifice on a considerable scale, he feels, to have had the "best job in Washington", where he defended an industry for which he has a virtually romantic affection.

After the Paris crash, Shaffer said that he would never have "sat around, fat, dumb and happy" if he had been aware that aircraft were coming out of the Douglas plant with cargo doors that were still unsafe. But that was afterwards: at the time, he expressed nothing but officer-like distaste for the grubby minutiae of inspection. His own summary of the conversation with McGowen is that "I rang him and said what the hell is wrong with your goddam plane? And he replied: 'Jack, we'll have it fixed by Friday night – '"

According to Shaffer, the term gentlemen's agreement is an unhappy one, conveying the incorrect impression that his transaction with Jackson McGowen amounted to a "hand-shake behind the barn".

Yet the fact is that at the time he agreed with McGowen that no AD was necessary, it would have been quite impossible for McGowen to have given him any detailed account of what might be done to make the door safe – for no one at the Douglas plant or in the FAA had yet worked out a detailed solution.

Shaffer covers this point by saying simply that "you have got to have faith in people". But Shaffer should have been aware that the summer of 1972 was a moment when nobody in the Douglas division of McDonnell Douglas could be expected to give an objective judgment on any matter which might involve publicity for actual or potential drawback in the DC-10.

It is hardly surprising that after this crushing defeat the Western office made no further attempts to issue ADs relating to the DC-10 door system. However, Sliff and his colleagues remained in touch with the engineers at the Long Beach plant, who did at least make some effort to honour the gentlemen's agreement that Jackson McGowen had made on their behalf.

It was, of course, obvious to any serious engineer that the situation could not be left as it stood on Friday June 16. In addition to the actuator rewiring, Douglas proposed three more changes to the door, all of which were sent out to the airlines by service bulletins from

Douglas over the next two months. But, unlike ADs, service bulletins are not mandatory.

These did not amount to a perfect solution. The DC-10 cargo door was not made totally fail-safe – as it is today – until after the Paris crash. But if the changes devised in July and August 1972 had been properly carried out on every DC-10 built and put into service, then the slaughter of March 3, 1974 might well have been averted.

The trouble is that they were not properly carried out. The most important of the early modifications – a support plate to be fitted inside each cargo door to strengthen the locking mechanism – was recommended by Douglas on July 2, 1972.

The recommendation was sent out to the airlines then operating DC-10s as a *routine* service bulletin with no indication that it was vital to the plane's safety.

As a result very few DC-10s were modified with any alacrity. Of the 39 DC-10s then in service – all with US domestic airlines – only five were modified within 90 days; 18 were not modified until 1973 and one DC-10 was still flying around without a support plate 19 months after the bulletin was issued.

The Turkish Airlines plane which crashed in Paris was also missing its support plate. It should have been modified by Douglas, because in the summer of 1972 the aircraft was still at the Douglas plant at Long Beach waiting for a buyer. The documentation issued by Douglas said that the work had been done, but that was a lie.

Because history is an unrepeatable experiment, we cannot prove that the extra urgency, legal weight, and publicity which go with Airworthiness Directives would necessarily have made the difference. But the crucial point is not so much the issuing or non-issuing of any particular directive, as the general determination on John Shaffer's part that the Douglas Company itself could be left to handle the matter in its own way. And, of course, the very way that the thing was done was bound to weaken the authority of Arvin Basnight and his staff.

And the secrecy in which the whole business was accomplished was damaging also: Douglas employees who should have "fixed" Turkish Airlines' plane later testified that they were simply unaware of the significance or the various things that were supposed to be done to DC-10 doors.

In the final article in the series, Insight examine why the DC-10 in question was considered safe to fly on March 3, 1974. In doing so they reveal a simple and shocking answer: because the plane's safety records had been amended in order to suggest the necessary safety modification had been made when it had not. It was an act that cost hundreds of lives.

◆

THE FALSE RECORDS OF SHIP 29

31 October 1976

THREE WEEKS after the world's worst air crash, McDonnell Douglas, the maker of the DC-10, called a press conference at its factory at Long Beach, near Los Angeles, California, to make a confession.

John Brizendine, president of the Douglas division, revealed that the Turkish Airlines plane which had crashed – known to Douglas as Ship 29 because it was the twenty ninth DC-10 to be built – had left Long Beach with a vital modification missing from its rear cargo door. Yet the company's records for Ship 29 said that the modification work had been carried out.

"This is a circumstance for which we do not yet have an explanation," Brizendine said. "We are investigating this matter vigorously."

He backed up that promise with a declaration: "We know that we have great responsibilities, and we take those responsibilities very seriously. You might remember – as we always do – that a Douglas aircraft is always a Douglas aircraft no matter who owns it, how long it remains in service, or what is done with it long after it's beyond our control. Our planes are part of our lives and part of our identity; that's one reason why we develop and build them with such care."

A little over a year later in Los Angeles Brizendine appeared before a much smaller but also much more critical audience. This one consisted primarily of American lawyers, hired by relatives of those who died in the Paris crash, who were attempting to extract compensation from McDonnell Douglas for what they considered to have been an eminently avoidable tragedy. We have been able to obtain Brizendine's secret testimony. This time his attitude was not quite the same.

If, in the interim, there had been a "vigorous" investigation into the falsification of Douglas's manufacturing records, Brizendine gave no indication that he had been very interested in the results.

And while he could not, apparently, throw much light upon the mystery of the false records, McDonnell Douglas's lawyers would not. They claimed that the internal investigation had been conducted by qualified lawyers and that the results were therefore "privileged" and need not be revealed in litigation.

As a consequence, vital questions about the reliability of Douglas's manufacturing inspection system must go unanswered. However, we have obtained some evidence about the creation of the false records. It does not solve the mystery – indeed in some ways it makes it even more puzzling.

In the summer of 1972, in the light of the Windsor incident when a DC-10 was forced to crash-land after its rear cargo door blew out over Ontario, all these cargo doors were supposed to be modified.

The plane, along with five others, had initially been ordered by a Japanese bank but the contract had been cancelled. The responsibilities for making the modification to Ship 29's door therefore belonged to Douglas.

One of the modifications recommended by Douglas called for a support plate to be fitted to the cargo door locking mechanism to strengthen it and prevent it from being forced – as had been the case in the Windsor incident. The records of Ship 29 claim that its support plate was fitted on July 18, 1972.

The records also claim that on the same day the installation was verified by three Douglas inspectors, each of whom applied a personalised rubber stamp to the paperwork, asserting that the modification had been properly carried out. Yet, as the wreckage of Ship 29 clearly showed, the support plate had not been fitted.

The US legal system provides for pre-trial proceedings – known as depositions – during which witnesses can be brought forward and examined on oath. In the Paris Air crash case the three inspectors – identifiable through their stamps as Edward M. Evans, Henry C. Noriega and Shelby G. Newton – were, naturally enough, among the first McDonnell Douglas witnesses to be interrogated.

It emerged that none of the three men could recall having worked on the cargo door of any DC-10 at any time in 1972. Nor could they recall any occasion whatever on which they had worked together – and they were certain they had not done so on July 18 of that year.

On July 18, Ship 29 was parked on the ramp outside building 54, of the Long Beach factory. Airplane workers, unlike men on the line in car factories, can usually identify the machines on which they have worked, and this makes it the more unusual that Edward Evans, like Henry Noriega, has no memory whatever of having set eyes on Ship 29.

Shelby Newton, who gave the most precise, but in some ways the most puzzling evidence, actually remembers Ship 29, but remembers with equal clarity that he did not work on it in July 1972.

However, Edward Evans's case differs slightly from the other two, in that the plant records do actually show that on the relevant day he could have been working on the airplane. Evans is the only one of the three who was a full-time inspector.

He was first assigned to DC-10 work in March 1972. He worked long days that summer, because he left home each day at 6.30am, travelled 20 minutes to the plant, and after work went straight to the college, where he was studying Quality Control, returning to his wife and small child at 10.30 in the evening. That particular day in July 1972, a Tuesday, he followed the usual routine, so far as he could recollect.

As Ship 29 was parked outside building 54, along with other DC-10s, it is possible that he could have been assigned to it.

Evans recognised his own stamp as being in Ship 29's records in a position suggesting that he had checked the installation of the support plate. As the stamp was there, he said, he accepted that he must have applied it.

Yet he had no recollection of ever having seen Ship 29. Nor did he have any recollection of having even seen a support plate before the Paris crash of 1974. He certainly could not recall that he had ever inspected any work on such an item, and indeed his evidence suggested that he would not have known how to do so.

His stamp, he said, had always remained in his pocket when not in use, and he had never allowed anyone else to use it.

After the Paris crash, Evans was taken off inspection work. But in the summer of 1974, feeling restless and anxious to get back to the work he felt he knew best, Evans had an interview with the president of the Douglas division, John Brizendine, and asked if he could have his stamp back.

Evans told the lawyers: "I told him [Brizendine] I have no idea how I bought that job off without those parts being installed, *if that is what I did*".

Henry Noriega's memory was more distinct than Evans's but that only made his account more puzzling. He is an electrician and during the whole of his 24-year career with Douglas he has, he said, worked only on electrical; never on mechanical installations. Yet his Q-stamp appears on Ship 29's records, validating non-existent mechanical work.

In his evidence Noriega recalled exactly what he was doing on July 18 – he was working on another DC-10 and never went anywhere near Ship 29. How, then, did his stamp appear on Ship 29's records?

All that Noriega could suggest was that perhaps a worker, superior to him – one who for some reason did not have a stamp and needed one to clear up a job – had borrowed his. Such an event, on Noriega's account, would have been almost unique and he could not recall any such thing having occurred on July 18 or any other day.

Both Evans and Noriega conveyed to the lawyers interrogating them that they were puzzled men, distressed and under strain. Shelby Newton, the third witness, made a sharp contrast. He is a young, articulate Black man, far better qualified in aeronautical engineering than either of his colleagues, and very precise in speech and memory.

On July 18 he was working, with a crew of 20 men under him, on another DC-10 several hundred yards away from Building 54, where Ship 29 was parked. He testified that his duties might have taken him through the ramp area of Building 54 but he was adamant that he never worked on Ship 29.

Newton said that neither he, nor any of his crew, had at any time done any work whatsoever upon a cargo door of any DC-10. Indeed, he said, he had never even seen anyone modifying a DC-10 door and, in July, 1972, would not have had any idea of how to carry out such work. He also said that he would not, under any circumstances whatever, have stamped off work which he had not seen done, with his own eyes.

Yet, his stamp appeared on Ship 29's records.

To begin with, when asked about the statements of Evans, Noriega and Newton, Brizendine seemed to have some difficulty in even remembering which of the three men was which. He said he had not questioned any of them directly and had only met Evans at Evans's own request. He recalled little about the interview and could not explain why, after it, Evans had no longer entertained any doubts that he had stamped Ship 29's records.

Brizendine said he was not aware that Evans had never inspected any work on any DC-10 cargo door before July 18 and he only held some vague recollection that Noriega was an electrical and not a mechanical inspector. Asked whether Noriega had had any experience of mechanical work, such as the fitting of a support plate, Brizendine said: "I couldn't tell you whether he did or not."

The only suggestion Brizendine could produce as to why Noriega might, after 24 years, have suddenly been switched to mechanical work was that he must have been given a special assignment.

It should be said that Brizendine was of the firm opinion that his company was not to blame for the Paris crash. He contended that the missing support plate, while an unfortunate lapse, was irrelevant because Ship 29's door had a far more deadly flaw. Indisputably, the "make-sure" locking device on the rear cargo door had been mis-rigged in such a way as to make it absurdly dangerous. McDonnell Douglas says that Turkish Airlines was responsible for the mis-rigging. Turkish Airlines, with equal vehemence blames McDonnell Douglas.

On the question of whether McDonnell Douglas could and should have anticipated the Paris disaster, Brizendine was equally unwilling to accept blame. It was pointed out to him by the interrogating lawyers that, almost two years before Paris, the tragedy was foreshadowed by the Windsor incident. On that occasion the plane, and the passengers, were saved but should not the incident have served as a warning?

Brizendine said that the crash in France really did not have all that much connection with the Windsor incident. Indeed, he seemed to think that Windsor demonstrated very little other than the excellence of the DC-10. He did not think that the pilot, Captain Bryce McCormick, had done anything very remarkable in bringing the plane down safely although he did allow that McCormick had "kept his cool and used the plane as it was designed to be used."

He was reminded that McDonnell Douglas had sent a special message to Captain McCormick congratulating him on his performance but Brizendine thought very little of the point.

"I would", he said, "also tell the guy that waxes the floor in my lobby that he had done a great job too".

If the Paris Air Crash case had gone to trial on the issue of liability, the plaintiff lawyers would have challenged McDonnell Douglas's claim that the results of its internal investigation are "privileged". But in May, 1975, while the depositions were still continuing, Douglas and its three co-defendants decided no longer to contest liability for the Paris crash and offered to settle the claims for compensation out of court.

At present there are still 80 families who have yet to agree with the settlement terms being offered and a liability trial is due to begin in Los Angeles on November 30. It seems, however, most unlikely that the trial will go ahead and if it does it will take years to resolve. We are therefore, for the time being, left with a disturbing mystery.

McDonnell Douglas's attitude toward the falsification seems to be that the event was an isolated, but totally mysterious failure in an otherwise excellent system. The attitude is understandable, but absurd, because it is impossible to know whether the failure was an isolated one without its causes being understood.

One obvious possibility is that the control of stamps within the Douglas plant was actually far more lax than the Douglas Quality Standards insisted upon: that people anxious to get work finished on time could find an appropriate stamp to complete the paperwork. Ship 29, when it eventually did find a buyer, found an impatient one, and when the plane was being readied in the late autumn of 1972, there was not very much time to spare. As there appears to have been no general knowledge among workers in the Douglas plant that the door modifications were of great importance, it is possible that someone may have decided in late 1972 to "clean up" the paperwork retroactively.

Although dishonest, the falsification might have been seen as an act of little consequence. Indeed, it would probably have never been discovered but for the crash that destroyed Ship 29 – and 346 lives.

1984
COLONEL GADDAFI AND
THE MINERS' STRIKE

In October, 1984, Britain was in the midst of a long strike by the National Union of Mineworkers (NUM), led by their president Arthur Scargill. The aim was to disrupt the British coal industry in protest against proposed colliery closures at the hands of Margaret Thatcher's government. The resulting turmoil seriously threatened to undermine Thatcher and destabilise the country.

Simultaneously, the UK was in the process of severing diplomatic ties with Libya, after a British police officer policing a protest outside its embassy in London was shot dead by an assailant firing from within the building. The protesters had been there to denounce the country's military dictator, Colonel Muammar Gaddafi.

Gaddafi, internationally condemned for his human rights record and corruption, had previously been accused of supplying money and weapons to the IRA as part of a long-running dispute with Britain. Now, he had discovered another strategy for manipulating British politics by financing Scargill's strike, according to a tip-off from French intelligence sources to Insight reporter Jon Swain.

Swain charmed his way into getting access to passenger manifests and hotel documents to prove that NUM executives were travelling to Libya to meet shadowy figures linked to the regime. This revelation caused a public relations disaster from which Scargill would not recover. The strike ended five months later.

SCARGILL: THE LIBYAN CONNECTION

———————•———————

28 October 1984

ARTHUR SCARGILL, the president of the National Union of Mineworkers, and Roger Windsor, the union's chief executive, have been holding secret talks with the Libyan government. Three weeks ago on October 8, the two men flew to Paris to meet Salem Ibrahim, who is described by French intelligence as Colonel Gaddafi's paymaster. Last Monday, Roger Windsor flew to Frankfurt and then on to Tripoli where he met Col. Gaddafi, the Libyan leader.

Windsor's visit was arranged by a Pakistani living in England, named Mumtaz Abbasi, who admits he is "European representative" of Al-Zulfikar, a Libyan-backed terrorist group which is dedicated to the overthrow of General Zia's regime in Pakistan. Windsor left Tripoli to return to England, by the same indirect route, on Friday. He was in the Libyan capital on Thursday when the high court in London ordered the sequestration of the NUM's assets.

None of the members of the NUM executive that *The Sunday Times* reached yesterday, including the union's general secretary, Peter Heathfield, was aware of the Libyan connection.

The sequence of events that *The Sunday Times* has pieced together began on Monday, October 8, when Scargill and Windsor flew from Manchester to Paris on Air France's early morning flight, AF964. Scargill's seat was booked under the name of "Smith", but he was recognised by a woman at the British Airways check-in desk and by the airport manager.

The *Manchester Evening News* was alerted, and was therefore able to report that Scargill's return to Manchester that night (on Air France's flight AF963) was delayed for nearly two hours by a baggage handlers' strike at Charles de Gaulle airport. As for what Scargill had been doing in Paris, the newspaper reported that: "The miners' leader was attending a meeting in the French capital."

Yesterday week, *The Sunday Times* attempted to reach Scargill to ask him what that meeting had been about, and whether he had met the coal board chairman, Ian MacGregor, who also happened to be in Paris on October 8. That night Maurice Jones, the editor of *The Miner*, the union's newspaper, telephoned to say that Scargill had not met MacGregor. Jones said that Scargill had told him he had gone to Paris to co-ordinate with the CGT, the French Communist union, about a convoy of lorries carrying food parcels which the union planned to send to striking British miners. (The lorries arrived in Britain the following weekend.)

However, when *The Sunday Times* contacted Augustin Dufresne, the CGT official responsible for organising the convoy, he said that there had been no such meeting. He insisted that, if there had been such a meeting, he would have known about it. He also said he was sure that Scargill had not even been in Paris on October 8 because if he had been "he would have called just to say hello".

In fact, Scargill and Windsor *were* at the CGT's headquarters, in the Paris suburb of Montreuil, for much of the day. According to our sources they met with a Pakistani, and a Libyan named Salem Ibrahim.

Ibrahim arrived in Paris on Sunday, October 7, the day before Scargill and Windsor, and checked into room 723 of the Hilton International, near the Eiffel Tower. His reservation had been made by the Rome Hilton, by telex.

The message said that he would be arriving from Tripoli, that his bill would be paid by the Bangladesh embassy, that he would be staying until October 10 and that he should be accorded VIP status.

Because of this last request, Ibrahim was not required to fill out the Hilton's registration card, which demands such details as passport number, nationality, date of birth and profession. Abrahim merely gave an address – "Shatt Street, Tripoli".

But his arrival aroused the interest of the French intelligence and security services. Salem Ibrahim is known to them as "Colonel Gaddafi's bagman" – the trusted confidant of the Libyan leader who negotiates and arranges the financial payments to the disparate groups and causes which Gaddafi supports, including terrorist groups in Europe.

Ibrahim checked out of the Hilton one day earlier than expected, on October 9, the day after his meeting with Scargill and Windsor. His bill, for 3,259.60 francs (about £300) was duly paid by the Bangladesh embassy in Paris. When we asked the Bangladesh ambassador why his embassy had paid Ibrahim's bill he denied it.

The Sunday Times has established that before he left the Hilton, Ibrahim made telephone calls from his room to two numbers. One of them, Tripoli 174982, is Ibrahim's home telephone number.

The second number, Doncaster 27068, is the home telephone number of a Pakistani exile named Mumtaz Abbasi. The terrorist group of which he admits he is the European representative was responsible for the hijacking of a Pakistan Airlines jet in March 1981. Abbasi is the crucial link in the NUM's Libyan connection.

Abbasi, who is married with five children, came to Britain about 18 years ago. He was, he says, a personal friend of Zulfikar Ali Bhutto, the prime minister of Pakistan, who was deposed in 1977 and executed – on the orders of Pakistan's president General Zia – in April 1979. At the time of the coup, Abbasi was in Pakistan and was arrested. He was later charged with treason, and sentenced to 25 years imprisonment.

In March 1981, Al-Zulfikar – which means "the Sword", and which is led by Bhutto's son Murtaza – hijacked a Pakistan Airlines internal flight and forced it to fly to the Afghanistan capital, Kabul. They demanded the release of all "political prisoners" in Pakistan, and gave the authorities a list of names. After five days on the tarmac, the hijackers murdered one of their hostages, a Pakistani diplomat, and then forced the pilot to fly the plane to Damascus. After 13 days – the world's longest hijack – General Zia caved in and ordered the release of 54 prisoners, who were flown to Damascus and exchanged for the hostages.

Abbasi was not among them, but he was released shortly afterwards as a result of pressure from, among others, the British government because he holds a British passport. He moved with his family to a modest terraced house at 77, Craithie Road, Doncaster. This summer he moved to a larger red-brick house at 133, Bennethorpe nearby.

He owns a small grocery shop, Express Foods, in Copley Road, Doncaster. But he is rarely there. An assistant at the shop said yesterday that this was because he "travels a lot". Neighbours say he went to Paris, West Germany and Libya.

His most recent trip to Libya began 11 days after the Paris meeting. He flew to Frankfurt on Friday October 19, and waited there over the weekend for his travelling companion.

Last Monday, Roger Windsor, the NUM's chief executive, set out on the same journey. Windsor has worked for the NUM for two years. Before that he worked for an international trade union organisation and lived in Stroud, Gloucestershire, where his wife, Angela, was secretary of the constituency Labour party.

If Windsor had travelled to Tripoli from London, where there is at least one direct flight a day, he would have run the risk of alerting Scotland Yard's Special Branch, which, since the siege in St James Square – and the virtual breaking-off of diplomatic relations between Britain and Libya – takes a close interest in all Tripoli-bound passengers.

Instead, he flew to Frankfurt on Lufthansa's evening flight, LH075. The next day he continued on to Tripoli, on Libyan Airlines flight LN113. His name was mis-spelled on the passenger manifest as "Windor". His single ticket to Tripoli was bought in Frankfurt, and paid in Libyan dinars.

The Sunday Times has not been able to establish which, if any, of the NUM's officials and staff, knew that Windsor had gone to Tripoli. When we telephoned his secretary on Wednesday she would only say that he was "away" and that she expected him back on Thursday. She had every reason to expect him on Thursday.

That was the day NACODS, the pit deputies' union, was due to strike, and the day that the high court was considering action against the union for non-payment of a £200,000 fine for contempt.

Yet Windsor stayed in Tripoli. The only account so far of what he was doing comes from the official Libyan news agency, JANA, which last Friday issued the following story under the headline, "Leader Receives NUM Envoy":

"Yesterday evening, the leader of the revolution received an envoy representing the British National Union of Mineworkers and inquired about the state of British miners who have been on strike for over eight months now.

"The leader expressed sympathy with the striking workers who suffer from abuse and exploitation at the hand of the exploiting ruling class in Britain.

"He also conveyed to the NUM envoy (Gaddafi's) solidarity with the striking miners' struggle to gain the legitimate rights and their rights in production, according to the 3rd universal theory dicta.

"The NUM envoy explained the hardship of the British miners, whose strike now entered its eighth month and continues because of the Thatcher government's obstinacy, its rejection of the workers' demands and closure of 20 pits, which led to the dismissal of 20,000 miners.

"The envoy also talked about the police daily repressive actions against the striking workers, explaining that the objective behind the strike, which is the longest in British history, is to reinstate miners to their jobs in Yorkshire, Wales, Scotland, Keith and Nottinghamshire.

"He said that the number of striking workers totals 80,000 who are daily facing multiple forms of oppression at the hands of the Thatcher Conservative government. The number of casualties has so far reached five, in addition to 30,000 other injuries and 8,000 imprisoned in British jails. The police action has also affected the NUM leadership, including the NUM president Arthur Scargill, who was beaten by British police.

"'The envoy added that he left miners' families a target of hunger and hardship, reaching the extent of their inability to feed their children or bury their dead."

Windsor and Abbasi returned from Tripoli together on Friday, again via Frankfurt on Libyan Airlines flight LN172. Abbasi was listed on the passenger manifest as "Abas". Windsor was listed as "Rougar". Two reporters and a photographer from *The Sunday Times* observed the arrival of the flight at Gate 33 of terminal B at 1.40 pm. Windsor and Abbasi left the plane together and were greeted by a Libyan official.

Windsor and Abbasi then spent the next three and half hours in the terminal, waiting for the connecting flight to Manchester. They passed the time looking in the duty-free shops and avidly reading British newspaper accounts of Thursday's sequestration of the NUM assets.

They travelled to Manchester on Lufthansa's flight LH074. At Manchester airport they got into a taxi together and travelled to their homes in Doncaster and Sheffield.

Windsor's Libyan trip was not known to members of the NUM executive whom *The Sunday Times* contacted yesterday. Trevor Bell, the leading moderate on the executive, said: "I know nothing about it. I am surprised that anybody would need to spend money going to Tripoli."

Yesterday *The Sunday Times* attempted to get explanations of the Libyan connection from Abbasi, Windsor and Scargill, and Salem Ibrahim.

Abbasi immediately admitted he had been to Tripoli last week for "personal and private reasons", to see a Pakistani exile and friend of his, Colonel Habib. He said he stayed at the Shatti Hotel.

He also admitted knowing Salem Ibrahim, who he described as vice-chancellor of Tripoli's Al Fatah university. He said they had known each other since 1972 and met regularly, either in Tripoli or when Ibrahim made one of his frequent visits to Europe. Indeed, he said, he saw Ibrahim in Tripoli last week "for a few hours", and in Paris in early September. But he denied that he was with him in Paris in October.

He also denied that he had any connection with the NUM, or that he knew or had met Roger Windsor: "I have no role in the NUM's business but I have full sympathy for their cause as long as they are fighting for their jobs," he said. "I have never met Scargill in this country or any other country. I have nothing to do with the union." He said the only contribution he had made to the miners' funds was 50p, which he had put in a collecting box in Doncaster.

Shown a photograph of Windsor, and asked if he knew him, Abbasi looked abashed. After a pause he said that Windsor looked like the man he had shared a taxi with from Manchester airport on Friday. He said they were "absolute strangers", going in the same direction.

When told that they had been seen together at Frankfurt airport, Abbasi changed his story: "We met completely by accident at Frankfurt airport checking flights to Manchester," he said. "When I arrived from Tripoli I wanted to check a Manchester flight. He was making the same inquiry."

Told that he had been observed with Windsor getting off the plane from Tripoli, and meeting a Libyan official, he categorically denied it. He then said he *may* have met Windsor on the plane from Tripoli: "I didn't take any notice. If I had known he was chief executive of the NUM I would have made a point of talking to him. It would have been an honour to meet a person of this stature."

Later he went back on his story yet again: "The first time I saw Mr Windsor was on German soil," he insisted.

Approached at his home in Sheffield, Windsor said angrily: "I have nothing to say. Are you going to leave my premises now, or do I have to call the police?" He refused to answer any questions, and shut the door.

The Sunday Times approached Scargill yesterday morning after he had addressed a miners' rally in the Lanarkshire steel town of Motherwell. Our reporter said: "Mr Scargill, have you anything to say about reports that you and the NUM recently sent a representative to Tripoli?"

Told that the reporter was from *The Sunday Times*, Scargill walked in silence for about 30 yards. When the question was repeated, Mick McGahey, the Scottish miners' president, who was accompanying Scargill, said "get tae hell" and told a bodyguard, "throw this man off the road." A *Sunday Times* photographer was jostled by the bodyguards and Scargill marched on in silence.

Reached at his home in Tripoli yesterday, Salem Ibrahim initially denied making a trip to Paris and claimed he had never met Scargill or Windsor.

He also denied knowing Abbasi. But when asked why he would not reveal what was discussed at the October 8 meeting he said: "Why should I?" He added: "Why don't you contact Scargill and Windsor. They will definitely tell you."

Insight: Jon Swain

1986
ISRAEL'S SECRET
NUCLEAR WEAPONS

On October 5, 1986, *Insight* finally confirmed what the world had long suspected: that Israel had the atom bomb. As well as establishing the existence of a secret nuclear weapons factory in Israel, *Insight* uncovered that far from being a "nuclear pygmy", the country owned the sixth-largest nuclear arsenal in the world (after America, the Soviet Union, Britain, France and China) and had been producing atomic weapons for two decades.

The investigation began with a tip-off from Mordechai Vanunu, a 31-year-old Israeli ex-nuclear technician who had worked at Dimona, Israel's Nuclear Research Centre. Vanunu, who had been made redundant after nine years of service over fear of his growing ties to West Bank Arab students, claimed to have secret photographs of a subterranean nuclear weapons factory hidden within Dimona.

Insight extensively interrogated Vanunu and his controversial claims, with the help of nuclear weapons experts. In doing so they were able to verify Israel's long-hidden capacity for this highly destructive material, as well as uncovering damning evidence that it had likely begun manufacturing thermo-nuclear weapons capable of destroying entire cities.

After blowing the whistle, Vanunu was abducted in Rome by Israeli intelligence operatives and spent 18 years in prison, 11 in solitary confinement, before being released under close surveillance in 2004.

INSIDE DIMONA: ISRAEL'S NUCLEAR BOMB FACTORY

---•---

5 October 1986

EVERY day at 7am a fleet of 40 blue and white Volvo buses speeds down the desert highway that cuts through the Negev desert. Nine miles out from the town of Dimona, the buses turn right into a side road and pull up after half a mile at an army checkpoint. Soldiers make a cursory inspection of security passes and the buses are waved through. Two miles further into the desert, they stop at another Halt sign, where security is more severely enforced.

Here an electrified fence extends into the dusty scrubland of the Negev. It surrounds Israel's most secret establishment. The sand within the perimeter is raked by tractor to betray intruders' footprints to the infantry and helicopter patrols. Observation posts are mounted on the hilltops nearby. Missile batteries have orders to shoot down any aircraft that stray into the airspace above, as one Israeli pilot discovered to his cost in 1967.

Officially, Dimona is run by the Israeli Atomic Energy Authority to conduct experiments into nuclear power. Its official title is Kirya-le-Mehekar Gariny or KMG – the Negev Nuclear Research Centre. The world knows it as Dimona, long considered to be Israel's nuclear bomb factory.

Dimona is a palm and concrete oasis reaching from the Beersheba to Sodom highway. The road is the closest anyone can get without a security pass. The handful of photographers who have evaded the patrols and succeeded in snatching a hazy shot from a speeding car charge exorbitant reproduction fees for their rare pictures.

The Volvo buses travel the route three times a day to service the 7.30am, 3.30pm and 11.30pm shifts. They carry 2,700 scientists, technicians and administrative staff. Secrecy demands that many people remain unaware of the duties performed within, by even long-standing colleagues. The penalty for loose talk is 15 years imprisonment.

Once off the buses, the workforce disperses to various *machons*, which are self-contained production units.

There are 10 machons in all. Machon 1 is the nuclear reactor itself, a silver-domed building 60ft in diameter. Machon 4 is where radioactive waste is immersed in tar and packed in drums to be sunk in the desert. But only a handful – 150 workers in all – are ever allowed to pass through the doors of the real secret within Dimona – Machon 2.

Outwardly, it is a crudely built and windowless concrete building, two storeys high – 80ft by 200ft – an apparently little-used warehouse and office block. Two details suggest otherwise: the walls are thickened to withstand bombardment and there is an elevator tower on the roof which seems unnecessary for such a small building.

For three decades this innocuous slab of concrete has hidden Israel's secrets from prying satellites and foreign nuclear energy inspectors. Above ground level the entire site is precisely what the Israelis say it is: an experimental nuclear power station. Intelligence agencies, scientists and journalists have attempted for many years to prove otherwise. But all have fallen down on one key question: Where is the technology that can transform the peaceful atomic research into a bomb factory? Machon 2 provides the answer.

False walls on the first floor above ground hide the service lifts that take men and materials to six subterranean levels, where the components of nuclear weapons are produced and machined into warhead parts.

The whistleblower

It was to Machon 2 that Mordechai Vanunu was first assigned in 1977. He is a 31-year-old Moroccan Jew, born on October 13, 1954, in Marrakesh, where his parents ran a small shop. In 1963, amidst increasingly anti-Jewish feeling, the family emigrated to Israel and settled in Beersheba. After three years conscription in the Israeli army, reaching the rank of first sergeant in a unit of sappers on the Golan Heights, Vanunu entered Ramat Aviv University in Tel Aviv. But he failed two exams after the first year of his physics degree course and returned home.

In mid-summer of 1976, he saw advertisements for trainee technicians at Dimona and, by chance, met a friend who was already employed by KMG. Vanunu collected an application form from the KMG offices in Beersheba, near the bus station on the main road to Tel Aviv.

His first interview was with security. Vanunu was asked about criminal offences, drug or alcohol problems and his political affiliations. A month later he received a letter of acceptance.

He went on the KMG payroll in November, 1976, by coincidence the same month that 13 American senators on a fact-finding visit to Israel were refused entry to Dimona. Vanunu was not taken out to the desert complex straight away. Instead he was sent back to school for a crash course in physics, chemistry, maths and English. He sailed through the initial entrance exam along with 39 of his 45 fellow candidates in January, 1977. In early February, Vanunu's intake boarded a Volvo bus for Dimona.

They were taken to a school on the site where their first duty was to sign the Israeli Official Secrets Act. Then he was given his security pass, number 9657–8, medically assessed to be fit and further schooled, under the auspices of a headmaster called Parahi, in elementary nuclear physics and nuclear chemistry with the emphasis on plutonium, uranium and radioactivity.

Vanunu was then given a further pass number, 320, for entry to Machon 2, and a locker (No. 3). The new intake were given 10 weeks to familiarise themselves with Machon 2. At the end of June, their initial training complete, they celebrated with a party.

There was one hiccup at this point. Vanunu was called up for a month's army-reserve duty with his engineer unit, but this seems to have been a mistake. When the nature of his job was discovered he was quickly released. Within seven days he was back in Machon 2, to be told that, after passing a final test, he would be working on the night shift, 11.30pm to 8am.

Vanunu satisfied a three-man examination board (an independent engineer, one of the Dimona school lecturers, and a specialist in handling radio-active materials). On August 7, 1977, he reported for his first full day's work as a *menahil* – a controller on the night shift. It was the start of a nine-year stint as a nuclear technician which was to take Vanunu throughout the labyrinthine Machon 2.

The history of Dimona

Dimona was secretly built by France between 1957 and 1964. It was originally claimed to be a textiles plant by Israel. When, in 1960, an American U2 spy plane photographed it for the first time, the incoming president, John F Kennedy forced the then Israeli prime minister, David Ben Gurion, to submit to regular inspections by US scientists to ensure that Dimona's true purpose remained peaceful nuclear research. Those visits gave Kennedy's successor, Lyndon B Johnson, sufficient assurance to publicly declare that Dimona really was a civilian reactor.

President de Gaulle added his reassurance, saying that France had stopped short of supplying the technology that could have transformed Dimona into a plant "from which, one day, atomic weapons could emerge".

But the official claims have never been accepted. It has long been suspected, but never publicly confirmed, that Israel has been using Dimona to produce materials for a simple atomic weapon. But the many speculative attempts to lift the curtain around Dimona have always foundered. Invariably based on the testimony of unidentified sources, they failed to explain how Israel obtains the fissile material needed for nuclear weapons.

Atomic bombs are made either from Uranium 235 or plutonium. But the production of Uranium 235 requires a huge gaseous diffusion plant or a large number of gas centrifuges. Plutonium, however, can be produced in a compact separation plant.

Plutonium is a by-product of the nuclear process, which in some types of reactor, like the one at Dimona, has to be separated from the uranium fuel rods after they have spent a period in the reactor core. In sophisticated weapons design, just 2 ½ kilograms of plutonium is enough to build a bomb.

France has always insisted that it had stopped short of supplying Israel with plutonium separation technology, which is thought to be the preserve of the major nuclear powers: America, the Soviet Union, Britain, France and more recently China. So most experts concluded that Israel, through the expertise and innovation of its scientists, had managed to extract only small amounts of plutonium using less efficient processes.

Though the inspections ended in 1969 after American scientists complained of unco-operative Israeli authorities, they never saw any evidence to suggest that Dimona housed the plutonium separation plant necessary to turn an ordinary research project into a significant atomic bomb factory.

At best, the CIA and the United Nations have concluded, Israel may have stockpiled enough plutonium in the past 22 years to build perhaps 10 but certainly no more than 20 primitive atomic bombs similar to the 20 kiloton device dropped on Nagasaki in 1945. That estimate is based on the greatest amount of plutonium that can possibly be extracted without the aid of sophisticated separation technology.

The general view has been that, while Israel does have an atomic weapons programme, it is still of a rudimentary nature. Similar suspicions are harboured against several other nations, including Argentina, Pakistan, India and South Africa.

However, Mordechai Vanunu's testimony, which has been checked with leading nuclear experts on both sides of the Atlantic, shows that one of the world's worst kept secrets is, in fact, one of the best kept confidences of the century. Far from being a nuclear pigmy, the evidence is that Israel must now be regarded as a major nuclear power, ranking sixth in the atomic league table, with a stockpile of at least 100 nuclear weapons and with the components and ability to build atomic, neutron or hydrogen bombs.

What the evidence showed

When French construction workers first bulldozed the desert scrub in 1957, they began excavating a crater 80ft deep in the sand. In it they buried Machon 2, the six-level concrete bunker, which was topped off with the two innocuous floors above ground. The false walls were built to hide the service lifts to the subterranean floors from the American inspectors. When the shell was complete, French engineers and technicians installed the technology de Gaulle claimed to have denied Israel. Vanunu's older workmates at Dimona fondly related stories of the Frenchmen who worked alongside them.

The six underground floors of Machon 2 are divided into numbered production units. There is also a demonstration room where visiting VIPs, confined only to the prime minister, the defence minister and the military top brass, are briefed on Operation Hump. That is the codename, says Vanunu, that Israel has given its latest bomb design programme.

In this room are boxed models of atomic devices and a wall-mounted floor plan of Machon 2. Workers are generally free to roam the plant during the long, tedious shifts. Vanunu regularly escaped the constant rounds of canasta played by his workmates to see what was going on.

He worked in, or visited, 33 production units in Machon 2. Unit 10, a ground floor, drive-in delivery bay received the trucks carrying the 100 large and 40 smaller fuel rods from the reactor core. A crane lowers the rods in baskets down through Level One which is a service floor, through Level Two which mainly houses the control room for the plant, to Unit 11 on Level Three.

Here the uranium fuel rods containing the plutonium by-product are chemically stripped of their aluminium coating. When stripped the uranium weighs 650 kilograms and is immersed in nitric acid. This is heated to 109 degrees centigrade for 30 hours to dissolve the uranium.

At this point the uranium content is 450 grams per litre and is transferred through pipes by vacuum to Units 12 to 22, the main treatment centre. This is so big that it occupies a huge production hall rising from Level Four to Level Two. During this process the liquid is treated to remove radioactivity and a mix of solvent and water is added. It is at this point that the plutonium, which mixes with the water, is separated from the uranium, which mixes with the solvent. By the time the mixture is pumped out of the main treatment centre it contains 300 milligrams of plutonium per litre.

In Unit 31 the liquid is further concentrated to two grams per litre and sent to Unit 33, where it is piped into 20-litre tanks and heated with, among other chemicals, hydrogen peroxide for four hours. After an eight-hour cooling period it is mixed with other chemicals which cause the powder to gather in lumps. This is drained and dried, leaving a 'cake' of plutonium, which is baked in Unit 37.

The baking process concentrates the metal into a solid button weighing 130 grams. Nine buttons of plutonium were produced each week, 1.17 kilograms a week for the 34 weeks a year that the process ran. (It shut down for four months for repairs and maintenance.)

The annual net result of this separation process is around 40 kilograms of plutonium a year, or nearly six times the most optimistic assessments of Israel's plutonium making capabilities.

In addition, further units were added between 1980–2, built and installed by the Israelis alongside the plutonium separation plant and monitored from the same control room. One of them, Unit 93 on Level Four, produces tritium. This is of immense significance, for it means Israel has the potential to produce thermonuclear weapons far more powerful than ordinary atomic bombs.

Sticks of lithium and aluminium radiated in the reactor produce the tritium as a by product. Heated in Unit 93 to 625 degrees centigrade, the sticks melt. Tritium is extracted.

In Unit 95, built alongside the three-storey main treatment plant in a disused lift shaft, lithium 6 was separated from commercially available lithium, producing 180 grams a day. Unit 98 is a deuterium production plant.

All of these components, plutonium, lithium 6, tritium and deuterium are taken to another section on Level Four code-named MM2, or Metallurgy, Machon 2. It is here that the raw materials are machined into the components of nuclear bombs.

The processes described above are a simplified precis of the detailed descriptions, flow rates, measures, temperatures and other scientific data that Vanunu, from his position in the control room and work in other units, was able to memorise over nine years and pass on to *The Sunday Times* Insight team, which in turn checked them out with nuclear scientists.

Vanunu never claimed to have seen a completed bomb and never claimed any special knowledge of precisely what the components were. He says the components were taken out of Dimona at regular intervals in a guarded fleet of trucks and hire cars to an unknown location in Haifa.

Our extensive debriefings of Vanunu, over a period of four weeks, produced estimates that Israel was producing 40 kilograms of plutonium a year, enough to make 10 bombs a year. During the period Vanunu worked there Israel therefore produced enough plutonium for 100 nuclear bombs of at least 20 kilotons, equivalent to the one dropped on Nagasaki. By using sophisticated designs requiring smaller amounts of plutonium, it could have produced enough to make 200 nuclear bombs.

Moreover, the production of lithium 6, tritium and deuterium means that Israel is producing the raw materials to make the components used to boost the yield of primitive atomic weapons to 10 times the 20 kiloton yield.

Two pictures in particular appear to show a lithium deuteride hemisphere which could be used in the construction of the most devastating weapon of all – the thermonuclear bomb – a weapon capable of yielding the equivalent explosive force of hundreds of thousands of tons of TNT. In the chilling jargon of the nuclear bomb makers, Israel has moved beyond the ability to produce small "suburb-busting" nuclear bombs to "city-busters".

There was one question that remained unanswered in Mordechai Vanunu's story. France built Israel a 26 megawatt reactor which can produce, at the outside, seven kilograms of plutonium a year. So how could Vanunu possibly report an annual amount of 40 kilograms?

His reference to 100 large and 40 small uranium fuel rods from the core and the subsequent amounts, in litres or grams produced in the separation processes, suggest a reactor of up to 150 megawatts – the right quantity to produce 40 kilograms a year.

Two events in the late 1960s explain the disparity. First, the Israel secret service, Mossad, masterminded the illegal acquisition of 200 tons of yellowcake – the raw material from which 123 tons of uranium fuel can be extracted – in late 1968 in an operation known as the Plumbat Affair.

Nobody has even been able to explain why Israel wanted so much. A 26 megawatt reactor requires only 20 tons of fuel a year. France had supplied the initial charge, Israel's own phosphate industry provided a further 10 tons a year and spent fuel was recycled to make new rods. So Dimona had more than enough uranium to fuel a 26 mw reactor.

A few months later Israel deliberately provoked the American scientists who inspected Dimona at intervals, harassing them to the point where they pulled out altogether. Since then no outside agency has been inside Dimona, thus leaving the Israelis free to upgrade their 26 megawatt core to 150 megawatts. British atomic energy scientists have confirmed that boosting Dimona's French reactor by a factor of five could have been achieved without rebuilding the reactor.

This is supported by evidence from France. Sources quoted in a recent book about French-Israeli nuclear co-operation said that the reactor built in the Negev had been far larger than admitted.

The sophistication and scale of Israel's nuclear weapons-making capabilities revealed by Insight makes it clear that Israel is now a major nuclear power. Its survival in the face of conventional defeat would seem assured, for no Arab nation could match its nuclear muscle.

China has approximately 300 warheads, France 500 and Britain as many as 700. Both America and the USSR are in a class of their own with about 27,000 each. Israel's projected arsenal of 100–200 weapons may be dwarfed by comparison but it is enough to make it the sixth most powerful nation on earth.

Ten days ago the outgoing prime minister, Shimon Peres, attended a regular briefing of Israeli newspaper editors. On the agenda was the upcoming *Sunday Times* Insight investigation. Though no editor will publicly reveal details of the conversation, it is believed that Peres, having told the editors of the forthcoming report, warned them of their obligations under the Official Secrets Act. He admitted that Insight had gained access to an inside source.

Insight: Peter Hounam, Robin Morgan, Max Prangnell, Rowena Webster, Peter Wilsher and Roger Wilsher. Additional research by Tim Brown, Mark Hosenball, Brian Moynahan and Jon Swain.

1994
CASH FOR QUESTIONS

In the summer of 1994 when Insight reporter Jonathan Calvert stepped foot inside parliament posing as a businessman, he was working on a worrying tip-off that its members had been engaging in morally dubious behaviour, right at the heart of British democracy, namely, that they were prepared to table questions in the House of Commons for money.

Knowing that the only way to uncover the truth and the proof to support it was subterfuge, Calvert approached Members of Parliament from both sides of the house pretending to be a businessman seeking information about a company he wished to invest in, and offered to pay them to table a question about it.

The investigation prompted a media storm, scandalised Westminster, and led to an investigation by the parliamentary privileges committee. The committee recommended the suspension of two MPs who were prepared to accept cash for questions, and both were barred from the Commons for limited periods. But the rebuke couldn't undo the damage on John Major's government, in part sowing the seeds for its eventual downfall in 1997.

The investigation also served as the impetus for the first report from the Committee on Standards in Public Life by Lord Nolan, in 1995, and the introduction of the Nolan Principles: seven principles which outline the ethical expectations on public office holders. It is a standard to which all political public figures are now held.

DISHONOURABLE MEMBERS?

———————•———————

17 July 1994

GRAHAM RIDDICK, Conservative MP for Colne Valley, was looking forward to a quiet weekend in his constituency as he sped home in his Audi 100 after a hectic few days in Westminster. There was no surgery with constituents to drag him away from his rose-covered cottage near Yorkshire's Denby Dale. The only distraction was to be an interview on his local radio station.

Waiting on the doormat as he arrived home that fateful Friday morning, however, was a token of what was to become one of the biggest follies of his political life. He had agreed to table a written question in return for a payment of £1,000. There, in an envelope, was the cheque. It was his reward for putting forward a 43-word question on how many contracts Githins Business Resources had undertaken for the department of social security.

When the department told him it had no knowledge of the firm, the MP returned the cheque. It was too late, though, to save his hopes of promotion in this week's government reshuffle and it was too late to stop John Major's government from being engulfed in new allegations of sleaze.

Last Sunday morning when Riddick picked up *The Sunday Times*, the full horror of what he had done was there in cold print. Githins, he realised, was an anagram of Insight, the *Sunday Times* investigative team – and he had made a fool of himself.

Not that Riddick yet had any remorse. "I have got nothing to worry about because I haven't taken your money. I haven't got an interest to declare," he told Insight last weekend. "I put one question down, which I was happy to do. Frankly, I am always happy to do that for anyone if it is going to help in the wealth-creation process . . . I certainly think it is perfectly all right for MPs to be involved in working with industry. Because it is industry that makes the world go round." It was a display of bravado he would come to regret.

It was over a lunch in January that a leading businessman confided to *The Sunday Times* that he had paid MPs to table parliamentary questions on his behalf. Such rumours had been floating around Westminster for several months. They had even been mentioned in a scholarly book on Commons procedure. But where was the proof?

Over the next few weeks the Insight team sifted through the records of thousands of questions dating back 11 years. The deluge of computer print outs spread across the office floor suggested that MPs had developed sudden, hitherto-unknown interests in everything from sewage treatment to ship repairs. A pattern began to emerge: several MPs known to have links with some of the 50 consultancy firms that hover around Westminster were asking questions of direct interest to the companies those firms lobbied for. It was circumstantial evidence; no more.

Moonlighting as a consultant has long been a way for MPs to supplement their salaries of £31,687 a year. "A bit on the side" was how Michael Connarty, Labour MP for Falkirk East, condemned it in the Commons last week.

Yet, having exhausted normal journalistic enquiries, there was still no conclusive proof of any kind of scam. A reporter could hardly approach an MP, introduce himself as a member of the Insight team and expect the MP to take £1,000 to table a question. The only recourse was to unconventional methods.

It is rare for journalists on a newspaper such as *The Sunday Times* to use subterfuge. The paper fully endorses the Press Complaints Commission's code of practice, which states that journalists should not generally obtain or seek to obtain information or pictures through misrepresentation or subterfuge. There are, however, exceptions. Clause 7 (iii) of the code says that "subterfuge can be justified only in the public interest and only when material cannot be obtained by any other means". Its use is permissible in detecting "a serious misdemeanour" and "preventing the public from being misled by some statement or action of an individual organisation".

Enter Jonathan Calvert, 31, a Yorkshire-born member of Insight and former Welsh newspaper reporter of the year, whose last acting role was in a university pantomime. The code of practice acted as his preliminary script. Now Calvert's role was to approach MPs with a view to tabling a question in return for cash.

Using his real name and at first assuming the identity of a road haulier from Cardiff, he made his initial contact with Ian Greer Associates, one of the biggest Westminster lobbying firms and one which has a track record for making "thank you" payments to MPs. Calvert was invited to their offices just around the corner from Buckingham Palace.

The reporter said he was the owner of Red Dragon Transport and he wanted to campaign against tolls on the Severn bridge. Clive Ferreira, Greer's personal assistant, bragged of the firm's achievements. "If you look at the early day motions and adjournment debates that we have introduced, I think you will find that it is a pretty impressive record."

Calvert was offered "political intelligence" and consultancy at a cost of between £4,000 and £5,000 a month. However, at about the same time, *The Cook Report*, the Central Television programme, was also visiting Greer's firm with an elaborate story about former Russian Communists using an American company and stolen art treasures to buy a British government agency. Insight withdrew and instead opted to approach MPs direct.

It was decided to test 10 Tory and 10 Labour MPs. There have been suggestions that David Tredinnick and Riddick, the two MPs exposed last week for agreeing to accept £1,000 each for tabling a question, were deliberately targeted because they were Lloyd's names and had lost money. This is not true: back-bench MPs were chosen at random. Indeed, Tredinnick was only approached after another Tory MP, Sir Michael Marshall, recommended him as someone who might raise a question for an investor.

As MPs queued up to exonerate themselves last week, there was confusion about who had been approached and who had not. Alan Duncan, Tory MP for Rutland and Melton, boasted to television cameras that his secretary had sent Calvert packing, but as nobody from Insight had spoken to him directly and his secretary had suggested writing to his office, he was not included in the survey. Henry Bellingham, Tory MP for Norfolk North West, told the Commons that he believed

Calvert had telephoned his office, but he had thrown away his pink message slip. Somebody must still be waiting for him to return a call, because nobody from Insight approached him.

Those MPs who were approached were told that Calvert was an investor who had inherited money and was looking for "a public affairs consultant with access to parliament" to table one question. Each MP had to be told a different story in case they all turned up to table the same question. All questions had to have one thing in common: the answers would only benefit the investor.

It was decided to use anagrams of the word Insight to press home how easy it was to table bogus questions, and initially Calvert posed as a potential investor in a drugs company that was developing a cure for a throat infection called "Thising disease".

Sir John Gorst, MP for Hendon North, was the first to be approached and he agreed to meet Calvert in the central lobby at the House of Commons on Wednesday, June 29. As with each subsequent visit he made to the House, Calvert showed his tape recorder to the security men at the entrance who asked him to switch it on to show that it was working and was not a bomb.

MP and "investor" sat on a bench while Calvert explained that he needed a written question to ask the department of health about the incidence of the disease and enquired if it was the sort of thing the MP could help with.

Gorst replied: "Yes, I could do, certainly. Though my preference is for doing things that are on a longer-term basis than just a sort of one-off particular question because my speciality, if I can call it that, has been more on giving advice than necessarily implementing it. Obviously, one can see that what you want is a bit of information."

Calvert: "Yes, a straightforward bit of information. It seems the only way I can get it is by asking a written question in parliament. I would be willing to pay for this."

Gorst: "Let's leave the question of that aside for the moment, because obviously the nature of one's position as a member of parliament is that it's legal, but it doesn't look very nice if you simply ask questions because you have been paid to do so."

Calvert: "It is worth £1,000 to me."

Gorst: "Let me put it this way. If you were interested in a sort of long-term relationship – public relations/public affairs advice – that would be more in my field. I am quite prepared to ask a question forgetting any question of a retainer or anything like that, simply in order to establish what the information is about this. And then, if at some subsequent stage you felt there was something we could make an arrangement about, we could discuss it on that basis. Simply in order to find out the answer to a question, I think that that would not be, in my view, a breach of the spirit of one's position as a member of parliament. If you tell me what you want to know I can easily table a question."

Calvert left, promising to send a fax which he never did. A curious Gorst, thinking his visitor "a slightly cranky individual of a type not unfamiliar to MPs from their surgeries", went to the well-stocked Commons library in search of a medical dictionary. There was no reference to Thising.

Nor, if he had looked, was there any mention of the drug Sigthin, which is what Tredinnick, MP for Bosworth, agreed to ask a question about when he met Calvert on the Commons terrace on July 7. Tredinnick, who took a spoonful of honey in his afternoon tea, was so relaxed with his visitor that he offered to buy him a cake.

Calvert handed him the 27-word question he wanted asked. Tredinnick pointed to the word Sigthin. "What is it?" he asked. Calvert told him it was a drug for a type of laryngitis and that he needed statistics on the illness's prevalence.

"I don't know if this is the sort of work you do," he said.

"It's hardly work," snapped Tredinnick, then smiled.

He was offered £1,000. Calvert said he had already made the cheque out.

Tredinnick, old Etonian and former Grenadier Guards officer, was appreciative. "I, em . . . That is very kind of you. I will, I will put the question down and you can send me a cheque."

He searched in vain through his pockets for a business card. Calvert handed him an envelope and the MP pulled a pen from his pocket and wrote down his address.

That evening the two spoke on the telephone. Calvert checked he had the right address to send the cheque. "I'm very grateful," said Tredinnick, who was rebuked by a Commons committee last month for failing to declare the numbers of his Lloyd's syndicates, "and hope that that works out all right."

Recalling the meeting on the terrace last week, Tredinnick said Calvert "seemed in a state of anxiety". With good reason. Two days earlier he had met Riddick on the same terrace and was apprehensive that he might bump into him again.

Riddick, too, had been quite willing to meet the "businessman". This time the story had been about Githins Business Resources and the desire to find out what contracts it had with the department of social security. Riddick, a former Coca-Cola sales manager, was at first happy to accept the £1,000. "Why don't you just send it to me? Do you want my home address?" he told the "businessman" in a phone call later that day. To Insight's chagrin, and despite the promise of £1,000, the question was tabled incorrectly and the firm's name was spelled as Gittins. Later Riddick was to post back the cheque, saying on reflection it was inappropriate. By then he had been told that the department of social security had no knowledge of the company.

Bill Walker, Tory MP for Tayside North, too, at first seemed ready to accept Calvert's money. "£1,000 would be fine?" the "businessman" asked him in his office at the Commons on July 5. "Yes. Let's see how it works out. I mean I am not going to bill you for £3,000. I wouldn't bill you for more than £1,000."

The next morning he telephoned Calvert's home to leave a message and in a subsequent conversation he said he wanted the cheque made out to the Air Cadet Glider Memorial Flight Fund.

All the 10 Labour MPs, however, refused to entertain the notion of tabling questions, on how many contracts a small motorway contractor called I T Singh had with the department of transport. In many cases they gave a firm "no" before the £1,000 could even be mentioned. "No, I don't do that sort of thing," said Roland Boyes, MP for Houghton and Washington. "No, I don't know anybody who does that sort of thing," said Norman Hogg of Cumbernauld and Kilsyth. "No, I am not a consultant," said Llin Golding of Newcastle-under-Lyme. "No, members of parliament do not deal with it in that way. I would see your local MP," said Gordon Oakes of Halton. "No, I am not a parliamentary consultant," said Geoffrey Robinson of Coventry North West. "Just ring up the department of transport. They will tell you. The contracts are all public information."

The balloon went up on Sunday morning when *The Sunday Times* published its story under the headline "Revealed: MPs who accept £1,000 to ask a parliamentary question". At first Tory Central Office said it was a parliamentary rather than a party matter. However, Major took time off from the G7 summit in Naples to discuss the matter on the telephone with Richard Ryder, the chief whip. Within hours Riddick and Tredinnick had both been suspended from their jobs as parliamentary private secretaries and were facing an internal party investigation if the Commons did not act. By Tuesday they – and the *Sunday Times* Insight team – were facing the might of an inquiry by the Commons committee of privileges.

All last week MPs were delving into statute books and Erskine May, parliament's "bible" of procedure, to establish what rules, if any, had been broken.

The answer is still unclear.

Erskine May sets out that "the acceptance by any member of either House of . . . any fee, compensation or reward in connection with the promotion of, or opposition to any bill, resolution, matter or thing submitted or intended to be submitted to the House or any committee thereof is a breach of privilege". Yet the register of members' interests allows MPs to do paid work provided they declare it.

The affair has opened a debate into parliamentary practice and whether MPs are at the Commons to do their constituents' business – or their own. More than half the MPs have commercial interests, holding between them more than 500 directorships and more than 400 consultancies.

Sir Michael Grylls, the Tory MP for Surrey North West, currently lists 11 companies and directorships, including Ian Greer Associates. David Evans, a millionaire Tory MP, suggested last week that the only way to solve the problem was to pay MPs £100,000 a year.

Many are already earning that. MPs are in big demand by businessmen. A consultancy can be worth £10,000 a year to an MP – and much more to the company paying him if it can use parliamentary questions to extract commercial information from inside government. Tim Smith, Conservative MP for Beaconsfield, when he was parliamentary consultant to Price Waterhouse, once tabled 38 written questions in a single day, asking each government department about management consultancy contracts. The data was useful for Price Waterhouse, which was drawing up a business plan for its computer consultancy division. Smith is now a Northern Ireland minister.

It is a world of small favours and large rewards. MPs can get lobbyists into the Commons under the guise of researchers. Politicians willing to help an airline find their tickets upgraded to first class when they next fly. The Commons was told last week that

Phil Gallie, Tory MP for Ayr, parliamentary liaison officer for Scottish Power, is provided with a car, he also gets private health care from the same source. Even Tony Banks, Labour MP for Newham North West, delights in getting 12 pots of honey a year as parliamentary adviser to the London Association of Beekeepers.

"It's hardly work" may go down as the epitaph on Tredinnick's political career, but it is also an accurate description of what an MP is asked to do in return for a large sum of money. When Sir David Steel stood down as leader of the Liberal party, he was approached by a consultancy firm that offered him at least £10,000 for one year simply to book rooms at Westminster for entertaining and to look after clients of a consultancy. He refused, but one former Tory cabinet minister is reputed to have signed a contract worth £24,000 with another firm just to host three dinners a year for leading businessmen. That is £8,000 a time every time he sticks his nose in the proverbial trough.

Four years ago Greer, a former Tory agent, told the select committee on members' interests that he had made six "thank you payments" to three MPs for introducing him to clients. He refused to name them, but one of the MPs was paid £10,000 for introducing Greer to British Airways.

Greer, whose clients include Coca-Cola and Cadbury-Schweppes, knows how to win friends and influence people. There is a division bell in his office so MPs who come to call can be summoned back to the House.

Last year he paid for the fringe conference agenda sent to 5,000 Tory delegates at Blackpool.

It is to Major, though, that he pays the most attention. He provided a Jaguar and chauffeur to take Major to meetings when he was seeking to become party leader, and even paid £5,000 to publish the prime minister's soapbox speeches from the 1992 election campaign.

When Ian Greer Associates celebrated its 10th anniversary last year with a party at the National Portrait Gallery, it was Greer, its £300,000-a-year boss, who remembered to bring the prime minister a gin and tonic – on a silver tray – because he knew his guest would prefer it to champagne.

Greer, too, is in the business of getting parliamentary questions asked.

In an unguarded moment, he admitted on camera to *The Cook Report* that he had the power to get questions tabled. "We would never go out and say we can arrange to have a question tabled, but actually we can. If we went out and said that, there's bound to be someone who would take great offence to think that a middle man could arrange such a thing but, as it happens, yes of course we do."

The revelations last weekend that some MPs are ready to accept money in return for tabling questions brought a howl of condemnation. However, the biggest howl within the Commons was aimed not at Riddick and Tredinnick but at *The Sunday Times* for its alleged use of entrapment and tape recordings to bring them to book. When Bruce Grocott, Labour MP for The Wrekin, suggested in Wednesday's Commons debate that the two were not of equal importance, he was deafened by a pantomime chorus of "Oh yes they are" from the Tory benches.

There was a feeding frenzy by MPs apoplectic with indignation. David Ashby, Tory MP for Leicestershire North West, who, this newspaper revealed, shared a bed with another man while on a foreign trip, said he had heard allegations that *The Sunday Times* intended to get rid of the government by causing by-elections.

Gorst, the MP prepared to ask a question for nothing, referred to a Murdoch empire "in the ascendant, that has a higher budget than the British Empire ever had in its decline".

Walker, the Tayside Tory MP, went one step further in a thirst for revenge: he read out Calvert's home address and ex-directory telephone number to the Commons. Within minutes Calvert's wife began to receive anonymous phone calls. When *The Independent* newspaper thought fit to print the address and telephone number the next day, Calvert received messages of support from its readers.

In contrast, when *The Sunday Times* responded to requests from other media to release tapes of the conversations with MPs in the interests of accuracy, it took pains to remove the home addresses supplied by the two MPs.

The tapes provided proof of what the MPs were trying to deny. Tredinnick turned up for a TV interview outside an empty House of Commons on Sunday to protest that he had never expected to receive a cheque, but in the transcript of the tape he says: "I will put the question down and you can send me a cheque."

Indeed, the revelations brought an admission from many at Westminster that MPs had long been aware of the scam, but nobody had provided the proof. Margaret Beckett, the acting Labour leader, said: "There have been rumours about this for some time. We have to look at any evidence that this is happening. MPs are sent to the House of Commons to represent constituents in a straightforward manner, not in a commercial fashion." An unnamed senior minister told *The Guardian* that it was common for his colleagues to accept "consultancy fees" in return for asking questions.

Tory MPs have been quick to raise the charges of bribery and entrapment against *The Sunday Times*. But George Galloway, Labour MP for Glasgow Hillhead, said: "There cannot be criminal intent in offering money to expose malfeasance or to expose an abuse in public life; that cannot be true. It is simply a contradiction in terms."

Clare Short, Labour MP for Birmingham Ladywood, said that the newspaper had done British democracy a favour. That did not stop Lord Brightman tabling an amendment to the Criminal Justice and Public Order Bill making it a criminal offence to "sell or offer to sell information" on someone's financial affairs when the information has been obtained by deception", a move which would kill much investigative journalism in Britain.

Press and public alike have recognised *The Sunday Times*'s argument that subterfuge was necessary to bring the scandal into the open. A telephone poll by LBC, the London radio station, showed that 79% of callers supported the paper and did not regard what had happened as entrapment. The *Evening Standard* in London, in a leader headlined "The papers got it right", said that blaming the press was a face-saving distraction: "Every political editor knows that businessmen pay for questions in the House, and that some politicians are particularly amenable to this sort of request. But it's not possible to say so, because the laws of libel are so stringent . . . We should all be grateful to *The Sunday Times* for bringing a matter which was known by a select few to the attention of the public."

The Guardian, normally no friend of this newspaper, was equally unequivocal. MPs "should not, not, not wallow in self-justifying outrage about the behaviour of *The Sunday Times*" proclaimed its comment column. It added: "Let nobody claim that newspaper reporters kicking politely at the front door would have been told the whole truth."

Betty Boothroyd, the Speaker, recognised the arguments on both sides when she announced a debate to refer the matter to the Commons privileges committee. She reminded MPs that there could be serious consequences if they believed that merely registering their interests discharged them from their public responsibility. They had to be careful not to bring parliament into disrepute. But she added that the conduct of the newspaper also merited further examination.

Was *The Sunday Times* more guilty in the methods it used to expose the scandal than the MPs who agreed to accept the cheques? Whatever the committee decides about the merits of the story, important reforms in the way MPs perform their duties are inevitable. Major has done little to disguise his anger at the way the two MPs' behaviour has damaged parliament's standing. He has let it be known that a tightening of the rules is urgently needed. If nothing else, the affair is likely to produce a new rule that MPs have to declare an interest when tabling a parliamentary question.

On Wednesday Riddick made an abject apology to the Commons. "Beyond the challenge to my own integrity, which I deeply regret, the thing that has mortified me the most is that my judgment may have undermined the general standing of members of parliament, and even perhaps have damaged the reputation of this parliament."

By then he was getting precious little support at home. His local newspaper, the *Huddersfield Daily Examiner*, which a few days before the scandal broke had recommended his promotion to junior minister, changed its editorial line with a headline: "Tragic errors of judgment by Graham Riddick".

Tredinnick, slumped on the Commons green benches where, according to Westminster legend, visitors are not allowed to sit lest they push a bribe down the back of their MP's seat, has kept his own counsel and remained quiet.

A committee of senior MPs will now be assembled to hear evidence from the MPs and *The Sunday Times* this autumn. Riddick said he was "thoroughly relieved" such a committee was to be set up. "It means that I will have my peers from this house, and not the press, sitting in judgment over me."

The problem now facing a parliament seemingly riddled with commercial and pecuniary interests is to find 12 good men and women true to sit on the committee of privileges. As Dale Campbell-Savours, the Labour MP, said last night: "I fear there may well be a stitch up."

Insight: Maurice Chittenden, Mark Skipworth, Jonathan Calvert and Randeep Ramesh

2002
TRACING THE 9/11 ATTACKERS

On September 11, 2001, hijackers deliberately crashed two planes into the two towers of the World Trade Center in New York. They killed 2,977 people, shaping the future of American and Western foreign policy like no other event in recent history, and provoked America into a messy and intractable war in Afghanistan.

Afterwards, it seemed unfathomable that a 33-year-old student and his band of even younger extremists could have planned and executed such a devastating attack on US soil. How could the US intelligence apparatus have entirely failed to register the groundwork for an attack of this size and sophistication? And who was lead terrorist Mohammed Atta, previously a complete unknown to America's counter-terrorism and homeland security departments?

Amidst the chaos, Insight went all over the globe to answer these questions. They uncovered, for the first time, the life story of lead terrorist Mohammed Atta. Through interviews with previous roommates, fellow students and old contacts, drawn from a complex web spanning Egypt, Germany, the US and Saudi Arabia, a portrait of Atta is laid bare.

Interwoven with this are the revelations of a series of opportunities to stymie the attack missed by the US authorities. These are framed by insider accounts of the Clinton administration – which left office shortly before 9/11 – detailing the budgetary issues and poor leadership that paved the way for a catastrophic attack to slip through the intelligence net.

THE ROAD TO GROUND ZERO

———————————————•———————————————

6 January 2002

MONDAY, SEPTEMBER 10 was a lovely, late summer day on the northeastern seaboard of America. From Portland, Maine, to Atlantic City, New Jersey, the sky was clear but for a few light clouds and temperatures were in the high seventies.

During the afternoon two young Arabs – an Egyptian called Mohammed Atta and a Saudi, Abdulaziz al-Omari – rented a four-door blue Nissan from an Alamo car hire office in Boston, Massachusetts, and headed for Portland. They cruised past a branch of Dunkin' Donuts and a Wendy's burger bar along US Highway 1A and out onto Interstate 95 for the two-hour journey north.

They crossed the Piscataqua bridge shortly after 5pm and about 45 minutes later were checking into the Comfort Inn in Maine Mall Road. The men shared a non-smoking room and paid their $149 bill in advance, saying they would be leaving early in the morning.

Nearly 300 miles away in his 34th-floor office in Manhattan, John O'Neill was thinking about the night ahead. He was dressed as usual in a black Burberry suit with a white shirt and a striped tie. It was the plain-clothes uniform he had worn for four years as the FBI's national security chief, and he was still wearing it on the eighth day of his new job as director of security at the World Trade Center. But he couldn't wait to change into his night uniform: the same black suit with a black shirt and no tie.

Heavily built and 6ft tall, O'Neill was a bulldozer of a figure, an Irish-American cop – but an unusual one. His FBI career was studded with successes and littered with enemies. Before leaving the agency he had been America's point man in the fight against terrorism.

"He knew more about Osama Bin Laden than anybody in the world," said his friend Howard Safir, the former top cop of New York. O'Neill believed he was on the Saudi terrorist's personal hit list. He also believed that bureaucratic rivals had blocked his investigations into some of Bin Laden's bomb attacks.

O'Neill was both smart and sensitive. He liked to have fresh flowers alongside the sword collection in his office. But he was also arrogant, secretive, restless and compulsively gregarious to a self-destructive degree. Even at 50, he was still running up debts and hurting those who loved him in order to party with the stars. The FBI had balked at his expenses for entertaining such contacts.

Just over a decade ago, stationed in Chicago, he had been offered a drink in a bar by a beautiful brunette called Valerie James. He had not told her until they were two years into a love affair that he had an estranged wife and family back in New Jersey. Valerie stuck with him and when his erratic professional behaviour finally exasperated even his most powerful friends last summer it was she who persuaded him to resign. "I am the FBI," he protested when she said it was time to quit. "I'm not in love with the FBI," she replied.

O'Neill promised to clean up his act and start coming home at night now that he had no need to entertain sources and colleagues from intelligence agencies around the world. But on the evening of September 10 he wanted to go uptown to the China Club, an exclusive night spot catering to celebrities.

Valerie was tired. They had already partied on Sunday at a big wedding at the Plaza hotel, and she wanted to stay home at their expensive apartment in Peter Cooper Village, lower Manhattan. (It had "the biggest collection of books on terrorism" – and of whisky bottles, she says.) She told O'Neill to go out on his own. In his black suit and black shirt he promised to be home by 11.30pm.

The China Club, in the theatre district near Times Square, has a long history as one of the hippest places to be seen. On Mondays, muscle magnifies the glamour. Millionaire professional athletes hang out there, attracting a large crowd of celebrity jocks.

That Monday night was O'Neill's last night alive. For four years he had warned that the Arab terror groups he was chasing had the capability and infrastructural support to attack America from within. He didn't know they were about to strike. According to friends, he stood at the bar drinking his usual Chivas Regal with water and a twist of lemon, smoking a cigar. Vindication was on his mind. "There were no attacks in New York on my watch," he told a friend.

In Portland, Atta and al-Omari were spending the evening killing time, cruising the streets in their Nissan. At 8.30pm, a security camera inside the Fast-Green cash dispenser on a restaurant car park caught the pair on film: al-Omari grimacing, then laughing. Atta appeared emotionless.

Their last supper consisted of a brief visit to Pizza Hut down the road from their hotel. By 9.20pm they were again caught on camera, at a Wal-Mart supermarket south of town. Atta, in a striped polo shirt, was carrying a plastic bag when they headed back to their mock-Andalusian motel.

O'Neill's former FBI colleagues have been unable to piece together the conversation between Atta and al-Omari that night. Al-Omari appeared to be only a junior member of Atta's gang, but he was once an imam at an Afghan training camp. Perhaps Atta, knowing he was only hours from death and troubled by memories of his own behaviour in Las Vegas strip clubs and Florida bars, was seeking some spiritual guidance. Did they follow the list of instructions to assassins later found in Atta's luggage, urging them to shave and to clean themselves ritually?

Midnight passed. At home in lower Manhattan, Valerie James awoke after 2am and found she was still alone. Too annoyed to go back to sleep, she started a game of solitaire on the computer. Eventually O'Neill returned. Staring drunkenly at the game, he put his arm around her and said sarcastically: "You're really good at that."

"F*** you," she replied. They slept apart.

Shortly after 5.30am, Atta and al-Omari left the Comfort Inn without breakfast. Twelve minutes later they went through security checks at Portland International Jetport for US5930, a hop to Boston where they had another flight to catch. A security camera recorded them. Atta strode purposefully forward. In Boston, Newark and Washington DC, 17 other young Arabs were dressing for the last time. It was another day of sunshine.

In Manhattan, O'Neill heard Valerie get up and go to her bathroom. He tapped contritely on the door and was forgiven – again. An hour later, they were racing against the morning rush-hour traffic. O'Neill pulled in front of her office in the garment district where she was an assistant fashion designer. They hurriedly said goodbye and O'Neill rejoined the traffic, heading for the Trade Center.

The skies of the eastern seaboard were busy with commuter airliners. In four of them death loomed.

Shortly before 9am, a colleague leant over Valerie's desk. A plane had hit one of the twin towers, she said, and there is a call for you. It was O'Neill. He had seen it all – and escaped. "It's terrible, there are body parts everywhere. My bosses are dead . . . Val, are you crying?" he asked. "No," she lied. She was overwhelmed that he was alive. She felt such relief. "I'll call you later," he said, and hung up.

Valerie and her colleagues moved into a conference room with a big-screen television. When she saw the first tower crumble, she crumpled into a chair. "John is dead," she said out loud. Rescue workers found his body nine days later. The 1,000 guests who had been invited to a planned retirement party on the top floor of the twin towers showed up for his funeral instead. "Some people have tried to suggest that Bin Laden was targeting John," says Valerie now. "I don't buy it. He may have known who John was, but he wouldn't kill 3,000 people to get just one man."

Even a Nostradamus would have blushed to predict the bizarre symmetry of O'Neill's death. Much more disturbing, however, is the story of what went on while O'Neill was still alive and commanding hundreds of agents as the FBI's top counterterrorist fighter.

He and a small number of other key figures in a covert American war on terror are now accused of failure. Were they to blame or were their warnings ignored? Was there a political failure under President Bill Clinton or did the shrewdest players of the intelligence community deliberately leave this messy anti-terrorist work to the O'Neills of their world? As one of them put it: "Careers were not made in counterterrorism."

Most disturbing of all is the story not of failure but of success – Mohammed Atta's success in leading the ruthless suicide assault on the bastions of American power, and Osama Bin Laden's success as the strategist behind the conspiracy.

He has acknowledged on tape that he was closely involved in the planning and that Atta led the hijackers. How could two religious maniacs – one an apparently effeminate Egyptian, the other a pampered Saudi millionaire – successfully cause such terrible and lasting damage to the secular world?

These stories of success and failure intertwine over several decades and over many thousands of miles before the climactic moment of fusion at 8.45am on September 11. One of the strands – which leads to an understanding of Atta's conspiracy – starts on the River Nile.

After flowing through half of Africa from its headstream in Burundi, the Nile splits at Cairo like a wishbone. Sluggish, brackish waters head northwest in one branch towards Alexandria; in the other, northeast towards Port Said.

Between the two branches, crisscrossed by a 19th-century network of irrigation channels, is the alluvial triangle of the Nile delta, one of the most densely populated areas in the world. Near its centre lies the agricultural centre of Kafr el-Sheikh, a sprawling settlement of crumbling concrete apartments, shacks and smallholdings.

In the town centre, amid the dust, donkeys and unrelenting heat, wooden stalls are heaped with citrus fruits, cucumbers, lettuces, potatoes and olives. The two mainstays of the local economy are rice and cotton cultivated on the waterlogged delta plains.

Those born in the town have slim prospects. Half of the population is illiterate and most of the youth face unemployment or at best a modest income from the land. There are some jobs in a small number of businesses in the town, including engineering and building companies, but those who want to be wealthy head for the capital on the Alexandria-Cairo train. Only the lucky few succeed.

Fifty years ago, Mohammed el-Amir Atta, a quick-witted teenager with slicked-back hair and an eye for an opportunity, was determined to be one of the lucky ones. He came from one of the more successful farming families on the delta, but he did not want to earn his living off the land. He aspired to the expensive suits and Mercedes cars of the rich Cairenes who drove along the pot-holed highway towards their retreats on the coast.

He had better prospects than the newborn John O'Neill, who had just arrived in the world nearly 6,000 miles away in Atlantic City, New Jersey, the son of a taxi driver who could barely pay the rent. As a boy, O'Neill would pin all his dreams on a television series called *The FBI*.

El-Amir was delighted when after finishing high school in Kafr el-Sheikh he passed the entrance examinations to Cairo University. His friendship with another student from his home town, Mohamed Sharake, who belonged to one of its most influential families, was to prove as important as his studies.

In the intimidating atmosphere of Cairo University, where many of the other students lived such lavish lifestyles as to be barely comprehensible to those back in Kafr el-Sheikh, el-Amir and Sharake forged a close friendship. During their holidays back home, el-Amir also became infatuated with Sharake's sister, Bouthaynai, who was 14. When he left university, he married her in a union that was brokered between the two families. Sharake opened a small legal business in the town and hired el-Amir.

Bouthaynai was not as enamoured with her ambitious and overbearing husband as her family was, but she settled down to life as a housewife. She gave birth to two daughters, Mona and Azza, and a son, Mohammed, born on September 1, 1968.

It was a time of high international tension and social unrest. The Soviet Union invaded Czechoslovakia. There were anti-government riots in western Europe, anti-Vietnam war demonstrations in Washington. In Atlantic City, a teenage and patriotic John O'Neill kept his head down and studied hard to join the FBI.

In Egypt, President Nasser had been humiliated by Israel in the six-day war in 1967 and had only two years to live, but his populist promises to stop rich Egyptians from carving up the country still strongly appealed to people from el-Amir's lower-middle-class background. Life was probably as good as it was going to get in Kafr el-Sheikh. El-Amir wanted to be in Cairo. As far as he was concerned, it was there to be taken.

El-Amir was a strict father who attended mosque every Friday and believed in academic excellence. His quiet, scrawny son never played football with the other boys, but would always be clutching a book on the way to school.

Ten years after Atta was born, El-Amir felt he had saved enough money and was established enough as a lawyer to leave Kafr el-Sheikh at last. The family moved to Abdeen, a central district of Cairo, near the presidential palace. It was a strange neighbourhood for the young lawyer to choose, one of the poorest. He was, however, not concerned with his neighbours. He established a law practice and ran his family life behind closed doors.

Young Atta went to the Ahmed Oraby state school opposite the Ministry of the Interior in a class of 25 other Mohammeds. Every year their teacher would ask what they wanted to do when they left school and Atta would reply: "I want to be an engineer when I grow up."

Other children changed their minds, but not Atta. He wanted to build things. Engineering was just the type of profession that his father approved of. The boy was also showing a talent for drawing.

After school he would hurry home through the rubble-strewn maze of streets with his head down, perhaps chatting briefly to his neighbour, Araby Kamel, who repaired cars. "I want to build new cities in the desert," Atta told him.

There seemed little else in his life. He never joined classmates on school trips to the beach. He would always carry a sick note saying he was unable to take part in sports. While the children ran around in the school compound, he would read a book or consult a teacher. Sometimes, in the warm evenings, he stood with friends on the main street where the air was thick with tobacco fumes from the coffee houses. Once he had been out for more than half an hour, the guttural voice of his father would be heard calling him home.

The neighbours felt sorry for Atta. His father was viewed by some as an overbearing snob. Nobody understood why el-Amir had chosen to live in Abdeen. He had the money to be in a better part of the city. He would never invite anyone into his home, which was two apartments knocked into one. When he bought a white Mercedes to replace his Fiat 132 it was seen as an unnecessarily ostentatious purchase by neighbours who could afford only rusting cars or donkeys.

When Bouthaynai came home with the shopping, prime cuts of meat and other delicacies would be piled high in her trolley; she declined the neighbours' offers of help.

Inside the eight-room apartment, El-Amir ruled. There were fierce rows. His wife told her relatives back in Kafr el-Sheikh that she was unhappy with the marriage. During the often turbulent family scenes, Atta, even as a teenager, regularly sat on her lap, much to the consternation of his father. "Toughen up, boy!" he would shout at his son. He already had two daughters and he did not want a third, he told his wife.

El-Amir was also prone to hectoring monologues and political rants. The plight of the Palestinians and the corrupting influence of what he called the "tyrant nation" – the United States, with its adultery and homosexuality – were two of his favourite topics. He shared many of the views of the Muslim Brotherhood, an organisation founded in 1928 with the written aim of "mastering the world" through Islam.

Although the brotherhood was outlawed in Egypt, it was still one of the most active political groups in the country. It fed on disillusionment. Many middle-class professionals like El-Amir were angered that the elite were once again enriching themselves on the back of increasingly cordial relations with the West initiated by Nasser's successor, President Sadat. Atta absorbed his father's views. The Palestinians and corruption among Cairo's "fat cats" would become his obsessions.

The Middle East was in turmoil throughout these impressionable years. In 1979 the Iranian mullahs had set up a religious dictatorship and were exporting Islamic revolution. In 1981 President Sadat was assassinated. In 1982 Israel invaded Lebanon in pursuit of the PLO. In Beirut, Islamic terrorists deployed a new tactic: the suicide bomber. Hezbollah fundamentalists carried out devastating suicide attacks, killing 299 Americans and Frenchmen, mainly military personnel, in October 1983.

By the time Atta began to study architecture at Cairo University in 1985, Islamic terrorist organisations including Egyptian Islamic Jihad – which had been blamed for Sadat's murder – were recruiting students. Egypt was one of the main sources of men for the Islamic jihad against the Soviet invaders of Afghanistan.

Atta was not an extremist, however, let alone a terrorist. Relatives said he was "like a girl" and female students in his class thought his baby face was cute. Male students noticed he hardly had any muscles on his upper body. When he graduated at the end of his five-year course, he was not politically or religiously active.

Egyptian fighters started to come home from Afghanistan after the Russian withdrawal, as the Soviet empire disintegrated. The Americans sent an army to Saudi Arabia to fight Iraq after its invasion of Kuwait. Atta remained uninvolved in protests. His personal upheavals were yet to come.

His father wanted him to study next in Germany. German, said el-Amir, was the language of engineers. A German tourist couple, identified only as Michaels, struck up a friendship with him in Cairo and agreed to sponsor him.

Atta arrived in Hamburg on July 24, 1992, in the middle of a heatwave. Packed in his bags were bundles of Egyptian pounds from his father, skilfully tailored leather jackets from the Cairo bazaars, family photographs and a copy of the Koran. He was overawed and already homesick.

He had the first chance in his life to be free of his father. El-Amir, however, still cast a long shadow. When Atta was refused a place to study architecture at the University of Applied Sciences despite passing the entrance examination, his father insisted on a legal appeal on the grounds of racial discrimination. The university quickly relented. Atta had by then won a place at the Hamburg-Harburg Technical University, however.

Hamburg was a bewildering place after Cairo, especially for a small, diffident 23-year-old. In the Egyptian capital there was no lurid red-light district and only the occasional drunken westerner. Hamburg had gaudy prostitutes, muggers and vagrant alcoholics.

It was also a thriving metropolis enjoying an economic boom because of the new markets opened up by the collapse of Communism in eastern Europe. Most foreign students found Hamburg intoxicating. Atta just missed home. He was particularly worried about his mother.

Atta put the snapshots of family and pictures of Cairo on his wall at his comfortable student lodgings at Am Centrumshaus, near the main square in Harburg, and studied hard. Slowly his personality started to change. With Germans he was polite and discreet. Margritte Schroeder, wife of the caretaker of the lodgings where he stayed from 1992–98, was the German who knew him best. To her, he was "perfect, without blemish, an exceptional young man . . . He invited us regularly to his flat to have a cup of tea and a chat".

She said: "He came back from Egypt with sweatshirts for my husband and he brought me a lucky charm – a little green statue of a mythic creature. His parents gave him an allowance, so he had no need to work to make money. He used to wear beautiful jackets of exquisite Egyptian leather. You couldn't buy quality like that here.

"So long as he lived here he had no television or video. The walls had pictures of Cairo, maybe some shots of his family. He never had a girlfriend so long as I knew him."

Once he moved out she saw much less of him, but "anybody who says he changed in the later months is just trying to make themselves sound important. I saw him here in early July (2001) and he was as nice as ever."

Muslim friends tell a different story. They say Atta became assertive, physically aggressive and fond of dabbling in "White trash" culture – while at the same time becoming belligerently religious.

Although none of his university friends in Cairo had thought him particularly devout, in Hamburg his religion became an important support. It was not uncommon for Muslim students to go through a period of extreme devotion in their early twenties. It was often connected to Salifism, a school of thought that relies on a literal interpretation of the Koran and emphasises the importance of jihad as an armed struggle. By their late twenties, many Muslims once again embraced western customs.

Atta, however, never lost this fascination with Muslim fundamentalism. His mother and sisters had never worn veils, but now he even had strong views on which materials Muslim women should wear: finely woven fabrics were too ornate, he said.

While studying, Atta started a part-time job at Plankontor, a planning company in Altona, a fashionable district of Hamburg. He took a prayer mat to work and scrutinised food to ensure it did not contain pork fat. His colleagues organised trips to football matches and the cinema, but Atta just went home. He did not even go to the annual office party. He did, however, earn his salary of £550 a month for a 19-hour week. He was a meticulous draughtsman and never missed a deadline. Wearing cotton slacks, a button-down shirt and jacket, he would pore over his work, poker-faced, drawing intricate plans of various towns. He signed them with his father's name.

The only occasion when Atta showed any sign at work of an inner life was when he presented a slide show of historic Cairo. In fluent German he spoke about the importance of preserving this architectural heritage. He was angered at plans for parking lots in Fatimid Cairo, one of the most historic districts, and a scheme to bulldoze ramshackle shops for a new open-air museum. Cairo's inhabitants should be spared "Disneyland" developments. He hated the towering office blocks and multistorey hotels that had sprouted up among Cairo's domes and minarets.

Atta was studying Islamic architecture in his degree, and in his dissertation he mapped out an entire section of the city of Aleppo in Syria, showing how many storeys each building had. He felt that taller buildings were an invasion because they overlooked the courtyards of traditional Arab homes.

Whenever Atta looked at Cairo and other Islamic cities, he told friends, he saw the unwelcome signs of what his father called the "thug" country, America. It was not only the new multistorey developments, but also the prevalence of the dollar and the Levi jeans coveted by female students at Cairo University. Although he accepted the education that the West had to offer, he began to refuse to wear jeans, the badge of America.

In Atta's world there were now no shades of grey. There was right and there was wrong. His views were crystallising on the template created by his father. But there was also a further dimension.

The acutely sensitive teenager despaired at what he saw as the inhumanity of the international community towards the Islamic world. In Bosnia, Iraq or Palestine it was Muslims who suffered. The United Nations did nothing and often the villain, so hated by his father, was America.

Atta hated Jews. The Palestinian issue was his predominant concern. "It is a conspiracy," he said. "Israel kills Muslims in the Palestinian territories with the sanction of the United States."

There was no point in the Oslo peace agreement between Israel and the PLO or any other deal. It was all a plot rigged against the Muslim world.

By 1995 – when he made a pilgrimage to Mecca, for which he grew a beard and wore a seamless white *ihraam* robe – his fundamentalist critique was complete.

On a study trip in Cairo that year, he applauded when an Egyptian academic was forced to divorce because he had applied the principles of literary criticism to the Koran. "Literary interpretation of the Koran is heresy," Atta emphatically told friends, sipping a mango juice in the 40C heat outside the Al-Azhar mosque.

He also railed against Cairo's wealthy elite. "They are bigwigs who scratch each other's backs when it comes to jobs and money," he said. "How can you hope to implement a fair social policy?" But he adored driving around the chaotic streets of the city in his yellow Fiat, listening to the Koran and blasting away at the horn with all the other drivers. He did not want to go back to Hamburg, he told his mother, who was going through a divorce from his father.

"I miss you," he told her. But both knew El-Amir would not tolerate disobedience. "Daddy wants you to go and you mustn't upset him," she said. "He's spent a great deal of money on your education and you must finish it."

He returned to Hamburg reluctantly. He realised he had embarked on a religious and intellectual journey that was likely to have an unpleasant denouement. He was still opposed to violence but his final transformation from wimp to bully and eventually to dogmatic killer was about to begin.

On the other side of the fence the "thug" country – America – had also been groping for bearings in a changing world. At the CIA, the operations department overflowed with officers who had returned home from covert assignment in the cold war after the Soviet Union collapsed in December 1991. Many had been involved in the war in Afghanistan where CIA agents working in Pakistan had shipped hundreds of millions of dollars of cash and weapons to the Islamic rebels. They knew that thousands of Arab rebels, who had been brought over to fight, largely funded by the government of Saudi Arabia, were now on the loose with their weapons.

CIA field officers in Africa were told to watch out for these weapons and warriors reaching Somalia, where American troops were trying to bring peace to a community riven by civil war. Most in the field regarded those intelligence warnings as simply another "CYA (cover your ass) operation" by the spooks, not a serious threat.

On the night of December 29, 1992, a bomb went off outside a hotel in Aden, Yemen, where American troops destined for Somalia had been billeted. At the headquarters of the CIA in Langley, Virginia, the news was received by the duty officer on the seventh floor. It was relayed two floors down to the counterterrorism centre, a multi-agency "fusion centre" where groups of anti-terrorism experts shared information and techniques.

Here was one open-plan floor divided into cubicles enclosing the cells which examined each terrorist problem. Desks overflowed with paper files, videos, video machines and television and computer terminals. Above the paths between the desks, signs hung from the low ceiling. Here was "Tamil Tiger Terrace" and over there "Abu Nidal Boulevard". As yet, there was no Bin Laden Street.

In charge of the CIA Near East desk – which included the Middle East and South Asia as far as Bangladesh – was one of the agency's most formidable Arab experts, a thoughtful and vastly experienced operative named Frank Anderson, who was in his last two years at the agency.

According to those close to Anderson, it was the bomb in Aden which first led him onto Bin Laden's trail.

"It was only after Aden that first word came through of Bin Laden's connections and how he might target America," agreed a former senior official of the CIA's department of operations.

However, in a pattern that was to become familiar over the coming years, the significance of the incident was quickly forgotten by the American political establishment.

In Washington the big news as December 1992 gave way to January 1993 was the change of power: the return of the Democrats after 13 years in the wilderness since Jimmy Carter. And, as everyone now knew, it was not foreign affairs that mattered in politics. It was "the economy, stupid" that had enabled the challenger Bill Clinton to defeat the incumbent President George Bush (senior), whose strong suit had been foreign policy.

The Gulf war had been won and the cold war was over and America wanted to sit back and make lots of money.

While the Washington inauguration parties continued, one man sat up working late each night. Richard Alan Clarke was one of the few survivors of the George Bush White House, a career civil servant, a foreign policy "geek" whom everyone needed. He was Mr Indispensable.

Clarke's desk was in the same suite of offices in which Colonel Oliver North had worked on the third floor of the Old Executive Office Building overlooking the White House west wing. It was the very den of White House conspiracies and plotting: a world of secure phones and specially toughened and insulated windows to protect from eavesdropping by foreign agents and rocket attack.

A bachelor and a 16-hours-a-day workaholic with an aversion for publicity, Clarke had the pallid appearance of a man with no life beyond his desk. Superficially, nobody could be more different from the gregarious, party-going John O'Neill of the FBI. In fact, professionally they were Tweedledum and Tweedledee. Clarke was another bruiser, a bull in the china shop who fought bureaucratic battles with sheer force of personality and deft manoeuvring.

As one of his old colleagues put it: "With a super-aggressive style, here is a man who inspires a reaction in anyone he meets. He has more friends – and more enemies – than anyone else around the White House. And this is a town of monstrous egos and bruisers."

Officially, Clarke was special assistant for global affairs. In fact, he became Clinton's most senior anti-terrorism adviser. Like O'Neill he was obsessed with Osama Bin Laden and knew all that could be known about him.

With one bruiser taking over anti-terrorism in the White House, another moving into the same slot at the FBI, why wasn't Bin Laden doomed before he even had a chance to recruit Atta? As we shall see, there were several reasons.

First, the CIA was about to be enfeebled by a series of internal crises. Second, despite Clarke's and O'Neill's individual brilliance and occasional successes, they suffered from the law of diminishing returns. The more they hectored their colleagues to try to get results, the more isolated they became. Energy was wasted on bureaucratic battles. Third, and crucially, there was no interest at the top. There was no strategic overview or willingness to take risks to ensure the terrorist threat to America would be met by a co-ordinated and successful response.

Bin Laden Street became a lonely place where Mohammed Atta and his team of terrorists could walk without being seen.

Insight reporters have fanned out through Europe, the Middle East, Asia and America seeking the key figures who know the hidden story behind the September 11 conspiracy. Stephen Grey interviewed Bill Clinton's most senior advisors, top congressmen, directors of CIA clandestine operations and former FBI counter-terrorism directors. John Ungoed-Thomas tracked down relatives and friends of Mohammed Atta in Egypt. Nicholas Hellen discovered Atta's associates and former teachers in Hamburg. Gareth Walsh interviewed Saudi sources about other conspirators. Joe Lauria heard the story of former counter-terror chief John O'Neill's last hours from his friends, son and girlfriend in New York.

Insight: Stephen Grey, Jon Ungoed-Thomas, Gareth Walsh, Nicholas Hellen, Richard Miniter, John Goetze, Nicholas Rufford, Uzi Mahnaimi, Ghulam Hasnain, Hartwig Nathe, Issandr el Amrani, Zoe Thomas and Ben Smalley

GOD'S WARRIOR

---•---

13 January 2002

FROM SUBURBAN Hamburg to the Afghan plains, a *Sunday Times* investigation finds the truth about the September 11 plotters

The white bungalow is one of many in a pleasant, leafy suburb in north Hamburg. It is surrounded by silver birches and there are two cars in the driveway, one of them an Audi. A couple in late middle age live there, both retired teachers.

The house is full of curiosities collected during their life together, including a large number of semi-precious stones. The least striking, but also least forgettable, of these mementos is the round Egyptian rug on the kitchen floor. It is brown and beige and it was a gift from Mohammed Atta, the leader of the September 11 attacks in America.

The couple are called Michaels, a common name in Hamburg. They do not want to be more closely identified – with good reason: they confirmed last week that they were the people who brought Atta to Germany, where he studied, worked and created the terrorist cell that carried out mass murder.

When the Michaelses first met him in Cairo a decade ago, Atta was a 22-year old architectural graduate, an apparently weak figure dominated by his father, a lawyer and a virulent anti-American. Their portrait of the young Atta gives the most intimate clues yet known about his character.

"The background to all this was that my wife and I had been organising an exchange of high school children – 16- to 18-year-olds – for a while," Herr Michaels said. "Our daughter had spent half a year [in Egypt] with a particular family. This Egyptian family, quite good friends of ours, knew Atta's father and through them we were asked if we would look after Atta. Before we agreed we asked if we could meet him and we did that in Egypt at our friends' house. He seemed modest, somewhat withdrawn but basically friendly. He wanted to study town planning – and, take it from me, Egypt needs that and we were happy to oblige.

"Atta's father was the one who forced him to come here to college. His exam results in Egypt were not so good. His degree was roughly equivalent to our Abitur [A-levels] with a score of about 3.0 [just above a pass]. With those results he would not have been able to continue studying in Egypt. His father wanted him to become more than just an architect – for him an architect was little more than a builder – and that was why he had to come to university here.

"He was very intelligent. He learnt German in one year to the standard where he passed all the tests to get the approval of the German authorities. To meet all the regulations he had to get a formal invitation from us and of course we offered him accommodation."

Atta moved into a 12ft by 14ft spare bedroom, placing his prayer mat on the parquet floor. He rang his father every week, and whenever his family rang Germany it was always one of his sisters who made the connection – in English.

Initially, he arrived on a tourist visa. Once he had passed an exam to study at university, he needed a residence visa. Herr Michaels, on another visit to Cairo, went to the German embassy with Atta's father to secure it.

Atta ended up studying at a technical university in Harburg, a suburb of Hamburg. "He was a very hard worker and he wasn't happy with the way the German students neglected their studies," said Michaels. "He complained that when there was a joint project, or a seminar the others often simply wouldn't turn up. He would spend many evenings when he was here just working by himself in his room."

The couple found that he "was a very ardent Muslim. We had an alsatian and whenever the dog tried to greet him he'd stick his hands up in the air so that they wouldn't be dirtied by the dog. We weren't too bothered by that; we had seen other Egyptians do the same."

Sex was more problematic. "On the television there were a number of films where it gets a bit saucy, the odd nude and so on, and he used to put his hands over his eyes. For all I know he used to peek between his fingers."

There were also problems with food: "During Ramadan he would cook at night. He would cook up lamb chops and the smell of it would really upset my wife. We never really anticipated that. I tried to make him a special version of our German food, for example replacing pork with sheep's cheese in a particular dish; but although I cooked him a special dish he refused to eat it, claiming that the pots would still be tainted by pork however much I'd scrubbed them out. He was an extreme believer from the very beginning."

Frau Michaels remembers: "We often discussed politics and he always gave me the impression that, although I was a woman, he took my opinion seriously. However, if I ever walked around the house without covering my arms the atmosphere got very unpleasant."

She also remembers his reaction to the news of some atrocities in Egypt. "He told me: 'It's terrible when people resort to violence. They should be able to sort out their problems in discussion – violence is never justified.'" He did not seem an idealist to her, however: "He was interested in earning money and furthering his career."

After about six months the cooking problem led them to ask him to move into student accommodation. "He left the house perfectly amicably," said Frau Michaels. When she discovered last September that he had become a mass murderer, she collapsed. "I had a nervous breakdown, a psychological breakdown whose effects continued until the end of November. I am still fighting it," she said.

"I still have to hope in the goodness of the human race because otherwise there would be no point, would there? I have to fight to stop myself being overcome by depression. The impact of this was like a split or a breakdown in everything which my life represented until then. It was as if a chain had snapped. For years I had made it my business to try to build up good contacts with people from abroad, whether that meant helping people here or simply making a point of sitting next to a foreigner, particularly including Arabs, when I was on the Underground, and just trying to chat to them nicely. Now I am not so open any more and of course that hurts me."

She added: "I don't blame myself for what happened – I understand that other people, professionals who ought to have noticed something, didn't."

The Michaelses last saw Atta in 1995 or 1996, a period when many of his acquaintances also saw their last of him. It was when the devout but career-centred student began his transformation into one of the Al-Qaeda terrorist organisation's most promising operatives.

After extensive inquiries in Germany, the US and the Middle East – tracking down former acquaintances of Atta and of his co-conspirators, and getting access to police and intelligence investigators – Insight can now tell the story of how the Egyptian was commissioned by Al-Qaeda and carried the plot to its terrible conclusion, while leaving a trail of clues that could have led to his arrest.

Western intelligence services believe two pilgrimages to Mecca provided Al-Qaeda with its best opportunity to recruit Atta. He shuffled his way with the throng into the 16th-century Grand Mosque in June 1995 and February 1996. Radical Muslims in Hamburg would have been able to provide the names of contacts in Saudi Arabia who were close to Osama Bin Laden, Al-Qaeda's leader.

When Atta returned to Hamburg from the second pilgrimage, still wearing the beard he had grown, he was thinking of death. On April 11, 1996, he wrote his will – a document he kept with him up to the morning he died. He said he wanted his corpse to be laid on its right side and pointed towards Mecca. Women should be barred from the burial and anyone who prepared his body or touched his genitals should wear gloves.

When the will was found in Atta's luggage after September 11, the first thing a former student friend, Ralph Bodenstein, noted was the date. On April 11, 1996, Israel launched a 16-day war against Lebanon, known as the "grapes of wrath". This enraged Atta, according to Bodenstein.

The will marked a watershed. Atta abandoned friends who were not equally devout and sought like-minded Muslims at the popular Al-Quds mosque among the sex shops and cheap hotels on Steindamm, near Hamburg's main station.

Al-Quds provided a key meeting point for the future ringleaders of the September 11 plot. Among them was a Lebanese student, Ziad Jarrah, who had known nothing but civil war during his early life.

Initially, Jarrah was no Atta. His doting parents thought of themselves as "secular Muslims". They sent him to a Christian school, evacuated him from Beirut to the Bekaa Valley and did their best to protect him from extremists who hailed suicide bombers as heroes.

Seven days before the grapes of wrath war he arrived, aged 20, in the east German town of Griefswald to study aeronautical engineering. His ambition was to be a pilot.

With him was his cousin Salim, also 20. They had played together as children and partied as teenagers in the Beirut nightclubs. They were now ready to enjoy life as students in a western city.

They moved into Papelalle Street in the student district and started a language course. Every Saturday night was disco night. They drank alcohol, rarely attended prayers and soon moved in with girlfriends. Jarrah's was Aysel Sengun, an attractive Turkish girl with German citizenship. He flirted with women in nightclubs and two-timed Sengun at least twice in their five-year relationship.

On their way to a disco with a girl on their arms, Jarrah and Salim were sometimes harassed by a classmate of Sengun's. "You are weak Muslims," he shouted. The two cousins would back away. They had nothing against devout Muslims. It was just not for them.

In the summer of 1997, when Jarrah's German was almost fluent, he won a place at the technical university where Atta was studying in Harburg. Sengun moved to Bochum, 180 miles away, to study medicine. The couple had exchanged rings but had not set a date for a wedding.

When Jarrah turned up at the home of a Hamburg landlady called Rosemarie Canel, she was captivated by his smile. He rented a room on Alte Landstrasse for two years. At weekends he joined Sengun in Bochum. His name was next to hers on her doorbell.

He seemed to have his future mapped out, but he started to lead a double life that was to consume him. It centred on the Al-Quds mosque. He met Atta and Said Bahaji, another technical university student and member of the mosque. A 22-year-old German-Moroccan, Bahaji had served in a tank unit in the German army and was fluent in four languages. He was to be the logistics officer of Atta's Hamburg cell.

Bahaji was a computer junkie. "I spend time at my PC with games, programs or the internet," he wrote on his personal web page. He also had more discreet interests, regularly visiting the website of Azzam Publications, a London company that gave information on "holy wars".

"The form [martyrdom] usually takes nowadays is to wire up one's body or a vehicle or suitcase with explosives in order to cause the maximum losses in the enemy ranks," says the company's guide on the "permissibility" of suicide operations. "There is no other technique which strikes as much terror into their hearts, and which shatters their spirit as much."

Jarrah became close friends with Bahaji and for the first time in his life he felt the pull of Islam. He obtained a prayer mat and during a visit home he sported a beard, taken as a sign of extremism in the Bekaa Valley.

"Shave it off," his perturbed father told him.

"It's an allergy, Daddy."

"Even if it's an allergy, I don't want to see it," said his father.

The beard was shaved off. But Jarrah wrote in one of his exercise books: "Tomorrow will come. The victors will come. We vow to vanquish you. The ground beneath your feet will tremble."

While Jarrah underwent his conversion, Atta's own transformation was gathering pace. In June 1997, the planning consultancy where he worked part-time while studying told him that his job could be done more effectively by computer. He seemed unperturbed and even sent back some of that month's salary. He had not worked for it, he said.

Nine months later he was in Afghanistan, arriving on the recommendation of a friend in Hamburg to train with Al-Qaeda.

This was a momentous time in Al-Qaeda. Bin Laden had been building up his terrorist training infrastructure in Afghanistan since being expelled from Sudan in 1996. America had failed to tackle him and had even turned down a Sudanese extradition offer.

On February 23, 1998, the apparently invulnerable Bin Laden delighted fundamentalists across the Islamic world by issuing a fatwa, urging Muslims everywhere to kill Americans. His associates were on the lookout for recruits who could operate inconspicuously in the West. Atta – with his middle-class background, aptitude for languages and cultivated manners – was an obvious choice.

About 60 miles southwest of Al-Qaeda's underground Afghan command complex in Tora Bora, a camp called Khalden once lay on a dusty, wind-blown plain. It is now obliterated, but for most of the past decade the mud-walled compound was at the centre of Bin Laden's jihad against the West. While recruits in other Al-Qaeda camps were trained for guerrilla conflicts such as Kashmir and Chechnya, Khalden was for terrorism in the West. It taught the sophisticated and covert skills needed to work undercover and to attack civilian targets.

Western investigators believe that it was here in the spring of 1998 that the September 11 plot was conceived. Intelligence sources say Atta's presence has been verified by former trainees. Among the recruits training with Atta were an Algerian called Ahmed Ressam and Zacarias Moussaoui, the Moroccan student now suspected of being his 20th hijacker. Ressam was arrested in late 1999 on his way to blow up Los Angeles airport. According to one source, he has identified both Moussaoui and Atta as fellow trainees at the camp that spring.

Khalden could handle up to 100 potential terrorists at a time. They were divided into cells, corresponding to the country they would target, and taught how to strike without mercy. Training included biological warfare, communications, explosives and forgery. Simulated targets included gas plants, airports, railway stations and large companies. They learnt to block roads and to attack buildings. Their assassination training was meticulous. Bin Laden, with a Kalashnikov slung across his shoulder, inspired each new intake with a tirade against the United States.

Atta's training team was led by Abu Zubeida, the Palestinian at the centre of most of Al-Qaeda's terror attacks on America. Days began with prayers before sunrise, followed by readings from the Koran and breakfast of dried dates. After training for three hours the men would lunch on roti (unleavened bread) and chickpeas, before further training, football and dinner.

Western recruits lived in mud huts while more hardy Afghan recruits slept under blankets in the open. "Non-Afghans were allowed to go to the local shops, which could be anything up to 10 miles away," remembers a British trainee. "There you could buy Mars bars or Pepsi, or something like that to ease the very basic lifestyle. For the first few days people from the West who had come to train would suffer fever, flu, stomach bugs, sprained ankles and infections." He said several western recruits headed home after seeing bodies brought back from fighting with the Northern Alliance.

Atta was ready to risk his life. He was asked to do more, however. Religious leaders told recruits that their jihad was sanctioned by Allah: for those who died, glory and paradise awaited. Atta was among a lucky few singled out as potential "martyrs" who would carry out suicide attacks. "Recruits were asked if they were prepared to take on a martyrdom mission. They were given four or five days to think about it. Then, if they said yes, they would begin a new phase of preparations for a specific task," said an intelligence source.

Once Atta had agreed to give up his life, a plan that had been developed and discussed by Bin Laden's most trusted lieutenants was presented to him: an aerial suicide attack on some of America's biggest buildings. He was not given specific targets.

"The plan to attack America was not Atta's invention," said an intelligence source. "It was handed to him in outline and was for him, as leader of the attack, to develop in detail." Atta was told to return to Germany, recruit his cell, prepare a final plan of attack and then return for a last briefing.

He was just the latest Khalden graduate to be tasked with a murderous mission. Ramzi Yousef was prepared there for the original attack on the World Trade Center in 1993. While Atta was in training, Liverpool-born Mohamed Rashed Daoud al-Owhali, another Khalden graduate, was in the final countdown for the August 1998 car bomb at the American embassy in Nairobi. Hitting Nairobi at the same time as Dar es Salaam, Al-Qaeda killed a total of 268 people.

When Atta returned to Hamburg as a terrorist commander for Al-Qaeda, he was a changed man. There was a swagger in his step. Committed to an attack on America, he started to toy with what he saw as its White trash vices. It was as if the trip to Afghanistan had dislodged one of the pressure valves within his pent-up personality. Or was he under orders to create a hedonistic cover persona to hide the religious warrior within?

His previously meek and precisely controlled persona started to slip. He drank lager on the Reeperbahn, the red light district where the Beatles had partied almost four decades earlier, and ate takeaways from the Batman halal kebab shop in the city centre. He would smoke the occasional joint. And he became addicted to Sony PlayStation games and Hollywood videos. Among the hired videos and games that he did not return were *Virus*, a movie about an alien plot to destroy mankind, and *Fighting Force II*, a combat game with skyscrapers on its cover.

His German lecturers noticed that his personality seemed harsher but were not alarmed. "He had no interest in exploring the higher culture of Germany, but at the time I didn't see anything wrong in that," said Professor Dittmar Machule, who grew close to Atta. "Part of our role here is to produce students from overseas to return to their country of origin. I thought he could be of greater use if he could speak to people in Egypt on their terms rather than as somebody who had been westernised."

At the university Atta concealed his contempt. With his fellow Muslims he was more forthright. "He didn't like Germany," said an Egyptian drinking friend. "He told me all Germans were Nazis."

Atta moved into a grim communal flat near Hamburg's docks. It was sparsely furnished with 11 mattresses strewn across the floor. Atta would get up at about 6am and return in the evening to cook for his housemates. They played Arabic music until 2am. As a boy he had always carried a sick note to school to avoid sports; now he started to play football with friends in the park. He was a striker.

He was biding his time, looking for a headquarters and gathering the key members of his fledgling terrorist cell. One recruit was Bahaji, the computer fanatic from the Al-Quds mosque. Another was Ramzi Bin al-Shibh, a slight 26-year-old economics student who came from Yemen, Bin Laden's ancestral home. Bahaji would become responsible for logistics for September 11 and Bin al Shibh was lined up as a pilot.

On November 1, 1998, these three signed an agreement to rent an apartment at 54 Marienstrasse, Harburg, for £300 a month. Atta signed the payment slips "Dar al-Ansar", Arabic for "house of supporters". It was the name Bin Laden had used for his headquarters in Pakistan during the Afghan war. Here in the faded yellow apartment block the September 11 attacks would be planned.

Two high-speed internet lines were installed. A neighbour in an overlooking apartment noticed that about six Arabs met regularly, sitting on the floor and drawing on pieces of paper, which they pinned to the walls. When they realised that he could see in, they stuck paper to the windows and hung up huge blinds. The Arabs left their shoes outside the door in a neat row. Neighbours got irate about the prayers at dawn and they hated the cooking. The whole block smelt of bones, they complained.

Although Jarrah was not living at the apartment, he was already one of the conspirators. His doting landlady noted his nocturnal excursions. He was, he said, going to visit friends in Harburg.

Another plotter was a bright student called Marwan al-Shehhi, who had been born in 1978 in Ra's al-Khaymah, the northern emirate of the United Arab Emirates. As a boy he spent many hours each week in the Al-Qusaidat mosque, where his father was the imam. He won a scholarship at the age of 18 to study abroad. Before leaving he married a woman called Fawzeyah at the insistence of his family. It was the right thing to do before heading to the West, they said.

Al-Shehhi had arrived in Germany in 1997, initially learning German at the University of Bonn. He was an outgoing student known for his sense of humour and Benetton shirts. A year later, having learnt German, he headed for Harburg to study shipbuilding at the technical university and met Atta.

Atta, Jarrah and al-Shehhi, the three men who would seize the controls of American Airlines flight 11 and United Airlines flights 93 and 175 on September 11, 2001, were now in the thick of the conspiracy.

German police had an opportunity to catch them. Seven weeks before the plotters moved into the Marienstrasse apartment, Mamdouh Mahmud Salim, 43, suspected of being Bin Laden's European financial chief, was arrested in Munich. He had the number of a Syrian businessman, called Mamoun Darkazanli, programmed into his mobile telephone. Investigators discovered that they shared a bank account.

Darkazanli was put under surveillance. Investigators found that he was a friend of the computer-mad Bahaji and that Bahaji was moving into 54 Marienstrasse. But the Germans are extremely careful not to use covert surveillance against innocent citizens – and they could find no evidence of a Bin Laden cell in their cursory inquiries. Salim was extradited to America, but further investigation of Darkazanli and his friends was called off.

Even after Darkazanli was a guest at Bahaji's wedding, with the plotters Jarrah and al-Shehhi, no eyebrows were raised. The terrorists' nest at 54 Marienstrasse was not to be disturbed. As we shall see, it would remain so until September 11, 2001, despite a display of compelling evidence that should have triggered police action.

Insight: Stephen Grey, Jon Ungoed-Thomas, Gareth Walsh, Nicholas Hellen, Richard Miniter, John Goetze, Nicholas Rufford, Uzi Mahnaimi, Ghulam Hasnain, Hartwig Nathe, Issandr el Amrani, Zoe Thomas and Ben Smalley

CLINTON'S SECRET WAR

———————•———————

20 January 2002

ON A cold afternoon in the last days of Bill Clinton's administration, Sandy Berger sat in his White House office with Condoleezza Rice, the woman who would soon be taking over his job as national security adviser.

All that most Americans knew about Rice in December 2000 was that she was Black as well as female. In Washington, however, she had a reputation as a patient and meticulous Kremlinologist; her friends knew she was also a superb classical pianist.

Berger glanced at her across the conference table in his office and gave a grim prediction that bore little relation to her skills: "Terrorism will consume far more of your time than you had ever imagined."

He revealed that America was locked into a messy battle with an unstable but brilliant set of terrorists. It was an improvisational, deadly game. Her eyes dropped to a list of names. The first was Osama Bin Laden. Her job was to advise the new president, George W Bush, how to fight him.

There was little time to prepare, and Rice was almost alone. The dispute over the presidential election result in Florida had dragged on for six weeks, and most of Bush's top advisers would not be selected, vetted and approved for months. Seeking more information, Rice sent for Dick Clarke, Clinton's counterterrorism "czar", to find out how the secret war against Bin Laden had gone so far.

Few in Washington had worked longer on counterterrorism than Clarke, and nobody at a more senior level. The son of a Boston chocolate factory worker, he had climbed to the elite of the American politico-military establishment by making himself indispensable to administrations since the Reagan era. He was a behind-the-scenes bruiser with many enemies, one of whom claimed he had survived by aping presidential sartorial styles and had even dyed his hair grey to match Clinton's silver mane.

Nobody worked with more intensity. Clarke was the master of the nuts and bolts of counterterrorism, and his small staff saw themselves as defenders of the free world. All the same, he had a less than glorious tale to tell Rice of America's failure to kill or capture Bin Laden.

Clarke's own personality is a key factor in the story, but so is the lack of sustained attention from the Oval Office as rival agencies squabbled over how to deal with a foe who – they eventually discovered on September 11 last year – had America implacably in his sights.

Some of the details of this failure have already been reported. As Insight revealed two weeks ago, Clinton turned down at least three offers involving foreign governments to help to seize Bin Laden. America also failed to secure intelligence files on Bin Laden and his network offered by Sudan. It failed to get Saudi Arabia's co-operation in the investigation into the deaths of 19 American servicemen in a truck bomb attack in Dhahran. And it failed to act on a warning of the bomb attack on the American embassy in Nairobi in 1998, which killed 213.

There was a great deal more to be embarrassed about in the unsuccessful secret war on Bin Laden, as Insight can now reveal.

Clinton's initial response to the attack in Nairobi – and the simultaneous bombing of the American embassy in Dar es Salaam, Tanzania – was to authorise Operation Infinite Reach, a retaliatory strike against Bin Laden in Afghanistan.

Clarke wanted much more. "He was after a comprehensive strike, one that would punish the Taliban for holding on to Bin Laden," said one national security council insider. But Pentagon top brass were reluctant.

In the end a unanimous proposal came to Clinton from Berger, William Cohen, the defence secretary, and Madeleine Albright, the secretary of state. A missile strike on an Al-Qaeda meeting would attempt to kill Bin Laden, his top lieutenants and about 300 followers. Missiles would also target a pharmaceutical plant in Sudan where CIA intelligence appeared to indicate that Bin Laden was preparing chemical weapons.

The report from Afghanistan of the Al-Qaeda meeting was probably the best advance intelligence the American military has ever had on Bin Laden's movements. But still the missiles missed; the terror leader had left hours earlier.

Worse, Clinton was accused of using the strikes to distract attention from the Monica Lewinsky affair. Daniel Benjamin, one of Clarke's staffers, says there was a loss of confidence inside the White House.

As Clinton's interest faded, Clarke continued the secret war. He was at the height of his powers. His team of antiterrorism specialists – the inter-agency counterterrorism strategy group (CSG) – mapped out a plan to get Bin Laden and disrupt his emerging conspiracies through an ambitious covert war.

Around his oval wooden table in what used to be Colonel Oliver North's office suite across from the White House, Clarke gathered America's top terrorist fighters. Michael Sheehan, a former special forces commander who served as the State Department's counterterrorism ambassador, and Cofer Black, a hulking man with slicked-back hair who led the CIA's counterterrorism centre, were regulars at Clarke's strategy sessions.

The Pentagon's representative tended to rotate among top officers, indicating Cohen's ambivalence about being sucked into a war on terrorism. According to one participant, "if they sent anyone under the rank of general, Clarke would throw them out. 'Get the hell out of here,' he would say."

The president wanted a continuing operation to find Bin Laden. In three memoranda of notification to the CIA, he had first authorised the killing of Bin Laden, then of several other senior Al-Qaeda leaders, and finally the shooting down of a private aeroplane that might contain Bin Laden. But when it came to actual operations, he was only prepared to authorise pin-prick cruise missile strikes that were focused on Bin Laden personally, not his organisation or the Taliban.

Two Los Angeles-class submarines were stationed permanently off the Pakistan coast, tracing giant arcs through the Indian Ocean as they waited to kill Bin Laden. Three times they received orders to prepare to launch. Hours of gruelling preparation followed, loading and arming missiles and synchronising the navigation controls. Each time, the strike was called off when the CIA cautioned that intelligence estimates of Bin Laden's whereabouts weren't sufficient.

Once, the CIA phoned the White House to report a camp in Afghanistan linked to Bin Laden where satellite photographs indicated a well-armed and equipped group were camped out in the desert, with some individuals appearing to be bodyguards for one central commander.

This was considered "all source intelligence" – leads were confirmed by satellite, telephone traffic and other methods. Clinton gave the order to prepare for a missile strike. Then, on closer inspection, the CIA analysts in Langley, Virginia, realised they were studying a wealthy sheikh from Dubai on a falconry expedition.

Two other false alarms – based on weak intelligence – rankled the navy: a planned attack on a tent in the Afghan desert and another on a compound of stone buildings believed to be an Al-Qaeda base. Analysts were unable to pinpoint Bin Laden in either place and the president called off the strikes.

The CIA was working with the military on preparations for a possible use of its secretive Delta Force. In a preparatory raid, operators from the CIA's Special Activities Division flew in to an abandoned airfield near the Taliban stronghold of Kandahar. They drew maps that planners would use to fortify its perimeter. The airfield could have been used as a forward base if an operation was launched to capture Bin Laden. But none was.

Intelligence agents were also air-dropped into territory controlled by the anti-Taliban Northern Alliance. The four-man team set up a listening post for the interception of Al-Qaeda communications and conducted a few days of training for Alliance personnel.

The training was almost worthless. "The briefing was conducted entirely in English," said Haroun Amin, the Alliance's ambassador in Washington.

The CIA managed to get an informant in Kandahar who had access to material at the Taliban's internal security office. Sometimes this source passed on information on Bin Laden's travels inside Afghanistan. But the information took too long to reach America's decision makers, who needed at least six hours' advance notice to launch a missile strike.

The Pentagon, headed by the chairman of the joint chiefs of staff, General Hugh Shelton, repeatedly resisted dispatching special forces into Afghanistan. Clarke and the national security council wanted a small operation – what army officials call "going Hollywood". Shelton and other defence officials cleverly resisted by asking leading questions of national security council staffers, who generally lacked military experience. What if a plane or helicopter malfunctions, don't you want a search-and-rescue team? And don't those rescue teams need carriers to take off from? And those carriers can't linger off the coast of Pakistan without giving away the game, can they?

Shelton showed he needed a cast of thousands to mount a proper operation and the sheer scale of such a venture deterred presidential approval. Clarke, according to his associates, concluded that the Pentagon was gun shy. "He basically told the Pentagon they were cowards, and that didn't go down too well," said one national security council staffer.

Another senior Clinton official said Clarke's criticisms were justified. "The Pentagon did nothing. They were paralysed by fear that something might go wrong like it did in Somalia. 'Gun shy' is not putting it hard enough."

Behind the scenes, Clarke was slowly trying to stiffen the administration's spine – and hunting for new options. To demonstrate America's vulnerability, he organised a group of government-paid hackers to break into the Pentagon's most secure computer systems in 1998. They gained control of the nation's military command centre systems – the very ones to be used to defend America during an attack. It took only three days and a batch of off-the-shelf PCs.

By the spring of 2000, the navy was weary of maintaining a submarine presence off Pakistan ready for a strike that was never ordered. They wanted a real plan or a ticket home. Clinton, now in the last year of his presidency, called Berger into the Oval Office.

"What else can we do to get Bin Laden? We've got to think of something new," he said. Berger passed the word to Clarke, who quickly convened his group to look for a solution.

As always, their brainstorming sessions were conducted in Clarke's office, over burgers and tuna sandwiches sent over from the White House canteen. Clustered around Clarke's whiteboard, the men drew up a shortlist of solutions to the Bin Laden problem. Albright used to refer to it as "Where's Waldo?" after a children's game.

Finally, Clarke came up with a solution: the Predator, the military's revolutionary unmanned plane. It would find Bin Laden. One participant said: "Dick loves technology. He was always asking what else can we do? What can be done next? He was saying, 'Why can't we do something?' He kept thinking about technology and asking what can we do that's practical. How can we get it together? We were drawing up the options on the board and that's how the Predator idea came up."

Until the spring of 2000, the Predator was not considered as more than a tactical eye in the sky. It had been used widely in the Kosovo war to spot troop movements, with great success. But, particularly given the ease by which it could be shot down or crash, its use had been confined to military tactical support, not as a covert intelligence asset. Clarke, however, saw its value in the war against terrorism.

According to one participant in the discussions: "The Predator itself was not new, but what was coming together at this time was an incredible improvement in video technology. You could see with incredible precision what was happening on the ground while the Predator itself could, with luck, remain completely unnoticed."

The group worked together with the CIA and the air force to set up a trial of the technology. General Anthony Zinni, head of US central command, which covers south Asia, had a close military-to-military relationship with the Uzbekistan government and, according to one source, it was persuaded to accept a secret airbase from which Predator missions could be flown.

By September 2000, after long bureaucratic delays, the project was up and running in a trial phase. The results were remarkable. As the Predator flew over Afghanistan, Clarke could watch the street bazaars of Kandahar and the terrorist camps around the town of Khost on a colour screen in Langley.

It would be daytime in Afghanistan but still dark in America. At 2am or 3am Clarke used to phone colleagues and ask if they wanted to come out and watch the action. Most were content with viewing the videos the following day. Clarke would show Berger and sometimes the president pictures from the missions.

One video showed a tall man in flowing robes moving through Kandahar. He was clearly seen with a small security detail that moved ahead of him, securing the street. "We were convinced it was him, Bin Laden himself," said one participant in the operation. Once again, however, Clinton did not authorise a strike: the analysts could not provide 100% certainty it was Bin Laden, and the military reaction time was too slow.

All the same, Clarke and his team were convinced that they would finally get the chance to kill Bin Laden in real time: to watch him on the screen while submarine-launched missiles were cruising across the desert to wipe him out.

In early October the Predator crashed. By official accounts the project was called off because of the crash, but insiders reveal it was only half the story.

The project was getting controversial. With Washington in full presidential election fever, it was bureaucratic infighting that finally shut down the Bin Laden hunt.

The CIA was getting restless at Clarke's ceaseless demands, and Cofer Black's relations with Clarke were turning sour.

"He was under pressure back at Langley, and Clarke saw this as Black becoming unnecessarily bureaucratic, of failing to support an unconventional approach. But Clarke's real beef was Jim Pavitt (the CIA's director of operations and Black's boss), who Clarke thought was the one blocking things," said one of those who witnessed their squabbles.

The CIA and the air force were telling Clarke there were operational reasons why the Predator programme had to shut down, but Clarke wasn't buying it. He knew there were other Predators available. "You're telling me it won't work. The real reason is that you don't want to do it!" shouted Clarke.

There was a dispute between the CIA and the air force over who should pay for the Predator. Simmering behind their budgetary concerns was growing resentment of how Clarke was calling the shots from the White House – exercising the sort of operational command, some suggested, that Olly North once had, and doing what Clinton had promised Congress that Clarke would not do when he was made counterterrorism co-ordinator.

"Basically, because there was no money specifically appropriated [allocated by Congress] for this project – and even if it was only a couple of million dollars – there was a hell of a fight over who should pay," said one senior White House official.

So the Predator vanished from Afghanistan's skies and Bin Laden disappeared from view. The Predator would not return until after September 11, 2001.

Insight: Stephen Grey, Jon Ungoed-Thomas, Gareth Walsh, Nicholas Hellen, Richard Miniter, John Goetze, Nicholas Rufford, Uzi Mahnaimi, Ghulam Hasnain, Hartwig Nathe, Issandr el Amrani, Zoe Thomas and Ben Smalley

THE HIGHWAY OF DEATH

27 January 2002

IN THE WEST of Saudi Arabia, the highlands of Asir flank the Red Sea, overlooking the same geological fault as the Great Rift Valley in Africa. On the eastern side of this range, volcanic rock falls to the largest sand desert in the world. The western side, however, is an area of breathtaking scenery renowned for its spices, honey and terraced smallholdings carved into the slopes.

Washed by downpours in March and April, Asir has the most rain in Saudi Arabia. The forests and farms of these cool mountains are a haven for families escaping the oppressive heat of Riyadh and the rest of the kingdom. Scenic cable cars, five-star hotels and bazaars fuel the fledgling local tourism industry but remain largely unknown to western eyes.

The region's capital, Abha, is a popular resort among Saudis. Fifteen miles east lies the town of Khamis Mushayt. In its most affluent quarter is the villa of Muhammad al-Shehri, one of the town's wealthiest businessman. Once an agent for Peugeot cars, he now has extensive property interests.

Last September 11, two of his sons, Wail, 25, and Waleed, 21, died in America. Both were hijackers on American Airlines flight 11, which ploughed into the north tower of the World Trade Center.

Three other men from the immediate Abha area and eight more from this same mountainous region also died on September 11. Most had been recruited as "muscle" to help Mohammed Atta, the Egyptian ringleader, carry the suicide hijackings to their conclusions.

These affluent young men had disappeared from their upland towns and villages to embark on what they saw as an honourable jihad – and had ended up committing mass murder. Why?

The reason lies partly in the idyllic surroundings, which mask a frustration among a local population who feel sneered at by Saudi Arabia's ruling classes and deprived of what they see as their share of the country's oil wealth. This alienation is compounded by the disproportionate number of families in the region who can trace their recent roots back not to the Saudi tribes, but to nearby Yemen.

The reason for their role in September 11 doesn't just lie in regional politics. It arises directly from imams preaching revanchist Islam, stirred by events in Afghanistan, and from the personal influence of Osama Bin Laden, the area's home-grown terrorist leader.

The road to the Asir mountains starts in Jeddah, the port where Bin Laden's Yemeni-born father started out working on the docks on his way to becoming one of the richest construction magnates in the country and a confidant of the royal family.

An eight-lane highway runs inland from Jeddah across the coastal plain towards Mecca, the holy city. About 15 miles before Mecca, a sign reads "Muslims only". The road splits and non-Muslims are guided around Mecca and towards the mountains.

The infidel road becomes a single carriageway, cutting a 30-mile detour south of Mecca across a plain strewn with boulders scoured clean by sandstorms. Wild camels graze on the roadside. The road starts to climb the steep rocky outcrops and rejoins the Muslim highway east of Mecca.

This is Route 15, which rides the ridge of the Asir mountains, snaking south through a series of switchbacks. The road clings precariously to the mountainside and at one point seems to leave it completely, supported by concrete struts. Once it reaches Al-Hada, a tourist resort at about 6,500ft, the road runs southeast towards Abha, a seven-hour drive away through a national park. Baboons watch tourists as they drive by.

This pioneering piece of highway engineering is the work of Bin Laden's father, who built the route from Mecca to Abha in the 1960s. Bin Laden himself, brought up in Jeddah, helped to carry out construction work on the road as a teenager.

Thirteen of the September 11 hijackers were born and brought up alongside Route 15.

Wail and Waleed al-Shehri grew up in Khamis Mushayt. Their prospects were excellent. Several of their nine brothers worked for the Saudi armed forces and their uncle is believed to have been a major in the kingdom's army and a director of logistics.

During their weekends, they would go down to the Red Sea with their family. Their elder brothers had travelled to America and spoke good English.

There was, however, little time for foreign languages in the Saudi school timetable, which focused primarily on Islam. During the younger al-Shehris' schooldays, there was a religious fervour running down Route 15.

In the 1980s some imams, notably Safar al-Hawali in Mecca, were urging young Muslims to fight against the Russians in Afghanistan. One of those who went was Bin Laden.

Before he left, he was seen as a gangly 21-year-old lucky enough to be born into one of the wealthiest families in the kingdom. Friends remember him driving his silver Mercedes 280 at reckless speeds around the streets of Jeddah. They also remember him as a keen football player, who excelled at headers because of his height.

Once in Afghanistan Bin Laden cultivated his image of a boy born into privilege who had traded it all in for a gun, rough quarters and a holy cause. Back home, tales of this humble warrior quickly spread along Route 15.

After the Soviet withdrawal from Afghanistan in 1989, Bin Laden returned a hero. Crowds would gather outside his home to meet him. But fighters like Bin Laden and extremist imams like al-Hawali needed a new enemy. The foe was at hand: the United States, which was amassing forces in Saudi Arabia to liberate Kuwait.

It was from the Saudi airbase close to Khamis that the American air force's 37th Tactical Fighter Wing launched the first airstrikes against Iraq.

Bin Laden had offered to repel the Iraqi threat himself with bulldozers and volunteers. Rejected, he began to address the crowds in the Jeddah mosques. When he was made to leave for Sudan in 1991, the cleric al-Hawali continued the anti-western campaign – until al-Hawali himself was put under house arrest in 1994 and sought refuge in London.

Bin Laden's message retained its resonance among young men like the al-Shehris. They became convinced Saudi Arabia's rulers had forged an unholy alliance with the US, based on oil and self-preservation.

One intellectual in Jeddah recalled: "Bin Laden was able to recruit a lot of high-school dropouts. These people love Bin Laden to death. They didn't have a goal in life and he gave them a goal." They were ready to fight jihad for him.

There was yet another factor at play, however: mental illness. Wail al-Shehri grew up into a charismatic but troubled adult with an incipient beard and wide, staring eyes. After graduating in 1999 from a teacher-training college in Abha he returned home as a PE teacher at his old school. Five months into his job his mental health began to deteriorate, eventually forcing him to take six months' unpaid leave.

Instead of turning to conventional psychiatry, he told his father he was seeking a form of exorcism. He had already consulted several Muslim clerics in the hope that they could cure him, and now he appeared to pin his hopes on a pilgrimage to the holy city of Medina with the less-religious Waleed, who dropped out of college to join him on the journey north.

Although the pair were later spotted in Medina, they appear to have had longer-term plans about which they told their father nothing. They confided in friends that they hoped to travel to Chechnya and seek martyrdom, fighting alongside others from their mosque. They wanted to learn to fight in Afghanistan.

In the spring of 2000, six young men gathered in the Al-Seqley mosque in Khamis Mushayt. The circle was led by Wail al-Shehri, who had renamed himself Abu Mosaeb al-Janoobi – "Mosaeb" after a follower of the Prophet Mohammed, "Janoobi" meaning "southerner". In the hush of the mosque he addressed the five others by their own noms de guerre and guided them as each swore an oath to die for Islam.

It is not known for certain who the others were; but when Wail disappeared soon afterwards so too did his brother, Waleed, and at least three other local youths: Ahmed and Hamza al-Ghamdi, and Ahmed al-Haznawi. It is reasonable to assume that, like Wail, they headed for Afghanistan. All became September 11 hijackers.

Intelligence sources say that Wail al-Shehri entered the Al-Farooq training camp, which sat on a plain between the tribal areas of Pakistan and a low range of Afghan hills. It was a favoured destination for young Saudis, Iraqis, Palestinians and Jordanians.

Wail lived in a compound of tents and mud huts surrounded by barbed wire. Each morning he learnt the theory of AK-47 rifles and anti-aircraft guns. In the afternoons, he put the morning's lessons into practice, firing live rounds and learning to throw grenades in the nearby hills.

Although basic training at Al-Farooq lasted little more than two weeks, Wail al-Shehri is believed to have spent several months in the camp, graduating to more advanced studies, such as hand-to-hand combat, bomb manufacture and making poisons.

Experts on Saudi society believe that recruiters for Bin Laden's Al-Qaeda first approached Wail at Al-Farooq. Afraid to recruit in Saudi Arabia itself, they operated in Afghanistan, Chechnya and the Balkans beyond the reach of Saudi agents.

Al-Qaeda needed recruits willing to be "martyrs" in the proposed attacks in America. During late 1999 Mohammed Atta had taken his key lieutenants, Ziad Jarrah and Marwan al-Shehhi, to Afghanistan from Hamburg where they had developed their conspiracy. Investigators believe Atta presented his detailed plans for approval at the highest level of leadership of Al-Qaeda, possibly including Bin Laden himself but certainly involving the late Mohammad Atef, the military commander.

According to an American intelligence report, dated November 2001, Atta may have travelled to Kandahar. Al-Shehhi, said the report, was also believed to have visited Kandahar, travelling under the name Abu Abdullah, and stayed in Bin Laden's compound, where he was treated for an unspecified injury.

American investigators have confirmed that at least four of the Saudi hijackers trained in Afghanistan, although the testimony of the family and friends of hijackers in Saudi Arabia suggests the real figure is at least double that.

One of them, Abdulaziz al-Omari, was imam at Al-Farooq when Wail was there. He led the camp's five daily prayer sessions. Eighteen months later, he died with Wail and Waleed al-Shehri on American Airlines flight 11.

Al-Omari, 23, was originally from Al-Makhwah, a town between Route 15 and the Red Sea coast, and had recently married. He had graduated from Imam Mohammed Bin Saud University at Buraydah, northwest of Riyadh, a hotbed of Wahhabism, the radical Saudi form of Islam. He became a follower of fundamentalist leaders including a

33-year-old cleric called Sheikh Suleiman al-Alwan, who preached in mosques around Buraydah.

In an interview with *The Sunday Times*, al-Alwan confirmed that al-Omari had been one of his students. Al-Alwan also confirmed that he had issued a fatwa calling on Saudis to fight with the Taliban. He insists, however, that he had no prior knowledge of al-Omari's decision to go to Al-Farooq or of the September 11 attacks.

Wail al-Shehri and Abdulaziz al-Omari were not the first Saudis from the Asir mountains to train at Al-Farooq.

Around four years ago Nawaq al-Hamzi, then 21, departed from Mecca for the camp. He is thought to have spent more than a year in Afghanistan. His brother Salem, four years younger, followed at the same time as Wail al-Shehri and possibly further future hijackers.

By then Nawaq al-Hamzi was living in America, and travelling the globe for Al-Qaeda. In January 2000, he and a man called Khalid al-Midhar (also a future September 11 hijacker) slipped through Kuala Lumpur's airport on tourist visas with a number of other men. According to one source, from the moment they left the aircraft they were under surveillance by the Malaysian security services at the request of the CIA.

They are believed to have tried to create a cover for themselves by pretending to be tourists. The true business of their visit, however, revolved around a meeting with one of Bin Laden's close aides, Tawfiq Bin Atash. Known in terrorist circles by his nom de guerre, Khallad, the Yemeni-born fighter had assumed control of Bin Laden's bodyguard and would go on to co-ordinate the attack on the American destroyer USS Cole in Yemen in November 2000, when 17 American servicemen died.

Malaysian security service cameramen snapped Bin Atash meeting al-Midhar in Kuala Lumpur. Information about the meeting was eventually shared with the American authorities, but it was not until around August last year that it would take on a greater significance, after the Americans had made the link between the Cole bombing and some of the characters in Kuala Lumpur.

Even now, the significance of the Malaysian meeting is hotly debated in Washington. Some CIA analysts think the Malaysian meeting was a planning session for the USS Cole and September 11 attacks. But a key American defence department official rejected that claim: "We have pictures. But we don't know what they were talking about."

Al-Qaeda was so well-disciplined that only a handful of men at the top had a clear picture of its plans. One of the many tragedies of September 11 is that the Saudi hijackers also seem to have been in the dark about what they would be involved in.

When they started to arrive in America last year, the young men from the cool Asir mountains had agreed to die, but did any know what was planned for them?

Insight: Stephen Grey, Jon Ungoed-Thomas, Gareth Walsh, Nicholas Hellen, Richard Miniter, John Goetze, Nicholas Rufford, Uzi Mahnaimi, Ghulam Hasnain, Hartwig Nathe, Issandr el Amrani, Zoe Thomas and Ben Smalley

A TRAIL OF MISSED OPPORTUNITIES

———————— • ————————

3 February 2002

ON OCTOBER 12, 2000, an American destroyer, the USS Cole, slipped into Aden for a refuelling stop known as a "gas-and-go". Two hours after docking, sailors on deck waved to two men approaching in a white skiff. The men waved back. Then, inexplicably, they stood to attention. There was a huge explosion as the skiff hit the destroyer. Seventeen sailors were killed and 39 injured by 500lb of plastic explosive.

Within hours of the attack John O'Neill, the FBI's New York chief of counter-terrorism, dispatched a dozen agents to Aden to find the killers. It was the start of the final inglorious episode in the Clinton administration's failed war on Osama Bin Laden. All attempts to kill the terrorist leader had failed, and his agents were attacking American interests with impunity. Secretly, the advance guard of a squadron of young suicide-terrorists was already in America.

On arrival in Aden, O'Neill's men sweated in the Movenpick, a "five-star" hotel. In their haste, the agents had neglected to bring any money. The nearest cash dispenser was 700 miles away, in Jeddah, Saudi Arabia. They wired back to New York for funds.

O'Neill, an aggressive but dapper figure, arrived two days later dressed for October in New York. The temperature in Aden was 102F, the humidity 99%. In suit and tie, O'Neill walked down the Movenpick's dank corridors to the room of Barbara Bodine, America's ambassador to Yemen.

Bodine, a career diplomat, had been in Yemen for three years. She had served in Kuwait City during the Iraqi occupation and had been co-ordinator for counter-terrorism at the State Department.

O'Neill found her barefoot in a polo shirt and blue jeans. "You'd better get rid of that suit," she thought to herself. "You'll die from the heat."

O'Neill said Bin Laden was behind the bombing of the Cole.

"He's out to get me," he added.

"Who?"

"Bin Laden. He wants to kill me," said O'Neill, exposing the pistol strapped to his ankle.

"He's after all of us," said Bodine. "He wants to kill any American. Besides, I have a slightly higher profile here than you."

O'Neill glared at her and exploded. It was the first of daily confrontations. They argued over the kind of guns his men could carry. He wanted them all to tote sub-machine guns. She said that would scare the hell out of the Yemenis. Eventually they struck a compromise: 24 FBI agents would carry long guns to protect a further 150 agents packing only pistols.

"O'Neill was rude. He was bullying . . . and he raised his voice with everyone," says Bodine.

The Yemenis had arrested some suspects, but at first would not allow the FBI to have direct access to them. Bodine says O'Neill's ways hadn't helped: "I had to act as a cultural interpreter. They have endured first British colonialism, and then the Soviets. These people have only had foreigners telling them what to do. Now O'Neill and his men were coming in, doing essentially the same thing."

After three weeks, Bodine asked the State Department to have O'Neill recalled. The attorney-general, Janet Reno, was a strong O'Neill supporter but she gave the order and he was back in New York for Thanksgiving.

"If O'Neill hadn't left, the entire investigation would have collapsed," Bodine says now.

Friends of O'Neill disagree.

"It was bullshit," said one former senior FBI man. "We needed those f****** guns in Yemen, and she wouldn't let him have 'em."

Porter Goss, chairman of the House of Representatives intelligence committee, says both were right – but O'Neill had a touch of Inspector Clouseau about him: "So we have got a kind of a Pink Panther scenario going."

The failure in Yemen may have blocked off lines of investigation that could have led directly to the terrorists preparing for September 11.

The FBI knew of a Yemeni whose phone was used by Al-Qaeda to exchange messages. Bin Laden had used his number. Now he was called by Khalid al-Midhar, who was both a relative and one of the future September 11 hijackers training in America.

If the number had been under surveillance or the Yemeni fully investigated, then al-Midhar might have been unmasked before September 11. There was also a failure of will. Michael Sheehan, Clinton's counter-terrorism ambassador, had warned the Taliban rulers of Afghanistan that they would face a military reaction if Bin Laden struck from Afghan territory. Yet there was no retaliation for Cole.

Here, newly installed officials of George W Bush's administration, which took power in January 2001, can take most of the blame. In February, the FBI and the CIA secretly told the Bush White House that Bin Laden's Al-Qaeda was responsible for the Cole attack; but the president and Condoleezza Rice, his national security adviser, decided against any immediate military response. That would have been no surprise to Bin Laden, who had long argued that America was a paper tiger that he could hurt with impunity. Al-Qaeda pressed ahead with a plan that would push the Cole incident into the footnotes – the attacks in America itself.

Mohammed Atta, the movement's Egyptian protégé, and his sidekick Marwan al-Shehhi had been in America since July 2000. After arrival from their base in Hamburg, they had begun $1,000-a-week flying lessons in Florida, using funds wired by a Bin Laden operative in the United Arab Emirates. In all, they received almost $90,000.

By the end of the year, they had their pilot's licences. Staff at Huffman Aviation in Venice, Florida, found Atta arrogant and inattentive. He and al-Shehhi caused panic at Miami international airport on Boxing Day 2000 when their light plane stalled while taxiing to the runway. "They were just sitting there, stupid as sitting ducks," said Rudi Dekkers, Huffman's owner. As darkness fell, they abandoned the plane among a log jam of airliners and paid a $200 taxi fare back to Venice.

One night last spring, Atta was driving through Tamarac, a town set in a belt of dull suburbia, when a sheriff's deputy pulled him over to check his documents. Atta had no driving licence with him. He kept his cool, however, and within minutes was on his way, having been issued with a summons – made out to a false address – to attend court and pay a small fine.

When Atta failed to appear, the court issued a warrant for his arrest. It was little more than a formality, however. The local backlog of unpaid traffic fines goes back to 1977, and is not on computer networks. This meant that, five weeks later, officers missed a chance to take Atta into custody when they stopped his white Chevrolet Malibu speeding through a 25mph zone. He was waved on his way with a standard printed police request to "try to help make our streets a safer place to be".

A third member of the Hamburg ring, Ziad Jarrah, arrived from Germany. He was joined by Ahmed al-Haznawi, a 20-year-old Saudi who would fly with him on United Airlines flight 93. It was time to start bringing in the footsoldiers, the Saudi-born or Saudi-educated men who would provide the gang's muscle when it came to seizing the airliners. Seven arrived in May and six in June.

Atta and al-Shehhi were now paying $840 a month for an apartment in a condominium in Coral Springs. Al-Shehhi spent his days washing piles of laundry for the gang in the development's washing machines. Atta was often in the parking lot, chain smoking.

Jarrah joined the US 1 Fitness Center in Dania Beach. The owner, Bert Rodriguez, remembers: "He wanted to learn about fighting and control – about being in control and how to control somebody."

Atta was on the move in and out of the country. There is evidence that a trip back to Germany was used as a final planning session.

At least two witnesses from Hamburg's technical university (FH-H) – where Atta had studied – have told German federal police (the BKA) that they saw Atta and al-Shehhi last June or July in the ground-floor workshops of the architecture department. The head of the workshop, Herr Kniephoff, witnessed them on at least two occasions with a scale model, measuring approximately 3ft square, of what he believes was the Pentagon.

Kniephoff told the BKA that the two men were joined by a third, unnamed person, whom he believed to be a current student at the university. He suspected that the model had been built elsewhere on the site and had been brought to the workshop for Atta to inspect. It is understood that Kniephoff told police he was struck by Atta's "evil" aura and by al-Shehhi's subservience.

Petra Louis, 32, an architecture student, also told the BKA she had seen them. "I saw both Atta and al-Shehhi here in the workshop with a white model of the Pentagon," she said. "What caught my eye was the way they were both wandering around, obviously looking for someone."

There are clues that they had not yet made a final decision on targets. According to two senior sources at the FH-H, between 60 and 80 slides of the Sears building in Chicago and the World Trade Center were found to be missing from the technical library after September 11. The library is 50 yards from the workshop where Atta and al-Shehhi were spotted. The disappearance of the slides has been reported to the BKA.

It may be that they were passed to the terrorists by a student who had a legitimate reason to use them for a seminar. According to Professor Gerd Kaehler, an Afghan student gave a talk on New York in July, attended by about 25 students. This provided a good reason to take out slides of the skyscrapers, although these were by no means the main point of the talk.

By August 6 Atta was back in Florida, where he rented a white Ford Escort. Over the next month he travelled 3,204 miles in it, co-ordinating the hijackers. He visited Las Vegas, as did other members of the gang. A stripper later complained that one of them paid her only $20 to lap dance for him.

In Washington, there had been celebrations in May when four followers of Bin Laden were found guilty of the bombing of two American embassies in East Africa in 1998. But there was still a lack of urgency about trying to discover what Al-Qaeda might be planning to do next.

When intelligence intercepts in May revealed that Bin Laden might be planning to strike at America itself during the July 4 celebrations, the White House's Counter-Terrorism Security Group did not formally meet to discuss the threat. The CIA seemed adrift – talking tough, while doing little.

There was also trouble at the FBI's counter-terrorism unit. In June, O'Neill ordered his empty-handed investigators back from Aden. Soon he would resign from the bureau, his life's passion, and take a job as chief of security at the World Trade Center.

At last, in July, the administration shifted into high gear after the CIA intercepted a mobile phone call in Milan that threatened Bush. It seemed that an Al-Qaeda cell was planning to assassinate the president during his first state visit to Italy. Bush fumed. He compared the previous plans to defeat Bin Laden to "swatting at flies". He demanded a strategy to "bring this guy down".

A plan was quickly developed to provide the CIA with some $200m to arm the Taliban's enemies and develop on-the-ground intelligence sources. General Wayne Downing, a retired special forces leader, was brought in. He had cultivated a relationship with the Iraqi National Congress to devise a secret military plan to topple Saddam Hussein. Now he was asked to work on a similar insurgent strategy to kill Bin Laden.

In August, an opportunity to find out what Bin Laden was planning inside America was wasted.

A man called Zacarias Moussaoui caused immediate suspicion when he enrolled at the Pan Am International Flight Academy near Minneapolis. He paid $6,300 in cash and became angry when questioned about his background. Instructors became deeply concerned about his interest in using commercial jet simulators, and one contacted a local FBI agent.

Moussaoui was arrested the next day. The FBI checked with foreign intelligence services and the French warned he might be linked to a terrorist group. But FBI agents were unable to persuade lawyers at the Justice Department to let them search his possessions, as the Foreign Intelligence Surveillance Act requires prima facie evidence that a suspect is an agent of a foreign power or terrorist group.

Moussaoui is now regarded as the "20th hijacker", as the hard drive of his computer might have revealed – along with sufficient evidence possibly to have forestalled the September 11 attacks. A prisoner in Seattle could have identified him for certain as an Al-Qaeda terrorist.

Ahmed Ressam, awaiting sentencing for his role in plotting a bomb attack on Los Angeles international airport, had begun co-operating with the FBI. After September 11, he was to identify Moussaoui as a militant he had seen at a terrorist training camp in Afghanistan. Too late. He was not asked about Moussaoui before September 11, say legal sources.

In early September, Atta's teams were making their final preparations. With just four days to go, a telling scene occurred in a Florida seafood restaurant, Shuckums.

Al-Shehhi was drinking screwdrivers (orange juice and vodka), while an unidentified companion drank rum and Coke. At the other end of the bar, Atta, in a dark blue shell suit, drank cranberry juice, played games on a video console and leered at passing waitresses. One later said she felt he was trying to "undress" her with his eyes.

Al-Shehhi got into a wrangle over his $48 bill, then ostentatiously pulled a wad of notes from his pocket and declared: "I'm an airline pilot." The group paid and walked out, insisting they were not just any airline pilots; they were American Airlines pilots.

The hijackers began positioning themselves for their last flights. Jarrah's team travelled to Newark. Another team led by Hani Hanjour, a mysterious figure who had entered America on a student visa but had never taken up his studies, was in Maryland, close to Washington's Dulles airport.

Al-Shehhi's and Atta's teams moved to Boston, where some of the junior members are thought to have hired a prostitute on at least two occasions. On September 9, the woman took a cab to the Park Inn and spent 20 minutes in a room with one of the hijackers, charging him $180. The cab driver later claimed he had taken the same woman to the Days Inn near Boston University, where she had spent time with another of the men.

In Washington, there was increasing concern about Bin Laden but no awareness of what was about to happen. In early September, the anti-Bin Laden plan of attack was approved by Condoleezza Rice. A strike against him by special forces and unmanned planes was ready. The proposal was due to be presented to the president on Monday, September 10; but Bush was travelling that day and did not receive it.

That night, as Atta spent his last hours in Portland, Maine, Jarrah and his team were in the Newark Airport Marriott hotel, just two minutes from the terminal from which they would set out to commit mass murder in the morning.

It was an expensive place to spend their last night alive. A three-tier chandelier hung over the polished marble of the lobby. Jarrah paid an extravagant $450 in cash for two no-smoking rooms, each with a double bed, on the third floor of the tinted-glass building. He chose rooms with a clear view of the Manhattan skyline, dominated by the twin towers of the World Trade Center.

The hijackers could see the television mast on the north tower, the office lights, now blinking out, one by one, as workers left their desks and headed for the subway below – and the red lights twinkling from the tops of the towers, warning aircraft to keep clear.

Insight: Stephen Grey, Jon Ungoed-Thomas, Gareth Walsh, Nicholas Hellen, Richard Miniter, John Goetze, Nicholas Rufford, Uzi Mahnaimi, Ghulam Hasnain, Hartwig Nathe, Issandr el Amrani, Zoe Thomas and Ben Smalley

2010–15
THE FIFA FILES

In the summer and autumn of 2010, the Insight team went undercover meeting officials from Fifa, the secretive body that runs international football, as eleven nations were competing for the honour of hosting the 2018 and 2022 World Cups. Their initial investigation uncovered extraordinary allegations of corruption and led to the suspension of eight Fifa officials including two from the powerful 24-man executive committee that would make the hosting decision. But it did not end there.

The announcement on December 2 that the tiny state of Qatar had been chosen to host the 2022 competition was greeted with shock and disbelief across the world. Of all the bids, the searing hot desert nation of Qatar was arguably the least competitive. It appeared to confirm the numerous allegations of vote rigging that Insight had picked up during their investigation and set its reporters on a four-year trail.

When hundreds of millions of secret documents were leaked to the team in 2014, a story of corruption, secret slush funds and bribery began to emerge. Insight spent two months examining tens of thousands of gigabytes of data using forensic-search technology, uncovering evidence which led back to the Fifa vice-president: a Qatari named Mohamed bin Hammam. He was at the centre of a murky web of clandestine transactions which, when tied together, told the story of how he had bought Qatar the 2022 World Cup.

The shock waves from the team's work would eventually lead to the toppling of the corrupt regime of Fifa president Sepp Blatter.

WORLD CUP VOTES FOR SALE

―――――――――― • ――――――――――

17 October 2010

A WORLD CUP official has been caught on film agreeing to sell his vote to one of England's rivals bidding to host the 2018 tournament.

The official, a member of the Fifa committee which grants the World Cup, guaranteed his vote to two undercover reporters after requesting £500,000 for a personal project.

A second member of the same committee was recorded asking for £1.5m for a sports academy from a reporter seeking his vote.

The *Sunday Times* investigation also uncovered allegations that supporters of two countries competing to host the World Cup have offered up to £750,000 a vote for personal "projects".

One former member of the Fifa committee warned that the failure of the England bid to offer such deals would be its downfall: "England have got all the good reasons why they should host it but they don't strike the deals . . . It's sad but true."

Our reporters spoke to six senior Fifa officials, both past and present, who offered to work as fixers for the World Cup bid. They all suggested paying huge bribes to Fifa executive committee members.

In seven weeks' time the 24-strong Fifa executive committee will decide by secret ballot which countries should host the 2018 and 2022 World Cups – prizes worth billions.

During our investigation, Amos Adamu, a member of the committee, was filmed negotiating a deal for his vote in which he would receive £500,000, half to be paid up front.

Reynald Temarii, a Fifa vice-president, was the second committee member asking for a payment, in his case to finance a sports academy. He also boasted that his confederation had been offered between $10m and $12m (£6m to £7.5m) by supporters of two bidding countries.

Our findings raise serious questions about the probity of some Fifa officials and cast doubt on whether England's bid will get a fair hearing. They come after David Cameron welcomed Sepp Blatter, Fifa's head, to Downing Street last week.

Bidding countries, officials and national football associations are strictly forbidden from entering into a deal or even the "beginning of a collaboration" to influence voting, according to Fifa's rules.

England is one of four contenders still bidding for 2018. It is competing against Russia as well as joint bids by Spain and Portugal and Holland and Belgium. On Friday the United States quit the race for 2018 and instead joined Qatar, Australia, Japan and South Korea in going for 2022 only. The bid committees have denied any improper approaches or wrongdoing.

The Football Association has mounted a vigorous campaign to stage the 2018 tournament in England and has always insisted it will not resort to bribery. Every Fifa official or adviser spoken to in the investigation agreed that England's bid had not involved bribery.

Our reporters posed as lobbyists for a consortium of American private companies who wanted to help secure the World Cup for the United States. The US bid committee's campaign has been completely above board and the reporters emphasised they were not connected with it.

The undercover reporters approached Adamu, the Nigerian president of the West African Football Union, who also serves as a Fifa executive committee member.

At an initial meeting in London, Adamu told the reporters that he wanted $800,000 to build four artificial football pitches in his home country. He wanted the money paid to him personally, adding: "Certainly if you are to invest that, that means you also want the vote."

The deal was sealed last month in Cairo when Adamu gave his "guarantee" he would vote for the United States in 2018. At the time it was still bidding for 2018. Adamu asked for the payments to be made through a relative who has a business in Europe. He also pledged his second preference for America in the 2022 contest but could not give his first. "I've already given my word to some other bid," he said.

Among the potential fixers who met the reporters were two Fifa committee members.

Amadou Diakite, on the referees' committee, advised the reporters that they should offer bribes of about $1m and he would make the introductions.

"I think that leaving the member to decide what he is going to do with the amount is the safest way to get his vote," he said.

In Paris the other serving official offered himself for hire for up to £300,000. Slim Aloulou, chairman of the Fifa disputes resolution committee, told the reporters they should not pay "peanuts" and recommended bribes of £1m a member.

The ethics code for serving Fifa members states: "Officials are forbidden from bribing third parties or from urging or inciting others to do so in order to gain advantage for themselves."

Temarii, president of the Oceania Football Confederation, asked one of our undercover reporters for NZ$3m (£1.5m) to fund a sports academy at its headquarters.

At the meeting in Auckland, New Zealand, he also claimed that supporters of two bid committees had offered Oceania between $10m and $12m.

Last night Fifa said it would examine the recordings provided by *The Sunday Times*.

Insight: Jonathan Calvert, Claire Newell, Solvej Krause and Cecile Schoon

FOUL PLAY THREATENS ENGLAND'S WORLD CUP BID

---•---

17 October 2010

DUSK WAS falling over the banks of the Nile when Amos Adamu, one of world football's most powerful men, met with two lobbyists for a highly confidential meeting.

Adamu escorted the pair to a quiet spot in the gardens of his luxury Cairo Marriott Hotel where the conversation would not be overheard.

"You know, one has to be very discreet about these things," he told the lobbyists.

The reason was that Adamu is one of just 24 people who will take part in a secret ballot in December that will decide which countries will host the World Cup finals in 2018 and 2022.

By the end of the meeting he had shaken hands on a deal that exposes corruption at the heart of the governing body of world football, Fifa.

The lobbyists were in fact undercover British reporters who said they were representing a consortium of American businesses who wanted to buy his vote for the USA.

In the gloom of the Cairo night, the 57-year-old Adamu was filmed agreeing to accept a payment of $400,000 (£250,000) before the vote and $400,000 afterwards.

The money was ostensibly to pay for artificial football pitches in Nigeria but Adamu wanted it to be paid to him personally rather than to his football federation.

He then went on to give an assurance about his vote.

Male reporter: You will vote for the USA, yeah?

Adamu: [Nods]

Female reporter: Because obviously that's what the consortium wants to guarantee.

Adamu: I know, I know, I know, that is a guarantee.

During a three-month investigation *The Sunday Times* was told that such shady deals were becoming commonplace and even encouraged by some of Fifa's own officials, past and present.

Our undercover reporters travelled around the world gathering evidence indicating that bribery and vote-buying are an acknowledged part of the contest to host the World Cup.

A winning bid requires just 13 votes from the 24 members of the Fifa executive committee who are eligible to vote. So perhaps it should be no surprise that one member said that his federation had been offered almost £8m for just his vote.

Others are said to have been offered personal payments of £750,000 each.

Former committee members named colleagues who they claimed had taken bribes in the past. Several former and current officials – including the chairman of another Fifa committee – were selling their services for exorbitant sums and offering advice on buying votes.

It is a story that will make depressing reading for the England team bidding to host the 2018 World Cup.

England's bid is widely regarded as one of the best for stadiums, infrastructure and organisation, but that is only half the battle.

In Auckland, New Zealand, we secretly filmed Ahongalu Fusimalohi, who for years served as the Fifa executive committee member of Oceania. He believed that England stood little chance because it was too careful to abide by the rules.

"England have got every reason why they should host the World Cup . . . but they don't strike the deals," he said. "You've got 24 members making that decision . . . Globally if you don't come up with something – although it's corrupt, it's only corrupt if you get caught – these people will go all over the world . . . to get it at any price. It's sad but it's true."

The fixers

The Fifa executive committee, which includes the president, Sepp Blatter, are some of the most pampered sports administrators in the world. They travel first-class, they stay in the best hotels, are paid $150,000 (£94,000) a year and receive a daily allowance of £300.

On December 2 they will take the multibillion-pound decision on the 2018 and 2022 World Cups. Russia and the joint bids of the Netherlands-Belgium and Spain-Portugal are in the running for both dates. England are now contesting just 2018 and Qatar, Australia, Japan and South Korea are going for 2022 only. As of Friday, the USA is bidding for just 2022.

The Sunday Times decided to investigate this summer after receiving allegations that dirty tricks were being used to win the World Cup.

Two reporters posed as lobbyists for a London company that had been hired by a consortium of US businesses who wanted to secure the World Cup for America.

It was made clear that this consortium was not connected with the official US bid committee whose campaign has been completely above board.

In order to get some intelligence on how World Cup bids really worked, we approached a number of football fixers with the inside track on Fifa.

The first was Michel Bacchini, a Swiss national and Fifa's tournament director for the Olympics, who had worked for bids in the past.

Bacchini was surprisingly direct. The way to win votes was to use big corporations to offer Fifa executive committee members business deals that would generate income for them, he said.

"[That way] you can't prove anything. What has this to do with football? You know, it's a nice income secured over several years. That's the way you have to do this," he said.

Two weeks later over lunch in Zurich he named current members of the committee who he claimed had taken money before. He singled out one wealthy representative who was made rich by the successful German bid for the 2006 World Cup.

Bacchini: I know how to get to him . . .

Reporter: What do we offer him. Is he someone who wants money?

Bacchini: Yeah, yeah . . .

Reporter: So how much do you think we might have to offer him?

Bacchini: . . . easily $1m.

After suggesting that we might make secret payments of between $2m – $5m, Bacchini cautioned: "Imagine if this comes out, disaster.

I mean this is a highly, highly politically sensitive issue. Imagine if one guy just drains the information to the press?"

Back in London, the reporters had dinner with a man who said he had seen it all before. Ismail Bhamjee, from Botswana, was a Fifa executive committee member for eight years before he was forced to resign over a ticketing scandal.

Bhamjee, 66, named three close colleagues from the committee who he claimed had been given cash in 2004 to vote for Morocco to host the 2010 World Cup. He believed the amount was $250,000.

He also identified a fourth committee member who he said was paid $1m to support Morocco but switched to the eventual winner South Africa at the last minute when he was paid more.

Bhamjee: I know they gave, they gave X [name withheld] personally a lot of money . . . But please, this is confidential.

Reporter: How much did they give him?

Bhamjee: He got, I think, a $1m-plus.

He was happy to contact some of the Fifa executive committee members. "We speak to them and say, 'You guarantee us your vote.' . . . We tell them: 'Look, we give you $200,000 and if we win the bid, we'll add on another $200,000'."

Bhamjee also said he had good intelligence on commercial interests who were attempting to buy votes for their country. The reporters asked how much the offers were.

Bhamjee: Anything from a quarter to half a million dollars.

Reporter: . . . Is that to invest in football? Or is that for them?

Bhamjee: No, no, no, no. This is separate from the football.

Reporter: That's for money, personal money?

Bhamjee: Yeah, they get.

However, later something spooked Bhamjee. The following morning he phoned the reporters in an agitated state, saying he hadn't slept all night and claimed to have suddenly discovered that nobody wanted any money for their vote. He sent the reporters a £100,000 invoice for his work.

The deal

The message had been clear. Some of the Fifa executive committee voters would have regional loyalties, some would vote politically or tactically and some would vote for the best bid. However, a few were in it for what they could get, whether it be finance for themselves or their federation. It was time to meet these men.

Adamu, president of the West African Football Union, has been a Fifa executive committee member since 2006.

In July he was quoted in a Nigerian paper saying: "The public sees every football administrator as a corrupt person, and I cannot explain why it is so. We should be transparent to prove them wrong."

Fifa had written to all its executive committee members ordering them to seek written permission before they met with bid committee representatives, following complaints about the high level of lobbying activity during this summer's World Cup in South Africa.

However, there was no problem in setting up a meeting with Adamu when he came to London in early September. Over coffee in a hotel bar, the reporters explained they wanted his vote and had backers willing to fund sports projects in his country.

According to Fifa rules, Adamu should not have entertained such an approach. But he appeared not at all surprised by the naked attempt to buy his vote. "You know, every bid campaign, they say, 'What can we do for you?'" He said he had recently visited Moscow, where supporters of the Russian bid had offered "co-operation" in building facilities and offering training to players. This again seemed to be a breach of Fifa's rules. However, England, he said, had made no such proposals.

Adamu leapt at the offer of funding and said he had his "own project" that required cash. He wanted to build four artificial football pitches, which would cost $200,000 each. The discussion turned to how the money would be paid:

Reporter: It can be paid in cash or it can be transferred.

Adamu: Yes.

Reporter: I didn't know whether it had to go via the Nigerian football federation, or it's better to you directly?

Adamu: Directly, directly.

He appeared to fully understand what was expected of him in return.

Reporter: Will it help you make your decision in favour of America in some way?

Adamu: Obviously. It will have an effect, of course it will have an effect. Because certainly if you are to invest in that, that means you also want the vote.

He wanted more time to consider the proposal and a second meeting was arranged for Cairo later that month.

Later he sent an email stating for the record that it was "against Fifa code of ethics to solicit, directly or indirectly" anything that would influence his vote. And yet, that's exactly what he was about to do.

The Cairo connection

The undercover reporters joined the great and the good of African football in Cairo three weeks later. The executive committee of the Confederation of African Football (CAF) was in town and that meant a number of Fifa executive committee members.

The reporters met Issa Hayatou, the long-standing Fifa executive committee member who is the CAF president. He was coy and said it would be indiscreet to say what offers had been made. "We know, but I can't say. Each makes their own offer," he said.

He probably didn't know it but one of the offers had been made the night before in the garden of a former palace that Fifa executive committee members were using as their hotel.

Adamu was careful as he talked through the illicit deal. He agreed to accept the cash for "football development" in Nigeria.

To give the transaction the cloak of respectability, he made it clear that money should not be seen "as a precondition for voting". However, this was exactly what the deal was.

Seconds later he gave his guarantee that he would vote for the USA (which at the time was bidding) for 2018. He put the reporters in touch with a relative and later suggested that the payment could be made through that relative's trading company in Europe.

Adamu was also happy to pledge that he would give his second-round vote to the USA for 2022, but he could not give his first. "I've already given my word to some other bid," he said.

Cairo had been full of talk about illicit payments. Amadou Diakite, who for many years had been Mali's man on the Fifa executive committee, had left the city with news that he spilt out to the reporters. He said he had heard that some of the voters were being offered personal payments of between $1m and $1.2m for their vote. In the course of seven telephone calls he named names, and gave details about the proposals.

Diakite, 56, who serves on the Fifa referees' committee, advised the undercover reporters that they should offer bribes of about $1m and he would make the introductions.

He said these bribes could be dressed up as "projects" but actually the money would go directly to the members.

"I think that leaving the member to decide what he is going to do with the amount is the safest way to get his vote," he said.

Later in Paris another current official was offering himself for hire for up to £300,000 for the World Cup bid and other work. This was Slim Aloulou, the 68-year-old chairman of the Fifa disputes resolution committee, who has been around Fifa for 30 years and spent 16 years on the executive committee before being made an honorary member of the organisation in 2004.

The undercover reporter asked him how votes had been acquired in the past and what was a reasonable offer.

Aloulou: What I can tell you is that a little while ago, these things were really not common, unlike what is said. Unfortunately, I hear that this kind of practice is spreading more and more. About amounts, I can't frankly tell you, but these amounts must be quite high. It's not for peanuts. I can make inquiries and try to figure that out.

Reporter: We thought of $800,000.

Aloulou: Yes, around $1m.

Reporter: Per member?

Aloulou: Yes, yes! Per member, I think, but the cost might be even higher than I think. I believe it could be around that level. You know, people invest much more than that to get the World Cup.

Securing a vote

Meanwhile, on the other side of the world in Auckland, one of our fictional lobbyists was attempting to find out what a Fifa vice-president, Reynald Temarii, wanted for his vote.

A former French footballer, Temarii has served on the Fifa executive committee since 2007 because he is head of the Oceania Football Confederation, which covers New Zealand and the South Pacific countries.

The reporter told him he wanted his vote for the USA and was willing to finance sports projects.

Temarii responded: "Your proposal, for sure, it's interesting. For me I just tell you that when the people come to see me I usually say:

'Okay, what will be the impact of your bid in my region?' If there is something concrete on the table, then it's interesting to discuss. If not, forget it."

He went on to explain that he was looking for NZ$3m (£1.5m) to build a sports academy at its Auckland headquarters.

Reporter: Is it something, for example, that our consortium might be able to finance?

Temarii: Yes, this kind of thing I am keen to discuss.

Temarii then told the reporter that there had been two other offers which he described as "huge".

Reporter: More than the NZ$3m?

Temarii: Yes, yes.

Reporter: How much are they offering you?

Temarii: No, no, I can't talk to you like that, but for me this is the basic approach when I talk with someone who wish[es] to get my vote.

At this point Tai Nicholas, Oceania's general secretary, entered the conversation to say "just for the regulations" that the cash offers to the confederation were not "formally linked" to the voting. "We are asking the bid teams to talk about 'If you win, what would you provide Oceania?'," said Nicholas.

It was far from clear how this would get around Fifa rules, which make clear that no offers should be made or discussed that could influence the voting. Indeed, Temarii then let slip that some of the offers for his vote were between $10m and $12m.

However, he went on to list his arguments for backing the USA as a second preference and ended with: "The third reason why we could vote for the States is because this kind of support coming from a private company would be useful, helpful for us."

His officials had become suspicious by the end of the meeting. Temarii said he would vote for the USA second because of the television revenues and in the latter part of the meeting said the financial assistance could not be linked to his vote.

Later Oceania sent an email saying that it was still interested in receiving cash from the consortium supporting America, but wanted to make clear this would not "influence" Temarii's vote.

The following day the reporter met Ahongalu Fusimalohi in an Auckland hotel. Fusimalohi was Temarii's predecessor on the Fifa executive committee – a position he held in 2002–7. He was keen to work as a £100,000-a-year consultant for our fake company to give advice on securing votes.

Fusimalohi said he knew all about dirty tricks because he had been offered cash bribes to vote for Morocco in the contest to host the 2010 World Cup.

"If I'd taken something, I would have taken, well, they were trying to buy me cheap but my selling price would have been a full retirement – and in shame, if I was to ever get caught . . .

Reporter: How much were they offering?

Fusimalohi: Well, something like $100,000 to $150,000.

Reporter: This is interesting for me.

Fusimalohi: And they'd put it in a separate bank account and I said, "Bullshit, if I get caught I mean that's a waste of my whole career. I'm not going to buy into this small-time petty cash money."

Reporter: If Fifa found out that . . . [one] were offering members incentives, would it be a problem?

Fusimalohi: Oh yes, it's going to be a big problem. It has to be strictly confidential . . . The 11th commandment of the CIA is just never get caught . . . It really is what's happening. Friday Fifa said it would examine *The Sunday Times*'s footage and tape recordings. We wrote to all the people recorded, asking them to explain their comments.

Fusimalohi and Diakite claimed they had made everything up because they were suspicious about whom they were dealing with.

Bacchini said he was recounting allegations he had read in a book and Bhamjee insisted that he had never uttered the words attributed to him. Aloulou said he never promised to secure votes and had only offered to make introductions. Temarii explained that his door was always open to anyone who wished to invest in his region.

Adamu insisted that he had merely been talking to the reporter's fictional company about business in Nigeria after the World Cup. He insisted he did not guarantee his vote. "My vote is not for sale," he said.

Off-side

Fifa rules prohibit bidding committees from offering voters money, or "any kind of personal advantage that could give the impression of exerting influence . . . or conflict of interest in connection with the bidding process, such as the beginning of a collaboration, whether with private persons, a company or any authorities".

Its code of ethics says Fifa officials may not accept bribes, gifts or other advantages offered or promised. They are also forbidden from bribing third parties or from urging or inciting others to do so in order to gain an advantage for themselves.

Insight: Jonathan Calvert, Claire Newell, Solvej Krause and Cecile Schoon

PLOT TO BUY THE WORLD CUP

———•———

1 June 2014

THE secret payments that helped Qatar to win the World Cup bid are revealed for the first time this weekend in a bombshell cache of hundreds of millions of documents leaked to *The Sunday Times*.

The files expose how Qatar's astonishing victory in the race to secure the right to host the 2022 tournament was sealed by a covert campaign by Mohamed Bin Hammam, the country's top football official.

The Qatari vice-president of Fifa, the governing body of world football, used secret slush funds to make dozens of payments totalling more than $5m to senior football officials to create a groundswell of support for Qatar's plan to take world football by storm.

This weekend and over the coming weeks this newspaper will expose how Bin Hammam exploited his position at the heart of world football to help to secure the votes that Qatar needed to win from the key members of Fifa's 24-man ruling committee.

The files unlock the mystery of how a tiny desert state with no football infrastructure won the right to host the world's biggest sporting tournament. This week they reveal how Bin Hammam:

- Used 10 slush funds controlled by his private company and cash handouts to make dozens of payments of up to $200,000 into accounts controlled by the presidents of 30 African football associations who held sway over how the continent's four executive (Exco) members would vote

- Hosted a series of lavish junkets for football presidents across Africa at which he handed out almost $400,000 in cash and met delegates privately to offer further payments while pushing for their support for the Qatar bid

- Paid out at least €305,000 in legal and private detective fees for Reynald Temarii, the disgraced Oceania Exco member, after he was suspended for telling undercover reporters that he had been offered $12m for his vote. Temarii refused to resign as an Exco member, thus preventing his planned replacement from voting for Qatar's rivals, Australia in 2022 and England in 2018

- Funnelled more than $1.6m directly into bank accounts controlled by Jack Warner, the Exco member for Trinidad and Tobago, including $450,000 before the vote

- Used his position in charge of Fifa's Goal Programme funds to channel $800,000 to the Ivory Coast FA, whose Exco member Jacques Anouma agreed to "push very hard the bid of Qatar". He also signed off two payments of $400,000 each to the federations of two other voters

- Hosted Issa Hayatou, the president of the Confederation of African Football (CAF), on a lavish junket in Doha at which delegates were lobbied over the 2022 bid. A month later the Qatar bid committee announced an exclusive $1m deal to sponsor CAF's annual congress in Angola, preventing rival countries including Australia from lobbying key figures from the continent.

This weekend football chiefs, politicians and anti-corruption experts called for the competition to host the 2022 World Cup to be rerun.

The documents were described as a "smoking gun" by Alexandra Wrage, a former member of Fifa's independent governance committee.

John Whittingdale, chairman of the Commons culture committee, said: "There is now an overwhelming case that the decision as to where the World Cup should be held in 2022 should be run again."

The disclosures come as the Qatar 2022 bid committee is facing a showdown with Fifa's top investigator Michael Garcia in Oman.

Sources say Garcia will interview the Qatar bid committee face to face for the first time as he nears the end of his two-year investigation into allegations of corruption in the bidding contests to be the host nation for the 2018 and 2022 World Cups.

It is understood that Garcia has no plans to interview Bin Hammam because the official Qatar bid committee has always insisted that he is an "entirely separate" individual who had nothing to do with the campaign to bring the World Cup to Doha.

The bid committee was quick to disown Bin Hammam publicly when he was banned from world football in 2011 after being caught bribing voters in his campaign to be elected Fifa president.

However, the leaked documents show how he worked with the leaders of the Qatar bid and lobbied the key voters, arranging lavish junkets paid for by the 2022 team, at which he offered football officials large payments in exchange for their support.

Fifa's rules ban bid committees, or any of their associates, from "providing to Fifa or any representative of Fifa . . . any monetary gifts [or] any kind of personal advantage that could give even the impression of exerting influence, or conflict of interest, either directly or indirectly, in connection with the bidding process . . . and any benefit, opportunity, promise, remuneration or service to any such individuals, in connection with the bidding process".

The revelations threaten to engulf Fifa as it prepares to gather for its annual congress in Brazil on June 10 ahead of the World Cup.

Facing pressure to rerun the bid, Sepp Blatter, the Fifa president, admitted last month that it had been a "mistake" to hand the tournament to Qatar after Fifa's technical assessors had said a Doha World Cup would be "high risk" because the searing desert temperatures of up to 50°C could be harmful to the players.

The files chart how Bin Hammam sought to secure support from the African voters, lobbying them on a string of junkets at which he showered them with gifts, lucrative benefits, private jet travel and extraordinary hospitality.

Emails, faxes, accounts and dozens of bank transfer slips show he bought support across the continent by handing out hundreds of thousands of pounds in cash to African football officials and making payments directly into their personal bank accounts. The money was paid from a series of slush funds controlled by his Kemco construction company, including his own and his daughter's bank accounts.

Buying support across Africa was central to Bin Hammam's strategy because the members of CAF exerted collective influence over how its block of four Exco members should vote. Several of the officials he paid held seats on CAF's ruling executive committee and another nine currently sit on standing committees of the Fifa executive.

The files reveal that Bin Hammam hosted three of the key African voters along with 35 other football officials on a junket in Doha in December 2009, which was bankrolled by the Qatar bid.

Email correspondence with some of the football officials afterwards reveals that he lobbied them to support the World Cup bid in exchange for large payments.

John Muinjo, president of the Namibian FA, emailed Bin Hammam afterwards promising that his federation "will always be behind you in its unequivocal support at all times" and adding that "we would want to be assisted with a once off financial assistance to the tune of $50,000" to build football pitches.

Bin Hammam responded personally, pledging that it would be "delivered as soon as possible". Last week Muinjo said the money had never reached his account.

The key Exco voter, Anouma, promised his support in correspondence with his Qatari colleague after a stay in Doha the same month.

He instructed his secretary-general at the Ivory Coast FA to write to Bin Hammam on his behalf promising to "push very hard the bid of Qatar" and later sent an email himself expressing "thanks and gratitude" for the hospitality he and his wife had received.

He went on: "I would like to assure you of my desire to ensure that the discussions we had together during this stay translate into concrete action. I would ask you to convey to His Highness the Emir of Qatar my sincere thanks and expression of my deep respect."

David Fani, president of the Botswana FA, also emailed Bin Hammam after the trip to Doha to say how impressed he had been by Qatar's preparations for the 2022 bid.

"I have no doubt that your country will be ready for the 2022 Fifa World Cup and, even without a vote, I pledge my support to you in this respect. If there is anything that I can do, no matter how small, to assist your course, I would be happy to oblige," he wrote. "I will write to you in the new year concerning assistance to Botswana Football Association as per our discussion of 21 December 2009."

The files also show Bin Hammam used his wealth to block a vote that would have gone to Australia, Qatar's rival for the 2022 World Cup, and England in the 2018 contest.

The opportunity was presented to him just two days before the vote when Temarii had decided to step down as an Exco member.

Temarii had been suspended over remarks made to a *Sunday Times* undercover reporter and was under pressure to stand aside so that his colleague from the Oceania Football Confederation (OFC) could take his place and vote.

However, the documents suggest there was a secret 11th-hour intervention by Bin Hammam. On the same day Temarii changed his mind and put out a statement saying that he was going to appeal his suspension.

This meant that OFC was disenfranchised – much to the anger of the Australian bid members who were expecting to receive the vote of Temarii's planned replacement as Oceania's Exco member. England lost out too as Temarii's would-be replacement was thought to favour its bid. It was one less vote for Qatar's opponents in the 2022 contest.

Bin Hammam's role in the affair is now likely to be investigated, as emails seen by *The Sunday Times* show he paid for Temarii to continue his appeal.

In the following months two Bin Hammam slush funds paid €200,000 and €105,000 in legal and detective fees on behalf of Temarii. The revelation will raise serious questions about the integrity of the voting process and how far it was compromised in favour of Qatar by Bin Hammam's cash.

Other suspicious payments to voters include two payments totalling $450,000 to Warner in the two years before the vote. Correspondence in the month after Qatar won the vote also shows Warner referred to Bin Hammam as "the only brother I have in football" and went on to send his bank details.

The email trail and bank documents also reveal the true story of a further $1.2m payment from Bin Hammam to Warner almost eight months after the bid when the two men had been suspended by Fifa for paying bribes to voters in Bin Hammam's campaign to unseat Blatter as the president of Fifa.

Bin Hammam declined to respond to correspondence and calls last week. His son emailed *The Sunday Times* to say that he and the family would not comment.

Last night members of the Qatar bid committee denied any link to Bin Hammam and said he had played no secret role in their campaign. They said they had no knowledge of any payments he had made and they had no involvement in any improper conduct.

Insight: Jonathan Calvert and Heidi Blake

CORRUPT FIFA CRONY PAID $450,000 BEFORE VOTE

1 June 2014

ONE of the most shocking revelations in the Fifa files comes from the forensic insight they provide into the murky relationship between Mohamed Bin Hammam and his fellow Fifa vice-president and crony, Jack Warner.

They show that Warner, the outspoken boss of Caribbean football, received a total of $450,000 from Bin Hammam before voting on the 2022 World Cup. It is the first concrete evidence to emerge that Qatari money was paid directly to one of the executive committee (Exco) voters in the crucial period before the secret ballot in 2010.

In 2011, Warner was sent a further $1.2m from Bin Hammam in equally murky circumstances.

It was paid after Fifa had suspended both men over allegations of bribery in the Qatari's failed attempt to become world football supremo.

The files show the frantic efforts that Bin Hammam's office made to evade international banking controls to wire the $1.2m to Warner, who had gone rogue and was publicly accusing Qatar of buying the World Cup.

Emails show that Warner's tone changed to private appeals to Bin Hammam for help, saying he was "financially desperate". It appears that controls were eventually sidestepped through a false invoice.

In happier times the two men had been close allies. In a leaked email Warner once described Bin Hammam as "my only brother in football". The Fifa files reveal just how far brotherhood went.

Warner first turns up receiving a sum of $250,000 in March 2008 as preparations were being made to announce Qatar's bid to stage the World Cup. In May 2010, a further $200,000 was paid to him.

Documents show that both sums were transferred into an account in the name of Concacaf, the American and Caribbean football federation, and are clearly marked in the correspondence as "payment to Jack A Warner" and "Jack Warner account". Warner was the president of Concacaf.

The 2008 payment came from Bin Hammam's presidential account at the Asian Football Confederation. No explanation was given for it.

The 2010 payment was even more suspect. It was transferred from an account controlled by Bin Hammam's Kemco construction company that he used as a "slush fund" to make payments to football officials.

A remittance slip confirming the bank transfer was sent to Warner by Najeeb Chirakal, Bin Hammam's personal assistant.

The purpose of the payment is never referred to in correspondence but at the time Bin Hammam was working hard to rally support for the Qatar bid with seven months to go before Fifa voted.

The 2010 payment is likely to interest Michael Garcia, the US lawyer hired by Fifa to investigate corruption in the 2018 and 2022 World Cup decisions, because it is the first evidence of a payment directly into an account controlled by one of the Fifa voters in the crucial period before the vote in December 2010.

Warner has claimed that he loyally voted for the United States to be the 2022 World Cup host. However, the voting went to three rounds and it is believed he used at least one of his ballot papers to back Qatar. The truth may never be known because it was a secret ballot.

A few weeks later, Warner emailed Bin Hammam's office, urgently seeking an email address for him in order to send a private message.

He then sent details of his personal bank account for Bin Hammam to make a wire transfer into it. It is not clear how much money, if any, was paid on that occasion.

Only months later, in May 2011, Fifa suspended Warner and Bin Hammam after they were caught paying bribes to Caribbean officials to support the Qataris' attempt to overthrow Sepp Blatter as the organisation's president.

Chuck Blazer, an American member of Exco, submitted evidence that they had offered delegates from the Caribbean football union cash payments of $40,000 each during a junket in Port of Spain.

After attending a lunch with Warner and Bin Hammam, the delegates were handed envelopes stuffed with $40,000. Warner told Fifa it was intended as a daily allowance.

The Fifa files contain a bank transfer slip showing that Bin Hammam put $363,000 into Warner's account after the junket to pay for the delegates' flights and accommodation.

A Fifa ethics committee report said there was "comprehensive, convincing and overwhelming" proof that bribes had been paid to officials to support Bin Hammam's campaign for the presidency, and that Warner had facilitated this.

When both were banned from football, Warner erupted furiously, threatening to unleash a "tsunami" of evidence of corruption inside Fifa and accusing Qatar publicly of paying for World Cup support.

In a fit of temper, he showed TV crews a private email from Jérôme Valcke, the Fifa general secretary, that said Qatar had "bought" the World Cup.

Addressing the cameras, Warner said: "You don't have to believe me, you don't have to like me . . . but Jesus Christ, take the truth when you see it."

Bin Hammam was quick to pacify him. The Fifa files show how within eight days of Warner's explosion, attempts were under way to pay him $1.2m from Bin Hammam's private Kemco account.

The payments were continually rejected by international money-laundering checks.

After an initial attempt to pay the money in three tranches to Warner's two sons and his assistant failed, he supplied the details of an account held by his company, J&D International, in Salt Lake City, Utah.

In an accompanying note, Warner appealed to Bin Hammam in conciliatory terms: "My dear brother, we have a serious problem in paying all our legal bills since the local bank did not release the transfer but instead returned it to your bank. In the circumstances, can you be kind enough to have the full sum wired to the under-mentioned account for which I do thank you kindly. Time is of the essence." The same day, he sent Bin Hammam a $20,000 bill from his lawyer, with the subject: "Help".

At the same time, the correspondence shows the two men were exchanging copies of the witness statements they would send to

Fifa to ensure they had their story straight about the cash-stuffed envelopes in the Caribbean.

The Salt Lake City transfer failed, so accounts in the Cayman Islands were tried with the appearance of success. Bin Hammam's assistant emailed Warner that the money had finally been paid and he shot back: "Allah is great ! ! !" His joy was misplaced: that transfer too eventually bounced back.

On July 7 an apparently successful transfer was made to a US account, but three days later Bin Hammam's assistant emailed Warner's secretary: "Just got a rude shock from our bankers that your bank has again returned the funds."

She responded: "We are working feverishly on our end to address this distressing situation," and quickly came back with a suggestion. The money should be sent "in parts rather than the entire amount, within at least one week of each other (500K, 212K, 500K) [or] be sent from another account, possibly one that is more directly related to football and the reason for sending same could be payment for advisory/professional services rendered".

Three days later, Warner chimed in with an email directly to Bin Hammam. "I'm financially desperate re the legal bills," he pleaded. The next day, July 14, another failed attempt was made to pay the money – this time into an account held by Warner in New York.

The correspondence shows that on July 26 the two men's assistants concocted a false invoice for "professional services provided over the period 2005–2010" as a fig leaf for the corrupt payment.

This time, the attempt to pay the cash appears to have been successful because the frantic email trail ran cold after the COD invoice was produced.

Insight: Heidi Blake and Jonathan Calvert

SOUTH SEAS SHIMMY PROTECTED QATAR BID

———•———

1 June 2014

OCEANIA is unlikely to spring to mind as a football powerhouse, consisting as it does of the South Pacific and New Zealand, a region better known for its hulking rugby players.

Nonetheless, Reynald Temarii, a former footballer from Tahiti, was a senior figure at Fifa in 2010 – and the files show that he played an extraordinary role in Mohamed Bin Hammam's secret campaign to bring the World Cup to Qatar.

Through Temarii, Bin Hammam paid out hundreds of thousands of euros to block a vote against Qatar's bid to host the Cup. In the process, he also blocked a potential vote for England, which was seeking to host the Cup in 2018.

Temarii, the central figure in this complex and subtle operation, is a former player in the French football league. At the time he was president of the Oceania Football Confederation (OFC) and a vice-president of Fifa with a vote on its executive committee (Exco).

During 2010, Bin Hammam flew the 43-year-old Tahitian to Doha, the Qatari capital, and arranged for him to meet the emir. In September that year, three months before the voting on the World Cup, a *Sunday Times* reporter met Temarii in Auckland, posing as a lobbyist for a consortium of US private companies that wanted to help secure the World Cup for America.

Temarii was secretly recorded asking for £1.5m for a sports academy. He also boasted that his confederation had been offered between $10m and $12m (£6m–£7.5m) by supporters of two bidding countries.

On November 18, following the publication of the article, Temarii was suspended for a year and fined 5,000 Swiss francs (£3,300) for breaching Fifa rules on loyalty and confidentiality. This meant that, if he did not appeal and resigned from the executive committee, he would be ineligible to vote in the World Cup ballot – which was only two weeks away. Furthermore, the vote would go to his deputy, who was thought to favour England for 2018 and Australia, one of Qatar's rivals, for 2022.

The files show that Bin Hammam leapt into action and played a pivotal role in Temarii's decision just two days ahead of the vote to appeal against his suspension.

His appeal, which shocked the football world, meant his deputy could not replace him and effectively blocked Oceania's vote. Both Australia and England were subsequently humiliated, crashing out in the first rounds with one and two votes respectively.

Each vote was absolutely vital in a very tight contest. The ballot was by single transferable vote and an eventual winner could, in theory, have prevailed after receiving just three votes in the first round.

The revelations will raise serious questions about the integrity of the voting process and how far it was compromised in favour of Qatar.

Leaked emails show the hectic activity behind the scenes as the Temarii drama was playing out in public. Initially, when Temarii was headline news across the world after the results of the undercover operation had been published in *The Sunday Times*, Bin Hammam did not contact him. But when the Tahitian was suspended for a year, and it was clear he would not be able to vote, Bin Hammam sent him an email.

"Dear friend," wrote the Qatari, "hope this mail finds you in good health and spirits. Having heard the news of *Sunday Times* I would like to extend to you my full confidence and support. Rest be assured that you have a brother in Qatar. Best regards Mohamed."

They spoke by phone the next day and Bin Hammam arranged for Temarii to fly immediately to Kuala Lumpur, the headquarters of the Asian Football Confederation (AFC) where Bin Hammam, the AFC president, has offices.

The documents show that Bin Hammam paid $19,875 to Voyance Tahiti, a travel agency, to fly Temarii business class to the Malaysian capital and to accommodate him and a companion for two nights in the opulent club suite at the five-star Mandarin Oriental.

He was also provided with a chauffeured car. Emails refer to Temarii and his companion as the "president's VVIP [very very important] guests". The payment was handled by Bin Hammam's Kemco construction company and taken from an account in the name of his daughter Aisha. The reason for the payment is simply stated as "business promotion".

After his visit to Kuala Lumpur, Temarii flew to Auckland where colleagues in the Oceania football confederation pressed him that weekend to resign as their president and not to appeal against his Fifa suspension.

David Chung, his deputy who had taken over as acting head of the OFC, flew to Fifa's headquarters in Zurich expecting to take Temarii's place on Exco and take part in the vote, which was only days away on Thursday, December 2.

On the Tuesday, Bin Hammam, in Kuala Lumpur, received an urgent email from Geraldine Lesieur, Temarii's Paris-based lawyer.

Writing in French, Lesieur said: "Reynald Temarii yesterday took the decision to stand down. I have requested him to delay his decision by 24 hours . . . I would like your help to convince Reynald not to give in to the pressure . . . I propose to you that I will call you at 19h Kuala Lumpur time (12h from Parisian time), knowing that there remains very little time before Reynald makes his decision."

Whatever persuasive powers were used, they certainly proved effective. Later that afternoon Lesieur released a statement to the media saying that Temarii had decided that he would not stand down. In the statement, Temarii said: "Despite pressures and issues at stake for the OFC, I decided not to waive this fundamental right to restore my honour, dignity and integrity following the calumnious accusations I suffered from *The Sunday Times*."

The announcement was heavily criticised in Oceania and Australia. One media outlet accused Temarii of sabotaging the Australian bid. What nobody knew was that Bin Hammam had made it possible for Temarii to continue his appeal by underwriting his hugely expensive legal fees.

On December 3, the day after Qatar was granted the 2022 World Cup, Temarii emailed Bin Hammam: "Dear Mohamed, just a few words to congratulate you and your team. I wish you all the bests [sic] for Qatar 2022. And once again, thank you for your kind support. Kindests [sic] regards, Reynald."

Two days later, Bin Hammam replied, saying: "Thanks for your congratulations on Qatar's bid to host World Cup 2022. I wanted to extend my sincere gratitued [sic] and appreciation for your support and I am confident that with your continued support and collaboration Qatar will stage an amazing World Cup of our beloved game."

A few weeks later Jean-Charles Brisard, a Swiss-based private detective firm, submitted a "budget" to Bin Hammam setting out Temarii's legal fees and other expenses amounting to €365,000 – to be paid by the Qatari.

Brisard's covering email said: "Per Mr Temarii's request, please find attached the current provisional budget for Mr Temarii's defense and the bank account details of my company following the signing of an administrative and financial management agreement between us."

The budget was for Temarii's travel expenses and legal fees dating back to late October, after the first *Sunday Times* article. It included €260,000 in fees for Lesieur, the lawyer who had sought Bin Hammam's help to stop Temarii stepping aside. There is no explanation as to why she was paid through Brisard's private detective company, JCB Consulting International.

Brisard, a French investigator better known as an expert on the financing of the terrorist group al-Qaeda, requested €30,000 from Bin Hammam for investigation work on Temarii's behalf.

He had carried out "Project Airtime", an attempt to discredit the *Sunday Times* journalists who wrote the original "World Cup votes for sale" story. *The Sunday Times* has seen a copy of his error-strewn report, which reveals he researched details of the journalists' homes, families and work as well as obtaining a private hotel bill.

This newspaper has previously reported that the work was commissioned by Temarii but the Fifa files reveal that it was paid for by Bin Hammam. In what appears to have been partial settlement of Brisard's €365,000 "budget", Bin Hammam's Kemco firm paid JCB Consulting €200,000 in February, using his daughter's account.

A second payment of €105,000 was made to JCB Consulting in April 2011 from a $1m "slush fund" operated by one of Bin Hammam's closest business associates.

An email sent to Bin Hammam's assistant details the payments alongside two others to be paid to football officials. It says simply: "Attached are the three telex transfers done as per Mr Hammam."

The payment to JCB Consulting came after Fifa had turned down Temarii's appeal.

The Tahitian was not the only football official who turned to Bin Hammam for help after being caught in *The Sunday Times*'s World Cup investigation.

Amos Adamu, the Fifa Exco member for Nigeria, had been filmed offering to sell for $800,000 his vote on the hosting of the 2018 World Cup. (His 2022 vote was not available because he had already pledged it to Qatar.)

When he realised he had been caught discussing the sale of his vote, he immediately contacted Bin Hammam, giving a fanciful account of the meeting with the undercover reporters and seeking Bin Hammam's opinion.

The Qatari's advice, if he gave any, is not in the email cache. Unlike some of those he "supported", he seems to have understood the need for discretion.

Adamu's fellow African football grandee, the former Botswanan Exco member Ismail Bhamjee, was also quick to turn to Bin Hammam after being filmed telling reporters Qatar was offering between $250,000 and $500,000 to the Africans for their votes.

The Qatar bid committee would later strenuously deny Bhamjee's allegations when they appeared in a submission to the British parliament. But, far from rebuking him for speaking out of turn, Bin Hammam supported Bhamjee and instead attacked *The Sunday Times* for "unethical" undercover journalism of a type that he said would rarely happen in the Middle East media.

After the scandal had broken and Bhamjee had been suspended, just 10 days before the World Cup vote, his son Naeem wrote to Bin Hammam. "I wanted to say a very big thank you for your continued support to my dad. He was so happy that you called," he wrote.

The correspondence reveals how close Bhamjee was to Bin Hammam. They were in regular email correspondence and met repeatedly. Bhamjee used Bin Hammam's assistant to book hotels.

When Bin Hammam announced his candidacy for the Fifa presidency in 2011, Naeem sent another email. "I cannot tell you the scenes in the Bhamjee household when we heard that you will be standing for Fifa presidential election – we were jumping for joy," he wrote.

Insight: Jonathan Calvert and Heidi Blake

SLUSH FUNDS AND HOSPITALITY: THE MASTERMINDING OF A DIRTY GAME

1 June 2014

MOHAMED BIN HAMMAM sat with quiet confidence in the front row of the hushed auditorium as the Fifa president Sepp Blatter tore open an envelope containing the name of the country chosen to host the 2022 World Cup.

Many hopes lay on this dramatic moment in December 2010. Prince William and David Beckham were in the audience – having just lost England's bid for the 2018 Cup – as were powerful figures from other countries bidding to stage football's greatest tournament.

It was the climax of years of effort. After a frenzied final round of top-level lobbying in Zurich's luxury hotels, members of Fifa's executive committee (Exco) had voted that afternoon at their headquarters in the Swiss city.

Now, with the world watching on live television, their decision on 2022 was imminent. Bin Hammam, 61, a dapper Qatari with silver hair and a neat goatee beard, was perhaps the calmest person in the room. He knew what was coming.

Behind him, a roar of delight erupted as Blatter declared the tiny, oil-rich Qatar the winner and its royal family leapt to their feet in celebration.

Bin Hammam hovered respectfully in the background as Qatar's ruling emir and his glamorous wife threw their arms around their fresh-faced son, 22-year-old Sheikh Mohammed bin Khalifa Al Thani, the nominal leader of the Qatari bid team.

Around them, the great and good of world football exchanged disbelieving glances in stunned silence.

How had a minuscule Gulf state, with virtually no football tradition or infrastructure, and searing summer temperatures of 50C, beaten footballing countries with much stronger bids?

No casual observer, watching Bin Hammam as he waited modestly for the Qatari celebrations to subside before stepping forward to kiss young Sheikh Mohammed discreetly on the cheek, would have guessed that he was the man who held the answer.

Now a cache of secret documents, leaked from the heart of world football by a senior Fifa insider, unmasks Bin Hammam as the mastermind of an extraordinary covert campaign using slush funds and secret deals to seal the support Qatar needed.

They also contain correspondence which reveals that some insiders realised what Bin Hammam had done. One lobbyist for a rival bid congratulated him on "a fine lesson in Machiavellian expertise ... remarkably executed, utterly accomplished".

How did the Qatari Machiavelli do it? And how can his country – an immensely wealthy absolute monarchy ruled by the same family since the mid-19th century – cling on to the Cup now that Bin Hammam's underhand game has been revealed?

The explosive revelations threaten to engulf Fifa as it prepares to gather for its annual congress in Brazil in 10 days' time in the glare of the world's media before the opening match of the 2014 World Cup in Sao Paulo on June 12.

Blatter, who has been Fifa's president for 16 years, is under mounting pressure to order a rerun of the 2022 vote.

He admitted last month that it had been a "mistake" for football's governing body to hand the tournament to Qatar after Fifa's technical assessors said the fierce desert sun posed a "high risk" to players.

The Fifa president is also likely to face calls for his own resignation. A growing number of influential figures in world football believe a new broom is needed to sweep out corruption at the heart of the sport's governing body.

All the nations bidding to stage the World Cup sign up to rules of conduct that ban them, or any of their associates, from providing any of Fifa's football officials with "any monetary gifts [or] any kind of personal advantage that could give even the impression of exerting influence, or a conflict of interest, either directly or indirectly, in connection with the bidding process".

Past investigations by this newspaper have shown that the rules are too often treated with contempt. Today's revelations will add to the groundswell of concern about how the World Cup was won.

Bin Hammam, a business magnate who made his fortune in the construction industry and property, had long been a powerbroker in the politics of world football when this scandal unfolded.

As bids for the 2022 World Cup were being prepared six years ago, he was head of Qatari football, president of the Asian Football Confederation and a vice-president of the Fédération Internationale de Football Association – to give Fifa its full name – with a vote in picking the top bid.

He portrayed himself as impartial and even privately promising he would vote for a rival bidder, Australia.

The Qatar 2022 bid team have always denied any connection with Bin Hammam, insisting he was an "entirely separate" individual. The Fifa files chart his movements in extraordinary detail as he flew around the world, often on the emir's private jet, meeting in secret with Exco members whose votes propelled Qatar to its victory.

The Fifa files overflow with astonishing revelations. This week, *The Sunday Times* focuses on how Bin Hammam secured the support of Exco's African members who were crucial to Qatar's success.

How Bin Hammam secured the vote

Using cash handouts and bank transfers from 10 slush funds controlled by his private company, Bin Hammam made dozens of payments to the presidents of more than 30 national football associations who held sway over Africa's votes.

To secure pledges of support for Qatar's bid from men he called his African "brothers" – and one formidable woman known as west Africa's "Iron Lady" – he handed out hundreds of thousands of dollars in cash and transferred sums of between $10,000 and $200,000 into bank accounts.

He invited African delegations to a string of junkets in luxury hotels and showered them with gifts, lucrative benefits, private jet travel and extraordinary hospitality.

And he exploited his position as chairman of Fifa's Goal Programme – which funds football development in poor countries – to channel $1.2m into football federations of three key African Exco voters.

Allegations that Qatar bribed all four of Africa's Exco members have dogged its bid since its shock victory.

Before the vote, two former Exco members and a retired Fifa secretary-general had told *Sunday Times* undercover reporters that the oil-rich Gulf state was offering the four Africans up to $1.2m. Soon afterwards, a whistleblower from inside the Qatari bid approached this newspaper to claim that two of them had been paid $1.5m each.

The allegations were published by a parliamentary inquiry in evidence submitted by *The Sunday Times*. But Fifa declined to investigate and the whistleblower retracted the allegations, later claiming to have done so after coming under pressure from Qatar.

In 2012 Fifa belatedly appointed Michael Garcia, a New York lawyer, to head its ethics committee and to look for evidence of wrongdoing. He is due to fly to Oman this week to interview members of the Qatari bid committee.

Sources say he will not grill Bin Hammam because he believes him to be unconnected with the World Cup bid. The Fifa files should make him change his mind. They contain the first evidence of direct payments to football officials in exchange for supporting the bid.

The evidence centres on bank transfer slips showing payments from 10 accounts controlled by Bin Hammam's private company – including his daughter's personal bank account – to football bosses across Africa.

They are accompanied by emails that show how Bin Hammam had offered payments at meetings in which he lobbied for support for Qatar. Other emails reveal how some senior figures repeatedly asked him for money.

Kalusha Bwalya, president of the Zambian FA and former international footballer, wrote to Bin Hammam after a meeting in 2009: "As per our conversation, please Mr President if you could assist me with about 50 thousand Dollars for my Football association and personal expenditures. I hope to repay you in the near future, as the burden is little bit too hard for me at this moment."

There is no evidence to suggest he ever repaid the debt. And in April 2011, he was again "a little thin on resources", as he told Bin Hammam's assistant. "Please speak to the President for help." Later that month, $30,000 dropped into his account.

Clearly, even a database this comprehensive cannot give the whole picture of Bin Hammam's operation. We do not know what was said in private conversations. But the Fifa files give an unprecedented insight into the nerve centre of the Qatari campaign.

After his success in winning the World Cup for Qatar, Bin Hammam overreached himself by trying to replace Blatter as Fifa president and was toppled from all his football posts for bribery. Some other officials named here have since fallen in local scandals.

Football's reaction to such embarrassments has always been to throw a culprit overboard and close ranks. Faced with the devastating evidence of the Fifa files, that game can no longer be played.

The African connection

The story of Mohamed Bin Hammam's secret campaign to bring the World Cup to the Gulf began on a humid June morning in 2008, at the headquarters of the Asian Football Confederation in the Malaysian capital, Kuala Lumpur.

Anyone strolling on the lawns in the tropical sunshine might have seen the neat figure of Mohammed Meshadi – one of the Qatari football chief's most trusted aides – slipping through the palms at the entrance to the glinting glass-fronted AFC building.

Meshadi was there to collect a package containing $100,000 in crisp banknotes withdrawn from expense accounts controlled by Bin Hammam in his role as president of the AFC.

Insiders say Bin Hammam ran the AFC like a personal fiefdom and had no qualms about draining its coffers of cash when the occasion demanded it. And this was a special occasion.

The debonair Qatari had invited the leaders of 25 African football associations to come to Kuala Lumpur on an all-expenses-paid junket and he was determined to make a favourable impression.

Accounts seen by *The Sunday Times* show a total of $200,000 was withdrawn to provide "cash advances for CAF guests" in the 48 hours before the visitors arrived.

CAF is the Confédération Africaine de Football, the sport's governing body in Africa, which is dominated by Francophone west African countries such as Cameroon and Togo.

The visitors, who received their spending money and gifts as they arrived, were treated to a trip to the exquisite Malaysian coastal resort of Malacca.

Even Izetta Wesley, the formidable Liberian Football Association president – known to her colleagues as the Iron Lady – was uncharacteristically gushing in her appreciation afterwards.

"I had a wonderful time and was previledge [sic] to sea [sic] that part of the world," she wrote in a leaked email. "I will always cherish these memories. Thanks for all the beautiful gifts."

Cash handouts and gifts were not all that was on offer. The correspondence shows that after the delegates left, Bin Hammam ordered his finance staff to transfer direct payments to Anjourin Moucharafou, the president of the Benin FA and a CAF executive committee member, and three other delegates.

Qatar's bid to host the World Cup in 2022 was not due to be submitted formally until March 2009, but it was vital to shore up support behind the scenes well in advance.

Another junket was organised in Kuala Lumpur only four months after the first. This time the African football chiefs were invited to bring their wives and daughters.

Meshadi was dispatched to AFC headquarters to collect another stack of dollar bills. Internal spreadsheets show that the visitors and their companions were to be presented with $5,000 each when they arrived, amounting to $195,000 in total.

A set of gifts was also prepared for each guest and packed up in Nike holdalls that were left in their five-star hotel rooms.

Among the guests on the list in line for Bin Hammam's beneficence was Lydia Nsekera, who was then the president of the Burundi FA and is now the first female member of Fifa's powerful executive committee (Exco).

Forty guests were treated to a private cruise on the blue expanse of Putrajaya Lake, south of Kuala Lumpur. Moving among them was Amadou Diallo, a French-speaking west African who acted as Bin Hammam's trusted bagman. Time was made for each of the delegates to have a private meeting with the Qatari.

Moucharafou of Benin was there again and the thank-you email he sent to Bin Hammam afterwards brings to the forefront the role of Issa Hayatou, the powerful Cameroonian who had been president of CAF since 1987 and was one of Africa's four Exco members with votes on who would get the 2022 World Cup. Hayatou has repeatedly shrugged off allegations of corruption and remains in office today.

"Your engagement in a partnership that is of profit to Africa next to President Issa Hayatou is for me a positive reinforcement of our future actions," Moucharafou wrote.

Soon afterwards, Hayatou's vice-president at CAF, General Seyi Memene of Togo, was paid $22,400 by Bin Hammam to fund a pilgrimage to Saudi Arabia for himself and his wife.

Requests continued to roll in. The president of the Swaziland FA and former senator, Adam "Bomber" Mthethwa, emailed Bin Hammam to thank him for an "unforgettable" visit to Kuala Lumpur.

He went on: "I am in dire need of finance in the region of $30,000. This arises from the fact that I've just retired from politics and my gratuity will only be paid to me when I reach the age of 55 in 2010." The documents do not record the Qatari's response, though he forwarded the email to be dealt with by his private staff.

Bin Hamman's next step was to build on the goodwill he had bought. In February 2009 he travelled to the CAF congress in Lagos, Nigeria. The emails show special care was taken to ensure that bagman Diallo was accommodated "in the same hotel where the delegates [are] staying".

A month later the Qatari football association formally registered its bid to host the World Cup, entering the race against the US, Australia, Japan and South Korea.

The rewards of the groundwork Bin Hammam had so carefully laid in Africa with Diallo's help were apparent as soon as the bid became public. Fadoul Houssein, the president of the Djibouti football association, emailed Bin Hammam the same day, ready to sign up for the fight and to bring east Africa onside.

"I was very pleased with you when I heard this news with our brother Diallo," he wrote. "I am ready to go with you to the end. I'm sure that Somalia, the Comoros . . . Sudan, Yemen [not a member of CAF] and Djibouti will support us. Count on me. I am already starting the war and I am sure you will win."

He was right: the football leaders of those countries all became close allies of Bin Hammam and were rewarded for their loyalty. Houssein himself solicited payments of more than $30,000 to fund expensive medical treatment for his association's general secretary.

The Somali football association had $100,000 paid into its bank account. When Sudan's association asked for help paying for its general assembly, Bin Hammam's staff asked it to provide bank details.

The Yemeni football association was paid just under $10,000 and emails show Bin Hammam's staff arranging another bank transfer to the Comoros, the island group off east Africa that, like Djibouti, is a former French colony.

Hammam's campaign intensifies

When Bin Hammam turned up at Fifa's annual congress at Nassau in the Bahamas in June 2009, he was ready to step up his campaign to cement the loyalty of his African brothers. The emails show he met a string of CAF delegates in private to discuss their financial needs. After the congress, Seedy Kinteh, the president of the Gambia football association, emailed Bin Hammam: "I really need your brotherly help again as per discussed in Bahamas and I hereby provide you with the full bank details that you can use for any transfer."

Just 10 days later another email dropped into Bin Hammam's inbox from Kinteh. "Many thanks indeed for your recent mail disclosing to me the transfer of $10,000," the Gambian wrote. "I must first of all express my profound gratitude to you for this very wounderful [sic] brotherly gesture that you have once again demonstrated."

Kinteh said he was sure the money would go a long way to develop the skills of Gambia's players – although the payment had gone into his own bank account. He signed off: "I have every reason to be grateful and indeed my President and Brother I AM !!!!"

Manuel Dende, the Sao Tome FA president, emailed Bin Hammam after meeting him in Nassau, asking for $232,000 to be paid into his personal bank account, ostensibly to build artificial football pitches in his country.

Perhaps the request for so much money was considered a touch audacious as Bin Hammam faxed a copy of it to his staff with the scrawled instruction: "I want to transfer $60,000 to this federation." The money was not immediately forthcoming and when Dende was eventually emailed with news that he had been paid only $50,000, his response was curt.

"Ok, tks," he replied.

Liberia's Iron Lady was more easily gratified. She received $10,000 into her personal bank account and responded: "I've received the transfer. Please convey my thanks and appreciations to Mohamed. May the Almighty Allah replenish his resources a hundred fold. I am so happy that I have a brother and friend that I can always depend on."

The Ivory Coast football association – fiefdom of Jacques Anouma, a key figure as he had a vote on Exco – received £22,000 from one of Bin Hammam's private slush funds, while the president of the Moroccan association, Said Belkhayat, received a payment straight into his personal bank account. The document trail does not show what this money was spent on.

Back in Qatar, the official team for the 2022 bid campaign was taking shape.

Persuasive hospitality

Sheikh Mohammed bin Khalifa Al Thani, the young son of the emir, had been anointed as chairman of the bid committee, while Hassan al-Thawadi, 31, the rake-thin, general counsel of Qatar's sovereign wealth fund, had been brought in as chief executive.

His more rotund deputy was Ali al-Thawadi, described by those who have met him as surlier than his silver-tongued namesake.

When their appointment was announced in September 2009, Ali al-Thawadi had just returned from Kuala Lumpur where he and three other members of the bid team had been entertained by Bin Hammam as "special guests".

The Qatari grandee – several decades older than the bid's fresh-faced leaders – had evidently impressed the younger men with his efforts to curry favour with his African brotherhood.

One of the committee's first moves was to set the ball rolling for another lavish junket for the CAF presidents hosted by Bin Hammam – this time in Doha, the Qatari capital, in December 2009.

The emails show how Bin Hammam's team worked closely with the official committee in organising the junket.

Hassan and Ali al-Thawadi were with Bin Hammam in November 2009 at the Asian Champions League final in Tokyo. The following month Ali al-Thawadi emailed Najeeb Chirakal, Bin Hammam's right-hand man at his private office in Doha, asking for "a list of all CAF federation's [sic] visiting doha [sic] high lighting the ones who confirmed up to date and updating it on a daily basis as confirmations are received from them".

Chirakal and "bagman" Diallo arranged for 35 African football association presidents and three key Exco voters to fly to Doha business class in groups throughout December and stay at the pyramid-shaped Sheraton hotel on the shores of the Gulf in the city's exclusive West Bay area.

Just before the guests began arriving, Bin Hammam's staff paid $50,000 straight into the bank account of Kalusha Bwalya, the president of the Zambian football association. The former Zambian winger had written to Bin Hammam in October to ask for "about 50 thousand dollars for my football association and personal expenditures".

Hayatou, the Cameroonian overlord of African football, was the first to arrive with his wife on December 6, followed by Amos Adamu, the Nigerian Exco member. Five days earlier, payments of $400,000 each had been channelled to their national federations from the Fifa Goal Programme fund controlled by Bin Hammam. The money was earmarked for works on their headquarters.

Jacques Anouma, the Exco member for Ivory Coast, also arrived and was not left out of the Goal Programme spending spree: his federation had already received $400,000 and was granted another $400,000 the next year.

Bin Hammam is likely to face questions about the conflict of interest in his position as chairman of the Goal Programme fund while secretly lobbying recipients of the cash to support the Qatar bid.

Ali al-Thawadi presided anxiously over the arrangements for the Doha junket, repeatedly asking Chirakal in Bin Hammam's office to send him the latest list of delegates who were expected, wanting to know the details of the programme arranged for them and instructing him to forward the invoices for all the flights and hotel rooms to the bid for payment.

"Please forward me the final list of CAF delegation arrival and departure. The full cost of their flight expenses and accommodation. The full program that has been arranged for them in their visit in Qatar," he wrote on December 16.

He wrote again at the end of the month: "Please provide us with the invoices regarding the African [sic] FA's visit last week from the accommodation and the travelling expenses in order to not delay those payments."

It is clear evidence of the closeness between Bin Hammam's secret operation and the official Qatari bid committee. The leaders of the bid will now be called upon to explain how much they knew about Bin Hammam's covert campaign to buy support for the 2022 Qatar World Cup.

They deny all knowledge of payments he made and say they were not involved in any such conduct and had no secret role in the bid.

Very little detail has survived about the hospitality the delegates enjoyed on the junket. What the documents do show beyond doubt is that Bin Hammam used the junket to hold a series of private meetings with the delegates at which he lobbied them to throw their support behind Qatar's bid at the same time as offering them handsome payments.

David Fani, president of the Botswana football association, emailed Bin Hammam afterwards to say how impressed he had been by Qatar's preparations for the 2022 bid.

"I have no doubt that your country will be ready for the 2022 Fifa World Cup and, even without a vote, I pledge my support to you in this respect. If there is anything that I can do, no matter how small, to assist your course, I would be happy to oblige," he wrote.

"I will write to you in the new year concerning assistance to Botswana Football Association as per our discussion of 21st December 2009."

John Muinjo, president of the Namibian football association, also emailed Bin Hammam to express his enthusiasm for the Qatar bid – at a price.

"Kindly take note that Namibia football association will always be behind you in its unequivocal support at all times," he wrote. He then added: "Dear President, allow me to sign off by humbly requesting you for the 2022 bid committee to consider as we discussed the legacy of putting up an artificial turf in the densely populated area of the north of Namibia which will positively score you points in the final analysis as you embark upon the mammoth task of securing the bid for vibrant Qatar in 2022.

"We would want to be assisted with a once off financial assistance to the tune of U$50,000 for the 2010 season to run our second division leagues that went crippled by the prevailing global economic melt down."

Bin Hammam responded personally: "I really appreciate your kind support to Qatar Bid for 2022 World Cup . . . As far as the request made by Namibia Football Association, I will see that it will be delivered as soon as possible."

Anouma of Ivory Coast was just as enthusiastic. His secretary-general, Idriss Diallo, wrote to Bin Hammam after the junket: "My president Jacques Anouma ask me to think about a strategy to help his very good friend President Bin Hammam. So . . . I send you in this mail a proposal to push very hard the Bid of Qatar 2022."

Anouma followed up with his own email: "After my recent stay in Doha at your invitation, I would like to express all my thanks and gratitude for the fraternal welcome you reserved for my wife and I and members of our federation.

"I want to tell you how much I appreciate your availability and your attention vis-à-vis African federations hereof. It is no doubt that the Doha meeting will contribute to tighten the bonds of friendship and brotherhood between, first, the African federations and your confederation, and secondly, between yourself and leaders of African football."

He went on: "I would like to assure you of my desire to ensure that the discussions we had together during this stay translate into concrete action. I would ask you to convey to His Highness the Emir of Qatar my sincere thanks and expression of my deep respect." The extent to which Bin Hammam and the Qatari bid committee had beguiled Africa's football barons became clear immediately.

Qatar secures CAF

On January 7, 2010, just days after the last of the delegates had returned home from the Doha junket, CAF announced that it had struck a $1m deal for the Qatar 2022 bid committee to sponsor its annual congress in Angola at the end of the month. The secretary-general emailed to all the other bid committees: "Kindly note that CAF has signed an exclusive sponsorship agreement with Qatar 2022 for the CAF Congress 2010, which as a consequence means that no other bidding nations for the Fifa World Cup will be allowed to make any presentations at the Congress.

"However, your delegation and representatives will be allowed to attend as 'observers', but without the possibility to organise press conferences, distribute any promotional material or erect stands to that effect within the venue and its vicinity on that day."

The announcement sparked fury among the other bidding nations which had intended to attend in order to promote their own proposals for the 2022 Cup. It was a masterstroke by Qatar in its strategy to use its financial muscle to lock down the four African votes.

Bin Hammam travelled to the congress in Angola with his bagman Diallo and the entire Qatar 2022 bid committee including Ali al-Thawadi, who was also looking for proposals to buy favour.

He offered $1m to Samson Adamu, the son of Nigeria's Exco member, to host a dinner in South Africa for African football legends.

As *The Sunday Times* later revealed, the deal would have allowed the recipient to cream off a huge profit on a dinner that would have cost only about $200,000 to host. However, the Qataris claimed they never actually paid the money after consulting Fifa's rules, and Adamu said that the deal had fallen through.

This newspaper's evidence was passed to Michael Garcia, Fifa's chief ethics investigator, and forms part of his continuing probe into vote-buying.

The Fifa files prove that the Legends Dinner was not the only deal on offer at the time of the Angola congress. George Weah, the former Liberian and English Premier League striker and one-time Fifa world footballer of the year, emailed Chirakal his bank details on the eve of the conference: "I write because after meeting with the President, he told me to pass on my contact and bank details information to you urgently."

Later that day Bin Hammam received a personal email from one of Weah's associates, Eugene Nagbe, a prominent Liberian politician.

"George has repeatedly spoken of his support for our future plans in world football and we all look forward to your ascendency," he wrote, adding that "conservatively, an amount of about USD 50,000 will be needed . . . to lock the election down" for Liberia's Iron Lady, Izetta Wesley.

"Please be assured Mr President, that this is just a step in the bigger scheme of things to come. George have lined up most of the other former stars and the federations in Africa and South America so that when we are ready, your victory will be assured."

The next month $50,000 was paid into Weah's personal bank account by one of Bin Hammam's slush funds, ostensibly for his "school fees".

Other delegates contacted Bin Hammam after the congress in equally gushing terms hoping for payoffs.

Muinjo, the Namibian FA boss, wrote: "Your delegation and their presentations left a lasting impression on the African continent. I have gathered from my many colleagues and I can confirm that too.

"I have also congratulated the Bid 2022 Ceo, Mr Hassan Al-Thawadi afterwards through e-mail correspondences. Mr President,

I am drafting these few lines as a follow up to our discussion with regard to the financial assistance please."

Seedy Kinteh of Gambia, who wrote to say he was having problems paying for his federation's annual congress, received a remittance slip from Chirakal showing a transfer of $10,000 into his personal bank account from Bin Hammam's daughter's account.

Ahmed Darw, the president of the Madagascar football association, said Bin Hammam had "promised to give me a help" with his own re-election. Asked by Chirakal how he would like the money paid, he provided two options: "by bank swift or I can take it in Paris with . . . Diallo".

The next big event on the horizon was the World Cup in South Africa in June–July 2010. With under six months to go before the 2022 winner would be chosen, Bin Hammam's generosity increased. Flying in to Johannesburg with his henchmen Diallo and Meshadi, he instructed his staff to pick up the bill for all his guests. One email shows that Bin Hammam bought 60 tickets costing about $3,800 and had them delivered to Hayatou, Cameroon's Exco member, at the five-star Michelangelo hotel in Johannesburg. Records of Bin Hammam's spending in the city show that he splurged $3,482 for "dinner for Exco members" and a further $4,331 on "rooms for Exco member".

During the tournament, Abdiqani Said Arab, Somali football's general secretary, emailed Chirakal his federation's bank details. Sure enough, $100,000 was paid from Bin Hammam's daughter's account.

Diallo, staying with African delegates as usual, put in a request for $50,000 to be paid to the Niger FA from the same account just after the tournament, and €10,000 was sent to Aboubacar Bruno Bangoura, then Guinean FA president.

Bin Hammam's loyal champion, Houssein of Djibouti, asked him to foot the bill for his wife and children to spend Ramadan in Doha and Chirakal was duly instructed to book them a suite in a hotel overlooking the Gulf. All the charges were to be settled by the Qatar FA. The month after their return, Houssein emailed Bin Hammam: "I think we have very good chance for to win the organisation WORLD CUP 2022 IN CHALLAH [sic]."

The final pay-off

Once the blare of the World Cup vuvuzelas had died away in South Africa, Bin Hammam embarked on an even harder push to assure himself of the support of Africa's four Exco voters in a rapid succession of direct secret meetings.

He flew Adamu of Nigeria and his Egyptian Exco colleague Hany Abu Rida to Doha by business class on August 15 and paid for their executive suites at the five-star Sheraton hotel. Anouma of the Ivory Coast was due to join them but was detained at the last minute by a political crisis at home.

Less than a fortnight later Bin Hammam flew on the emir's private jet to Cairo to collect the African kingpin, Hayatou of Cameroon, and bring him back to Doha.

Then, on September 3, he arranged for the leaders of the Qatari bid committee to fly with him on the royal jet to the Cameroonian capital, Yaoundé, to meet Hayatou again on his home ground.

Yet another private meeting was set up between Bin Hammam and Hayatou in Cairo on September 15. Days later Bin Hammam was secretly catching up with Anouma in Doha.

However, while the football diplomacy forged ahead, a shock awaited the Qataris. In mid-September, less than three months before the crucial vote, Fifa inspectors visited Qatar to assess its suitability to host 2022.

The emirate's ambitious $50m proposal to build collapsible air-conditioned stadiums that would shut out the searing summer heat would finally be put to the test.

The visit was a disaster. The inspectors slammed Qatar as a "high risk". The technical assessors balked at the challenges of having to build nine stadiums from scratch and said the fierce desert sun posed a "potential health risk" to players.

It was not the only misfortune to befall the Qatari bid that month. Adamu of Nigeria had promised his 2022 vote to Qatar, but *Sunday Times* undercover reporters caught him offering to sell his 2018 vote for $800,000 and he was suspended by Fifa – knocking out a guaranteed backer for Qatar.

The Qataris were undeterred. They batted off the criticism of their bid, insisting their air-conditioned stadiums would shut out the fierce heat, and rolled out the red carpet for their African brothers one last time. The venue was a friendly match between Brazil and Argentina in Doha on November 17. Diallo made the arrangements on Bin Hammam's behalf and the guests were luxuriously accommodated in the Ritz Carlton.

After the match Bin Hammam's inbox was flooded with messages from his guests. Houssein of Djibouti was particularly eloquent: "If god wills it we will win, president. Thank you for protecting us from all that is bad."

The long wait was nearly over. Bin Hammam's two-year campaign of munificence was about to pay its dividends.

The leading lights of world football were descending on Zurich to hear who would host the 2018 and 2022 tournaments. The bidding nations fielded glittering entourages of football stars, celebrities and statesmen. David Cameron joined David Beckham and Prince William for England's last push for 2018.

Chirakal had arranged for the Qatari bid committee and their entourage to stay in magnificent style at the Baur au Lac, Zurich's finest five-star hotel, running up bills of more than $340,000 which were charged to Hassan al-Thawadi at the bid committee. The emails show that Bin Hammam was with them, attending to the final preparations for the bid's last stand before the votes were cast.

Qatar's final presentation to a packed auditorium in Zurich was a slick affair with high-budget promotional films and polished performances from a crisp-suited Sheikh Mohammed Bin Khalifa Al Thani – figurehead of the Qatari bid – and his elegant mother, Sheikha Mozah.

Hassan al-Thawadi, the bid chief executive, made a final effort to dismiss the safety concerns raised by Fifa's inspectors. "Heat is not and will not be an issue," he promised.

They had no need to break into a sweat, however. As Bin Hammam filed out of the main auditorium to cast his ballot in secret with his 22 fellow Exco voters, he could congratulate himself on a job well done.

He was confident of African votes – and he had good reason to feel relaxed about the other eight votes that he would need to win, as we will reveal in coming weeks.

When the result was announced to a stunned crowd, Bin Hammam was inscrutable. Some in the room, however, were in on his secret – and his correspondence afterwards shows how his friends across Africa were only too quick to queue up for their rewards. Seedy Kinteh of Gambia emailed Bin Hammam the day after the vote to congratulate him.

Two days later, he followed up with an email to Bin Hammam's assistant: "I write to find out about the progress of my appeal concerning the Vehicle. I have already got in my possession a colosal [sic] sum of ten thousand US dollars . . . and any assistance will be of immense value to me."

Kinteh said that he needed the car to travel to football projects in the Gambian countryside. Three months later, $50,000 was paid to him directly from Bin Hammam's daughter's account.

Nicholas Musonye, the general secretary of the Council of East and Central Africa Football Associations (Cecafa), wrote to Bin Hammam: "This is a glorious moment to all of us in our zone and we congratulate you for the hard work and all the efforts you put in this bid.

"Your many years of hard work have been rewarded and you will go down in history books for what you have achieved for Asia and the people of Qatar."

Two days later he forwarded Cecafa's bank details to accompany a request for $200,000 to fund a tournament in Tanzania. The money was paid.

The requests kept rolling in, but Bin Hammam did not lose patience. He responded to each email from the African football bosses, thanking them in turn for their "invaluable" support, and he kept the money flowing. After all, it had been worth it.

When Izetta Wesley got in touch in the new year with the message, "CONGRATULATION for winning your World Cup Bid", Bin Hammam's response said it all.

"Thank you very much for your kind greetings," he wrote to the Iron Lady. "I would not have succeeded if not for the support from friends and believers like you."

Insight: Heidi Blake and Jonathan Calvert

THAIS ROLL INTO QATAR, OUT ROLLS A CHEAPER GAS DEAL

7 June 2014

ALTHOUGH the novelty of Doha's pyramid-shaped Sheraton hotel overlooking the Gulf had faded in the nearly three decades since it had been built, Mohamed bin Hammam favoured it for his extremely important guests.

They followed the same routine: after strolling past the palm trees lining the lobby they would be welcomed warmly and placed on his charge account before being ushered to a luxury suite.

Among those who arrived on a sweltering evening in August 2010 was Worawi Makudi, the long-established president of the Football Association of Thailand.

Like Bin Hammam, he was a member of Exco, the powerful executive committee of Fifa, with a crucial vote on who would host the World Cup. He knew the Arab world well. A member of Thailand's Muslim minority, he was educated in Kuwait in the 1970s.

Also on the Qatari's charge account at the Sheraton was Sim Hong Chye, Makudi's chief adviser at the Thailand FA. A venture capitalist, he was more commonly known as Joe Sim, "the Casino King".

They had a third figure staying with them at the Sheraton on Bin Hammam's account. His name was Brian Teo, and his job – working for a company that sold equipment to the oil and gas industry – gave a clue to their reason for being in Qatar. The emirate's vast gas fields are the chief source of its unrivalled per-capita wealth.

The Fifa files reveal how Bin Hammam used his power and influence to usher Makudi's team into talks about a large gas deal with top Qatari government officials and members of the Qatari royal family.

This summit came at a time when Thailand had been seeking to save tens of millions of dollars on its supply of liquefied natural gas from Qatar.

Bin Hammam's secret role as fixer behind these top-level talks on an energy deal raises serious questions about his use of Qatar's energy muscle to try to influence key voters in its bid for the 2022 World Cup. It also shows the close connections Bin Hammam had to the Qatari bosses despite denials that he had anything to do with the official Qatari bid to host the World Cup.

The morning after their arrival, Sim and Teo took the half-mile taxi ride to the diplomatic district of Doha. There, inside the mirrored Navigation Building, they met Abdullah bin Hamad Al Attiyah, the then deputy prime minister and energy and industry minister.

Leaked emails show that Al Attiyah, who has no connection to football, was there to discuss an arrangement between the Qatar Football Association and the Thai FA and a deal over liquefied natural gas. In other words, just four months before Exco was to vote on the bids for 2022, Bin Hammam had ushered a right-hand man to one of the crucial Exco voters into talks at the highest levels of the Qatari government about a major gas deal.

At the time, energy officials in Thailand were renegotiating terms they had struck with Qatar to purchase 1m tons of liquefied natural gas each year at a contracted price. Gas prices had plummeted by 20% since the deal was first discussed, leaving Thailand to pay way above the odds.

Thai energy officials had been hoping to persuade Qatar to release them and allow them to buy at the market price, which would potentially save Thailand tens of millions of dollars but yield no benefit to Qatar. Bin Hammam's football connections provided an opportunity to discuss this.

Makudi and his team flew out of Doha the day after the meeting. The next day Sim followed up with an email to Al Attiyah, which he copied to Bin Hammam and Abdul Aziz Al-Malki, director of the office of the deputy prime minister.

He wrote: "It was a great honour for me to have an audience with your excellency on 16 Aug 2010. My team, sincerely, would like to thank your royal highness for all your kind supports in promoting the bilateral co-operations in soccer developments and activities between the Qatari FA and Thai FA.

"With your excellency granted permission, I will liaise with the CEO of Qatargas Operation Company Limited for a meeting to conduct all the follow up actions on the LNG sale. Your excellency. I have the honour to remain yours humbly, Joe Sim, chaiman [sic] of Venture Group."

State-owned Qatargas is the largest liquefied natural gas company in the world.

Under Fifa's rules, bidding nations must not offer Exco members or their associates any opportunities that could influence them in deciding how to cast their ballot.

The Qatar FA and anyone associated with its bid committee were banned from providing to an Exco member or "any of their respective relatives, companions, guests or nominees ... any kind of personal advantage that could give even the impression of exerting influence ... and ... any benefit, opportunity, promise, remuneration or service to any such individuals, in connection with the bidding process".

Nonetheless, Sim, the right-hand man of Thailand's Exco member was being given the opportunity to play a pivotal part in a major deal with Qatar's sovereign gas company. Furthermore, his involvement was expressly designed to foster close relations between the Qatar FA, of which Bin Hammam was president, and the Thai FA, of which Makudi was (and still is) president.

The leaked documents show that Sim also followed up his meeting with an email to Sheikh Khalid Al Thani, the chief executive of Qatargas, who is a son of the then emir and brother of the chairman of Qatar's 2022 bid committee. Bin Hammam was copied into the correspondence.

Sim wrote: "Your excellency. His excellency deputy premier Abdullah bin Hamad Al Attiyah has directed me to liaise with your excellency on the LNG sale. Your excellency has mentioned next week would be a good time to meet.

"Kindly grant me the permission for a meeting for me to discuss follow up actions with your excellency and co-coordinating [sic] staff appointed by your excellency. Your excellency I have the honour to remain yours humbly Joe Sim."

The meeting was scheduled for early September. Sim returned to Doha seeking a meeting with Bin Hammam the night before it was scheduled to take place. The documents trail ends there.

In the following months the energy agreement with Qatar was amended, and Thailand has gone on to buy millions of gallons of gas from Qatargas at the much cheaper spot-price. The details of the negotiations are not known.

Last week the Thai state-owned oil and gas company, PTT, denied any suggestion that its deal with Qatargas was in exchange for supporting Qatar "to host the Fifa World Cup in 2022". Makudi also denied this suggestion.

Makudi, a key ally of Hammam in the cut-throat world of Asian football politics, is known to have voted subsequently for Qatar's bid.

He later was to become embroiled in controversy over his dealings with Lord Triesman, the former England bid chairman.

Using parliamentary privilege, Triesman alleged that Makudi had demanded the TV rights to a friendly fixture with the Thai national team in return for his vote in the contest to host the 2018 World Cup.

Makudi tried to sue Triesman but his legal action proved unsuccessful.

Insight: Jonathan Calvert and Heidi Blake

PACT WITH ENEMY SEALED BIN HAMMAM VICTORY

—————————•—————————

7 June 2014

THE soaring voice of a renowned soprano floated on the warm night air as Mohamed bin Hammam stepped onto the lantern-lit veranda of the Johannesburg Country Club. Dapper in a crisply cut suit, the silver-haired football grandee joined the illustrious guests milling around on lawns sloping gently to the lake.

It was July 5, 2010, with only six days to go before the World Cup final in the Soccer City stadium. Sumi Jo, the Korean diva, had been hired to entertain the football powerbrokers who descended on the club in Auckland Park.

Bin Hammam, head of Qatari football, was at the club as the special guest of Chung Mong-joon, a fellow member of the executive committee of Fifa, the sport's international governing body.

Neither man was overawed by the wealth flaunted around them. Both were well acquainted with the power of money. The Qatari had made his fortune in construction and property. Chung, a South Korean, was the majority shareholder in Hyundai, the car and engineering giant.

They were also well-versed in the art of shifting alliances. Indeed, no stranger watching them chatting amicably would have realised that they had recently been sworn enemies.

In 2009 they were locked in a bitter war of words as Chung allegedly bankrolled a campaign against the Qatari.

"This man knows nothing about football," Bin Hammam briefed at the time. Chung went further, accusing the Qatari of "suffering from mental problems".

In 2010 there was further cause for enmity. South Korea and Qatar were bidding to become the hosts of the 2022 World Cup, pitting Chung and Bin Hammam against one another again.

Yet they were all but inseparable during the World Cup games in South Africa. Leaked documents show they travelled together between matches on Bin Hammam's private jet, shared the astonishing luxury of Fifa's VIP hospitality suites during important games and dined together in the neo-renaissance splendour of Johannesburg's Michelangelo hotel.

Last week, we revealed Bin Hammam's operation to buy support across Africa for Qatar's bid using slush-fund payments of as much as $200,000 at a time.

Our second tranche of Fifa files show that masterful diplomacy, extravagant largesse and Machiavellian strategy played a crucial part in securing Asia's votes. Bank transfer slips and emails also reveal that Bin Hammam made payments totalling $1.7m to football bosses across Asia from the same secret slush funds he used in Africa.

The documents lay bare in astonishing detail how the Qatari football boss spread his private wealth between officials across the continent in return for their loyalty.

Chung was the key to Bin Hammam's game plan. He is a respected figure in Korea, an accomplished former sportsman and a politician with presidential ambitions.

The shrewd Qatari used just the right bait to lure him. As with so many of Bin Hammam's operations uncovered from the Fifa files, it is a complex story of skulduggery in luxurious settings – and it has a sting in its tail.

Power in world football arises not from skill on the pitch but from becoming boss of a national football association and then president of a regional confederation to claw one's way onto Fifa's 22-man executive committee (Exco).

Bin Hammam held one of Asia's four seats on Exco and was also president of the Asian Football Confederation (AFC), an unwieldy, 47-member organisation covering a swathe of the globe from Syria to Australia.

In early 2009, he received intelligence that Chung was supporting a plot to topple him from the AFC. A rival from Bahrain, another Gulf statelet even smaller than Qatar, was allegedly being bankrolled by the South Korean.

The Qatari hired Peter Hargitay – a lobbyist and former aide to Sepp Blatter, the Fifa president – to conduct covert surveillance on Chung and his delegation as they arrived in Kuala Lumpur for the AFC congress in May that year, when member countries would vote on Asia's four Exco seats.

Bin Hammam had been tipped off that Chung's associates were offering development grants of up to $200,000 to Asian national football associations to back Bahrain's campaign. He was looking for hard proof.

"Below please find a first input re S-Korean delegation with initial descriptions of the assignment, private mobile numbers, arrival dates," Hargitay wrote to Bin Hammam on April 29.

To help win the vote, Bin Hammam also used the services of Manilal Fernando, a rotund Sri Lankan hustler and long-standing ally, who was employed by Fifa as its South Asian regional development officer.

Fernando's emails reveal that his electioneering methods were far from straightforward. He sent Bin Hammam one report guaranteeing the votes of 12 AFC countries, adding: "I am sure of Pakistan and Afghanistan because I sent a mobile phone and both photographed the ballot paper inside the booth and showed it to me."

The documents show that Fernando also received a payment of $23,000 from Bin Hammam's slush fund as reimbursement for a cash gift he said he had given to Alberto Colaco, the general secretary of the Indian football association – after winning a guarantee of his support.

A bitter war of words erupted between Chung and Bin Hammam after the Qatari made public allegations about vote-buying. It threatened to drive a wedge through the heart of Asian football. The South Korean accused the Qatari of "acting like a head of a crime organisation" as president of the AFC.

Blatter intervened, publicly reminding the warring parties of "the fundamental principles of discipline and respect for opponents".

In short order the attempted coup fizzled out, and Bin Hammam won the vote. Few were surprised when Fifa's ethics committee cleared all concerned of wrongdoing. That was the way of handling spats in the Fifa "family".

With his presidency secure, Bin Hammam had a new project to attend to: Qatar's bid for the 2022 World Cup.

Strategy documents show that, as early as June 2008, the Qatari had concluded that buying up support in Asia and Africa was crucial to winning the right to host a World Cup.

The files show that in 2009 he made a string of unexplained payments from accounts held by his private company, Kemco, to football bosses across Asia. Among them was Mari Martinez, president of the Philippines football association. An unknown sum was paid into his wife's bank account, and he went on to receive $12,500 in his own.

Ganbold Buyannemekh, president of the Mongolian FA, arranged payments of more than $40,000 to his daughter. Rahif Alameh, president of the Lebanese FA, had $100,000 paid into his personal account – the first tranche of $200,000 from Bin Hammam.

The core targets of Bin Hammam's strategy, however, were his three fellow Asians on Exco: Chung, Worawi Makudi of Thailand, and Junji Ogura of Japan.

Bin Hammam could count on the unfailing loyalty of Makudi, a long-term ally. But Chung and Ogura presented a knottier problem as both Korea and Japan were also in the race for 2022. And in Chung's case, the rivalry was not just patriotic but personal.

Nonetheless, Bin Hammam focused on Chung as the powerful figure he had to bring onside. The Qatari was not one to allow old enmities to stand in the way.

The files reveal a marked change of tack towards Chung as summer turned to autumn in 2009. In October, the month after Qatar set up its 2022 bid committee – in which Bin Hammam had no formal role despite being boss of Qatari football – one of his closest aides arranged for Chung to travel to Kuala Lumpur on AFC business.

The aide emailed instructions to upgrade Chung's room at the five-star Shangri-La hotel to a suite and ensure he was given a dedicated car – all expenses paid.

The two rivals breakfasted together in the hotel's Lemon Garden restaurant on the morning of November 24. From that occasion onwards, whenever Chung visited Kuala Lumpur he was lavished with the hospitality that Bin Hammam reserved for his closest friends and allies.

Bin Hammam's aide later instructed staff in the AFC's logistics department: "Please ALWAYS accord Dr Chung the presidential suite. This is a standing instruction." And then: "Following my earlier email, please also ensure that the car for Dr Chung is Hyundai (highest-range model) or if that is not available, then a Mercedes 300 or 500 model (newest model). This is also a standing instruction." The extra cost was all to be charged to Bin Hammam's presidential account at the AFC.

The lavish hospitality was reciprocal. The two men's assistants were soon arranging for Bin Hammam to travel to South Korea in February to be hosted by Chung at the five-star Grand Hyatt hotel with dazzling views of Seoul's futuristic cityscape.

Chung arranged for Bin Hammam to meet the South Korean president, Lee Myung-bak, a former top executive at Hyundai.

"Our meeting at the presidential Blue House was arranged by none other than my good friend and comrade-in-arms Dr Chung Mong-joon," the Qatari gushed afterwards on his blog.

"What impressed me during the meeting was the Korean president's vision for football . . . No wonder Korea's bid for the 2022 Fifa World Cup has his full and unqualified support."

Leaked correspondence shows that an alliance had been cemented. The documents record an intriguing deal in which Bin Hammam appears to have won Chung's loyalty by offering to help him secure his re-election as vice president of Fifa in a ballot of AFC members that was due in January 2011.

By doing so, he established a vital claim on Chung's loyalty that would pave the way for a vote-swapping pact which helped seal Qatar's victory in the 2022 World Cup.

In another twist, Bin Hammam gifted Chung the use of his trusted electoral fixer, Manilal Fernando, who had scuppered the South Korean's attempted coup in 2009.

The Sri Lankan set to work lobbying voters, and not just to back Chung for Fifa vice-president and Bin Hammam for AFC president – Fernando himself was seeking a seat on Fifa's Exco.

"I have just returned from Dubai, where I had a meeting with my group," he wrote in an email to Chung on October 20. "All these countries agreed to support Mr Bin Hammam for president, you for Fifa vice-president and myself for Fifa Exco member. Allready [sic] Sri Lanka, India, Bhutan, Nepal and Tajikistan have signed your nomination. In addition Afghanistan, Bangladesh, Maldives, Usbekistan [sic] and Pakistan will send your nominations directly to the AFC to Mr Bin Hammam.

"Mr Bin Hammam is campaigning very hard for you . . . You are in a strong position with Mr Hammam, myself and Warawi [Makudi] all supporting you . . . Like I worked for Hammam last time I will work for him and you this time, do not worry we are winning."

While there is no evidence that Chung knew about Fernando's underhand tactics or had solicited the use of them, in emails to Bin Hammam the Sri Lankan sought large rewards for the countries he had locked down.

Fernando had an official role with the Goal Programme, the Fifa fund for football development in poor countries chaired by Bin Hammam. He sent Bin Hammam a list of Goal Programme payments of $400,000 each to countries in his group – Pakistan, Afghanistan, Nepal, Bhutan, Kyrgyzstan, Uzbekistan and Sri Lanka – asking the Qatari to use his position to obtain approval from the Goal Bureau.

Fernando was also keen that another source of football development money was generously lavished on key voters, writing to Bin Hammam in August to recommend loosening the purse strings of the AFC's Aid 27 budget. "Until elections are over we must see that all funds due from Aid [27] to countries are paid without making it difficult for them with too many questions asked," he suggested.

Bin Hammam continued to lavish football bosses with direct payments from the network of slush funds operated by Kemco. Asatulloev Zarifjon, president of the Tajikistan football federation, received $50,000 in June 2010. The next month, Fernando's ally, Nidal Hadid of the Jordan FA, received $50,000 into his personal bank account from the account of Bin Hammam's daughter, Aisha.

Another loyal ally of Fernando was handsomely rewarded for backing Bin Hammam. Ganesh Thapa, president of the Nepalese FA, was paid a total of £115,000 from two separate Kemco accounts in March and August 2010. He said last week that the money was paid as part of a business arrangement he had with Kemco.

Bangladesh received $25,000 in November 2010, while Pakistan received about $15,000 in the same period. Afghanistan was paid $40,000 from the Kemco account. The documents do not record how the money was spent.

Behind the scenes, Bin Hammam and Chung were talking. The documents show how Bin Hammam had devised a vote-swapping deal that would give Qatar the absolute majority that sealed its 2022 victory. The foundations of his understanding with Chung appear to have been laid during a string of private meetings during the World Cup in South Africa.

Chung, his wife, two daughters, niece and two assistants shared Bin Hammam's private jet between games and were invited to enjoy VIP hospitality alongside the Qatari crown prince, Sheikh Tamim bin Hamad bin Khalifa Al Thani, at a match in Cape Town.

In early June, Chung called Asia's four Exco voters together for a summit over dinner at the Michelangelo hotel. It ought to have been a tense gathering – with the most senior officials of three rival bidding countries in one room representing interests which, on the face of it, were diametrically opposed. In the event, the chronology of the Fifa files suggests the meeting led up to the formation of a crucial pact that would ultimately sweep Qatar to victory.

On July 2, Chung had emailed Bin Hammam a friendly message: "There will be the quarter final between Uruguay and Ghana in Soccer City today. I would like to go with you and watch the game together. On the way, we can talk about various topics of mutual interest."

They had much to discuss. Minutes of a meeting of the AFC executive committee in Kuala Lumpur the next month show a deal was on the table between the Asian members to back each other's 2022 bids in the event that their home countries failed to survive the early voting rounds.

The host of the 2022 tournament was to be decided by a secret multiple-round ballot of Fifa's 22 Exco members in December. The bidding nation that received the fewest votes in each round would be eliminated until a single candidate emerged with an absolute majority of 12.

Bin Hammam could be confident that he had enough African votes in his pocket for Qatar to do well in the first round. But, to reach an absolute majority in the final round, he needed pledges from Exco members to support Qatar once their first choices had been eliminated.

Four members of the Asian federation were vying for 2022: Qatar, South Korea, Japan and Australia. Bin Hammam discounted Australia, as it had no Exco vote, but needed the other two.

Documents record that he told those gathered at the AFC meeting, including Ogura and Chung: "We have four Asian nations bidding and three are represented in the Fifa executive committee.

I, Dr Chung and Mr Ogura will be supporting our respective nations, Qatar, Korea Republic and Japan.

"But we should promise each other that if any of our bid loses, then the support will be switched to the other bidders not only by voting but also by campaigning for each other. I think this is the one thing we owe to our continent."

He knew that if he got their pledges, they would have no chance because he had already stacked the decks in Qatar's favour with the African votes, as *The Sunday Times* revealed last week. Furthermore, by seeking their pledges, Bin Hammam was entering a grey area.

Fifa rules banned member associations and bid committees from striking "any kind of agreement with any other member association or bid committees as regards to the behaviour during the bidding process [which] may influence the bidding process". However, private agreements between Exco members of bidding countries were impossible to police and in effect fell outside the rules.

The ploy appears to have worked – with both Chung and Ogura widely acknowledged to have pledged their loyalty to their fellow Asian bids if their own countries dropped out.

Presenting his bid to the Asian Football Federation the same month, Ogura said: "The AFC President has made it clear that he will support Qatar. While I will surely vote for Japan, Dr Chung must be on his own country's side . . . but no matter what, what is most important for the Asian football family is seeing the World Cup back on Asian soil." It was a decisive moment.

When, on the bitterly cold night of December 2 in Zurich, members of Exco began to cast their secret ballots, Qatar stormed into the lead with 11 votes in the first round – just one shy of the 12 it needed for victory. Japan was level with the US on three while South Korea had four. Australia crashed out of the running with a single vote.

In the second round, Qatar dipped to 10, while Japan fell out with just two and South Korea clung on with five.

With Japan out of the race, Qatar regained a vote in the third round, while South Korea was eliminated.

In the fourth and final round, three votes swung to Qatar, propelling the tiny Gulf state to a victorious total of 14, six points ahead of the US.

The sting in the story came in the Asian elections the next month. Fernando won his Exco seat and Bin Hamman was re-elected AFC president. But, despite all Fernando's best lobbying efforts, the Asian federation members handed Chung's Exco post to a Jordanian prince.

It was clearly a sore blow. But Bin Hammam had not forgotten Chung's loyalty. The correspondence shows that soon after Chung lost his seat, Bin Hammam visited him in Seoul and made him a promise. The Qatari wrote to him after the meeting in February to thank him for the "fabulous" hospitality he had received on the visit. "I will do my best in Zurich and hope it will be successful," he added.

The pledge is revealed in correspondence from Chung's assistant, ES Kim, later that month. "During his visit to Korea, President Hammam mentioned ... that he would propose Dr Chung as honorary Fifa vice-president at the upcoming Fifa Exco meeting and Dr Chung is deeply appreciative of this kind gesture from the AFC president," he wrote. In relation to this matter, Dr Chung would like to send a letter to some of the Fifa Exco members, who, in his opinion, would support President Hammam's proposal. Before sending out such a request letter, Dr Chung would like to sound out the opinion of the AFC president about his plan."

Bin Hammam agreed and, sure enough, Chung got his wish. He was named Fifa's only honorary vice-president later that year, a position he still holds today.

And the real sting is that both Bin Hammam and Manilal Fernando have since been banned for life from world football. In the Qatari's case, this was for a "conflict of interest"; in the Sri Lankan's, for corruption including conflict of interest, bribery and accepting gifts.

Chung and Ogura did not respond to requests for comment last week.

The official rules of conduct

Ethical behaviour: The member association and the bid committee shall conduct any activities in relation to the bidding process in accordance with basic ethical principles such as integrity, responsibility, trustworthiness and fairness. The member association and the bid committee shall refrain from attempting to influence members of the Fifa executive committee or any other Fifa officials, in particular by offering benefits for specific behaviour.

Gifts: The member association and the bid committee shall refrain, and shall ensure that each entity or individual associated or affiliated with it shall refrain, from providing to Fifa or to any representative of Fifa, to any member of the Fifa executive committee, the Fifa inspection group, Fifa consultants, or any of their respective relatives, companions, guests or nominees:

i) any monetary gifts;

ii) any kind of personal advantage that could give even the impression of exerting influence, or conflict of interest, either directly or indirectly, in connection with the bidding process, such as at the beginning of a collaboration, whether with private persons, a company or any authorities, except for occasional gifts that are generally regarded as having symbolic or incidental value and that exclude any influence on a decision in relation to the bidding process;

iii) any benefit, opportunity, promise, remuneration or service to any of such individuals, in connection with the bidding process.

Unfair collaboration: The member association agrees to refrain from collaborating or colluding with any other member association or any other third party with a view to unfairly influencing the outcome of the bidding process.

Insight: Heidi Blake and Jonathan Calvert

SECRET DEALS TURN HEAT ON WORLD CUP

———●———

8 June 2014

THE secrets of how Qatar's top football chief exploited his nation's vast sovereign wealth to help win crucial votes for its World Cup bid are revealed in explosive documents leaked to *The Sunday Times*.

Fresh disclosures from the Fifa files show how Mohamed bin Hammam, the disgraced Fifa vice-president, pulled strings at the top of government and with the country's royal family to arrange meetings and favours for key voters in the months leading up to the World Cup ballot.

The Qatar 2022 committee has maintained it has no links to Bin Hammam since this newspaper last week exposed the slush funds he used to make secret payments of more than $5m in his campaign to seal support for the tiny country's World Cup dream.

But fresh disclosures from the documents today threaten to blow a hole in its claims that he was an "entirely separate" individual with "no official or unofficial role in the bid". Pressure on world football's governing body, Fifa, to take action over this newspaper's evidence intensified last night when the first of its big sponsors, the Japanese electronics giant Sony, broke ranks and called for the damning disclosures to be "investigated appropriately".

Ed Miliband, the Labour leader, piled on further pressure, telling *The Sunday Times* there would be an "overwhelming case for the bidding process to be reopened immediately" if the "startling" evidence in the Fifa files was proven.

The cache of hundreds of millions of documents leaked from the heart of world football today reveals that Bin Hammam:

- Brokered government-level talks for the Thai member of Fifa's executive committee (Exco) to push a gas deal that was potentially worth tens of millions of dollars to Thailand
- Was invited to visit Vladimir Putin to discuss "bilateral relations" in sport between Qatar and Russia a month before their landslide victories in the 2018 and 2022 votes
- Invited the former Exco member Franz Beckenbauer to Doha with bosses from an oil and gas shipping firm, which was employing him as a consultant, to discuss Qatari investments in the maritime sector
- Fixed discreet meetings with the Qatari royal family for at least seven key Exco members, including the Fifa president, Sepp Blatter
- Shored up his own seat on Exco by using secret slush funds to make payments totalling $1.7m to football officials across Asia.

The contents of the Fifa files have reverberated around the globe since *The Sunday Times* revealed last week Bin Hammam's secret campaign to buy up support for the Qatar World Cup bid.

Blatter has maintained a public silence on the allegations since the story broke, despite mounting pressure to strip Qatar of the 2022 World Cup and order a rerun of the vote. He is also facing growing calls for his own resignation.

Michael Garcia, Fifa's in-house investigator, further enraged critics last week by announcing that he would cut short his investigation into corruption in the World Cup bidding process ahead of Fifa's congress in Sao Paolo on Tuesday without reviewing the fresh evidence obtained by *The Sunday Times.*

Miliband joined the attack on Garcia last week, saying: "Few people will have much confidence in the investigation being conducted by Fifa unless it takes full account of the evidence uncovered by *The Sunday Times.*"

He said the Fifa files contained "startling evidence that the decision to make Qatar the host for the World Cup in 2022 may have been corrupted".

The new revelations from the files threaten to throw Fifa's annual congress into disarray before the first match in the 2014 World Cup on Thursday.

Leading Exco members are under intense scrutiny over their secret dealings with Bin Hammam as they gather before the kick-off.

The documents shed new light on how a tiny desert state with virtually no football infrastructure and sweltering summer temperatures of up to 50°C – but an immense treasure chest financed by its vast oil and gas reserves – walked off with the rights to host the world's biggest sporting tournament.

Leaked emails show that Bin Hammam brokered two secret meetings with Qatari royals to discuss a major gas deal with a senior aide to Worawi Makudi, the serving Thai Exco member, in the critical final months before the ballot.

Joe Sim, a businessman and Makudi's chief adviser at the Thai football association, met Qatar's deputy prime minister and the chief executive of Qatargas, the state gas company, in August and September 2010 to discuss a sale of Qatar's liquefied natural gas reserves.

Documents show that the meetings were aimed at "promoting the bilateral co-operations in soccer developments and activities between the Qatari FA and Thai FA".

The exact nature of the deal on the table is unclear, but it came as Thailand sought to save tens of millions of pounds by renegotiating an arrangement with Qatar to purchase 1m tons of liquefied natural gas each year at a fixed price that it considered too high.

When confronted by this newspaper on Friday, Makudi denied that he had received a personal "concession" from his involvement in the gas deal but declined to elaborate.

The documents also reveal for the first time the high-level secret dealings between Qatar and Russia shortly before they swept to victory in the races for 2022 and 2018 – with Russia demolishing England's 2018 bid in the process.

Emails show that Russia invited Bin Hammam to a summit to discuss "bilateral relations" in sport between their two countries on October 30, 2010, a month before the vote on the bids. Two days later, Qatar's ruling emir also flew to Moscow for talks about joint gas production deals between the two countries.

The leaked correspondence shows that Vitaly Mutko, Russia's Exco member and 2018 bid chairman, hailed Bin Hammam's meeting with Putin as "a chance to further promote bilateral relations between our nations in the areas of sport".

Michel Platini, the former French football star who is now president of the European football federation (Uefa), confirmed last week that Bin Hammam had arranged for the Qatar bid committee to meet him in Switzerland.

Bin Hammam was not present at their meeting and did not lobby him, he said, but Platini's revelation puts in question Qatar's claim that its football boss had nothing to do with the World Cup bid.

Flight itineraries, emails and hotel bookings also reveal that, after the bid was won, Franz Beckenbauer, the former German star who had also been a member of Exco, travelled to Doha accompanied by Erck Rickmers, owner of the German shipping firm ER Capital Holding.

The company had hired Beckenbauer as a consultant after he stood down from his Fifa Exco seat in April 2011.

The two men were accompanied by Beckenbauer's agent, Marcus Hoefl, and three other executives from the shipping company, which owns a fleet that transports oil and gas on the high seas.

A spokesman for the firm confirmed last week that they were there to discuss Qatari investments in the maritime sector, but said no contract was signed as a result of the meetings with senior Qatari officials, which Bin Hammam did not attend. Beckenbauer declined to comment.

The documents lay bare the extent to which Bin Hammam used his connections to usher key football figures into the inner sanctum of Qatari society for meetings with the emir, the crown prince and other senior royals as part of the campaign to secure support for the bid.

The evidence that Bin Hammam was able to go straight to the top in his campaign to seal support for the 2022 bid undermines Qatar's claim that the disgraced football official had no role in its campaign.

The files show that Bin Hammam was fixing the meetings for members of Qatar's ruling family with football's most powerful men at the same time as using a network of secret slush funds to buy up a groundswell of support among the bosses of national football associations.

This week's Fifa files reveal details of the $1.7m he paid from the funds, controlled by his private company Kemco, often into the bank accounts of officials whose support he was seeking across Asia.

The glut of Asian payments came as Bin Hammam was campaigning for both the Qatar World Cup bid and for his own re-election to the post of president of the Asian Football Confederation.

The Qatar bid committee denies all wrongdoing.

Insight: Heidi Blake and Jonathan Calvert

SECRET TAPES REVEAL FIFA COVERED UP CORRUPTION

<hr>

7 June 2015

SENSATIONAL allegations about bribes in the contest to host the 2010 World Cup, even including a claim that a rival bidder actually won the vote before it was then rigged in South Africa's favour, are revealed today in extracts from secret tapes released by *The Sunday Times*.

The tapes expose the alleged World Cup bribes that are now at the heart of the US investigation into Fifa, but were suppressed by the sports body and its president, Sepp Blatter, for five years after they were handed to Fifa by *The Sunday Times*.

Top Fifa officials were filmed by undercover reporters from this newspaper talking candidly about the million-dollar bungs to host the World Cup.

They include an extraordinary allegation by one of the 24 Fifa executive committee (Exco) members who took part in the ballot for the 2010 World Cup that the contest was rigged and Morocco had actually beaten South Africa. South Africa, which denies the claims, went on to host the tournament.

Ismail Bhamjee, an Exco member from Botswana, said he and his colleagues conferred after the vote and realised Morocco had won the secret ballot. "After talking with everybody . . . Whose votes went where? We're all colleagues, you know. And then we found out that actually Morocco won by two votes," he said.

He admitted it was possible some Exco members might have lied about their votes. But he went on to list those he understood had supported Morocco and seemed convinced the north Africans had won. He speculated that the ballot papers, which were tallied behind closed doors, could have been deliberately miscounted. He added: "Please, this is very secret."

The tapes were first handed to Fifa by this newspaper in October 2010 with a request it should investigate the serious allegations of corruption they contained.

In light of the US investigation into the 2010 World Cup, last night *The Sunday Times* posted some of the more shocking allegations on its website. Among the clips are claims by ex-voters and senior officials that:

- They themselves had been offered bribes by Morocco; they also named other Exco voters who had taken the money from the north African country and South Africa.
- The Exco members conferred after the 2010 vote and worked out that Morocco had won the right to host the 2010 tournament by two votes.
- Jack Warner, the former Fifa vice-president, had accepted a $1m bribe from the Moroccan bid.
- Warner had double-crossed his Moroccan bribers and voted for rivals South Africa because they offered even more money.
- Morocco offered to pay a former Fifa general secretary to approach Exco members and offer them bribes.

Neither the bids nor the Exco members were ever investigated by Fifa. The newspaper did not circulate the tapes more widely for legal reasons.

The tapes also contained previously published allegations that Qatar was offering bribes of up to $1.2m in the contest to host the 2022 World Cup. Qatar has always strongly denied this.

When the four former Fifa officials were secretly filmed in 2010 they talked openly about the vote that had taken place in May 2004. Officially, South Africa triumphed by 14 votes to 10.

The contest is now central to the US inquiry, which is examining similar claims made by Chuck Blazer, the former American Fifa Exco member, that Warner was offered $1m by Morocco but switched his vote when South Africa promised him $10m.

The failure by Fifa to act on the tapes may leave the sports body open to further action from the US authorities. Prosecutors in America are considering charges against Fifa for obstruction of justice for overlooking a litany of corruption allegations over the years, many of which have been brought to its attention by this newspaper.

The video recordings were made during an undercover investigation by *The Sunday Times* in the months before the December 2010 ballot to host both the 2018 and 2022 World Cups. Reporters posed as lobbyists working to promote one of the bids to penetrate the secretive world of the Fifa Exco.

They offered to hire a series of former Fifa officials as "consultants" and each one openly acknowledged that Exco members had been paid for their votes in the past.

In the first of the meetings, Bhamjee told the reporters about the $1m bribe Warner has allegedly been paid by Morocco for his vote. "I know they gave Jack Warner personally a lot of money for the Concacaf [Warner's North America confederation]. But please, this is confidential," he was recorded saying.

He said Warner "ditched" Morocco because the South Africans offered him a bigger bribe. The money took a few years to arrive in his account and at one point he phoned Bhamjee by mistake, believing he was talking to his South African contact.

Bhamjee recalled: "[Warner said:] 'Where is my money?', you know. And I said, 'Hey, this is Ismail.' [Warner replied:] 'Ahhh, I speak to you later', and he turned down the phone."

His claim about Warner was corroborated by Michel Bacchini, a former Fifa director of competitions, who had worked as a consultant to the Moroccan bid team. Bacchini told the undercover reporters: "But, Jack, they [the Moroccans] were paying him and at the end when they were voting here in Zurich, you know, he was making a big scene, he was running out of the hotel complaining that somebody was cheating.

"He was the guy who cheated, he was making a big scenario out of it. I know a hundred per cent that he was voting for the South Africans and pretended to vote for the Moroccans. I always said you never have to pay any money upfront."

In another recording, Ahongalu Fusimalohi, the former Fifa Exco member from Tonga, said Morocco had offered him a $150,000 bribe for his vote. He had refused but other members had accepted.

Despite repeated requests and letters to Fifa, the sports body defiantly refused to take any action about these allegations despite being handed the tapes five years ago. The evidence was also submitted to the inquiry into World Cup corruption by Fifa's ethics investigator, Michael Garcia, which was completed last year, but he too disregarded it.

On Friday, Fifa issued a short statement in response to our question of why it had sat on the evidence.

It said: "It cannot have escaped even *The Sunday Times*'s attention that these matters are being investigated by the proper authorities, ie, government agencies, not newspapers. And Fifa is fully co-operating with these investigations."

Insight: Jonathan Calvert

2015
THE DOPING SCANDAL

The biggest leak of blood-test data in sporting history, revealed to Insight, showed that athletes competing at some of the world's most prestigious sporting events were cheating on an extraordinary scale. A third of medals, including 55 golds, had been won in Olympic and world championship endurance events by athletes with suspicious test results, yet the authorities had failed to take any of those medals away. There was also a dangerous side to the glory: many athletes were found to be risking death or disability by recklessly using transfusions or banned red-cell-boosting drugs.

Following the investigation, the head of the international governing body for athletics, Lamine Diack, was arrested. In 2020, he was found guilty of accepting bribes from athletes in exchange for covering up positive drug tests which allowed them to continue competing in major competitions, including the London 2012 Olympics. As well as exposing corruption at the head of the very association tasked with regulating cheating and dangerous doping, Insight's work also formed part of a wider argument that Russia was involved in systematic doping. This resulted in the country's ban from the 2016 Olympics.

REVEALED: SPORT'S DIRTIEST SECRET

—————●—————

2 August 2015

SECRET data revealing the extraordinary extent of cheating by athletes at the world's most prestigious events can be disclosed for the first time today, after the biggest leak of blood-test data in sporting history.

The Sunday Times and the German broadcaster ARD/WDR have been given access to a database containing more than 12,000 blood tests from 5,000 athletes, including many household names from across the world.

The blood-doping data reveals that a third of medals, including 55 golds, have been won in endurance events at the Olympics and world championships by athletes who have recorded suspicious tests – yet the authorities have failed to take away any of the medals.

The data shows that athletics is in the same "diabolical state" as cycling in the scandal-hit era of Lance Armstrong, according to world experts who describe the findings as a "shameful betrayal" of clean athletes.

Several British athletes have lost out in major events to competitors who were under suspicion. They include Jessica Ennis-Hill, the star heptathlete, who believes she was robbed of a gold medal in the world championships.

Many athletes are risking death or disability by recklessly using transfusions or banned red-cell-boosting drugs such as erythropoietin (EPO) which make their blood so thick they should be seeking hospital treatment rather than competing.

The data in the files has been kept under lock and key for years at the International Association of Athletics Federations' (IAAF) Monaco headquarters, but was released by a whistleblower seriously concerned about its "disturbing" content.

Two of the world's foremost anti-doping experts, who reviewed the files for this newspaper, said the data provided compelling evidence that the IAAF had failed to take sufficient action against athletes with highly suspicious tests.

Robin Parisotto, a scientist who regularly reviews athletes' blood tests, said: "Never have I seen such an alarmingly abnormal set of blood values ... So many athletes appear to have doped with impunity, and it is damning that the IAAF appears to have idly sat by and let this happen."

The second expert, exercise physiologist Michael Ashenden, who gave evidence against Armstrong, was equally appalled: "For the IAAF to have harvested millions of dollars from the broadcasting of athletics events around the world ... yet only devote a relative pittance of those funds towards anti-doping, when they could see the terrible truth of what lay beneath the surface, is ... a shameful betrayal of their primary duty to police their sport and to protect clean athletes."

The disclosures raise serious questions about whether results can be trusted at the biennial world athletics championships which will be held in Beijing in three weeks' time. The files include the following incendiary revelations:

- More than 800 athletes – one in seven of those named in the files – have recorded blood-test results described by one of the experts as "highly suggestive of doping or at the very least abnormal"

- A top UK athlete is among seven Britons with "suspicious" blood scores. The athlete scored the single most abnormal blood score of all the 490 tests on British athletes

- Ten medals at London 2012 were won by athletes who have had dubious test results

- Twenty-one athletes recorded blood values so extreme they risked heart attacks or strokes, and should have been given emergency treatment to have their blood drained

- Star names such as Mo Farah and Usain Bolt, who have been the subject of whispering campaigns, emerge as clean with no abnormal results

- More than a third of the world's fastest times in endurance events were achieved by athletes whose tests have triggered suspicion.

The IAAF threatened to take out an injunction preventing *The Sunday Times* from publishing details from the files, but it dropped its action at the eleventh hour on Friday. It said the newspaper "is in unlawful possession of the IAAF's entire blood-testing database of over 12,000 samples covering the years 2001–2012, or at least a very substantial part of it".

Yesterday Ennis-Hill, the face of the London 2012 Olympics, called on the IAAF and the World Anti-Doping Agency to address the problems highlighted in the files. Ennis-Hill narrowly lost out on gold in the 2011 world championships to a Russian athlete who had recorded abnormal blood results, according to the files.

She said: "It is never good to hear of new possible doping offences in my sport, but if we are to stop a few athletes thinking cheating is acceptable, we have to explore all information that comes to light, however damaging it is for the sport as a whole."

Ashenden and Parisotto examined the blood tests of athletes who won medals in endurance events at the Olympics and world championships between 2001 and 2012. They flagged up many athletes who were "likely" to have doped and should have faced a potential ban as they were able to rule out all other factors. Others were classified as "suspicious" requiring further investigation.

They found that doping had become so widespread that 146 medals fell into these two categories, including the 55 golds. Half the star athletes who had won at least two gold medals at the world championships had recorded likely doping or suspicious blood-test results.

The experts were disappointed that new measures introduced by the IAAF to crack down on unscrupulous athletes by using a biological passport had had only a limited effect.

Unlike other sports, athletics has allowed athletes with highly abnormal blood scores to continue to compete. This meant that before the introduction of the biological passport in 2009, the IAAF had no way of sanctioning athletes who transfused their own blood to boost performance.

Urine tests targeted at such athletes might detect the blood-boosting drug EPO, but would not catch those using their own blood to cheat. After 2009, Ashenden says that despite the introduction of the biological passport, his analysis of the data shows nearly 70 athletes with suspicious blood-test results still escaped censure.

Russia emerges from the files as the blood-doping centre of the world, with more than 80% of the country's medals won by athletes who had given a suspicious blood test at some point in their career. Kenya, renowned for producing great distance-runners, is also a doping hotbed, with questions over 18 of the country's medals.

Last week, an IAAF spokesman said: "The IAAF has always been at the forefront in combating doping – researching and implementing new analytical techniques and methodologies."

The IAAF said that before the introduction of its biological passport in 2009, its testers had followed up all "atypical" results with urine tests for the blood-boosting drug EPO and then target-tested those athletes over time. Since 2009, the IAAF said it had "pursued more cases under the passport system than all other anti-doping organisations together". It says it is spending $2m (£1.3m) a year on combating cheating. "As a percentage of overall annual budget, this is the highest of any sport," it said.

The disclosures come as the IAAF is preparing to elect its new president in two weeks, with Britain's Lord Coe standing against the Ukrainian former pole-vaulting star Sergey Bubka.

Coe, an IAAF vice-president, has called for the sports body to spend more money on the fight against drugs cheats, and has vowed to set up an independent anti-doping agency for athletics. "The gap between the positive test and sanction must be reduced," he said earlier this year. "It would cost more money, but I'd find it. I'd have to. It would remove the conspiracy theories."

Insight: Jonathan Calvert and George Arbuthnott

A CLEAN SWEEP IN THE DIRTIEST RACE

2 August 2015

THE flash bulbs popped as the fast-moving pack of elite female athletes jostled for position in the Helsinki Olympic stadium. At stake was sporting immortality: world champion in arguably the toughest track race of all, the 1500 metres.

Summoning up her last reserves of energy, Maryam Yusuf Jamal, a young Ethiopian in her first professional season, quickened her stride and battled to the front.

Then the extraordinary surge happened. Four women in the red, white and blue of Russia surrounded Jamal and pushed her off-balance as they powered to the front.

Millions of television viewers worldwide saw the Russians sprint to the first three medal positions and also take fifth place – an unparalleled triumph for the Russian team.

Experts watching in the stadium that afternoon at the 2005 world championships scratched their heads. Was this extraordinary achievement the result of advanced training and discipline, a freak of nature – or some other, more murky reason?

The anti-doping unit of the International Association of Athletics Federations (IAAF) should have been aware of the precise answer to that question. It had the results of eight blood tests the Russians had undergone since arriving in Finland.

Those test results have now been reviewed by one of the world's foremost experts in blood-doping who has concluded that the Russian performance was a "slam dunk" case of cheating.

The women's tests indicated that they had probably injected themselves with the banned blood-boosting drug erythropoietin

(EPO) or transfused a bag of their own blood into their veins to enhance their performance.

Yet despite having the test results, the IAAF said nothing at the time of the event, and the medals from the "dirtiest race" in the 2005 world championships remain on the record book today.

The injustice at Helsinki was not just a question of medals. As the Russians surged to the front, Britain's Helen Clitheroe struggled at the back of the pack, finishing 10th. It was a career-defining defeat for her as she was no longer able to attract funding to continue in the event she loved.

This was an unfair outcome. Experts say that blood-doping can cut a 1500 metres runner's time by several seconds. For athletes running clean, this could have made the difference between 10th and 1st place.

After being told about the Russian women's blood-test results last week, she said: "I didn't think there was any cheating going on. After that race I just thought, well, maybe I'm just not as good as them.

"It is disappointing because perhaps I was as good as them after all. That's the disappointment. But that race is something I can never change."

The Helsinki blood tests have been a closely guarded secret until now. They are contained within the biggest leak of doping test data in sporting history, which has been handed to *The Sunday Times* and the German broadcaster ARD by a whistleblower.

The data covers the results of 12,359 tests from more than 5,000 athletes conducted over an 11-year period from the 2001 world championships, when the IAAF started taking blood samples, up to the eve of the 2012 London Olympics.

In the opinion of two experts, the data shows that 146 world championship and Olympic medals in endurance events such as long-distance running were won by athletes whose blood-test results were considered to be suspicious on one or more occasions in their career.

This amounts to a third of all medals in endurance events during that time.

Hundreds of top competitors recorded abnormal results. In some cases, the results were so abnormal that the athletes risked death from a stroke or heart attack.

The data shows that star British endurance athletes such as Jessica Ennis-Hill and Mo Farah are clean from blood-doping but unknowingly competed against athletes who are suspected of cheating.

In the London 2012 Olympics, 10 of the medals in endurance events were won by athletes who had recorded suspicious test results at some point in the preceding years.

The data suggests that the use of banned performance-enhancing substances such as EPO and the outlawed practice of boosting blood counts with transfusions were just as commonplace in athletics as they were in the scandal-hit years of cycling.

Despite the introduction of the "biological passport" in 2009 to crack down on doping, the cheats are still often not being caught. The experts who reviewed the files pinpointed dozens of cases where highly suspicious test results had not led to any ban or suspension.

The disclosures are a damning indictment of the IAAF, which for years has kept this toxic information under lock and key at its palatial villa headquarters in Monaco, taking action against only a small proportion of the athletes under suspicion.

There are now calls for reform as the IAAF prepares to elect a new president this month. Britain's candidate, Lord Coe, is leading the charge by campaigning for more money to be spent creating an independent anti-doping tribunal.

Questions will continue to be asked, however, about whether clean athletes will again lose out at the next world championships in Beijing in only three weeks' time.

If analysts need a past case for comparison, the women's 1500 metres in Helsinki 10 years ago is the most egregious. The Russians' blood tests were so abnormal that they should have tripped every alert on the IAAF anti-doping team's checklist.

The test for blood-doping involves cross-referencing the numbers of new and old red cells in an athlete's blood. The result is called an "off-score". Any score above 103 is abnormal for women athletes, but the Russians were way above that.

The winner, Tatyana Tomashova, who was the world champion and Olympic silver medallist, had an extraordinary off-score of 129 on the day of the race.

Yuliya Chizhenko-Fomenko was even higher with a score of 140. She finished second but was disqualified for pushing and her silver medal went to Olga Yegorova – who in 2001 had tested positive for EPO but got off on a technicality.

Yegorova's off-score at Helsinki was 124. Yelana Soboleva, who came fifth, scored 136.

The figures were so extreme that one of the Russian women should have had her blood drained in hospital because the haemoglobin concentration was perilously high, experts say.

Athletes sometimes argue that their high off-scores are natural, particularly if the tests are taken after a race.

The probability of Tomashova's and Yegorova's results being natural were close to one in 100,000, however. And when an off-score is over 131 – as it was for the other two Russians – there is just a one-in-a-million chance of it being due to natural causes, according to one of the biggest scientific studies of elite endurance athletes undertaken, which was published two years before the Helsinki race.

The odds against all four teammates in the same race having naturally high off-scores was in the trillions. There could only be one conclusion given the improbable coincidence of such outlandish results across the team. The experts believe they were cheating.

The four Russian women were not the only athletes with jaw-dropping blood scores at Helsinki. Rashid Ramzi, a 25-year-old Moroccan athlete representing Bahrain, stunned the world by taking gold in both the men's 1500m and the 800m, an unprecedented achievement in the modern era.

Ramzi had had an unremarkable career but his fortunes had changed when he went to Bahrain to train alongside Brahim Boulami, a Moroccan world record holder who had been caught using EPO.

Steve Cram, the British former 1500m world champion, would later write of Ramzi's triumphs in Helsinki: "He almost embarrassed his competitors with his ease of victory. New-found ability in your mid-twenties has the odour of North Shields fish quay on a warm day."

There was certainly more than a whiff of scandal about his doping test results, which can now be revealed. For men, any off-score over 119 is regarded as abnormal. On the day that Ramzi cruised to victory in the 1500m, his off-score was 158. When he won the 800m it was 148.

Both results were a one-in-a-million chance of being natural. He too was competing with a dangerously viscous blood that should have put him in hospital.

The IAAF was aware of how abnormal the blood-test results for the four Russians and Ramzi were compared with the majority of other athletes in Helsinki. It says now that it did follow up with urine tests on all five athletes, which proved to be negative. They were targeted for further testing and ended after failing those tests.

At the time, the IAAF had no procedure for sanctioning athletes on the basis of their blood tests alone. Athletes who were using blood transfusions could have sky-high scores and never be banned.

In 2009, Ramzi tested positive for CERA, a previously undetectable successor to EPO, following his gold at the 2008 Beijing Olympics. The four Russian women were caught substituting their urine with someone else's in tests designed to detect EPO. But all five were allowed keep their world championship medals from 2005.

None of the Russian athletes or Ramzi responded last week to our requests for comment on their abnormal test results.

Their cases are just the tip of an iceberg. This newspaper's analysis shows that every world championship and Olympic Games since 2001 has been contaminated by athletes with suspiciously high off-scores.

More than 800 athletes – one in seven of those named in the data – have recorded one or more blood-test results deemed to be abnormal. The baseline for abnormal is any score that has less than a one-in-100 chance of being natural. Many athletes were way beyond that point.

The worst offenders were from Russia, which accounted for 415 of the abnormal tests, followed by Ukraine (102), Morocco (82), Spain (81), Kenya (77), Turkey (52), Greece (42), Belarus (42), Romania (32), Portugal (32), and the US (32).

Twelve athletes from Britain were found to have given 19 abnormal test results. They include a successful athlete who on three occasions recorded off-scores that had a less than a one-in-1,000 chance of being natural. The athlete, who cannot be named, denies cheating and has threatened legal action.

The data containing these revelations has been leaked by an anonymous whistleblower who is concerned about the IAAF's apparent failure to clamp down on many blatant cases and wants to see genuine reform in the federation's anti-doping work.

The whistleblower believes that athletes with abnormal results may be under pressure from national training programmes, and has requested that they are not humiliated by being named.

The Sunday Times disclosed only the identities of a handful who were subsequently banned.

This newspaper asked two of the world's foremost experts on doping detection, Robin Parisotto and Michael Ashenden, to review the data relating to medallists at the world championships and the Olympics between 2001 and 2012. Both were shocked by the evidence.

Parisotto, a stem-cell scientist, and Ashenden, an exercise physiologist, have been called upon many times to give opinions in anti-doping cases since they jointly developed the first test for EPO 15 years ago.

Parisotto currently sits on the International Cycling expert panel and Ashenden has been a member of a similar body at the World Anti-Doping Agency.

They have asked that their judgements on individual athletes not be published except for a few extreme cases and be used only to show a more general picture of suspicious activity across athletics.

They employed a simple colour-coded formula when analysing the athletes on the files. Red was for an athlete who was "likely to be doping" requiring potential disciplinary action, and yellow for those whose tests were "suspicious" and therefore warranted further investigation.

A third of all medals were won by athletes who were found to have had a suspicious test at some stage in their careers. Some tests had been recorded at the time of the medal win, while others were at different events or when the athlete was in out-of-competition training.

The total of 146 medals awarded to 76 athletes who had given dubious blood tests included 55 golds. In more than half of these cases, at least one of the experts concluded that the athletes were "likely" to be doping and the others should have merited urgent follow-up investigations. A small number of these competitors have been banned over the years, but only four medals have been stripped by the authorities.

The experts found that, astonishingly, 80% of Russia's medal-winners had recorded suspicious scores at some point in their careers. The remarkable achievements of Kenya's runners, which academic studies have tried to explain by climate, culture or genetics, may also have a sinister side. No fewer than 18 of the country's medals were won by athletes with suspicious blood-test results.

Ashenden said he had been taken aback by some of the results, which were "grotesque in their extremity" and "quite easily the worst I have ever seen". He told this newspaper: "The database reveals that at every world championships and Olympic Games since Sydney 2000, medals have been won in at least one of the distance events by an athlete who at some point in their career had most probably engaged in blood-doping.

"Often two out of the three medallists had probably engaged in blood-doping at some point in their career. In one event the entire podium comprised athletes who at some point had most probably engaged in blood-doping."

His comments were echoed by Parisotto, who described the database as both "damming and disturbing".

"Never have I seen such an alarming abnormal set of blood values," he said. "Damning in that so many athletes appear to have doped with impunity without repercussions but more damning in that the IAAF appears to have idly sat by and let this happen.

"Disturbing in the sense that so many clean athletes appear to have been cheated out of winning medals but perhaps more disturbing that many athletes had willingly placed themselves at significant risk to their health.

"It is inexplicable that over 800 athletes within the database demonstrated blood results highly suggestive of doping or at the very least abnormal."

He added: "In no fewer than four world championship races all podium winners showed evidence of doping. Was nobody watching?"

The data shows that 21 athletes had such sludgy haemoglobin levels that they risked fatal heart attacks and should have been taken to hospital to have their blood drained.

Parisotto said the IAAF should be made accountable for reckless levels of apparent doping which have "blossomed" over the years on its watch. "With so many athletes at risk of suffering heart attacks, strokes and potentially even death, where is the duty of care in all of this?" he asked.

The IAAF said last week that it "has always been at the forefront in combatting anti-doping, searching and implementing new analytical techniques and methodologies".

It said that before the introduction of the biological passport in 2009 its testers had followed up all results that were deemed "atypical" with immediate urine tests for EPO and then target-tested those athletes in and out of competition. Athletes would not have been banned for one abnormal test alone, the IAAF says.

Since the introduction of the passport, the IAAF now passes those "atypical" results to three scientific experts for analysis and will ban athletes if "there is an overwhelming likelihood that the athlete engaged in prohibited doping".

The IAAF said it had "systematically pursued all passport profiles flagged as atypical" and had taken "more cases under the passport system than all other anti-doping organisations together".

It also said it had committed $4m to its anti-doping budget in 2014 and 2015. "As a percentage of overall annual budget, this is the highest of any sport," it said.

Insight: George Arbuthnott, Jonathan Calvert, David Collins and Bojan Pancevski

SHADOW OVER THE LONDON MARATHON

———•———

9 August 2015

THE London marathon was won seven times in 12 years by athletes who have recorded suspicious blood scores that indicate they could have doped, according to the biggest leak of drug test data in sporting history.

The tally represents nearly 30% of winners in the 24 men's and women's races. The data reveals the extent of suspected cheating by elite athletes in the six internationally famous city marathons around the world.

One in four was won by athletes who had given blood tests that suggest they may have doped to improve their performance over time.

In the wake of last week's revelations about widespread cheating in the Olympics and world championships, eight British athletes, including Mo Farah, are publishing their blood test data to show they are clean.

Their decision to publish flies in the face of efforts by the International Association of Athletics Federations (IAAF) and British Athletics to persuade the athletes to keep the results hidden from public view.

On Friday the World Anti-Doping Agency (WADA) announced it would launch an "urgent" investigation into allegations of widespread doping made by this newspaper last weekend. The IAAF has agreed to hand its full database, seen by this newspaper, to the anti-doping body.

This weekend *The Sunday Times* makes fresh disclosures based on an expert analysis of the IAAF's database which include:

- The winners of 34 big city marathons – one in four – should have faced censure or at least been investigated over evidence of potential blood-doping within their test results
- The organisers of the London and Chicago marathons say the IAAF and the national anti-doping authorities failed to tell them that some athletes were competing with blood so heavily doped that it threatened their health
- The former world No 1 marathon runner Liliya Shobukhova recorded extreme blood scores for nine years before action was finally taken against her. Two of her scores had a billion-to-one chance of being natural
- Athletes with suspicious blood scores collected more than £3m for winning city marathons
- Only a third of the 105 athletes who were identified as likely cheats since the IAAF brought in new anti-doping measures have been banned.

The House of Commons culture, media and sport committee is set to hold a hearing into widespread doping in athletics in the autumn and is likely to call Lord Coe, the IAAF vice-president, who said last week that this newspaper had declared "war on athletics".

Jesse Norman, chairman of the committee, has expressed his concern about evidence that suggests the athletics authorities were doing too little to combat the blood-doping cheats. "If these allegations are true, they paint a damning picture of the state of world athletics and the IAAF in particular," Norman said.

The IAAF last week again sent a legal letter to this newspaper asking it to destroy any copies of the blood-doping data – a database containing more than 12,000 blood tests from 5,000 athletes, including many household names from across the world.

The data, which does not prove doping, was leaked by a whistleblower who was seriously concerned about the "disturbing" content and was analysed by two of the world's foremost doping detection experts, Michael Ashenden and Robin Parisotto. Their analysis of the data indicated that a third of all medals in the Olympics and world championships endurance events were won by athletes with suspicious blood results between 2001 and 2012.

These findings were based on a range of blood scores for each athlete rather than just one as the IAAF attempted to claim last week.

The marathons worst affected were Chicago, London, New York and Boston. In London seven wins, six second places and seven third places out of 24 male and female races were secured by athletes whose blood tests were deemed suspicious by the experts. A total of 32 suspicious athletes finished in the top three positions at the marathons. Some of the abnormal blood tests were recorded at the time of the event and others at some point in their career.

A number of the athletes appeared to be risking a stroke or heart attack by using blood transfusions or banned red-cell-boosting drugs such as erythropoietin (EPO) that made their blood so dense they should have been seeking hospital treatment rather than competing.

The results show the extent of blood test abnormalities registered by Shobukhova, who was the best-performing female marathon runner in the world for several years.

She is a three-times winner of the Chicago marathon and also a victor in London in 2010 – netting a total of more than £1m in prize money.

Shobukhova had recorded extreme blood scores for nine years before the athletics authorities took action against her in 2014.

Her blood was dangerously thick from doping when she recorded her first victory at Chicago in 2009 and two years later when she ran the second-fastest time for a woman at the same event. Both tests had a one-in-a-billion chance of being natural.

However, organisers of the Chicago marathon were not told about the blood scores carried out by the IAAF and the United States anti-doping authorities that suggested her life was in danger.

"We never received any information indicating that Liliya Shobukhova's Chicago blood test results were abnormal," said a Chicago marathon spokeswoman.

The London marathon also said it had been kept in the dark about the suspicious blood tests discovered by the IAAF.

Nick Bitel, the London marathon chief executive, said the race had a zero tolerance of doping.

"We will certainly be asking the IAAF for their reaction to this and trying to understand what lessons have to be learnt for the future," he said.

The IAAF said yesterday that it had written to some athletes advising them not to compete because of their blood scores.

"It is then up to the athlete, in full knowledge of the risk, to decide whether or not to compete," said a spokesman.

The IAAF said on Friday that it was "fully co-operating" with the independent investigative team set up by WADA.

It added that it will open its full database, including pre-2009 test results, to WADA and "will invite WADA officials to study that material with the support of relevant IAAF anti-doping experts with immediate effect".

Insight: Jonathan Calvert, George Arbuthnott and David Collins

ANOTHER MARATHON VICTORY –
AND A PERSONAL BEST FOR CHEATING

9 August 2015

THE word "money" momentarily wrapped itself around the midriff of Liliya Shobukhova when she broke the tape at the London marathon on a grey April day five years ago.

It was a serendipitous moment: the 32-year-old Russian athlete was in the best form of her career and it was making her rich. But Virgin Money, the sponsor whose emblem was on the finishing tape, cannot have known the truth behind her victory.

Shobukhova was showered with more than £1m in prize money as a result of performances in London and Chicago, and she enjoyed lucrative sponsorship by Nike.

The evidence against her had been accumulating since she recorded exceptionally suspicious blood-doping scores in 2005. It is in the data of the International Association of Athletics Federations (IAAF) examined by *The Sunday Times* and the German broadcaster ARD/WDR.

Yet the athletics authorities did not strip her of her marathon victories until last week– after we had taken the lid off the extent of blood-doping among long-distance runners by revealing that a third of endurance medals at the Olympics and world championships between 2001 and 2012 went to athletes with suspicious blood test results.

This weekend we can disclose what two of the world's foremost anti-doping experts concluded when they looked at the blood data for the male and female winners of the big city marathons: London, New York, Chicago, Boston, Berlin and Tokyo.

They found that from 2001 to 2012 the London marathon was won seven times by athletes who had recorded suspicious blood tests at some point in their careers. As there were 24 male and female golds in those 12 years, this is more than 29% of the total.

Worldwide, of the 142 male and female winners in the six big city marathons over the same period, the winners of 34 showed evidence of potential blood-doping within their test results. They collected more than £3m in prize money for their victories.

For several years Shobukhova was the top female marathon runner in the world. Yet when she stepped up to marathons from her previous distance of 5,000 metres, there was already enough data in the IAAF's records to suggest she was cheating.

In endurance events, especially the marathon, athletes can significantly improve their performance by taking the banned drug erythropoietin (EPO) or by extracting their own blood and re-infusing it days before a race.

Blood samples are taken so that testers can cross-reference the numbers of new and old red cells in an athlete's blood. The result is called an "off-score". Any score above 103 is abnormal for female athletes.

When Shobukhova won the European Cup 5,000m in Florence in 2005 her off-score was 127, and it had risen to 135 by the time she competed in the 5,000m at the world championships in Helsinki that year, finishing ninth.

These figures should have raised the alarm among the testers. When an off-score is over 131 there is a one-in-a-million chance it is natural, according to one of the biggest scientific studies of elite endurance athletes undertaken. It also represents a thickening of the blood that could be fatal.

Shobukhova continued competing and her off-score was 132 when she finished fourth in the European Cup in Munich in 2007.

The IAAF says it would have targeted any athlete with such suspicious blood scores for further testing, but the data records only one further blood test on Shobukhova in the two years and four months after Munich.

It is likely that she was given extra urine tests but these would not have helped the testers to discover whether she was illicitly undergoing blood transfusions, say our experts.

When Shobukhova began running marathons in 2009, her blood scores started to soar even further. In October 2009, she powered to victory in the Chicago marathon with an off-score of 153. It had a less than a one-in-a-billion chance of being natural.

Other sporting organisations conducting blood tests – such as the International Cycling Union (UCI) – had for years barred any competitor whose blood was as viscous as Shobukhova's was in Chicago.

In 2009 the IAAF introduced a biological passport system, which gave its testing unit the power to recommend banning an athlete if a panel of experts agreed a series of off-scores suggested "an overwhelming likelihood" of doping.

Six months later she won her third successive Chicago marathon in a time that made her the second fastest female in history.

Only Britain's Paula Radcliffe has run a better time.

It was the pinnacle of Shobukhova's career – and also a personal best for her off-score, which was 156.

The IAAF had more than enough data to take action against the Russian champion.

However, she escaped censure and the following year she was free to compete in the London Olympics. She was one of the favourites to take the gold but pulled up with a thigh strain during the race.

Another two years passed before the athletics authorities finally took action against Shobukhova. In April last year the Russian athletics federation announced that she was to be banned for two years for "abnormalities" in her biological passport.

Radcliffe, a long-time anti-doping campaigner, was unforgiving when the news of the ban broke.

"Finally exposed as a drug cheat. Fraud on so many levels, so much money effectively stolen in appearance fees, winnings and endorsements," Radcliffe tweeted.

But it was not until three days ago – in the wake of this newspaper's story about blood-doping, and after we had approached her about her off-scores – that the IAAF at last stripped Shobukhova of all her marathon titles from 2009 and banned her for three years.

The IAAF's apparent failure to clamp down hard on this and other blatant cases lay behind the decision of an anonymous whistleblower to show the association's leaked data to *The Sunday Times*. The whistleblower wanted to see genuine reform in its anti-doping work.

Two experts on doping detection – Robin Parisotto and Michael Ashenden – have helped *The Sunday Times* by analysing the data.

Parisotto, a stem cell scientist, is on the UCI's expert panel; and Ashenden, an exercise physiologist, has been a member of a similar body at the World Anti-Doping Agency.

At the request of the experts and the whistleblower, names of athletes with consistently abnormal off-scores are not being published unless they have been publicly punished by IAAF.

Besides Shobhukhova, Abderrahim Goumri, a Moroccan, is in this category. He came second in the London marathon in 2007 and third in 2008. Yet he had recorded highly abnormal test results since 2003. He was finally suspended in 2012 for fluctuations in his biological passport.

When Shobukhova won the 2009 Chicago marathon, Goumri finished second in the men's race. His off-score was 166. Men's off-scores are naturally higher than women's but scores above 119 are abnormal.

Goumri's blood score was the second highest of all the 6,600 male tests on the IAAF's anti-doping files.

His training partner and friend, Rashid Ramzi, a double world champion and Olympic silver medallist, was eighth on the same list with an off-score of 158.

Insight: Jonathan Calvert, George Arbuthnott and David Collins

2012 MEDALLISTS 'PAID BRIBES' TO BE AT GAMES

8 November 2015

GOLD and silver medal winners at the 2012 Olympics are on a list of eight athletes who are alleged to have escaped bans for doping after huge bribes were paid to the heads of world athletics so they could compete at the London Games.

The allegations are being investigated by French prosecutors who suspect the former president of the International Association of Athletics Federations (IAAF) and its ex-head of anti-doping took bribes totalling €1.2m (£857,000) on behalf of the athletes.

The revelation sheds new light on the IAAF's failure to crack down on widespread doping in athletics as detailed in an investigation by *The Sunday Times* and the German broadcaster ARD/WDR in the summer.

This newspaper has obtained the list of eight Russian athletes who prosecutors claim should have been banned by the IAAF prior to the London Olympics.

However, they escaped censure after a deal was allegedly done so they could compete at the 2012 Games.

In return, senior figures in the Russian athletics federation are alleged to have paid Lamine Diack, then IAAF president, €1m with a further €200,000 going to Dr Gabriel Dollé, the body's former anti-doping chief.

Both men have been arrested and put under formal notice of investigation by the office of the Parquet National Financier, which investigates serious financial crime in France. Diack, who faces charges of corruption and aggravated money laundering, has described the allegations as "surreal".

The investigation by French prosecutors began in August when it was passed evidence by investigators working on behalf of the World Anti-Doping Agency (WADA).

The investigators will tomorrow reveal the results of their inquiry, which is set to expand the scandal further. Richard McLaren, a member of the WADA inquiry panel, said the report would be "a real game-changer for sport".

"Here you potentially have a bunch of old men who put a whole lot of extra money in their pockets – through extortion and bribes – but also caused significant changes to actual results and final standings of international athletics competitions," he said.

He added: "This is a whole different scale of corruption than the FIFA scandal."

Diack, from Senegal, was in the final weeks of his 15-year reign as president of the IAAF when *The Sunday Times* and ARD revealed widespread doping among elite athletes after being leaked the sports body's blood test data from between 2001 and 2012.

He described as "laughable" allegations that the IAAF had failed to tackle cheating in athletics properly.

However, evidence gathered by French prosecutors suggests a number of the athletes identified by this newspaper as suspected blood-doping cheats may have evaded a ban because of corruption.

According to sources close to the French prosecution, the IAAF's panel of experts investigated a number of Russian athletes for blood-doping prior to the 2012 Olympics under the newly introduced "biological passport" that allowed it to ban competitors whose red cell count was abnormally high.

A high concentration of red cells indicates that an athlete may have used a banned substance such as EPO or had an illegal blood transfusion.

The panel recommended that action should be taken against eight athletes but, according to the source, Diack's personal lawyer, Habib Cissé, took charge of the cases.

"What surprised a lot of people was that the Russian case was given to Cissé," said the source. "He is a lawyer but he had nothing to do with anti-doping procedure."

He claimed Cissé then did a deal with the Russians.

"As you know, a year after it was the Olympics in London and it was very important for the Russians to have their athletes competing in the Games."

The Sunday Times has seen all the test results of the Russian athletes and many recorded blood scores that had less than a one-in-a-million chance of being natural.

Cissé, who is also under formal investigation, gave the list to the Russian athletics federation and later travelled to Moscow, said the source.

Neither Dollé nor Cissé has commented on the allegations.

The athletes were allegedly told they faced a ban that would prevent them from competing in the London Olympics the following year.

Last year one of the athletes, the marathon runner Liliya Shobukhova, claimed two members of the Russian athletics federation had extorted €450,000 for covering up her highly suspicious test results.

French prosecutors believe the other athletes on the list also paid senior figures in the Russian federation to avoid a ban. All competed in the London Games; one won a gold medal and another took silver.

When the Russian federation did not ban the athletes the IAAF should have taken the case to the Court of Arbitration for Sport, but it failed to do so.

The source alleged: "It was the Russian matter to punish [the athletes] but they didn't do it because . . . Diack had a deal with the Russian athletics federation not to punish them."

Shobukhova's payment came to light after she was finally banned for doping last year. A documentary by ARD/WDR revealed that €300,000 had been returned to her after the ban with the knowledge of a senior IAAF official.

Last week Kipchoge Keino, the chairman of Kenya's Olympic committee, warned WADA was "seriously considering" recommending Kenya be banned from all competitions for four years unless it urgently cleans up its act.

The Sunday Times's doping files revealed 18 Olympic and world championship medals had been won by Kenyan athletes with suspicious blood test results. Yet not one of those medals had been stripped.

Lord Coe, the IAAF president and former chairman of the organising committee for the 2012 Games, was questioned voluntarily last week after the IAAF's Monaco headquarters were raided by police.

He said yesterday the extortion allegations were "abhorrent", but insisted no doping results had been covered up and every athlete found in violation of the IAAF's biological passport system had been charged and sanctioned.

"We are not complacent," Coe said. "Where there are fragilities in the system that may have allowed extortion, no matter how unsuccessful, we will strengthen them." An independent tribunal would be established to hear "all integrity-related violations," he added.

Insight: Jonathan Calvert, George Arbuthnott and David Collins

2017–20
WAR CRIMES AND
THE SAS

The Special Air Service (SAS) regiment of the British Army is known for two things: its tough soldiers, capable of operating in the most high-risk and hostile environments, and its extreme secrecy. In a four-year investigation, Insight dug into allegations that a group of these elite soldiers had "gone rogue" during the war in Afghanistan, and committed serial war crimes.

In 2017, Insight uncovered details of an internal investigation carried out by the Royal Military Police (RMP) into allegations of abuse by SAS soldiers. This had followed complaints from the families of murdered Afghan civilians and also whistleblowers from within the British army itself. Despite the failure of the RMP investigation – known as Operation Northmoor – to secure any prosecutions in relation to the allegations, Insight continued to investigate the Afghans' stories. They pieced together a bloody picture. The SAS unit was alleged to have executed unarmed Afghan civilians after they had been detained; doctored mission reports to implicate their Afghan special forces partners; and planted weapons on the civilians' bodies. The team further uncovered evidence that the RMP investigation into the "serial murders" had been prematurely shut down by the government to avoid embarrassment.

Despite his case being thrown out by Operation Northmoor; one young man whose family had been shot dead in Afghanistan pushed for it to be heard in the High Court. Partly on the basis of The Sunday Times's reporting of a cover-up by the special forces, the appeal was successful. By August 2020, evidence supporting Insight's reporting had come spilling out in confidential emails from within the SAS, which showed that its commanders had major concerns that the unit in question had been committing war crimes.

ROGUE SAS UNIT ACCUSED OF
EXECUTING CIVILIANS IN AFGHANISTAN

---•---

2 July 2017

MEMBERS of Britain's Special Air Service (SAS) are alleged to have covered up evidence that they killed unarmed Afghan civilians in cold blood and falsified mission reports in a war crimes scandal that the government has tried to keep secret.

The allegations have emerged in a classified multimillion-pound Royal Military Police (RMP) investigation, Operation Northmoor, which has been run from a secure underground bunker in Cornwall for the past year and a half.

Senior military police and defence sources with a detailed knowledge of the investigation have said that evidence gathered of war crimes by the SAS is "credible". Part of the inquiry is said to have focused on a particular SAS squadron, which has been described as a "rogue" unit.

A source close to Operation Northmoor says there is strong evidence that unarmed Afghan civilians, suspected of being Taliban insurgents, were murdered rather than captured during night raids on their homes.

In one 2011 case under investigation, special forces soldiers are alleged to have handcuffed and hooded some of the victims before later shooting them dead.

The detectives gathered evidence that appears to show top-secret SAS mission reports had been doctored to make it look as if its Afghan special forces partners, rather than the British regiment's soldiers, had carried out the shootings. This meant the killings were not investigated at the time.

Operation Northmoor is said to have acquired drone and other video footage – nicknamed "kill TV" – that shows British soldiers opening fire and contradicts the SAS account that their Afghan partners were responsible. An examination of bullets taken from some of the victims' bodies revealed they were of a type used by the SAS.

Northmoor also acquired photographs, taken by the SAS, of shooting scenes in which the victims are holding a Makarov pistol – a weapon favoured by the Taliban leadership – that was allegedly planted by the special forces unit to give the false impression that the person they had shot was an armed Taliban commander rather than a civilian.

Operation Northmoor, set up in 2014, was investigating dozens of alleged unlawful killings between 2010 and 2013 by special forces and had become one of the largest military police investigations, with more than 100 RMP officers involved.

The inquiry had been expected to take several more years with provision made for the work to continue until late 2021. But the Operation Northmoor team was instructed by the Ministry of Defence (MoD) to conclude the vast majority of cases by this summer. A military police source said this demand meant the team had been given insufficient time to investigate properly.

The source said there was a desire in the MoD "to just make it go away". He believes officials were desperately trying to "avoid any of the detail of the accusations getting into the press and thereby undermining, in their view, national security, public trust, [and] work with allies".

A senior Whitehall source revealed that the MoD and the army's most senior generals had regarded the evidence of "mass executions" emerging from Operation Northmoor as "credible and extremely serious". The source said it was "seen as a potential disaster for the government" so there were attempts "to keep it under control by reducing the scale of the investigation".

In February, Sir Michael Fallon, the defence secretary, publicly announced that the Operation Northmoor inquiry – which included lesser offences of false imprisonment and assault – would be reduced by 90% in a matter of months. Now the inquiry's workload has been slashed from an initial investigation into 52 deaths to one case of unlawful killing. It is understood that the one case that has survived the cull is an investigation into the alleged shooting of four family members during a night raid on their homes in Qala-e-Bost, east of

Lashkar Gah, southern Helmand province, in February 2011. It is the only case of the 52 alleged killings which is currently subject to a civil claim and the details were expected to become public.

In a series of Skype interviews, family members and local officials have claimed to this newspaper that at least two of the four victims had been held at gunpoint and handcuffed with plastic ties before being shot dead. The RMP is arranging to travel to Afghanistan to interview the witnesses.

It is understood that many of the killing allegations in Northmoor related to special forces' night raids, which became a key tactic in the later stages of the Afghanistan war. The aim was to break down the Taliban leadership by waging a relentless campaign of raids in which suspected insurgents would be plucked from their beds at night and taken to detention centres.

However, British Army officers interviewed by this newspaper believed the SAS raids were often based on unreliable intelligence and raised suspicions that the soldiers set out to kill rather than capture Taliban suspects in contravention of the rules of engagement. The officers said this led to the shooting of innocent civilians with no connection to the Taliban insurgency.

One ex-SAS officer has suggested that what at times was in effect a "shoot-to-kill" policy may have been caused by frustration in the ranks that those captured would be freed soon afterwards without yielding useful intelligence.

Night raids and other search operations by British, American and other special forces units led to 295 civilian deaths between 2009 and 2012, according to the United Nations Assistance Mission in Afghanistan.

The deaths led to a series of complaints from serving members of the British Army and from the International Committee of the Red Cross working in Afghanistan. This triggered the RMP's investigation three years ago. Ministers were informed and the chief of the general staff's office allocated a separate budget for the investigation, which included a £7.6m computer system, such was its seriousness.

As the investigation grew, the RMP detectives were moved to a bunker at RAF St Mawgan to keep their work secure.

The RMP is understood to have made a breakthrough when it acquired classified "after-action" reports on killing incidents from the SAS.

According to a military police source who has a detailed knowledge of the investigation, some of the reports had not been filed to the regular army command because the SAS claimed that the victims had been shot by Afghan special forces who often attended the raids as back-up or interpreters.

However, according to the source, the RMP examined the bullets found in some of the victims and discovered that they were British Army issue 5.56mm – a type of ammunition used by the SAS at the time and not by the Afghan army which typically used 7.62mm rounds.

Sometimes the SAS would give orders for the Afghan forces to stay outside the compound while they went in for the raid, according to the source. This may have been because they had "decided rather than capture, they'll kill". The detectives acquired footage of the incidents from drones and other cameras showing British troops present at a shooting.

The source said: "Well, hang on a second, it says [in the after-action reports] only the Afghan partners fired . . . he's dressed in British military equipment, and the guy was shot and killed with a 5.56".

A British special forces officer said that at one point the Afghan CF 333 commando unit refused to patrol with the SAS because of concern about their conduct. One CF 333 commando told this newspaper that in 2010 he had witnessed SAS soldiers planting drugs and guns on a victim who had been shot needlessly at a checkpoint.

The inquiry has examined the activities of an SAS unit which is said to have gone "rogue". The unit has been accused of having routinely carried a Russian Makarov "kill pistol" during the night raids because it could be photographed with the corpse if an unarmed Taliban suspect was gunned down.

The British special forces officer alleged that the pistol was planted to make it look as if the victim had been a high-value target as the Makarov was commonly used by senior Taliban and al-Qaeda leaders. It also made it appear that the suspect had been armed, allowing the soldiers to claim that they had fired to defend themselves.

The source added that one of his friends in another special forces unit had been asked to carry a similar "kill pistol" and had refused.

The concern was echoed by the military police source. "How do you justify in an after-action report that it was right to kill someone? You photograph them with a gun . . . There were issues being investigated about what's called 'drop weapons'," the source said.

The sources also claimed the soldiers had attracted suspicion by placing the pistol in the left hand of the victim on too many occasions and by using the same gun serial number when compiling mission reports on the killings.

On Friday a spokesman for the MoD said that more than 90% of the 675 allegations being examined by Northmoor had been discontinued and fewer than 10 investigations remained. He added that the decision to dismiss the cases had been taken solely by the RMP and the government had not influenced the decision.

In a statement, the MoD said: "The Royal Military Police has found no evidence of criminal behaviour by the armed forces in Afghanistan."

However, it is understood that before Fallon's February statement the RMP reported two cases to the Service Prosecuting Authority (SPA) in which detectives believed the weight of evidence meant British servicemen should have stood trial. However, the SPA did not believe there was a realistic chance of conviction at that stage.

In one of those cases, senior RMP officers had expected a special forces soldier would be prosecuted for multiple murders. The other cases in the wider investigation had even stronger evidence of war crimes, according to the source, raising questions about why they were later dropped.

The source claimed it was difficult to find a court-martial military jury with the required security clearance that was properly independent of the SAS and that this could have influenced the SPA's decision not to prosecute.

Revealed: how inquiry into SAS unit accused of executing civilians was 'made to go away'

From the fortified security of a concrete bunker on a Cornish airbase scores of detectives from the Royal Military Police (RMP) have been working on one of the biggest multiple-murder investigations in modern-day Britain.

Their task has been a closely guarded secret. The investigation began in March 2014 but it took 18 months for the government to acknowledge publicly that there was an inquiry, called Operation Northmoor.

The Ministry of Defence said Northmoor was looking into 675 allegations of abuse by British soldiers during the 13-year war in

Afghanistan. Among those allegations were accusations that soldiers killed 52 people unlawfully. There was little further information released. However, these scant details caused an outcry from politicians and the media, who assumed many of the accusations had been made by ambulance-chasing lawyers seeking compensation for undeserving clients.

The same criticism had been levelled at the Iraq Historic Allegations Team (Ihat) investigation which was assessing 2,000 abuse allegations generated by one law firm: Public Interest Lawyers (PIL), whose leading partner, Phil Shiner, was eventually struck off for dishonesty.

But Northmoor was a substantially different inquiry and it was causing concern at the heart of government. In December 2016, a well-placed government source told The Sunday Times that the inquiry was "X-rated" because it threatened to engulf Britain's most famous regiment, the Special Air Service (SAS), in a huge war crimes scandal.

"Investigators are looking at a number of extremely serious allegations relating to the actions of British special forces in Afghanistan," the source said. "Some of those allegations relate to mass executions which, if proven, would be tantamount to war crimes. The SAS are one of a number of special forces units implicated."

The source continued: "There has been a series of meetings at a very senior level across Whitehall about how to handle the potential fallout of these allegations being made about high-profile units such as the SAS. Northmoor is seen as a potential disaster for the government, so the military is trying to keep it under control by reducing the scale of the investigation." The source added that the investigation's outcome would "more than likely be guided by the Ministry of Defence".

An investigation by The Sunday Times reveals today why the allegations were considered so explosive. Our account has been based on interviews with more than 50 military police officers, special forces soldiers, senior army commanders, government officials, lawyers and witnesses.

A military police source said the "majority" of the 52 alleged unlawful killings were claimed to have been carried out by special forces. The RMP has been investigating claims that unarmed civilians were woken in the night and summarily killed in raids that were sometimes based on false intelligence.

As its inquiries continued, the RMP is also understood to have discovered evidence of planted pistols and falsified mission reports, which would suggest that SAS soldiers may have attempted to cover up their involvement in war crimes.

The overall picture that emerges from the sources is one of a huge murder investigation with several interlinking cases that were being pursued rigorously by the RMP. The cases were considered all the more serious because they originated from complaints by soldiers and humanitarian bodies, including the International Committee of the Red Cross, rather than claimant lawyers.

The RMP was given a separate budget from the chief of the general staff's office and was provided with a new £7.6m forensic computer system to investigate the claims in early 2016. By last summer more than 100 detectives were working on the case from the inquiry's Cornish hideaway at RAF St Mawgan.

It became the biggest RMP investigation and the work was expected to take another two to five years. Then everything changed.

In October last year senior officers at Northmoor were instructed by the MoD that the investigation should be wound down by this summer. It was followed quickly by a reshuffle of the top officers leading the investigation.

In February this year, a parliamentary report condemned the MoD for paying "ambulance-chasing lawyers" to bring thousands of "spurious" cases against troops who had served in Iraq.

Sir Michael Fallon, the defence secretary, reacted to the report by announcing that the Iraq investigation was shutting down and surprisingly, as it had no connection to the parliamentary report, he said that nine in 10 of the Afghan cases being examined by Northmoor would be discontinued by the summer.

In recent months the RMP has been jettisoning Northmoor cases at a rate of five per working day. A military police source suggested the number of cases being dropped had been speeded up by scrapping a process that had required consultation with an independent lawyer and a military prosecutor before a line of inquiry was jettisoned.

On May 12 the MoD indicated Operation Northmoor was still examining 190 of the 695 abuse allegations, but on Friday it announced that fewer than 10 cases were still being scrutinised. It was further confirmed that only one case of unlawful death remained.

The surviving case is believed to be an incident in which four family members are alleged to have been shot dead during a night raid on their homes in southern Helmand province, in February 2011. Unlike most of the other killing cases in Northmoor, this case was brought by a firm of lawyers seeking compensation for the family of the deceased.

A military police source with a detailed knowledge of Northmoor told *The Sunday Times* that there was a desire within the MoD to close down the inquiry. "I think it was driven by the collapse of PIL and the desire of everyone in the MoD to just make it go away," he said.

The source said the government set an arbitrary date of the summer to wrap up the majority of cases, without providing resources to get through the heavy workload.

"That means only one thing: that you're not doing as much as you would have done to investigate the cases in the time allowed," he said.

"What they're desperately trying to do is trying to avoid any of the detail of the accusations getting into the press and thereby undermining, in their view, national security, public trust, [and] work with allies."

Insight: David Collins, George Arbuthnott and Jonathan Calvert

AS THEY DRANK TEA, THE BOYS WERE SHOT IN THE HEAD – AND BLOOD FILLED THEIR CUPS

———————————— • ————————————

17 November 2019

THE Royal Military Police (RMP) believed it was a murder of children by a British soldier.

On the night of October 18, 2012, a highly trained Special Air Service (SAS) soldier burst into a room in an Afghan village and shot three boys and a young man in the head and neck from close range. The incident was over in seconds. The teacups the boys had been drinking from only moments earlier were filled with blood. Relatives of victims were left to mop up shattered teeth and brain flesh from the heavily stained carpet.

The victims were aged 20, 17, 14 and 12. The government would claim all four of them were Taliban insurgents but no evidence has been produced to suggest that they were anything other than a shopkeeper, a farmer and two schoolboys.

The events that evening should have been a cause célèbre raising questions about covert operations by our special forces in Afghanistan. Was the soldier acting in self-defence, was it a mistake or should it have been tried as a war crime?

Detectives from the military police's special investigation branch believed from the evidence that it was a multiple murder, sources say. The investigators referred the case against the soldier to the Service Prosecuting Authority, recommending war crimes charges.

They had also discovered that the soldier's special forces unit had compounded the alleged crime by trying to cover up its role in the killings. As a result, the military police referred the officer in charge of the SAS mission to prosecutors, alleging that he had falsified documents. They suspected that the cover-up had gone all the way to the top of the military. In a move unprecedented in modern British military history, the detectives recommended that one of the SAS's most high-ranking officers should be put on trial for conspiracy to pervert justice. The case is shrouded in the blanket of official secrecy that often surrounds those involving special forces – especially embarrassing ones. None of the soldiers was prosecuted and the Ministry of Defence told this newspaper: "The RMP has found no evidence of criminal behaviour by the armed forces in Afghanistan."

However, an investigation by *The Sunday Times* and the BBC's *Panorama* programme has pieced together a detailed account of that evening and subsequent events from documents, military sources and witness statements.

Contrary to the MoD's statement, the RMP did find evidence. As part of our joint investigation we invited Lord Macdonald of River Glaven, the former director of public prosecutions, to look over the case. His view, based on the available information, was that the soldier's account was inconsistent with the physical evidence at the scene and the prosecutors' suspicions should have been heightened by the attempted cover-up. He believes that there are grounds to reopen the case.

Frank Ledwidge, a barrister and former justice adviser to the Army in Afghanistan, said: "If British forces are using the technique of death squads in counter-insurgency as a policy, in my view that requires investigation. And this should be taken extremely seriously."

The following is an account of the events on that evening based on sources and documents seen by this newspaper and *Panorama*.

Night raids

It was the autumn of 2012 and the SAS were in the thick of a campaign of night raids on the homes of Afghan men identified as Taliban insurgents. The campaign was controversial because large numbers of suspects were targeted each night, often as a result of sketchy intelligence from local warlords, who may have been using the Army to settle scores with rivals.

Yet the reliability of the intelligence was crucial because, while many of the targets were captured and taken back to base, a significant number were killed in their homes after, apparently, resisting arrest. Detectives would later investigate whether these deaths were killings to decapitate the Taliban leadership.

Darkness had fallen on the evening of Thursday, October 18 when the SAS unit left its base at Camp Bastion accompanied by Afghan soldiers and tanks for the 12-mile journey to the village of Loy Bagh in Helmand province.

The village was regarded as a relatively safe place in a hostile area. A British army base was situated less than a mile from its centre and checkpoints at either side of the village were equipped with tethered Zeppelin-style spy balloons fitted with cameras. They gave the Army a bird's-eye view over the village's single-storey, mud-built compound homes and the events that happened that evening.

The soldiers entered the village looking for a Fazel Mohammed, 20, who was said to be a Taliban leader. His family said Mohammed, a father of two, had spent the day buying fabric to sell in his shop before attending prayers at the mosque at about 7.30pm. He returned home to his parents' compound accompanied by his brother Naik, 17, a cotton farmer, and two boys who were studying at the local madrasah. They were Mohammed Tayeb, 14, and his friend Ahmad Shah, 12. The two younger boys were planning to head home the next day as the Eid holidays had begun.

When they sat down to have tea in the guest room, news was spreading in the village that soldiers were searching houses. A neighbour directed the troops to Mohammed's home. The guest room is a featureless mud building about the size of a domestic garage with a single doorway and a window. It stands apart from the main house on a compound wall just yards from the entrance where the soldiers began to enter. Most of the troops headed across the courtyard to the house but one peeled off to check the guest room, according to Mohammed's mother.

The shooting

There was no hesitation. The soldier barged through the hanging cloth on the doorway and began shooting at targets three or four yards from the muzzle of his rifle. As an expert special forces soldier, his bursts of gunfire were unerringly accurate. Photographs of the four victims show that each of them, including the 12-year-old, had at least one bullet hole in their head. The high-velocity bullets ripped through their victims and embedded in the mud walls.

Photos of those walls show clusters of bullet holes mostly less than a yard from the floor. The downward angle of the shots suggests that the victims must have been sitting down or kneeling when they were killed.

Before leaving the soldiers dragged the bodies across the blood-soaked carpet into a neat line. When the family encountered the grisly scene there was an outpouring of grief followed by rage.

By morning the roads were blocked with people clamouring to march on the army base and officers were summoned by the local governor. The governor and family were convinced that there had been a grotesque mistake, as they were sure the boys were not Taliban members.

However, the Army declined to meet the governor and a new story emerged the next day – which was almost certainly why the SAS officer in charge òf the mission would later be accused of falsifying documents. After a mission, army officers are required to fill out a report describing incidents of note. If civilians are injured this normally triggers a serious incident report that would activate an RMP investigation. But this did not happen. Instead, an email was sent to the International Security Assistance Force headquarters to 30 senior officers describing only an Afghan-led mission with civilian casualties. The SAS were said to have merely mentored the Afghans that evening.

The RMP only learnt about the incident two months later when a complaint was made to the British government on behalf of the victims' family by Public Interest Lawyers. The law firm's partner, Phil Shiner, was later struck off for paying fixers to find clients in Iraq but there was no suggestion of wrongdoing in this case.

The RMP began looking into the incident in December 2012 and a year later the case was considered sufficiently serious to be rolled into Operation Northmoor – an Afghan war crimes inquiry that had just been set up.

The claim that there had been no SAS involvement in the killings quickly unravelled. A source close to the investigation said video evidence showed soldiers wearing British equipment, and the bullets found at the scene belonged to a British calibre rifle. The Afghans used a wider calibre weapon.

The detectives interviewed the SAS soldier who carried out the shooting under caution. He said he had gunned down the first two victims because they were by the window holding long-barrelled weapons and he feared they might shoot at his colleagues in the courtyard. According to his account, the other two victims then emerged from the shadows in the guest room. He said he shot the first and then fired jointly at the second along with a non-UK soldier who had arrived at his side.

Treasury solicitors acting for the government would later justify the shooting by claiming Mohammed and his brother were Taliban commanders who had plotted roadside bombings. This is denied by their family and local politicians who were on the side of the British.

Drop weapons

The family also reject the soldier's claim that the victims were armed. One of the wider allegations investigated in Operation Northmoor was that the SAS had deposited "drop weapons" next to bodies to make it appear as if their victims had been armed. It is not known whether this happened in this incident.

The RMP did not believe the soldier's account. In February 2014, the soldier was referred to the service prosecutor over four allegations of murder. The officer in charge of the mission and one of the SAS's most high-ranking officers were also referred to the prosecutor by their commanding officers.

The mission leader was accused of making a false record, and the high-ranking officer was alleged to have attempted to pervert the course of justice.

A service prosecutor wrote to the victims' family in March 2015 to say no action would be taken against the SAS soldier. The letter cited "insufficient evidence" but emphasised that this did not mean the soldier's account was believed.

Last week Lord Macdonald expressed surprise at the prosecutors' decision. He said: "The soldier claims he fired these rounds in circumstances where men came at him out of the shadows, presumably on their feet because they were advancing towards him, holding weapons. In those circumstances it's very difficult to see how the bullet marks end up, clustered in the wall a metre from the ground." He concluded: "I would have very grave suspicions about the case, and it's a sort of case that one would expect to see advanced further."

The leader of the mission and the high-ranking officer were also never charged. Two years later in 2017, Operation Northmoor was effectively wound down by Sir Michael Fallon, defence secretary at the time. The RMP had been investigating 52 deaths, mainly by special forces. All the cases were dropped.

A military police source with a detailed knowledge of Northmoor accused the government of "desperately trying to avoid any of the detail of the accusations getting into the press and thereby undermining, in their view, national security, public trust [and] work with allies."

Insight: George Arbuthnott, Jonathan Calvert and David Collins

This reporting eventually became part of an appeal by a young man whose family had been killed in Afghanistan, to get his case heard in the High Court. It was successful, and during the course of the proceedings incendiary evidence emerged from within the SAS regarding the allegations. The following reporting on that evidence is perhaps the pinnacle of Insight's years of investigation into what really went on in Afghanistan.

◆

ROGUE SAS AFGHANISTAN EXECUTION SQUAD EXPOSED BY EMAIL TRAIL

1 August 2020

THE HELICOPTERS were deafening as they swooped down over Gawahargin village in southern Helmand province. Shrieks of fear rang through the building below as the inhabitants woke to find themselves surrounded by dim figures emerging from the dark. Red and blue laser gunsights probed the openings of the mud-built home and a booming megaphone ordered the family to come out into their courtyard. One by one, family members tentatively stepped out into the open with their hands in the air.

The soldiers placed black hoods over the heads of the men of the house and bound their hands with plastic ties. The women and children, including 19-year-old Saifullah Yar, were ushered to a guest room on the outer wall of the family's compound. While they were being detained, they heard bursts of gunfire.

When the helicopters flew off, Saifullah headed back to the house in search of his father, whom he had last seen being handcuffed and hooded by the soldiers. He found his father – a farmer – slumped against his bedroom wall with eight to 10 bullets holes in his head.

His cousin had been killed in his own bedroom in the adjoining compound. So many bullets had ripped through his neck that his head was hanging loose from his shoulders. Saifullah's two brothers were later discovered dead. Their bodies were riddled with bullet holes and lying outside the compound.

Within a couple of hours, the Chinook helicopters had offloaded the Special Air Service (SAS) troops at their secret base in Afghanistan, where news soon began circulating about yet another "kinetic" – military slang for lethal force – raid by the crack special forces regiment. When a computer link to the mission report was circulated early that morning, an SAS troop sergeant-major inquired by email at 6.56am: "Is this about . . . latest massacre! I've heard a couple of rumours."

Rogue unit

The events of that early morning on February 16, 2011 were first reported in 2017, when we wrote a series of stories revealing the SAS was being investigated for committing war crimes during the 13-year Afghanistan campaign. It was alleged innocent civilians were killed in cold blood and weapons planted beside their bodies to make it look as if they had put up a fight.

The Ministry of Defence refused to comment on the killing of Saifullah's family when we approached it three years ago. But last month a cache of extraordinary secret documents from inside the special forces was disclosed in the High Court, giving eye-opening new details that appear to support allegations this was a quadruple murder by UK troops. It is rare that such highly confidential communications between troops and senior members of the special forces are released.

They record the fears among senior officers that there may have been a pattern of behaviour by a "rogue" SAS unit that had killed 33 people on 11 night raids on homes in the first three months of 2011. They included 10 near-identical killings that had happened after the SAS had captured a male family member and sent him back into his empty home to clear the way for a search of the premises.

The secret review of the raids found that in each of the incidents the SAS unit claimed the captured man had conjured up a weapon from inside the building despite having the special unit's guns trained on his head. He was then shot dead. The officer conducting the review concluded: "We are getting some things wrong right now."

One email shows that one of the most senior commanders in special forces headquarters in Britain had become deeply concerned about the killings and his misgivings were reported to the special forces directorate in central London.

He wrote that the actions had been reported to him as "possibly a deliberate policy among the current unit [name redacted] to engage and kill fighting-aged males on target even when they did not pose a threat". He said the "disturbing" allegations could be "explosive" because it suggested SAS troops had "strayed into indefensible" behaviour that could be "criminal".

Later every one of the dozens of SAS soldiers and servicemen involved in the operation who were interviewed by military police claimed they had no memory of their actions on the night of the killings. A judge questioned the plausibility of this "collective amnesia".

The new information emerged only after the government's lawyers misled a High Court hearing in a case that had been brought seeking a proper independent investigation into the killings on behalf of Saifullah, who is now in his late twenties and still lives in Afghanistan. The lawyers had argued there had been no complaints about the killings at the time, but the documents they were then forced to disclose contradict that claim.

The judge in the second hearing – held by video conference 10 days ago – has demanded a witness statement from Ben Wallace, the defence secretary, to explain why the government withheld this crucial information. "What has happened in this litigation is out of the ordinary," Mr Justice Swift told the hearing.

You couldn't make it up

While Saifullah and his family were mourning the deaths of their relatives at dawn on the day of the shootings – Wednesday, February 16, 2011 – the documents show that British special forces soldiers at base camp were becoming increasingly incredulous about the nature of the killings by the SAS unit.

The emails, notes and mission reports have been redacted by the government to conceal names, and contain military terms, but their meaning is clear.

The troop sergeant-major had asked about the "latest massacre" that morning because he could not open the link to the mission report on his computer. A colleague, a senior non-commissioned officer, wrote back to fill him in on the events hours earlier. He began by describing the death of Saifullah's cousin Ahmad Shah in the adjoining compound. "Basically, for what must be the 10th time in the last two weeks, when they sent a B [Afghan man] back into the A [a building], to open the curtains(??) he re-appered [sic] with an AK [AK-47 assault rifle]," he wrote.

He went on to describe what the SAS unit claimed had happened to Saifullah's father, Abdul Khaliq, aged about 55. "Then when they walked back in to a different A [building] with another B [Afghan] to open the curtains he grabbed a grenade from behind a curtain and threw it at the c/s [call sign ie: SAS soldier]. Fortunately, it didn't go off . . . this is the 8th time this has happened.'

The email ends with a reference to the shooting outside the compound of one of Saifullah's two brothers, Saddam. "And finally they shot a guy who was hiding in a bush who had a grenade in his hands. You couldn't MAKE IT UP!"

Eyebrows were also being raised further up the chain. There was an email exchange about the incident between some of the most senior officers in the special forces command in Afghanistan that day. One senior commander made clear that he had doubts about the way the SAS unit had been reporting incidents in which Afghan men had been captured before being killed. "If accurate," he said of the reports, then "TB [Taliban] appear to have become more militant and less careful of life than previously".

He asked his colleagues for their "thoughts". Another senior special forces officer quickly replied with a tone of disbelief. "Has anybody come up with an explanation as to why all TB are beginning to adopt the previously unobserved TTPs [tactical practice] of: 1. re-entering buildings during the search phase and coming back out with a weapon against an overwhelming force 2. keeping grenades in their pockets?" he wrote.

The SAS unit's official version of the night's mission was set out more fully in a "first impression report" produced by the Army a few days later. It states the raid on Saifullah's house was part of a search for his brother Saddam, who was suspected of being a member of an enemy gang that was planting roadside bombs. Saddam was the only target for the raid.

The report says that Saifullah's father was escorted back into his house after capture and was instructed to open the curtains in the third room they entered. "As he does so," the report continues, "he pulls a grenade from behind the curtains and moves to throw it at the team. He poses an immediate threat to life and is engaged with aimed shots. The assault team members take cover. The grenade malfunctions and does not detonate."

Saifullah's cousin moved behind a table and picked up an AK-47 assault rifle when he was taken back into his house, according to the SAS unit's account. He was shot instantly.

Saddam was killed after the soldiers allegedly found him outside the compound with a grenade in his hands, and the other brother, Atta Ullah, is said to have died after emerging from under a blanket with an AK-47 near a compound about 300 yards away.

The SAS troops took photographs of the family's weapons to show they had acted in self-defence. The two assault rifles and two grenades were, however, the only weapons recorded as being found in the two adjoining compounds, which made it all the more remarkable that four family members had managed to get their hands on one during the surprise raid in the middle of the night.

Assassination

Contrary to the claims made by the British government's lawyers in court, the documents show the SAS unit's version of events came under question immediately on the morning of the shootings in angry exchanges with the troops' coalition partners.

As was common on night raids, the Afghan partner unit (APU), consisting of special forces, had been supporting the SAS troops when they surrounded Saifullah's home and the adjoining compound. One note shows that soldiers who were present had told their commanding officer four innocent civilians had been murdered that night.

The job of placating the APU fell upon a senior officer from the Special Boat Service (SBS) – the SAS's maritime sister regiment. The SBS had close relations with the APU because it had been deployed to do mentoring and training work with the Afghans.

In a note written on the day of the killings, the officer said he had just had a "very difficult" meeting with the colonel in charge of the APU. The colonel brought along nine of his soldiers, one of whom was a relative of Saifullah's family and who gave assurances that the dead men were teachers and farmers, not Taliban supporters.

The colonel said his soldiers had reported that nobody had fired at the coalition forces, but the men "were shot anyway". The note added: "He suggests that 2 men were shot trying to run away, and that the other 2 men were 'assassinated' on target after they had already been detained and searched."

As the meeting became more heated, one of the Afghan soldiers drew his pistol and asked permission to shoot his SBS mentors. The SBS officer wrote: "He [the colonel] repeatedly asked me to explain to the officer (present in the room) why his family had been first detained, and then killed by the British, particularly as there was no evidence."

In an email note of a second meeting, the APU colonel made clear his troops would no longer work with the SAS until the issue was resolved and said he was going to raise the matter with a special unit of the Afghan police that deals with serious crime.

The matter was already being taken up on the day of the shootings by a security adviser to Gulab Mangal, then governor of Helmand province, who phoned a general in command of coalition forces in the region to inquire about the civilian casualties, according to an army report. The general assured the adviser the matter had been taken care of by the British.

However, the governor was still not satisfied with the answer three days later, the first impression report produced by UK special forces shows. "On the 19 Feb Gov Mangal indicated through Col [colonel's name redacted] that during the operation in the early hours of the 16 Feb, four innocent civilians were killed by CF [coalition forces]."

Alarm bells

The alarm bells were ringing at special forces headquarters in the UK about a pattern of behaviour by the SAS unit. A long note has been disclosed from one of the most senior figures in special forces, containing incendiary information.

The note states that in April that year a senior commander had been to a dinner and had been taken to one side for a private chat by a fellow high-ranking officer. He had heard disturbing reports from Afghanistan from his men.

The men reported that there appeared to be a deliberate policy by the current SAS unit on tour in Afghanistan of killing "fighting age males... even when they did not pose a threat". The senior commander told the officer he had heard "similar unease" and headquarters had noticed an upward trend in the numbers of enemies being killed.

The commander's note went on to explain that in February he had been forced to raise two particular issues "that are fuelling our concern". The first was the disparity between the number of weapons recovered from the enemy and the number of bodies.

The second concern was "the number of instances where the 'head of family' Bs [Afghan men] were being invited to lead the compound clearance and were subsequently being engaged and killed". He said that after a period of restraint since the February incident, there had been another case on April 2 when two Afghan men had been captured and then killed when they were asked to help clear their homes.

The officer he talked to had previously been on a special forces tour in Afghanistan. The commander wrote that the officer "recounts that during his [team's] tour there was not a single incident when the B [Afghan man] chose to take aggressive action against what were clearly impossible odds. He is therefore surprised that there have been multiple examples of this happening during the current [redacted] tour."

The commander said he found the information "very disturbing" even if the reports were second-hand. He said it might be a new enemy tactic but it did not seem to be necessary, as the Taliban understood the "limitations" of the UK's detention system.

The Insight team has previously been told by an SAS officer that the regiment's soldiers had at times adopted "a shoot to kill" policy, which may have been caused by frustration that people caught in night raids were often released after a few days without yielding useful intelligence.

The commander's note ends with his concern that the incidents threatened to damage the plan to hand over power to the Afghans and to sour British relations with the ministry of the interior.

Not enough guns

On the same day – April 7, 2011 – a special forces major was finishing a review for his superior of all the raids carried out by the SAS unit since December 2010. He set out his findings in an email to his superior that afternoon, and they were startling.

He wrote: "I counted 10 separate incidents (spanning eight separate operations) in which the TTP [tactic] of sending a B [Afghan man] back into a building to assist with clearing it resulted in that same B getting killed ('reaching for an AK-47 behind a blanket' etc being the sort of comment in the OpSum [operational summary])."

These incidents happened between January 8 and April 2, 2011. The major highlighted five other incidents during the same period when the number of people killed was far higher than the number of guns the SAS unit said it had found at the scene. While noting that there could be many explanations for the mismatch, his review showed that in just three of those operations 23 people were killed and only 10 guns recovered.

The major concluded his email that: "In my view there is enough here to convince me that we are getting some things wrong right now".

Four days later, instructions were emailed to the commander of special forces in Afghanistan to carry out a review of the tactic of sending the head of the household back into the building. The email – marked "Secret UK Eyes Only" – said "there have been several instances in which [redacted name of unit] have been forced to engage and kill the nominated Afghan male because he had reached for a concealed weapon in the accommodation area, either as he returned into the compound or during the clearance phase. This is a relatively new trend."

The dossier noted that the UK's Afghan partners believed that the SAS had been "overly kinetic" during these operations. This was weakening the relationship between the two governments and "if allowed to deteriorate, could undermine [redacted] the transition in Afghanistan".

The commander was asked in the email to assess the "severity of concerns" and report any criminal act that might have been committed to the Royal Military Police (RMP). However, it appears that no crimes were reported and the matter might have ended there.

Cover-up

More than two years later Saifullah's uncle made a claim against the UK government for unlawful detention and mistreatment, as he had been imprisoned for 20 days after the raid by the SAS and then released without charge.

As part of the litigation, the allegation about the four civilian killings was passed on to the special investigation branch of the RMP, who felt the claims were sufficiently serious to launch an investigation in March 2014.

It was the beginning of a large-scale war crimes inquiry, which was expanded to look at 52 suspected murders by British special forces in Afghanistan. By 2017 sources close to the inquiry told us that the RMP were seriously looking into allegations that the SAS killed unarmed Afghan civilians in cold blood, planted weapons on victims and falsified mission reports to cover its tracks.

While the RMP's investigation, Operation Northmoor, was wound down under pressure from the government that year, inquiries into the deaths of Saifullah's relatives continued until last summer, when the RMP concluded their work, admitting that they had not even been able to identify the alleged offenders who had carried out the shooting.

Saifullah's law firm, Leigh Day, launched an application for judicial review in September, claiming that his right to a prompt and effective independent investigation had been breached. In initial submissions to the judge in November, it emerged that the RMP had interviewed almost all the 54 military personnel connected to the incident. "None of those personnel could specifically remember the operation under question," the government's lawyers said.

The request for a judicial review was denied and so an oral appeal hearing was held in March in front of Mr Justice Jay, who allowed the case to go forward. The judge found that Saifullah's lawyer had a reasonable case to argue based on the allegations of a cover-up that had been previously made in a joint investigation in *The Sunday Times* and by the BBC's *Panorama*, and the fact that soldiers had shown "collective amnesia" when asked about the shooting. A "wall of silence" that was "deeply suspicious" was another way it was described in court.

One of the key assertions was a claim by the government's lawyers that the MoD was unaware of complaints about the killings until the claim by Saifullah's uncle in late 2013.

This was misleading, as the government's lawyers soon realised when they reviewed the paperwork that needed to be disclosed after the judge's decision to allow the review to go ahead. It was then that they found the documents quoted in this article. Saifullah's lawyer has expressed "grave concern" that it was almost shut out from bringing the case because the contents of the document had not been given to the court.

The defence secretary has until the autumn to write a witness statement explaining to the court how the error happened. There will also be fresh questions for the heads of Britain's special forces as to why the killings were not investigated at the time, but covered up.

This weekend Lord Macdonald, a former director of public prosecutions and one of the country's leading criminal lawyers, said: "The way a nation wages war tells you all you need to know about its attachment to the rule of law. It is bad enough if British soldiers were systematically murdering civilians in Afghanistan – making themselves liable to criminal proceedings in the UK.

"But this is compounded if their superior officers and government officials deliberately failed to investigate suspected war crimes, and then tried to conceal evidence that they had occurred from the courts."

A former senior military officer with knowledge of such operations told this newspaper of his doubts about the SAS claims that many of those killed had single-handedly decided to take on the unit in their own homes after being captured. He said it "defied logic" for someone to launch an attack against impossible odds when their family is in the hands of the enemy just metres away.

"It's just not going to happen. There could be retribution taken against your family. It's just ridiculous," he said. "The chance of somebody being aggressive against you when you have their family is minimal."

He said the SAS's mission reports were "highly incredible". "There's overwhelming force. Everyone's been detained. You know you're going to die if you do it. What advantage is there? There is no advantage. Even if you're a member of the Taliban, your best chances are going into the detention system, get processed, no one knows who you are and you get released. It happens all the time. Why would you risk this? This is a thin veneer of an excuse."

The MoD said: "This is not new evidence, and this historical case has already been independently investigated by the Royal Military Police as part of Operation Northmoor. It has also been subject to four reviews conducted by an independent review team.

"These documents were considered as part of the independent investigations, which concluded there was insufficient evidence to refer the case for prosecution. The Service Police and the Service Prosecuting Authority of course remain open to considering allegations should new evidence, intelligence or information come to light."

Insight: George Arbuthnott, Jonathan Calvert and David Collins

2020–21
FAILURES OF STATE: THE COVID-19 PANDEMIC

In the early months of 2020 the UK was waking up to the overwhelming scale of the coronavirus pandemic. Hospitals were overrun, health care services lacked adequate resources, and the country foundered in the absence of a confident pandemic response.

The Insight team immediately began investigating why the UK had been caught so unprepared, and how the public were so quickly plunged into an unprecedented crisis. It was the first major national press investigation to cast serious doubt over the government's handling of the pandemic.

Insight revealed for the first time that Boris Johnson had failed to heed warnings and had lost a crucial five weeks of preparation for the coming storm. It exposed a deep complacency within the government epitomised by the Prime Minister's failure to attend the first five Cobra meetings on the virus. The article sent shock waves through Downing Street and the Department of Health.

A month later, Insight produced a second major investigation which set the agenda over the months that followed by revealing that more than a million infections had been allowed to spread across the country as the Prime Minister dithered over lockdown. His inaction led the country to suffer the worst death toll and economic fallout in Europe.

Next, Insight went back to the beginning of the pandemic and produced a world exclusive about China's cover up over the virus that was the closest match to Covid-19 and therefore the best clue to the origins of the outbreak.

Then, Insight's work on the fallout from the first wave revealed how intensive care had been rationed for the elderly despite claims by ministers that the NHS had coped. It exposed how many thousands had been left to die without life-saving treatment, including care-home residents who were barred from receiving hospital care, due to the unmanageable deluge of patients caused by Johnson's inaction.

38 DAYS WHEN BRITAIN SLEEPWALKED INTO DISASTER

———————•———————

19 April 2020

ON THE third Friday of January a silent and stealthy killer was creeping across the world. Passing from person to person and borne on ships and planes, the coronavirus was already leaving a trail of bodies.

The virus had spread from China to six countries and was almost certainly in many others. Sensing the coming danger, the British government briefly went into wartime mode that day, holding a meeting of Cobra, its national crisis committee.

But it took just an hour that January 24 lunchtime to brush aside the coronavirus threat. Matt Hancock, the health secretary, bounced out of Whitehall after chairing the meeting and breezily told reporters the risk to the UK public was "low".

This was despite the publication that day of an alarming study by Chinese doctors in the medical journal, The Lancet. It assessed the lethal potential of the virus, for the first time suggesting it was comparable to the 1918 Spanish flu pandemic, which killed up to 50 million people.

Unusually, Boris Johnson had been absent from Cobra. The committee – which includes ministers, intelligence chiefs and military generals – gathers at moments of great peril such as terrorist attacks, natural disasters and other threats to the nation and is normally chaired by the prime minister.

Johnson had found time that day, however, to join in a lunar new year dragon eyes ritual as part of Downing Street's reception for the Chinese community, led by the country's ambassador.

It was a big day for Johnson and there was a triumphal mood in Downing Street because the withdrawal treaty from the European

Union was being signed in the late afternoon. It could have been the defining moment of his premiership – but that was before the world changed.

That afternoon his spokesman played down the looming threat from the east and reassured the nation that we were "well prepared for any new diseases". The confident, almost nonchalant, attitude displayed that day in January would continue for more than a month.

Johnson went on to miss four further Cobra meetings on the virus. As Britain was hit by unprecedented flooding, he completed the EU withdrawal, reshuffled his cabinet and then went away to the grace-and-favour country retreat at Chevening where he spent most of the two weeks over half-term with his pregnant fiancée, Carrie Symonds.

It would not be until March 2 – another five weeks – that Johnson would attend a Cobra meeting about the coronavirus. But by then it was almost certainly too late. The virus had sneaked into our airports, our trains, our workplaces and our homes. Britain was on course for one of the worst infections of the most deadly virus to have hit the world in more than a century.

Last week, a senior adviser to Downing Street broke ranks and blamed the weeks of complacency on a failure of leadership in cabinet. In particular, the prime minister was singled out.

"There's no way you're at war if your PM isn't there," the adviser said. "And what you learn about Boris was he didn't chair any meetings. He liked his country breaks. He didn't work weekends. It was like working for an old-fashioned chief executive in a local authority 20 years ago. There was a real sense that he didn't do urgent crisis planning. It was exactly like people feared he would be."

Inquiry "inevitable"

One day there will be an inquiry into the lack of preparations during those "lost" five weeks from January 24. There will be questions about when politicians understood the severity of the threat, what the scientists told them and why so little was done to equip the National Health Service for the coming crisis. It will be the politicians who will face the most intense scrutiny.

Among the key points likely to be explored will be why it took so long to recognise an urgent need for a massive boost in supplies of personal protective equipment (PPE) for health workers; ventilators to treat acute respiratory symptoms; and tests to detect the infection.

Any inquiry may also ask whether the government's failure to get to grips with the scale of the crisis in those early days had the knock-on effect of the national lockdown being introduced days or even weeks too late, causing many thousands more unnecessary deaths.

We have talked to scientists, academics, doctors, emergency planners, public officials and politicians about the root of the crisis and whether the government should have known sooner and acted more swiftly to kick-start the Whitehall machine and put the NHS onto a war footing.

They told us that, contrary to the official line, Britain was in a poor state of readiness for a pandemic. Emergency stockpiles of PPE had severely dwindled and gone out of date after becoming a low priority in the years of austerity cuts. The training to prepare key workers for a pandemic had been put on hold for two years while contingency planning was diverted to deal with a possible no-deal Brexit.

This made it doubly important that the government hit the ground running in late January and early February. Scientists said the threat from the coming storm was clear. Indeed, one of the government's key advisory committees was given a dire warning a month earlier than has previously been admitted about the prospect of having to deal with mass casualties.

It was a message repeated throughout February but the warnings appear to have fallen on deaf ears. The need, for example, to boost emergency supplies of protective masks and gowns for health workers was pressing, but little progress was made in obtaining the items from the manufacturers, mainly in China.

Instead, the government sent supplies the other way – shipping 279,000 items of its depleted stockpile of protective equipment to China during this period, following a request for help from the authorities there.

Impending danger

The prime minister had been sunning himself with his girlfriend in the millionaires' Caribbean resort of Mustique when China first alerted the World Health Organisation (WHO) on December 31 that several cases of an unusual pneumonia had been recorded in Wuhan, a city of 11 million people in Hubei province.

In the days that followed China initially claimed the virus could not be transmitted from human to human, which should have been reassuring. But this did not ring true to Britain's public health academics and epidemiologists who were texting each other, eager for more information, in early January.

Devi Sridhar, professor of global public health at Edinburgh University, had predicted in a talk two years earlier that a virus might jump species from an animal in China and spread quickly to become a human pandemic. So the news from Wuhan set her on high alert.

"In early January a lot of my global health colleagues and I were kind of discussing 'What's going on?'" she recalled. "China still hadn't confirmed the virus was human-to-human. A lot of us were suspecting it was because it was a respiratory pathogen and you wouldn't see the numbers of cases that we were seeing out of China if it was not human-to-human. So that was disturbing."

By as early as January 16 the professor was on Twitter calling for swift action to prepare for the virus. "Been asked by journalists how serious #WuhanPneumonia outbreak is," she wrote. "My answer: take it seriously because of cross-border spread (planes means bugs travel far & fast), likely human-to-human transmission and previous outbreaks have taught overresponding is better than delaying action."

Events were now moving fast. Four hundred miles away in London, from its campus next to the Royal Albert Hall, a team at Imperial College's School of Public Health led by Professor Neil Ferguson produced its first modelling assessment of the impact of the virus. On Friday, January 17, its report noted the "worrying" news that three cases of the virus had been discovered outside China – two in Thailand and one in Japan. While acknowledging many unknowns, researchers calculated that there could already be as many as 4,000 cases. The report warned: "The magnitude of these numbers suggests substantial human-to-human transmission cannot be ruled out. Heightened surveillance, prompt information-sharing and enhanced preparedness are recommended."

By now the mystery bug had been identified as a type of coronavirus – a large family of viruses that can cause infections ranging from the common cold to severe acute respiratory syndrome

(Sars). There had been two reported deaths from the virus and 41 patients had been taken ill.

The following Wednesday, January 22, the government convened the first meeting of its scientific advisory group for emergencies (Sage) to discuss the virus. Its membership is secret but it is usually chaired by the government's chief scientific adviser, Sir Patrick Vallance, and chief medical adviser, Professor Chris Whitty. Downing Street advisers are also present.

There were new findings that day with Chinese scientists warning that the virus had an unusually high infectivity rate of up to 3.0, which meant each person with the virus would typically infect up to three more people.

One of those present was Imperial's Ferguson, who was already working on his own estimate – putting infectivity at 2.6 and possibly as high as 3.5 – which he sent to ministers and officials in a report on the day of the Cobra meeting on January 24. The Spanish flu had an estimated infectivity rate of between 2.0 and 3.0, whereas for most flu outbreaks it is about 1.3, so Ferguson's finding was shocking.

The professor's other bombshell in the report was that there needed to be a 60% cut in the transmission rate – which meant stopping contact between people. In layman's terms it meant a lockdown, a move that would paralyse an economy already facing a battering from Brexit. At the time such a suggestion was unthinkable in the government and belonged to the world of post-apocalypse movies.

The growing alarm among scientists appears not to have been heard or heeded by policy-makers. After the January 25 Cobra meeting, the chorus of reassurance was not just from Hancock and the prime minister's spokesman: Whitty was confident too.

"Cobra met today to discuss the situation in Wuhan, China," said Whitty. "We have global experts monitoring the situation around the clock and have a strong track record of managing new forms of infectious disease . . . there are no confirmed cases in the UK to date."

However, by then there had been 1,000 cases worldwide and 41 deaths, mostly in Wuhan. A Lancet report that day presented a study of 41 coronavirus patients admitted to hospital in Wuhan, which found that more than half had severe breathing problems, a third required intensive care and six had died.

And there was now little doubt that the UK would be hit by the virus. A study by Southampton University has shown that 190,000 people flew into the UK from Wuhan and other high-risk Chinese cities between January and March. The researchers estimated that up to 1,900 of these passengers would have been infected with the coronavirus – almost guaranteeing the UK would become a centre of the subsequent pandemic.

Sure enough, five days later on Wednesday, January 29, the first coronavirus cases on British soil were found when two Chinese nationals from the same family fell ill at a hotel in York. The next day, the government raised the threat level from low to moderate.

The pandemic plan

On January 31 – or Brexit day as it had become known – there was a rousing 11pm speech by the prime minister promising that withdrawal from the European Union would be the dawn of a new era unleashing the British people who would "grow in confidence" month by month.

By this time, there was good reason for the government's top scientific advisers to feel creeping unease about the virus. The WHO had declared the coronavirus a global emergency just the day before and scientists at the London School of Hygiene and Tropical Medicine had confirmed to Whitty in a private meeting of the Nervtag advisory committee on respiratory illness that the virus's infectivity could be as bad as Ferguson's worst estimate several days earlier.

The official scientific advisers were willing to concede in public that there might be several cases of the coronavirus in the UK. But they had faith that the country's plans for a pandemic would prove robust.

This was probably a big mistake. An adviser to Downing Street – speaking off the record – said their confidence in "the plan" was misplaced. While a possible pandemic had been listed as the No 1 threat to the nation for many years, the source said that in reality it had long since stopped being treated as such.

Several emergency planners and scientists said that the plans to protect the UK in a pandemic had once been a top priority and had been well-funded for the decade following the 9/11 terrorist attacks in

2001. But then austerity cuts struck. "We were the envy of the world," the source said, "but pandemic planning became a casualty of the austerity years when there were more pressing needs."

The last rehearsal for a pandemic was a 2016 exercise codenamed Cygnus, which predicted the health service would collapse and highlighted a long list of shortcomings – including, presciently, a lack of PPE and intensive care ventilators.

But an equally lengthy list of recommendations to address the deficiencies was never implemented. The source said preparations for a no-deal Brexit "sucked all the blood out of pandemic planning" in the following years.

In the year leading up to the coronavirus outbreak key government committee meetings on pandemic planning were repeatedly "bumped" off the diary to make way for discussions about more pressing issues such as the beds crisis in the NHS. Training for NHS staff with protective equipment and respirators was also neglected, the source alleges.

Members of the government advisory group on pandemics are said to have felt powerless. "They would joke between themselves, 'Haha, let's hope we don't get a pandemic', because there wasn't a single area of practice that was being nurtured in order for us to meet basic requirements for a pandemic, never mind do it well," said the source.

"If you were with senior NHS managers at all during the last two years, you were aware that their biggest fear, their sweatiest nightmare, was a pandemic because they weren't prepared for it."

It meant that the government had much catching up to do when it was becoming clear that this "nightmare" was becoming a distinct possibility in February. But the source said there was little urgency. "Almost every plan we had was not activated in February. Almost every government department has failed to properly implement their own pandemic plans," the source said.

One deviation from the plan, for example, was a failure to give an early warning to firms that there might be a lockdown so they could start contingency planning. "There was a duty to get them to start thinking about their cashflow and their business continuity arrangements," the source said.

Superspreader

A central part of any pandemic plan is to identify anyone who becomes ill, vigorously pursue all their recent contacts and put them into quarantine. That involves testing and the UK initially seemed to be ahead of the game. In early February Hancock proudly told the Commons the UK was one of the first countries to develop a new test for the coronavirus. "Testing worldwide is being done on equipment designed in Oxford," he said.

So when Steve Walsh, a 53-year-old businessman from Hove, East Sussex, was identified as the source of the second UK outbreak on February 6 all his contacts were followed up with tests. Walsh's case was a warning of the rampant infectivity of the virus as he is believed to have passed it to five people in the UK after returning from a conference in Singapore as well as six overseas.

But Public Health England failed to take advantage of our early breakthroughs with tests and lost early opportunities to step up production to the levels that would later be needed.

This was in part because the government was planning for the virus using its blueprint for fighting the flu. Once a flu pandemic has found its way into the population and there is no vaccine, the virus is allowed to take its course until "herd immunity" is acquired. Such a plan does not require mass testing.

A senior politician told this newspaper: "I had conversations with Chris Whitty at the end of January and they were absolutely focused on herd immunity. The reason is that with flu, herd immunity is the right response if you haven't got a vaccine.

"All of our planning was for pandemic flu. There has basically been a divide between scientists in Asia who saw this as a horrible, deadly disease on the lines of Sars, which requires immediate lockdown, and those in the West, particularly in the US and UK, who saw this as flu."

The prime minister's special adviser Dominic Cummings is said to have had initial enthusiasm for the herd immunity concept, which may have played a part in the government's early approach to managing the virus. The Department of Health firmly denies that "herd immunity" was ever its aim and rejects suggestions that Whitty supported it. Cummings also denies backing the concept.

The failure to obtain large amounts of testing equipment was another big error of judgment, according to the Downing Street source.

It would later be one of the big scandals of the coronavirus crisis that the considerable capacity of Britain's private laboratories to mass-produce tests was not harnessed during those crucial weeks of February.

"We should have communicated with every commercial testing laboratory that might volunteer to become part of the government's testing regime but that didn't happen," said the source.

The lack of action was confirmed by Doris-Ann Williams, chief executive of the British In Vitro Diagnostics Association, which represents 110 companies that make up most of the UK's testing sector. Amazingly, she said her organisation did not receive a meaningful approach from the government asking for help until April 1 – the night before Hancock bowed to pressure and announced a belated and ambitious target of 100,000 tests a day by the end of this month.

There was also a failure to replenish supplies of gowns and masks for health and care workers in the early weeks of February – despite NHS England declaring the virus its first "level four critical incident" at the end of January.

It was a key part of the pandemic plan – the NHS's Operating Framework for Managing the Response to Pandemic Influenza dated December 2017 – that the NHS would be able to draw on "just in case" stockpiles of PPE.

But many of the "just in case" stockpiles had dwindled, and equipment was out of date. As not enough money was being spent on replenishing stockpiles, this shortfall was supposed to be filled by activating "just in time" contracts which had been arranged with equipment suppliers in recent years to deal with an emergency. The first order for equipment under the "just in time" protocol was made on January 30.

However, the source said that attempts to call in these "just in time" contracts immediately ran into difficulties in February because they were mostly with Chinese manufacturers who were facing unprecedented demand from the country's own health service and elsewhere.

This was another nail in the coffin for the pandemic plan. "It was a massive spider's web of failing, every domino has fallen," said the source.

The NHS could have contacted UK-based suppliers. The British Healthcare Trades Association (BHTA) was ready to help supply PPE in February – and throughout March – but it was only on April 1 that its offer of help was accepted. Dr Simon Festing, the organisation's chief executive, said: "Orders undoubtedly went overseas instead of to the NHS because of the missed opportunities in the procurement process."

Downing Street admitted on February 24 – just five days before NHS chiefs warned a lack of PPE left the health service facing a "nightmare" – that the UK government had supplied 1,800 pairs of goggles and 43,000 disposable gloves, 194,000 sanitising wipes, 37,500 medical gowns and 2,500 face masks to China.

A senior Department of Health insider described the sense of drift witnessed during those crucial weeks in February: "We missed the boat on testing and PPE . . . I remember being called into some of the meetings about this in February and thinking, 'Well, it's a good thing this isn't the big one.'

"I had watched Wuhan but I assumed we must have not been worried because we did nothing. We just watched. A pandemic was always at the top of our national risk register – always – but when it came we just slowly watched. We could have been Germany but instead we were doomed by our incompetence, our hubris and our austerity."

In the Far East the threat was being treated more seriously in the early weeks of February. Martin Hibberd, a professor of emerging infectious diseases at the London School of Hygiene and Tropical Medicine, was in a unique position to compare the UK's response with Singapore, where he had advised in the past.

"Singapore realised, as soon as Wuhan reported it, that cases were going to turn up in Singapore. And so they prepared for that. I looked at the UK and I can see a different strategy and approach.

"The interesting thing for me is, I've worked with Singapore in 2003 and 2009 and basically they copied the UK pandemic preparedness plan. But the difference is they actually implemented it."

Working holiday

Towards the end of the second week of February, the prime minister was demob happy. After sacking five cabinet ministers and saying everyone "should be confident and calm" about Britain's response to the virus, Johnson vacated Downing Street after the half-term recess began on February 13.

He headed to the country for a "working" holiday at Chevening with Symonds and would be out of the public eye for 12 days. His aides were thankful for the rest, as they had been working flat out since the summer as the Brexit power struggle had played out.

The Sunday newspapers that weekend would not have made comfortable reading. *The Sunday Times* reported on a briefing from a risk specialist which said Public Health England would be overrun during a pandemic as it could test only 1,000 people a day.

Johnson may well have been distracted by matters in his personal life during his stay in the countryside. Aides were told to keep their briefing papers short and cut the number of memos in his red box if they wanted them to be read.

His family needed to be prepared for the announcement that Symonds, who turned 32 in March, was pregnant and that they had been secretly engaged for some time. Relations with his children had been fraught since his separation from his estranged wife Marina Wheeler and the rift had deepened when she had been diagnosed with cancer last year.

The divorce also had to be finalised. Midway through the break it was announced in the High Court that the couple had reached a settlement, leaving Wheeler free to apply for divorce.

There were murmurings of frustration from some ministers and their aides at the time that Johnson was not taking more of a lead. But Johnson's aides are understood to have felt relaxed: he was getting updates and they claim the scientists were saying everything was under control.

400,000 deaths

By the time Johnson departed for the countryside, however, there was mounting unease among scientists about the exceptional nature of the threat. Sir Jeremy Farrar, an infectious disease specialist who is a key government adviser, made this clear in a recent BBC interview.

"I think from the early days in February, if not in late January, it was obvious this infection was going to be very serious and it was going to affect more than just the region of Asia," he said. "I think it was very clear that this was going to be an unprecedented event."

By February 21, the virus had already infected 76,000 people, had caused 2,300 deaths in China and was taking a foothold in Europe, with Italy recording 51 cases and two deaths the following day. Nonetheless Nervtag, one of the key government advisory committees, decided to keep the threat level at "moderate".

Its members may well regret that decision with hindsight, and it was certainly not unanimous. John Edmunds, one of the country's top infectious disease modellers from the London School of Hygiene and Tropical Medicine, was participating in the meeting by video link but his technology failed him at the crucial moment.

Edmunds wanted the threat level to be increased to high but could not make his view known as the link was glitchy. He sent an email later making his view clear. "JE believes that the risk to the UK population [in the PHE risk assessment] should be high, as there is evidence of ongoing transmission in Korea, Japan and Singapore, as well as in China," the meeting's minutes state. But the decision had already been taken.

Peter Openshaw, professor of experimental medicine at Imperial College, was in America at the time of the meeting but would also have recommended increasing the threat to high. Three days earlier he had given an address to a seminar in which he estimated that 60% of the world's population would probably become infected if no action was taken and 400,000 people would die in the UK.

By February 26, there were 13 known cases in the UK. That day – almost four weeks before a full lockdown would be announced – ministers were warned through another advisory committee that the country was facing a catastrophic loss of life unless drastic action was taken. Having been thwarted from sounding the alarm, Edmunds and his team presented their latest "worst scenario" predictions to the scientific pandemic influenza group on modelling (SPI-M) which directly advises the country's scientific decision-makers in Sage.

It warned that 27 million people could be infected and 220,000 intensive care beds would be needed if no action were taken to reduce infection rates. The predicted death toll was 380,000. Edmunds's colleague Nick Davies, who led the research, says the report emphasised the urgent need for a lockdown almost four weeks before it was imposed.

The team later modelled the effects of a 12-week lockdown involving school and work closures, shielding the elderly, social distancing and self-isolation. It estimated this would delay the impact of the pandemic but there still might be 280,000 deaths over the year.

Johnson returns

The previous night Johnson had returned to London for the Conservatives' big fundraising ball, the Winter Party, at which one donor pledged £60,000 for the privilege of playing a game of tennis with him.

By this time the prime minister had missed five Cobra meetings on the preparations to combat the looming pandemic, which he left to be chaired by Hancock. Johnson was an easy target for the opposition when he returned to the Commons the following day with the Labour leader, Jeremy Corbyn, labelling him a "part-time" prime minister for his failure to lead on the virus crisis or visit the areas of the UK badly hit by floods.

By Friday, February 28, the virus had taken root in the UK with reported cases rising to 19 and the stock markets were plunging. It was finally time for Johnson to act. He summoned a TV reporter into Downing Street to say he was on top of the coronavirus crisis.

"The issue of coronavirus is something that is now the government's top priority," he said. "I have just had a meeting with the chief medical officer and secretary of state for health talking about the preparations that we need to make."

It was finally announced that he would be attending a meeting of Cobra – after a weekend at Chequers with Symonds where the couple would publicly release news of the engagement and their baby.

On the Sunday, there was a meeting between Sage committee members and officials from the Department of Health and the NHS which was a game changer, according to a Whitehall source. The meeting was shown fresh modelling based on figures from Italy suggesting that 8% of infected people might need hospital treatment in a worst-case scenario. The previous estimate had been 4%–5%.

"The risk to the NHS had effectively doubled in an instant. It set alarm bells ringing across government," said the Whitehall source. "I think that meeting focused minds. You realise it's time to pull the trigger on the starting gun."

At the Cobra meeting the next day with Johnson in the chair a full "battle plan" was finally signed off to contain, delay and mitigate the spread of the virus. This was on March 2 – five weeks after the first Cobra meeting on the virus.

The new push would have some positive benefits such as the creation of new Nightingale hospitals, which greatly increased the number of intensive care beds. But there was a further delay that month of nine days in introducing the lockdown as Johnson and his senior advisers debated what measures were required. Later the government would be left rudderless again after Johnson himself contracted the virus.

As the number of infections grew daily, some things were impossible to retrieve. There was a worldwide shortage of PPE and the prime minister would have to personally ring manufacturers of ventilators and testing kits in a desperate effort to boost supplies.

The result was that the NHS and care home workers would be left without proper protection and insufficient numbers of tests to find out whether they had been infected. To date 50 doctors, nurses and NHS workers have died. More than 100,000 people have been confirmed as infected in Britain and 15,000 have died.

A Downing Street spokesman said: "Our response has ensured that the NHS has been given all the support it needs to ensure everyone requiring treatment has received it, as well as providing protection to businesses and reassurance to workers. The prime minister has been at the helm of the response to this, providing leadership during this hugely challenging period for the whole nation."

Insight: Jonathan Calvert, George Arbuthnott, and Jonathan Leake

22 DAYS OF DITHER AND DELAY ON CORONAVIRUS THAT COST THOUSANDS OF BRITISH LIVES

———•———

24 May 2020

THERE IS a simple mathematical truth that would have caused alarm about the coronavirus pandemic if it had been more fully appreciated when it was first flagged up in reports from China in late January. The number of people infected appeared to double in as little as three days. The maths was remorseless. It meant one case would become eight in nine days, and after 21 it would be 128. In less than nine weeks, one case could infect a million people.

So time was already running out for Britain when, amid the last of the late February storms, Boris Johnson returned from his working holiday at the state-owned Chevening residence to face opposition accusations that he was a "part-time" prime minister.

On Monday, March 2, the virus had been in the country for almost five weeks and was multiplying fast. This was an important day as Johnson had decided to get a grip on the crisis by doing something he had notably failed to do since it started. "I have just chaired a Cobra meeting on coronavirus," he declared in a video message to the nation.

Standing in front of a Downing Street bookcase full of leather-bound volumes, the prime minister warned that the virus was likely to become a more significant problem and added "this country is very, very well prepared . . . we've got fantastic testing systems, amazing surveillance of the spread of disease". Widespread testing and contact tracing would, however, be abandoned in just over a week.

Johnson had agreed an "action plan" with his fellow members of the Cobra emergency committee that morning but new measures, to prevent the spread of the virus, would be introduced later only if needed. It would be a notable feature of the prime minister's televised press briefings over the next crucial three weeks until lockdown that key actions would be deferred until future dates. Meanwhile, the virus was spreading rapidly.

Inexplicably, the final sentence of the March 2 video message has been lopped off the version posted on the prime ministerial Twitter page. It was: "I wish to stress that, at the moment, it's very important that people consider that they should, as far as possible, go about business as usual."

Having delivered Brexit on January 31, Downing Street was keen to foster a mood of buoyancy and optimism as the nation began its new future of self-determination. In the following days, Johnson initially epitomised the upbeat spirit, shaking hands and attending the rugby at Twickenham, in a clear signal that life should go on despite the virus.

Life did go on as usual at the beginning of March. The bars and trains remained packed and mass sporting events were attended as normal. Many people are likely to have paid with their lives for commuting on packed trains, drinking in pubs and attending events such as the Cheltenham Festival during this period.

Across the world, many governments would be grappling with the fast-moving crisis and few would emerge from the coming months without mistakes. In Britain, the government's response was to replace "Let's get Brexit done" with a new mantra: "We're following the science". But was that what the decision-making team – Johnson, key advisers such as Dominic Cummings, and ministers, including the health secretary Matt Hancock, as well as the chief scientific and medical advisers – were actually doing?

The big lockdown gamble

An Insight investigation has talked to scientists, politicians, academics, emergency planners and advisers to Downing Street about the government's response to the coronavirus crisis in the three weeks from March 2.

We found that a key government committee was informed at the beginning of the month by its two top modelling teams that Britain was facing a catastrophic loss of life without drastic action. By then, however, any hope of containing the virus through contact tracing had fallen through because the government had failed to adequately increase its testing capacity in January and February.

Caught in the headlights, the government was intent on pursuing a "contain" and "delay" policy of allowing the virus to spread through the population, with the intention of shielding the vulnerable and elderly and introducing new measures to slow the rate down at some future point when it looked as if the NHS might be overwhelmed.

This approach was based on the flu model, which was designed to cope with an infection that was very infectious in a similar way to the coronavirus but less deadly. In the Far East, countries such as Taiwan, South Korea, Vietnam and Singapore based their approach on lessons learnt combating the Sars crisis of 2003 and other viral outbreaks that emerged from China. They were better prepared to move fast, particularly in their use of tests and tracing to restrict the spread.

In the UK it was hoped that antibody resistance would be built up in the population – herd immunity – in order to avoid a second outbreak later in the year that might be even worse. This, however, was a big gamble as there was no clear evidence that people who had suffered the virus would have lasting antibody protection. Despite using the term at the time, the government denies it had a policy of herd immunity.

The government pursued its contain and delay strategy through the first two weeks of March despite the strong warnings from its two main modelling teams that it could lead to a catastrophic number of people being killed by the virus. The teams from Imperial College London and the London School of Hygiene & Tropical Medicine (LSHTM) both concluded separately that if the mitigation measures under the delay strategy were followed, it could result in about 250,000 deaths. They delivered papers detailing those findings to a meeting of Sage, the scientific advisory group for emergencies, on March 3, attended by government officials.

It was only in the middle weekend of March that the key decision makers would fully engage with the fact that their mitigation measures risked a death sentence for a quarter of a million people and something far tougher was required.

What is more, this realisation came only after the academic teams took it upon themselves to model a lockdown as the only solution that could avoid overwhelming the NHS – showing how deaths could be kept to the tens of thousands.

There was a key meeting of the prime minister's close team on the morning of Saturday, March 14, after the modellers' new projections on the lockdown solution had been delivered. By this point European countries were hastily introducing lockdowns and there was growing support among Johnson's team for the move.

After being initially hostile to the idea, the prime minister put his libertarian instincts to one side and agreed in principle that a lockdown would be necessary. However, rather than locking down immediately, there was a further nine-day delay as he deliberated over how and when a lockdown should be introduced.

That prevarication proved, for some, to be fatal. New back-dated modelling assessing the historic spread of the disease which is published for the first time today – estimates the number of people infected in the UK was indeed doubling every three days during late February and early March, just as some of the initial reports from China in late January had suggested they might.

The work, produced jointly by an Imperial College London team led by Samir Bhatt and Oxford University, suggests that on March 3 – the day the government committee gave the warning about the dire consequences of a mitigation approach – there were about 14,000 infections in the UK. Such was the speed of the spread of the virus that 200,000 people were estimated to be infected by the time the government began to change its mind about its policy on Saturday, March 14.

The last nine days while Johnson wrestled over the decision on when and how to go for lockdown were particularly brutal. By the time the lockdown was announced on Monday, March 23, such large numbers were doubling over such a short period that infections are estimated to have soared to 1.5 million.

According to the data, no other large European country allowed infections to sky-rocket to such a high level before finally deciding to go into lockdown. Those 20 days of government delay are the single most important reason why the UK has the second highest number of deaths from the coronavirus in the world.

Getting in front of the virus

A few hours before Johnson attended Cobra on March 2 another leader was holding her own press conference on the response to the coronavirus crisis on the side of the world where the sun rises first.

With slow precision Jacinda Ardern, the New Zealand prime minister, read out a raft of measures her small island nation was taking to protect health and business because "the precautionary approach is best".

Travel from China had already been banned for a month and 8,000 New Zealand nationals returning home from the area and Iran had been self-isolating for two weeks. That day Ardern said travellers from Italy and South Korea would be required to self-isolate for two weeks. "It is too early to say what the impact will be, but regardless, we are getting in front of this issue," she added.

The early intervention would prove highly successful and enabled New Zealand to start to return to normality last month after a relatively short lockdown with just over 1,500 cases and 21 deaths.

By contrast, the island of Britain was in a far more exposed position than New Zealand as an international air hub with 23.7 million people arriving in the UK in the first three months of the year.

So it was perhaps all the more surprising that so little had been done in the five weeks before March to prepare the UK for a pandemic while our borders were kept open, despite warnings from scientists.

A statement on March 2 by the government's scientific pandemic influenza (SPI) group on modelling had advised that it was "almost certain" there would be sustained transmission of the coronavirus in the UK and it was "highly likely" to be already happening. It estimated that the time taken for cases to double was about four to six days – a rate that had been revised downwards from initial estimates in January on the spread of the disease in Wuhan, the Chinese city where the outbreak is thought to have begun.

However, the recent research from Imperial College London and Oxford University has been able to make more accurate estimates by using the dates when people died from the virus to look back and work out the likely rates of infection in the past. This appears to confirm that infections were in fact doubling every three days and an estimated 11,000 people were already infected on March 2 – and could soon become millions.

While the government's modelling committee may have underestimated the speed of the spread of the virus, it was not blind to the scale of the problem faced in Britain. It warned of a worst case scenario of 80% of the population becoming infected.

The Cobra plan

Given the grim predictions and the near-certainty of sustained transmission, it might have been expected that the prime minister would announce concrete and immediate steps when he returned back to Downing Street via the network of corridors from committee room B, where he had attended his first Cobra meeting on the crisis.

But the action plan that emerged from the meeting amounted to a series of measures that would only be taken at some future date to halt the spread of the disease. It puzzled Lord Kerslake, who would have been responsible for implementing such a plan when he was the head of the civil service under David Cameron. "If ministers believe that emergency measures will be necessary, they should act now," he told *The Guardian* that day, adding that the only reason for holding back was if "you don't believe they are necessary in the end".

The full details of the government's action plan were set out in a lengthy document from the Department of Health and Social Care on March 3 that introduced its "contain, delay, research, mitigate" strategy. It notes ominously that "if the disease becomes established in the UK . . . it may be that widespread exposure in the UK is inevitable".

Officially, the country was still in the "contain" phase, in which the contacts of anyone who had contracted the virus would be tracked down and tested. But that battle had already been lost. Such was the rapid spread of the virus that it had almost certainly reached one of Johnson's own ministers, Nadine Dorries, the health minister, who would start to go down with symptoms two days later.

Given that widespread exposure appeared highly likely, it would have been possible to have moved on swiftly to the delay strategies outlined in the document, which included: "school closures, encouraging greater home working, reducing the number of large-scale gatherings". But, according to the document, the government was planning to weigh up the trade-off between the "social and economic impact" of such measures and "keeping people safe". It decided to wait. And wait.

True to form, the prime minister was in a characteristically upbeat mood when he presented the action plan at the first of his daily press conferences on March 3 flanked by two doctors who were to become household names. Likeable, earnest and articulate Professor Chris Whitty, the chief medical officer for England, and Sir Patrick Vallance, the chief scientific adviser, would be used as the government's human proof that it was "following the science".

Johnson told the journalists sitting shoulder to shoulder in the wood-panelled 9 Downing Street room that the coronavirus was "overwhelmingly a disease that is moderate in its effects" before repeating his misplaced faith in the UK's testing and surveillance systems. "This country is going to get through coronavirus, no doubt at all and get through it in good shape," he added.

The prime minister said the plan was not a list of actions the government "will do" but rather it was what it "could do at the right time". He said: "Our plan means we are committed to doing everything possible based on the advice of our world leading scientific experts to prepare for all eventualities."

Sage advice on modelling

It has now emerged that earlier that same day some of those world-leading scientists had presented data to a meeting of the Sage advisory group showing the alarming consequences of the mitigation measures being proposed by the government.

The renowned pandemic modelling teams from Imperial College London and LSHTM had been asked to assess the effects of strategies to mitigate the virus such as social distancing, school closures, whole household isolation and banning mass gatherings. Their findings were a stark warning to the government about the policy it was pursuing.

If there were no interventions then there could be as many 500,000 deaths. But the figures were still frightening when they factored in the mitigation measures. The teams both found that no matter how they modelled the measures – singly or in combination – the death toll was huge: more than 200,000 could lose their lives in the LSHTM calculation, and 250,000 according to Imperial.

A source close to the two teams said Professor Neil Ferguson of Imperial, and Professor John Edmunds of LSHTM – who had both attended Sage meetings at the time – became increasingly concerned after the figures had been calculated. It seemed that all the scenarios the teams were asked to model were insufficiently draconian to avert a disaster. "We looked at the mitigation strategies one by one and in combination and we realised that they would still likely result in large numbers of deaths," said Edmunds.

However, the source said the government did not even ask the teams to model whether a lockdown might be the solution and instead only commissioned them to look at increasingly finer-grained versions of mitigation in early March. "I think a sense of, 'It can't really be that bad' was important in explaining the delay," said the source. "The [modellers'] central estimates of severity were viewed as a 'reasonable worst case' by the government – not the most likely scenario. It took them a while to be convinced."

The source added: "I think an overarching concern – and why so much time was spent looking at alternatives involving mitigation and shielding – was that everyone, especially Chris Whitty, Patrick Vallance and the policy people, knew what the economic and social costs of lockdown would be."

The modellers would later take matters into their own hands.

UK is open for business

In the first week of March the number of officially confirmed cases rose significantly from 36 to 206. By the weekend of Saturday, March 7, the scale of the catastrophe facing the UK and its speed could be seen just a thousand miles away in Italy where cases had risen fivefold to 5,800 and the deaths had increased eightfold to 233 in just six days that week.

There was no clear reason to assume the UK would escape the pandemic more lightly than Italy. That weekend the Ireland versus Italy Six Nations rugby match in Dublin was called off because of fears that it might help spread the virus. Across the UK, hundreds of thousands of people attended sports events as usual.

On Sunday, March 8, France banned public gatherings of more than 1,000 people but that same day thousands of French fans were allowed to mingle in the 67,000 crowd at Murrayfield, Edinburgh, for their team's Six Nations game with Scotland.

The prime minister made his own statement the previous day about Britain being open for business by joining the 81,000-strong crowd that watched England beat Wales at Twickenham.

Across the world people had been replacing handshakes with awkward waves or the knocking of elbows in an attempt to limit the spread of the infection. In the UK the SPI behavioural group, which reports to Sage, the key committee informing the political decision makers, made clear recommendations that the "Government should advise against greetings such as shaking hands and hugging, given existing evidence about the importance of hand hygiene."

But Johnson was determined to carry on as normal. "I'm shaking hands," he had told the March 3 press conference on the day the behavioural group's guidance came out. "I was at a hospital the other night where I think there were a few coronavirus patients and I shook hands with everybody, you'll be pleased to know."

A couple of days later during an appearance on ITV's This Morning he bounded over to Phillip Schofield and seized his hand when the presenter had deliberately kept his arms by his side. Schofield pointedly inquired whether Johnson had washed his hands before grabbing him.

Unrepentant, Johnson then posted on Twitter a video of himself eagerly shaking hands with five female rugby players at Twickenham on Saturday, March 7. It was curious behaviour bearing in mind Johnson's repeated statements that he and the government were following the advice of the scientists on the crisis.

A source who was advising Downing Street at the time said: "The handshake – you can't minimise how important that is. He was the ultimate example of somebody saying, 'This is a mild illness, the scientists are overstating this.'"

Gunmetal skies at Cheltenham

Three days later the gunmetal skies and threat of drizzle did little to damp the ardour of the horse-racing enthusiasts as more than 60,000 people flocked to the opening of the four-day Cheltenham festival on the morning of Tuesday, March 10.

The Cheltenham festival had once been cancelled for foot and mouth, a livestock disease, but it was not going to stop for the coronavirus, especially with the prime minister sending out messages that Britain was open as usual. On the opening day of the event, Ian Renton, the festival's director, sent a letter to concerned local councillors setting out the reasons for going ahead.

It said: "As with events from England v Wales attended by the prime minister at Twickenham on Saturday to 10 Premier League games around the country this weekend, the government guidance is for the business of the country to continue as usual while ensuring we adhere to and promote the latest public health advice."

Bottles of hand sanitiser were placed in the washrooms and around the racecourse for the crowds who mingled and pressed together in the enclosures drinking and eating. One of those people was Jules Annan, a 55-year-old freelance photographer, who worked on all four days taking photographs of celebrities, tycoons and royals who had joined the throng. Ten days later he found himself struggling for breath as he was rushed to Cheltenham General Hospital and placed on oxygen. "My lungs basically gave up," he said. "I knew I was in a bad way."

He cannot be certain about how he became infected with the virus, which he eventually shook off, but he believes he may have become infected during the races. "There was a guy in the bed opposite me at the hospital who was at the races too and thinks he got it there."

Gloucestershire would later experience a spike in hospital death rates and the effects of the event may have spread across the country. Two racing enthusiasts who attended the festival died on the same day at the end of March.

They were Paul Townend, 61, a racehorse owner from Stratford-upon-Avon, who had his ventilator switched off in Warwick Hospital, and David Hodgkiss, a 71-year-old chief executive of a steelmaking firm and chairman of Lancashire cricket club, from Cumbria.

Townend's widow, Geraldine, blames her husband's death on the government's failure to bring in the lockdown earlier. "I don't know why we were so late?" she said. "Other countries were in lockdown well before us. The writing was on the wall."

One of the last sporting fixtures played this year was on March 11, when 3,000 fans came over from Spain to watch Liverpool play Atlético Madrid in the Champions League. According to the Imperial College London and Oxford University estimates, Spain had 640,000 infections at the time compared with 100,000 in Britain, although it was just a week ahead in terms of the spread of the virus such was its unchecked growth across the UK during that period.

Edge Health, which analyses health data for the NHS, carried out modelling that estimated that the match and the Cheltenham festival are linked to 41 and 37 additional deaths respectively at nearby hospitals between 25 and 35 days later, compared with similar hospital trusts that were used as a control. And that was just the local hospitals.

The herd immunity problem

Back in London on the day before the Cheltenham festival began, the chief scientist Vallance had been put forward to express the scientific view that mass gatherings were not a big problem. Vallance, who had left a £780,000-a-year job in the pharmaceutical industry a year before to take the job advising ministers, explained that gatherings "actually don't make much difference".

He said: "There's only a certain number of people you can infect. So, one person in a 70,000-seater stadium is not going to infect the stadium. They will infect potentially a few people they've got very close contact with. That's true in any setting: in the house, in a church, in a restaurant."

Sir David King, one of Vallance's predecessors as chief scientific adviser and a critic of the current administration, is scathing about the reasoning on mass gatherings. His son was at the Cheltenham festival and later suffered coronavirus symptoms, which took him three weeks to recover from.

King said: "If you've ever been to a race meeting or football match, you would normally meet your friends in a pub beforehand, then you often need to get a train – there are long queues and big crowds. Anyone who has attended any of these events knows you are in contact with a very large number of people.

"But worse than that the people at these football matches and horse races come from all over the country and return to all over the country. It's the ideal way to spread the virus. My only sensible interpretation is that is what you would advise if you were aiming for herd immunity."

The news from the government was becoming increasingly gloomy that Monday, March 9. After chairing another Cobra meeting, Johnson had been forced to announce that attempts to contain the virus were unlikely to succeed on their own.

Johnson said measures would inevitably have to be introduced to delay the spread of the virus and he would follow the scientific advice and act when the time was judged to be right. Whitty told journalists that the first of those measures – asking anyone with respiratory symptoms or a fever to self-isolate – would be the next step, but not for another 10 to 14 days.

The delays and the toleration of mass gatherings in a way fitted with the same policy. There was a view within the team advising the government that once contact tracing had failed to contain the outbreak then a burgeoning number of cases was inevitable – even desirable.

The plan – which the modellers had already estimated would cause more than 200,000 deaths – was to allow the virus to infect large parts of the population, while shielding the old and the vulnerable, and bringing in measures to slow down the rate of infection when it looked as if the numbers of cases might overwhelm the NHS.

The thinking behind this approach was that any attempt to shut down the virus completely would have repercussions later, with a likely second outbreak that might cause an even greater death toll in the autumn and winter, as insufficient numbers of people would have acquired immunity to the virus. This was the implicit herd immunity aspect of the policy that became so controversial when it became explicit as the second week of March wore on.

Vallance told the Monday press conference: "What you can't do is suppress this thing completely and what you shouldn't do is suppress this thing completely because all that happens is that this thing pops up later in the year when the NHS is in a more vulnerable stage in the winter."

A source who was advising Downing Street at the time said that herd immunity was central to the government's plans in late February and early March. "There was always this message coming straight down of, 'We've all got to get it,'" the source said. "And I remember having a conversation about how, 'I don't like this and this chicken pox party thing.' In February and March it was like, we've all got to get it at some point and that was just a sort of mantra."

But patience was running out with the government's delays and inaction. On Wednesday, March 11, Anthony Costello, professor of global health at University College London and a former World Health Organisation director, tweeted what many experts were thinking.

"We're simply not doing enough now. We shd [sic] ban mass gatherings, close parliaments, alert all health workers about protective equipment and hygiene, close schools/colleges, promote home working wherever possible, and protect workers in the gig economy. Every day of delay will kill."

On Thursday, March 12, there was a deepened gravity in the prime minister's voice when, standing in front of two Union Jack flags, he told the nation: "This is the worst public health crisis for a generation . . . I must level with you, level with the British public – more families, many more families are going to lose loved ones before their time."

Only nine days earlier he had described the virus as a "moderate illness". But by that Thursday the number of confirmed cases had jumped from 51 on March 3 to 596 and there had been 10 deaths. The contain strategy had not worked and contact tracing was abandoned – as the failure to increase testing capacity during previous weeks made it impossible.

By then it would have been futile anyway because the Imperial and Oxford back-modelling estimates predict by that day 130,000 people had caught the virus. This suggests that the contact testing programme had only picked up 0.5% of the infections when it was finally discarded.

The government had clearly misread the speed of the virus's acceleration. So the first of the mitigation measures was finally brought in that day when people were told to self-isolate at home if they had symptoms. Just three days before, Whitty had said this measure would be introduced in 10 to 14 days.

Two other measures would also be brought in – the banning of mass gatherings and isolation of whole households if one person had symptoms – but again the government stressed these would be delayed to the "right time" in the future.

Vallance and Whitty explained the staged timing by saying people might tire of such social distancing measures if they were brought in too early and lasted a long time. "If people go too early they become very fatigued. This is going to be a long haul. It is very important we don't start things in advance of need," Whitty said.

The newspapers the next morning, Friday the 13th, were withering. "Johnson's response has not been to lock down entire cities or even the whole country, as China, South Korea and Italy have done. He has not ordered the closure of schools, as Ireland and Denmark did yesterday. Nor has he ordered the cancellation of large public events, as France and even Scotland have done," complained *The Times* leader.

"Instead, his response was to announce that Britain would stop testing all but those exhibiting the most severe symptoms of the virus . . . This is a remarkable gamble by Mr Johnson, albeit one that the government insists is informed by science."

That morning Vallance went on Radio 4's *Today* programme and dug an even deeper hole for his colleagues by mentioning the phrase the spin doctors did not want the public to hear. The government's aim, he said, was to suppress the virus but not completely and "to build up some degree of herd immunity" while protecting the vulnerable. Later, on Sky News, he said that herd immunity would require 60% of the population to contract the virus.

That would be 40 million people – of whom 1% were likely to die, based on events in China and Italy. It was quite a gamble as it had not yet even been established whether people would develop long-running antibody resistance after contracting the virus.

The solution

The days were ticking by quickly. Despite repeated assertions by the government it was following the scientific advice, there was increasing concern among its two university modelling teams that their warnings were not being heeded that the death toll would still be horrendous even if the mitigation measures were introduced.

They took matters into their own hands and, without being commissioned to do so, began crunching the numbers on a lockdown from their campuses in London. The first results were contained in an LSHTM study – co-authored by Edmunds and his colleague Nicholas Davies. This was communicated to the government's advisory modelling committee on Wednesday, March 11, according to Davies. Modellers at Edinburgh University, led by Professor Mark Woolhouse, confirmed the findings.

The report advised that the death rate could be drastically cut with more severe measures to suppress the virus. It predicted that intermittent periods of intensive lockdown-type measures would prevent the NHS from being overwhelmed.

Ferguson and his team at Imperial drew similar conclusions that week in an equally devastating report. The early results of that work were discussed in Sage that week and provided to the government that weekend. A draft was also sent to the White House as it predicted up to 1.2 million deaths in America under a mitigation strategy.

The team estimated that the number of UK deaths could be cut to about 30,000 with a series of lockdowns over a two-year period, whereas the government's preferred mitigation measures could allow hundreds of thousands of deaths. The two reports were the beginning of the end for the government's strategy.

World closes down

The world was closing down by Saturday, March 14. France said it was shutting non-essential public locations, Spain went into lockdown that evening, America had announced a ban on flights from the UK and the Italians were already holding impromptu concerts from their balconies after the whole country had been confined to their homes since Tuesday.

In the UK many people had given up waiting for the government to take action and were already taking matters into their own hands. Firms were encouraging employees to work from home, and suddenly that Saturday's sporting fixture list was looking threadbare as the leagues cancelled games of their own volition despite the huge losses in revenues.

The government's strategy was in shreds: ripped apart by its own modelling scientists and looking creepily Darwinian after the unfortunate introduction of the words "herd immunity". More than 200 scientists and academics signed a letter condemning the delay policy and saying thousands of lives could be saved by introducing stricter social distancing measures immediately.

These were the problems confronting Johnson when he summoned a meeting of his inner team at 9.15am that Saturday morning. By then it is understood that his most influential adviser Cummings had gone through a "Domoscene conversion" to being a strong advocate of the kind of suppression strategy that would lead to lockdown.

A source who attended Cobra meetings at the time said: "The libertarian in Boris didn't want lockdown." However, Johnson is said to have been won over at the meeting because of the seriousness of the threat, and a decision was made in principle to lock down Britain. He told those around him "we need to be taking all measures necessary".

But the key issues of how and when to introduce a lockdown would not be resolved for another nine days. A senior Tory source said Johnson "bottled" lockdown during the following week because of concerns about the economy.

The failure to seize the initiative and go into lockdown at that point was a decision that cost many lives. After deliberating over the weekend, the government waited until the evening of Monday March 16 to introduce a package of advisory measures. People were told to work from home if possible, avoid pubs and restaurants and self-isolate at home if someone in their household was ill.

Even scientists on the government's own advisory committees were alarmed by the delays in introducing more stringent measures. Professor Peter Openshaw, a member of the government's Nervtag (new and emerging respiratory virus threats advisory group) committee said: "Many of us on the scientific advisory committees were quite keen that action should be taken a couple of weeks before action actually was taken.

"I think that critical period of delay made the big difference to the peak numbers, both of hospitalisations and of deaths. I think everyone would accept now in retrospect that if we'd gone for lockdown a couple of weeks earlier that would have greatly reduced the numbers of hospitalisations and deaths."

Every day was vital now as the UK already had an estimated 320,000 infections on March 16, according to the Imperial and Oxford back-dated modelling, and it would double again almost every three days despite the advisory measures which were introduced.

Final days to lockdown

The final week before lockdown was played out in slow motion. There had been a fundamental pivot in government policy towards more draconian actions but the prime minister is said to have still been uncomfortable with the idea of a full legally enforced shutdown, which many of his advisers now saw as an unfortunate necessity.

It was to be a week of more delays and more drip feed measures. The big announcement on Wednesday was that finally schools would be closed indefinitely but that would not take place until Friday afternoon.

The measures to close cafés, pubs, bars, clubs, restaurants, gyms, leisure centres, nightclubs, theatres and cinemas would not take effect until midnight that evening. Isolation to protect the 1.5 million people identified as extremely vulnerable as a result of existing conditions would not be announced until Sunday, March 22.

While many people were already working from home and starting to stand their distance from others in social situations, there were reports that many commuter buses and trains were still packed in central London, which had more than a third of known cases. Google data tracking people's movements suggests the use of public transport was down by only a third across the UK by Wednesday, March 18. It was clear not everyone was following the government's advice.

Having backed the government's earlier strategy, Cummings was said to now be convinced it wouldn't work and was advocating a lockdown, starting with restricting traffic in and out of London. Military chiefs are said to have been put on notice that their troops might be needed to enforce a lockdown in the capital starting at midnight on Saturday.

A government insider said the prime minister looked "haunted" as he wrestled with the big decision of what to do next. His attempts at jollity had backfired at the beginning of the week when he described the effort to equip the NHS with more ventilators to meet the coming blizzard of respiratory illnesses as "operation last gasp".

The gearing up of the NHS had one particularly ill-thought-out and reckless consequence. On Thursday, March 19, the health department announced 15,000 people should be discharged from hospitals into the community and care homes to free up beds for coronavirus patients. This was without a mandatory requirement that they be tested for the virus.

On Friday, March 20, Dr Jenny Harries, deputy chief medical officer for England, reassured the country that there was a "perfectly adequate supply of PPE [personal protective equipment] for care workers and any supply pressures have been completely resolved". The lack of PPE and the failure to protect the elderly in care homes would shortly become the next national scandal to haunt the government and expose its lack of planning since January.

At the Downing Street press conference, Harries advised people to stay two metres apart during walks while standing at a lectern less than a metre from the prime minister.

By that day, the number of infections had doubled during the midweek to an estimated 790,000, according to the Imperial and Oxford data. Despite the growing dangers, many people popped out for a last drink before the pubs shut overnight.

The clement spring weather that weekend brought thousands of people out into parks and open spaces in the new world where they could no longer congregate in sports clubs, pubs or restaurants.

Johnson skipped the daily press briefing on Saturday, March 21 and took a break with his fiancée Carrie Symonds in the prime minister's second home at Chequers. He returned the following day to host a press conference where he made the same mistake as Harries – standing a metre away from his colleagues while imploring the nation to stay two metres apart.

Inside Downing Street there was a growing realisation Britain was now on a trajectory to be "Italy, at least" in terms of cases and fatalities, according to a source advising the top team. The final straws were the crowds out in the fresh air on Mothering Sunday and the still considerable commuter traffic on Monday morning with half of workers still travelling to their offices. Johnson was forced to finally announce the lockdown that evening.

When the new measures came in on the evening of Monday, March 23, the infections had almost doubled again since the previous Friday and there were an estimated 1.5 million across the UK, according to Imperial and Oxford's new data. Close to 1.2 million of those infections had happened since Johnson resisted calls to lock down on Monday, March 16.

An analysis of the data shows the lockdown swiftly reduced the spread of the virus but was introduced so late that Britain had a higher number of infections than every other major European country at the time they took the same emergency measures. For example, Italy had an estimated 1.2 million at its lockdown on March 10 and Germany, which locked down a day earlier than the UK on March 22, is estimated to have had just 270,000 infections.

Sir David King said the lockdown delay was "grossly negligent". "The fact they were short of PPE, the fact they were short of testing equipment. The response of the government has not just been tardy. It has been totally disrespectful of British lives," he said. "We created an unmanageable situation."

There had been too much delay. The sheer number of people who had been allowed to become infected meant the country was riddled with the virus and the only defence was the workers of the NHS, who had been left critically short of testing and protective equipment.

To date, 36,675 people in Britain have been confirmed as having died from the virus, including more than 300 NHS staff and care workers. Within four days of lockdown the infection had found its way to the very top of government when the prime minister himself tested positive for the coronavirus.

Last night a government spokesperson said: "Our strategy has been designed at all times to protect our NHS and save lives. Our response has ensured that the NHS can provide the best care possible for people who become ill, enabled hospitals to maintain essential services and ensured ongoing support for people ill in the community.

"It has been vital through this global pandemic to make interventions which the public can feasibly adopt in sufficient numbers over long periods. The Government has been very clear that herd immunity has never been our policy or goal."

Insight: Jonathan Calvert, George Arbuthnott, Jonathan Leake and Dipesh Gadher

REVEALED: HOW ELDERLY PAID PRICE OF PROTECTING NHS FROM COVID-19

25 October 2020

ON THE DAY Boris Johnson was admitted to hospital with Covid-19, Vivien Morrison received a phone call from a doctor at East Surrey Hospital in Redhill. Stricken by the virus, her father, Raymond Austin, had taken a decisive turn for the worse. The sprightly grandfather, who still worked as a computer analyst at the age of 82, was not expected to survive the day. His oxygen levels had fallen to 70% rather than the normally healthy levels of at least 94%.

Vivien says she was told by the doctor that her father would not be given intensive care treatment or mechanical ventilation because he "ticked too many boxes" under the guidelines the hospital was using. His age, sex, high blood pressure and diabetes would all have counted against him under the advice circulating at the time. His family fear the hospital was in effect rationing healthcare while infection levels approached a peak. "He was written off," she said.

Unusually, Vivien and her sister were allowed to visit their father one last time, provided they did so at their own risk, wore personal protective equipment (PPE) and scrubbed down afterwards.

What they saw horrified them. Vivien described it as a "death ward" for the elderly in a complaint she later made to the hospital. Inside, were eight elderly men infected with the virus who she describes as "the living dead". As they lay "half-naked in nappies" in stifling heat, it was like a "war scene".

While the sisters sat by their father, the man in the next bed died alone. They found an auxiliary nurse in tears outside the ward. "We said, 'Are you all right? What's the matter?' And she just said: 'They're all going to die and no one is doing anything about it.'"

Their father died later that day without being given the option of intensive care, which the family believes might have saved him. They fear he was a victim of triaging guidelines that prevented many elderly patients from being given the care they would have received before the pandemic's peak.

An Insight investigation can today reveal that thousands more elderly people like Raymond were denied potentially life-saving treatment to stop the health service being overrun – contrary to the claims of ministers and NHS executives.

The distressing and largely untold story of the lockdown weeks is how the NHS was placed in the impossible position of having to cope with an unmanageable deluge of patients. Despite warnings the prime minister had procrastinated for nine days before bringing in the lockdown and during this time the number of infections had rocketed from an estimated 200,000 to 1.5 million.

It meant Britain had more infections than any other European country when they took the same drastic decision, as well as fewer intensive care beds than many. Before the pandemic hit, the UK had just 6.6 intensive care beds per 100,000 people, fewer than Cyprus and Latvia, half the number in Italy and about a fifth of that in Germany, which had 29.2.

As a result, the government, the NHS and many doctors were forced into taking controversial decisions – choosing which lives to save, which patients to treat and who to prioritise – in order to protect hospitals. In particular, they took unprecedented steps to keep large numbers of elderly and frail patients out of hospital and the intensive care wards so as to avoid being overwhelmed.

In effect, they pushed the problem into the community and care homes, where the scale of the resulting national disaster was less noticeable. Downing Street was anxious that British hospitals should not be visibly overrun as they had been in Italy, Spain and China, where patients in the city of Wuhan were photographed dying in corridors.

During this time, a veil of secrecy was placed over the hospitals, and the government would emerge from the crisis of those early spring months to claim complete success in achieving its objective. "Throughout this crisis, we have protected our NHS, ensuring that everybody who needed care was able to get that care," the health secretary, Matt Hancock, proudly declared in an email to Conservative supporters in July. "At no point was the NHS overwhelmed, and everyone who needed care had access to that care."

But could this claim be true?

They ran out of body bags

As part of a three-month investigation into the government's handling of the crisis during the lockdown weeks, we have spoken to more than 50 witnesses, including doctors, paramedics, bereaved families, charities, care home workers, politicians and advisers to the government. Our inquiries have unearthed new documents and previously unpublished hospital data. Together, they show what happened while most of the country stayed at home.

There were 59,000 extra deaths in England and Wales compared with previous years during the first six months of the pandemic. This consisted of 26,000 excess fatalities in care homes and another 25,000 in people's own homes.

Surprisingly, only 8,000 of those excess deaths were in hospital, even though 30,000 people died from the virus on the wards. This shows that many deaths that would normally have taken place in hospital had been displaced to people's homes and the care homes.

This huge increase of deaths outside hospitals was a mixture of coronavirus cases – many of whom were never tested – and people who were not given treatment for other conditions that they would have had access to in normal times. Ambulance and admission teams were told to be more selective about who should be taken into hospital, with specific instructions to exclude many elderly people. GPs were asked to identify frail patients who were to be left at home even if they were seriously ill with the virus.

In some regions, care home residents dying of Covid-19 were denied access to hospitals even though their families believed their lives could have been saved.

The sheer scale of the resulting body count that piled up in the nation's homes meant special body retrieval teams had to be formed by police and fire brigade to transfer corpses from houses to mortuaries. Some are said to have run out of body bags.

NHS data obtained by Insight shows that access to potentially life-saving intensive care was not made available to the vast majority of people who died with the virus. Only one in six Covid-19 patients who lost their lives in hospital during the first wave had been given intensive care. This suggests that of the 47,000 people who died of the virus inside and outside hospitals, just an estimated 5,000 – one in nine – received the highest critical care, despite the government claiming that intensive care capacity was never breached.

The young were favoured over the old, who made up the vast majority of the deaths. The chief medical officer, Chris Whitty, commissioned an age-based frailty score system that was circulated for consultation in the health service as a potential "triage tool" at the beginning of the crisis. It was never formally published.

It gave instructions that in the event of the NHS being overwhelmed, patients over the age of 80 should be denied access to intensive care and in effect excluded many people over the age of 60 from life-saving treatment. Testimony by doctors has confirmed that the tool was used by medics to prevent elderly patients blocking up intensive care beds.

Indeed, new data from the NHS shows that the proportion of over-60s with the coronavirus who received intensive care halved between the middle of March and the end of April as the pressure weighed heavily on hospitals during the height of the pandemic. The proportion of the elderly being admitted then increased again when the pressure was lifted off the NHS as Covid-19 cases fell in the summer months.

The government's failure to properly equip the NHS with adequate PPE or testing equipment made an impossible job even harder. Not only were doctors and nurses overrun with patients, but they themselves were exposed to the virus, and the lack of testing meant that thousands had to spend time isolating at home, as they did not know if they were infected. It left hospitals dangerously understaffed.

All the while, seven Nightingale hospitals – in London, Manchester, Harrogate, Bristol, Birmingham, Exeter and Sunderland – stood mostly empty, suffering from the same shortage of intensive care staff. Those vacant beds would be used by the government to make the claim that the NHS was never overwhelmed.

Dr Rinesh Parmar, chairman of the Doctors' Association UK, which represents frontline NHS medics, said his members had reported that many dying patients had been deprived of access to care they would have normally received at the beginning of the pandemic.

"In reality, the late lockdown allowed far more infections to spread across the country than the NHS had the capacity to cope with," he said. "It left dedicated NHS staff in the invidious position of having to tell many critically unwell patients who needed life-saving treatment that they would not receive that treatment. Those staff will be mentally scarred for a long time as a result. They dedicate their lives to caring for people and never expected to be left in such a situation."

Dr Chaand Nagpaul, chairman of the British Medical Association (BMA), said: "It is manifestly the case that large numbers of patients did not receive the care that they needed, and that's because the health service didn't have the resources. It didn't have the infrastructure to cope during the first peak."

The Doctors' Association and the BMA believe there should have been an independent inquiry into the handling of the pandemic by the government so that its lessons could be applied to the second spike, which is rising fast.

Parmar added: "Without learning from this, the government appears to be repeating the same mistakes by overruling its own scientific and medical advisers, failing to take action and knowingly walking into another disaster in this second wave of the pandemic with its eyes wide open."

'Critical incident' declared

In the week before the lockdown, the pandemic had hit the NHS in London – the first hotspot for the virus – like a hurricane. Despite the warnings about the threat, the government had not provided hospitals with sufficient PPE and its decision to stop contact tracing blindsided the NHS as to where and when the first wave would crash down.

The answer came on Thursday, March 19, when Northwick Park Hospital in Harrow, northwest London, declared a "critical incident". Cases had been building at the hospital since it had been designated as the screening centre for people with Covid symptoms arriving at Heathrow.

But the population in the surrounding boroughs served by the hospital was already badly affected by the contagion. Hundreds came to the hospital seeking treatment for the virus in a fortnight and more than 30 people died in the area from infections that week alone. It meant Northwick Park had more patients than it could cope with and it began shipping them out to the surrounding hospitals.

The incident was a demonstration of how harrowing and time-consuming it would be for NHS staff to treat large numbers of patients. Nursing staff would have to sit holding the hands of dying patients in plastic gloves because their relatives were not allowed onto the wards.

Drastic measures were needed to keep the numbers down in hospitals so that clinicians could deal with the first wave of cases, which had come significantly earlier than the government had anticipated. In the last week of March, the numbers of daily deaths from Covid-19 in the capital hit triple figures and would surge even higher.

The London Ambulance Service had prepared by increasing the threshold for the severity of symptoms that a coronavirus patient would have to typically exhibit before they would be taken to hospital. The service uses a simple chart called News2, which scores each of a patient's vital signs and gives marks on breathing rate, oxygen saturation, temperature, blood pressure, pulse rate and level of consciousness. Abnormal indications are given a higher mark. A score of five is usually sufficient for a patient to be taken to hospital.

However, on March 12 that threshold score was increased to six. "I believe it was changed because of the volume of calls and the capacity issues," one London ambulance paramedic explained. "There were so many people to go to. There was just a period before the lockdown where no one really knew how to deal with it." As a result, many seriously ill people were left in their homes – a policy that was dangerously selective, according to medics.

Dr Jon Cardy, a former clinical director of accident and emergency at West Suffolk Hospital, said that in normal times patients would often be referred for critical care if they scored just five on News2. "If I had a patient with an early warning score of six," he went on, "I'd be saying: 'This person certainly needs hospital treatment.' You can't leave them at home with a cylinder of oxygen and a drip. They could easily deteriorate into multi-organ failure."

Indeed, for many people in the initial deluge of cases, it was too late by the time their condition was deemed so serious that a paramedic team was rushed out to them. Shortness of breath was one of the key criteria for taking people to hospital, but many suffered a condition known as "happy hypoxia". Their oxygen levels would drop dangerously without them noticing.

These people often suffered heart attacks before an ambulance could reach them – and they would not necessarily receive quick treatment because in London the average call out time for an ambulance almost trebled to more than an hour in late March.

An ambulance clinician in south London at the time said: "I saw a lot of Covid deaths in people's homes. Too many. The critical care paramedics on call would just go from cardiac arrest to arrest to arrest. They were seeing five, six, seven of those patients a day, back to back, in their areas."

The guidance was then changed on April 10 to advise that people scoring between three and five should be taken into hospital for assessment. The paramedic said it was changed because too many patients who needed urgent care "were just being left at home".

Deaths from heart problems doubled compared with previous years during those early weeks of lockdown, according to figures from the Office for National Statistics (ONS). An adviser to the Cabinet Office said mortuary staff were shocked by the number of bodies being delivered from homes by special recovery teams that had been set up to handle the surging body count.

"The staff were seriously questioning why so many deaths were taking place at home," the source said. "We did not explain to the public that this was the delicate balancing act – we've reduced the likelihood of getting an ambulance but we've increased the response teams to pick up bodies in people's homes."

Patients cleared out

In the last weeks of March, the hospitals were in the process of clearing out patients at the government's request in readiness for the expected big surge in infections in early April. Sir Simon Stevens, the NHS chief executive, wrote to health trust chief executives outlining plans to free up a third of the UK's 100,000 hospital beds.

His letter said he had been advised by Whitty and the government's scientific advisory group for emergencies (Sage) that the NHS would come under "intense pressure" at the peak of the outbreak.

He asked hospitals to assume that they would need to postpone all non-urgent operations by mid-April or earlier, which would save

15,000 beds, and ordered that 15,000 "medically fit" patients should be ejected from the beds and found places in the community.

The health secretary presented emergency legislation to parliament that week to slash "administrative requirements" to help facilitate the mass discharge.

As hospitals continued to fill, the prime minister held a brainstorming session on the phone with his director of communications, Lee Cain, and key advisers from the general election and the Vote Leave campaign to create a new slogan for its fight against the virus. They came up with the words "Stay at home, save lives", and "protect the NHS" – a key policy from the Conservatives' successful election campaign – was suggested.

The now familiar slogan "Stay at home, protect the NHS, save lives" was launched at a Downing Street press conference by the prime minister the following day, Friday, March 20. Later, it would be heavily criticised because it could be read as a simple instruction telling everyone to keep out of hospital to preserve the NHS.

This was, after all, a key government objective, especially when it came to intensive care beds. That day, a meeting of the government's moral and ethical advisory group (MEAG) was told that Whitty's office had been working with a senior clinicians group to devise ways to "manage increased pressure on staff and resources" caused by Covid-19. He wanted advice on the ethics of selecting who should be given intensive care treatment – and who should not.

It was total anarchy

The evening of March 23 was an extraordinary moment in the nation's history. The prime minister had been at his most headmasterly when he sombrely announced from his antique desk in Downing Street: "From this evening I must give the British people a very simple instruction – you must stay at home."

Two days later, Whitty dialled into an important meeting. He had asked the members of MEAG, who include academics, medics and faith leaders, to consider a controversial document that had been prepared in response to his request for ethical guidance on how to select which patients should be given intensive care in the pandemic.

The document – obtained by Insight – is highly sensitive because it recommended giving a score to patients based on age, frailty and underlying conditions, to see whether they should be selected for critical care. It was intended to be used as a triage tool by doctors, and the initial version under consideration that day effectively advised that many elderly people – who were the vast majority of patients being treated for serious infections of Covid-19 – should not be given intensive care treatment.

Since any total over eight meant a patient would be given ward-based treatment only, the over-80s were automatically excluded from critical care because they were allocated a score of nine points for their age alone. Most people over 75 would also be marked over the eight-point threshold when their age and frailty scores were added together. People from 60 upwards could also be denied critical care if they were frail and had an underlying health condition.

The document – headed "Covid-19 triage score: sum of 3 domains" – had been created the previous weekend by Mark Griffiths, a professor of critical care medicine at Imperial College London, after Whitty's request to MEAG. The professor has declined to discuss the document.

Twenty members of MEAG attended the meeting, with Whitty acting as an observer. Some of those present expressed concern about the use of age as an "isolated indicator of wellbeing" and questioned whether such selection might cause distress to patients and their families. One member later expressed their outrage that the triage tool discriminated against the weak and disabled.

A second version of the document, entitled the "Covid-19 decision support tool", was also drawn up and circulated in the days after the meeting. This raised the score for specific illnesses, but lowered the marks given for age.

It was still effectively advising that anyone over the age of 80 who was not at the peak of health and fitness should be denied access to intensive care – as would anyone over 75 years old who was coping well with an underlying illness. A source says a version of this document with the NHS logo was prepared for ministers for consideration on Saturday, March 28.

According to Professor Jonathan Montgomery, MEAG's co-chairman, the documents were not formally approved or published at the time. He said they were designed only to be used if intensive care capacity had been reached – which the NHS says never happened. But Montgomery acknowledged that they had been distributed to doctors and hospitals as part of the consultation process. "We were aware that some of them were looking at that tool and thinking about how they might use it," he said. "Some of them were using it."

A source involved in drawing up the triage tool from the Intensive Care Society said it was sent to "a wide population of clinicians" from different hospitals, including specialist respiratory doctors dealing with the most seriously ill Covid-19 patients.

Insight's research suggests that two versions of the triage tool were in circulation during the height of the pandemic. In late April, the largest health region in Scotland, NHS Highland, even posted a version of the original document, which excluded 80-year-olds, on the patient information section of its website, with its logo emblazoned on it. The only significant change from the original document was that women scored one less point than men.

This was marked as the document's fifth version, which would be reviewed again in July. NHS Highland now says the publication was "in error" and was not used, but it refuses to explain how it came to be published or which part of the government or health service had passed the document on to it.

Doctors elsewhere in the country have confirmed their hospitals did use the type of age-based system proposed by this government-commissioned triage tool to prevent intensive care beds being filled beyond capacity by the elderly. One doctor said he had been told by other medics the triage tool's age-based criterion was applied at hospitals in Manchester, Liverpool and London at that time.

The doctor described how the tool was followed so carefully at his large Midlands hospital that dozens of intensive care beds were kept empty in readiness for younger, fitter patients. He said almost all patients in his hospital aged over 75 died in the non-critical care wards without emergency treatment during that period.

If they had been given intensive care, they might have survived. In the few cases in other hospitals where patients over 80 with the virus were given intensive care, 38% survived and were discharged alive during the first wave of the outbreak, according to figures from the Intensive Care National Audit and Research Centre.

April the cruellest month

The death toll from the virus was rising steeply to hundreds each day by the last weekend in March. The lockdown had been a success in its first week by swiftly cutting the rate at which the virus was reproducing, but the large numbers of people who had caught the disease before the measures were introduced meant that April would indeed be the cruellest month.

There were two key places where infections remained high. The Sage committee was seriously concerned about how hospitals were becoming breeding grounds for the virus because of the lack of PPE and insufficient testing capacity to check whether staff were infected.

Many staff were unable to work after contracting the virus and others self-isolated needlessly because they or their family had symptoms that might have been ruled out by a test. NHS staff absence rates were a record 6.2%.

The other place where Covid-19 seemed to be thriving was in the place that was supposed to be sorting out such problems: No 10. As the virus swept through the cramped Georgian building, from the prime minister down, it meant that, as April began, there was a vacuum at the top of government. There were also 13,000 people in hospital with the virus and more than 600 dying each day. It was only going to get worse.

The prime minister was isolated in his flat above No 11 Downing Street with food being left at his door but was still nominally in charge. An ashen-looking Hancock, who had also contracted Covid, returned to work on Thursday, April 2, and made the bold claim that there would be 100,000 virus tests a day by the end of the month. He acknowledged that it had been his decision to prioritise giving the tests available to patients rather than NHS staff. Despite the obvious problems caused by the lack of testing, he claimed: "Public Health England can be incredibly proud of the world-beating work they have done so far on testing."

Age discrimination

While it was always inevitable that the virus-stricken prime minister would be given an intensive care bed, others were not so fortunate. The selection of patients for intensive care was already taking place and the methods being used bore a remarkable similarity to the recommendations in the triage tool that MEAG members had discussed a week earlier.

This hidden triaging approach was spotted by two of the country's leading experts in the critical care field: Dr Claire Shovlin, a respiratory consultant at Hammersmith Hospital and professor of clinical medicine at Imperial College London, and her colleague Dr Marcela Vizcaychipi, an intensive care consultant at Chelsea and Westminster Hospital, who lectures in critical care at Imperial.

They were shocked to see that in the first week of April large numbers of people were dying from Covid-19 without being given access to intensive care. They did an analysis of the national figures and set out their concerns in a letter to the Emergency Medicine Journal two weeks later.

Their study showed only a small proportion – less than 10% – of the 3,939 patients who were recorded as having died of Covid-19 by Saturday, April 4, had been given access to intensive care. This was particularly worrying, according to their study, because a separate analysis of those who had survived showed the "crucial importance" of intensive care in providing support for patients "most severely affected by Covid-19".

When they then compared the numbers of deaths from the virus in the normal wards with the number of intensive care beds said to be available in the UK, they came to a disturbing conclusion. Hospitals not only appeared to be withholding intensive care from patients who might benefit from such treatment, but they were actually being too overzealous and doing so more than was necessary given the available capacity.

This led the two experts to question what criteria the clinicians were using to choose which patients should be denied potentially life-saving treatment. In their study they expressed particular concern about "a Covid-19 decision support tool" that had been "circulating in March", noting that it used a number of factors that meant men, the old, the frail and those suffering from underlying illnesses were less likely to be admitted to intensive care. Their description exactly mirrors the tool commissioned by Whitty and submitted to MEAG.

The medics wrote: "Implementation of such tools could prevent healthy, independent individuals from having an opportunity to benefit from AICU [adult intensive care unit] review/admission by protocolised counting of variables that do not predict whether they would personally benefit from AICU care."

Their paper concluded: "Current triage criteria are overly restrictive and [we] suggest review. Covid-19 admissions to critical care should be guided by clinical needs regardless of age." Their study was published on May 4, but the highly selective triaging would continue – and it was already too late for many patients.

Death ward

It was a feature of the darkest weeks of the pandemic that patients would be informed of key life-and-death decisions without their families present, as the wards would be mostly off-limits to visitors because of the risk of infection.

The NHS withdrew into itself as the waves of cases hit the hospitals. It suspended the publication of critical care capacity figures, which meant nobody outside the corridors of power would be able to tell whether hospitals were being overrun, and issued a general ban on information to the media without sign-off from central command.

Pressure was also exerted on NHS staff to prevent public disclosure of problems on the wards. Some trusts were alleged to have trawled staff social media accounts and given dressings-down to medics who mentioned PPE shortages or staff deaths. One surgeon working at a hospital in west London said: "There was an active drive by certain trusts to tell doctors to shut up about it because they didn't want the bad publicity."

So while most of the UK were hunkered down in their homes, few knew what was actually going on inside the hospitals.

When Vivien and her sister were allowed in to see their father Raymond in East Surrey Hospital they found a red "do not enter" sign emblazoned on the door to his ward and a porter guarding the entrance.

Vivien, a 54-year-old charity volunteer, says the scene was heartbreaking: "To see people just dying, all around you . . . It was like something out of a Victorian war scene. With nobody doing anything to help them." Vivien's sister was furious: "My sister said to one of the nurses, 'Why are you allowing them to suffer? You wouldn't treat a dog like this.'"

Their father passed away that day without being taken into intensive care. The family complained to the hospital and received a profusely apologetic letter back written by the health trust's chief nurse, Jane Dickson, on behalf of the chief executive.

"I want you to know how sorry I am that we let your father down," she wrote. "We have been reflecting on our initial response to the Covid-19 pandemic and I regret to say there are aspects of our care that we got wrong." Dickson conceded that "routine tasks of supporting our patients to eat and drink suffered" because staff were "overwhelmed" and there was a shortage of staff with the necessary skills.

The letter stated the clinical team did not think "a more intensive level of care was appropriate given [Raymond's] level of frailty". The hospital said later in a statement that he had not been "denied the care he needed". It added there was sufficient capacity to treat him in intensive care if this had been appropriate.

Raymond's family find it mystifying that more was not done to get oxygen into his body. "There were other options they could have tried that may or may not have worked," said Vivien. "But there was not that option. It was just that he wasn't on the list."

The family also queried why Raymond or the other patients in his ward were not taken to the Nightingale Hospital in London, which was fully equipped with oxygen and ventilators and was supposed to have a capacity of 4,000 beds – but only ever treated 54 people. "To me [the Nightingale] was like a bit of a smokescreen, a facade, because I don't understand why they didn't use it," said Vivien.

The doctors on the ground say the Nightingale was beset by problems from the start. There was a struggle to recruit adequately trained staff from other hospitals that were already overstretched and medics were reluctant to refer patients because of concerns over the unknown standard of care.

One ambulance clinician who was drafted to work at the Nightingale explained that it was mainly set up to treat "younger patients who were on less respiratory support" and fewer underlying illnesses.

"But, actually, those patients were few and far between and they got prioritised on hospital intensive care units anyway because they were more likely to have a good outcome," the clinician said. "And actually people who are a bit older or had more co-morbidities were the ones we were having those more realistic discussions with."

The NHS said it had never been the case that Nightingale hospitals were "mainly equipped" for young patients.

A stark contrast

Data obtained by Insight show that many other patients of Raymond's age were denied access to intensive care at the height of the pandemic. The figures highlight a stark contrast that more than half of those who died of the virus in hospital during the first wave were aged over 80 and yet only 2.5% of patients of this age group were admitted to intensive care.

The data comes from the government's best monitor of what happened in hospitals during the outbreak. It was collected from 65,000 people who were admitted to hospital with the virus up to the end of May and were analysed by the Covid-19 Clinical Information Network (Co-Cin), which reports to the Sage advisory committee.

The figures show that there was a significant decrease in the proportion of people in England and Wales who had received intensive care before they died as the outbreak progressed. In the two middle weeks of March, 21% of those who died of the virus in hospital had been given intensive care treatment.

Yet as the pressure on the NHS increased through April, the proportion of critically ill patients who received intensive care before they died dropped to just 10% by the beginning of May. However, when the hospitals began dealing with far fewer patients in July, the numbers dramatically increased to 29%.

The main reason for this appears to have been that some hospitals were rationing the numbers of patients over the age of 60 who were given access to intensive care. In the middle weeks of March, 13% of that age group admitted to hospital with the virus were given an intensive care bed. By the start of May, that figure had more than halved and was down at 6%. Once again, as the pressure eased on hospitals in July, this increased back to 11%.

The official version given by ministers and the NHS was that critical care beds were still available throughout the height of the outbreak, which was certainly true for some hospitals in areas less badly hit by the virus.

But we have spoken to a number of doctors who paint a harrowing picture of the extreme choices that were being taken on the wards in virus hotspots in central and southeast England that were overrun with patients needing intensive care. At their request, we have protected their identity because they are afraid their NHS management teams could take disciplinary action against them for speaking out.

A senior intensive care doctor who was working in the same southeast region as the East Surrey Hospital where Austin died confirmed that medics were forced to choose between patients who needed intensive care beds contrary to claims that everyone received the care they required. "I don't think the public have ever been aware of just how bad things were and indeed how bad things could get again," she said. "Hospitals had to ration intensive care admittance. I hate to use the word ration, but it's what was happening."

She described how by early April her bosses realised that her hospital's intensive care capacity would quickly be breached if they admitted all the Covid patients who would normally receive that level of care. So they began using the parameters of age, clinical frailty score and co-morbidities to help choose between patients – the same variables recommended by the government-commissioned Covid-19 triage tool.

She said that in normal times those who were very frail would sometimes not be offered invasive ventilation because of their low survival chances and the health complications the procedure can cause. But, she added, what was happening on the Covid wards was very different to that.

"The respiratory physicians and the ward medics were finding this incredibly, incredibly difficult," she said. "They were having to turn people down for critical care and the respiratory physicians were getting upset, because usually we would give those people a shot."

The rationing of intensive care to elderly people who would have been given such treatment if there was more capacity was "widespread" within hospitals at the time, she says. "Colleagues in intensive care reached out to me from across the country for support. They were saying, 'This is going on at my hospital, this is feeling really bad.'"

She and fellow doctors were angered by the government's positive messages about how the NHS was coping. "Every evening at the [televised media] briefing you just couldn't recognise anything that they were saying. It was so discordant with what we were seeing. They'd made it all up. It was completely bizarre – picking certain statistics to highlight how well they were doing versus other countries when actually, particularly in London, it was an absolute car crash."

London bore the initial brunt of the first wave with the highest number of intensive care admissions and the doctors found the extent of the triaging they were forced to do particularly tough. A surgeon working at a hospital in the west of the city said: "A lot of patients who we will in normal times say, 'Okay, we'll admit them to intensive care to give them a chance in the knowledge that they might well not make it' . . . for those patients that chance was not given."

This is confirmed by Professor Christina Pagel, director of University College London's Clinical Operational Research Unit. "There is no doubt that there are people that would have got intensive care at the beginning of March or in June that didn't get it in April because of capacity," she said.

By Wednesday April 8, the numbers of people dying of the coronavirus each day exceeded a thousand and hospitals in other areas were beginning to take drastic measures. A senior doctor working in the intensive care wards of one of the major hospitals in the Midlands has described the difficult decisions that were taken.

"We were limited by the capacity, the number of beds we had and the worry that if we filled our intensive care units up with frail, older patients we'd be unable to take the younger patients," he recalled. "As we got busier, our admission criteria and the people that were being admitted significantly changed to not admitting those that were elderly."

He said his hospital's admission criteria were based on a version of the 'Covid-19 Decision Support Tool' which had been prepared for ministers on March 28. The management of his NHS trust had sent the tool to medics saying "it had been produced to help guide decision-making regarding admissions to critical care," he said.

As a result of applying the scores in the tool, he says, "we got to the point where we almost didn't have anyone in critical care who was over 75. Whereas we had been admitting that age group at the beginning." But the tool was applied so rigorously that the hospital kept dozens of intensive care beds free that were not used for the over-75s.

The elderly, he says, were not even offered non-invasive ventilation as they were left to die in the non-intensive care wards. As a result, 90% of the hospital's deaths from the virus happened on the wards and just 10% received intensive care during the height of the pandemic in April.

He admits that his colleagues would often have to tell a "white lie" to patients suggesting it was in their best interests to be cared for on the wards. "But the reality of the situation was actually it was because we were facing multiple admissions of younger, fitter patients at that point, and we just couldn't accommodate the elderly at the rate that they were coming in."

But he says it was easier to exclude the elderly from intensive care because the fear of infection meant there were no families visiting who might challenge the decision. "Certainly for some of the fitter 75-year-olds we could have taken, we should have taken [into intensive care] and we probably would have done as a result of pressure from families," he said.

This selective approach continued into May and the elderly were only admitted to intensive care again when patient numbers began to drop in the summer.

The clinician blames the prime minister's late lockdown for placing doctors in such an invidious position during those months. "We would have had fewer patients admitted in that short period of time so we would have been able to offer the best in terms of intensive care capacity for each and every single one of them."

Identify the frail

The prime minister was touch and go for a while but was able to return to the ward from intensive care on Thursday, April 9. On that day an extraordinary document was distributed by the Buckinghamshire NHS Trust asking clinicians and GPs to urgently "identify all patients who are frail or in the latter stages of life and score them based on their level of frailty". The purpose was to draw up a list of those who might stay at home when they became seriously ill rather than be taken to hospital.

The document made clear that the move was necessary because intensive care was "expected to far outweigh capacity by several thousand beds over the next few weeks in the southeast region due to Covid-19" and that there was "a limited staff base to look after sick patients in our hospitals". It said the approach it was setting out was being adopted by clinical commissioning groups across England.

The trust was asking doctors to scour the lists it was providing from registers of care home, palliative, frail and over 80-year-old patients and give them a score. If the patients scored seven on the frailty scale – which was anyone dependent on a carer but "not at risk of dying" – the trust recommended that it would be better that they remained at home rather than be taken into hospital.

The document said that the decision should take into account the patient's circumstances and family's wishes when deciding on hospital admission but it was "ultimately a decision for the clinicians involved". In a statement last week the Buckinghamshire trust said every patient who needed hospital treatment was admitted.

However, this type of selection made some doctors feel uneasy. One GP in Sutton, south London, described how his health authority had made "inappropriate" demands on his practice to contact elderly and frail patients to discuss their future care plans in a way that ruled them out for hospital treatment and told him "we're going to be analysing the numbers".

He said the authority had identified dozens of his practice's patients who would be asked to accept "do not resuscitate" orders or agree that they would forgo hospital care in the future. The health authority instructed him to talk to the patients and log their decisions on a centralised system named Coordinate My Care, which ambulance staff could then access to see whether a patient had opted out of hospital care, according to its website.

The doctor said he was "told to get a certain percentage" of patients on the authority's list "signed up". In the end, he only contacted a handful because he felt the conversation was "damaging to patient-doctor relationships" and he says his practice was ticked off by the health authority for not fulfilling their instruction.

Similarly difficult conversations appear to have taken place across the country. The Coordinate My Care system has been in operation for ten years but there was a huge increase of 34,000 patients added to its list in the first six months of this year.

Last week, Dr Dino Pardhanani, GP lead for Sutton on behalf of NHS South West London, defended the approach. He said the discussion of future care plans with patients was "established best practice and the Covid-19 outbreak did not change that".

As the crisis was reaching its height on April 10, Good Friday, NHS England weighed in with its own advice to health authorities setting out the groups of elderly people across the country who it said "should not ordinarily be conveyed to hospital unless authorised by a senior colleague"

The list was very broad. It included all care home residents and patients who had asked not to receive an intravenous drip or to be resuscitated. It effectively suggested that those who had accepted do not resuscitate orders might be denied general hospital care. There was also an exclusion for dementia patients with head injuries and people who had fainted and appeared to have "fully recovered" – but only if they were over the age of 70.

The advice was withdrawn in just four days after there was an angry backlash. Martin Vernon, the NHS's former national clinical director for older people, said it had been a "flagrant breach" of equality laws. "It seemed to suggest that people in care homes and older people generally have less value, and therefore it's quite reasonable to exclude them from the normal pathway of care," he said.

An NHS statement said the advice had been brought in to make sure that ambulance crews consulted with senior control room colleagues about whether patients could be more safely treated outside of hospital.

But there was no doubt that the measures to protect the NHS did have a significant effect. Just 10% of the 4,000 Covid deaths registered in the last week of March and first week of April occurred outside hospitals, according to figures from the ONS. Yet in the fortnight spanning the end of April and beginning of May, some 45% of the 14,000 people who died of the virus had not been taken into hospital.

They were people like Brian Noon, a "fit and strong" 76-year-old RAF veteran, who had tested positive for the virus after attending the A&E department at the Lancaster Royal Infirmary on Good Friday.

The hospital sent Noon home and arrangements were made for him to be checked twice a day by a rapid response nursing team who were already visiting to monitor his terminally ill wife, Desley, 77. On Easter Sunday, his daughter Kerry says she spoke to one of the nurses and was told she needed to talk to him about agreeing to a "do not resuscitate" order. The nurse warned, Kerry says, that an ambulance would refuse to take him to hospital if he did not have such an order in place.

The family initially decided not to discuss the issue with Noon because he had a "fear of death" and it might upset him. The next day the nurse returned to say their father would no longer be sent to hospital if his condition worsened. "It was not a discussion," his eldest daughter Maria said. "We were told there had been a change to the plan and Dad wouldn't be going to hospital."

They were not aware at the time just how sick their father had become. It was only weeks later that they were shown the rapid response team's logs, which recorded a plummet in his oxygen from 91% on Easter Sunday to 79% the following Tuesday.

The guidance from the British Thoracic Society is that oxygen levels below 94% are abnormal and require assessment for urgent treatment. However, his nursing team had repeatedly written "oxygen therapy not required" in his records and despite his desperate condition noted that "no further escalation [of treatment] is intended or considered appropriate".

His oxygen levels had dropped to 44% when he died on Wednesday April 15. His family were left in the dark as to why he was not given the treatment he required. His GP told them that "vulnerability scores" were being used by the health service in the area but it is not known whether Noon was assessed in this way.

If they had applied the Covid-19 Triage Tool seen by Insight, Noon would have been excluded from intensive care because of his age, frailty and diabetes. The family now wants a full explanation.

"Dad did not receive timely and crucial medical care and as a direct result, he died a horrific and excruciatingly painful death," said Maria. "We feel like Dad's been murdered. They were killing off the elderly and the vulnerable. If you're elderly, don't you need more care, don't you need more compassion?"

Dr Shahedal Bari, medical director of University Hospitals of Morecambe Bay NHS Foundation Trust, which was responsible for Noon's care, said it was "working with the family to answer all of their questions".

Ultimately thousands of frail and elderly people across Britain died at home without hospital treatment. Caroline Abrahams, director of the charity Age UK, has accused the government of being too fearful of the "endless news coverage of people dying outside in hospital corridors or banked up in ambulances" and alleges that older people were "considered dispensable" as a result. "The lack of empathy and humanity was chilling. It was ageism laid bare and it had tragic consequences," she said.

Carnage in care homes

The discharge of up to 25,000 hospital patients into care homes during the pandemic's height was becoming a highly controversial move. By Friday, April 17 there had been almost 10,000 excess deaths in the homes and yet the policy of allowing patients to be transferred into them without first being tested for the virus had only ceased the day before.

Indeed hundreds of patients were also being sent to homes even though they had tested positive. In response to a request from the department of health to make more beds free in hospital, councils such as Bradford instructed the care home sector to bear the responsibility for looking after hospital patients for the duration of their illness.

Such policies wreaked havoc in the homes where staff had even less protective equipment than the hospitals and would often spread the virus as they worked shifts in different premises. A third of all care homes declared a coronavirus outbreak, with more than 1,000 homes dealing with positive cases during the peak of infections in April, according to the National Audit Office. During the three months of the first wave of the pandemic, 26,500 more people died in care homes than normal.

Many of those who died were simply refused care. David Crabtree, an owner of two care homes in West Yorkshire, is angry about the way many of his residents were left to die and were denied access to hospital.

A hospital patient had been forcibly discharged back into one of his homes without a test and developed symptoms for Covid-19 at the beginning of April. As the patient's condition deteriorated, the home called an ambulance but a clinician on the end of the phone refused to send one. "We were told there was a restriction on beds and to treat as end of life," Crabtree said. The resident died a few days later in the second week of April.

The single infection had already spread quickly to others in the home. In the days that followed a total of seven more residents died from the virus and not one was admitted to hospital. "I couldn't believe what we were being told," he said, "they were denying people because of age."

But in the middle of the month, the policy of the hospital changed and infected residents were admitted. "The peak dropped so I don't think there was pressure on beds. After April 15 we were able to get people into hospital." He said five infected residents from his home were admitted to hospital at the end of the month and they all survived – raising the question as to whether the other eight would have still been alive if only they had been treated.

An Amnesty International report published this month cited research from the Health Foundation that found the numbers of care home residents admitted to hospital decreased substantially during the pandemic, with 11,800 fewer admissions during March and April in England compared to previous years.

Medics have also described how the care home sector was left to fend for itself. An intensive care doctor in the Midlands said: "I can't remember seeing anybody from a care home who had tested positive who was brought into hospital, not a single one."

Turned away

At Johnson's first prime minister's questions in the Commons on Wednesday, May 6 after his return to work the previous week, he conceded that there had been a tragedy in the care homes. "There is an epidemic going on in care homes, which is something I bitterly regret," he said.

However, there were still very sick people who were being turned away from hospitals. Betty Grove, 78-year-old grandmother from Walthamstow, northeast London fell ill at the end of April with a cough and low oxygen levels and went to Whipps Cross Hospital in east London on the advice of her GP.

The hospital found she had pneumonia and a collapsed lung and, yet, still sent her home four hours later because, according to her daughter Donna, they feared she might become infected with Covid-19. She may well have already had the virus, especially given her symptoms. But Donna says the hospital refused to test her mother because they would have to admit her to do so. It was a Catch-22.

Over the next ten days, Betty, a retired Co-op worker of 25 years, "grew weaker" and began struggling for breath. Donna says she called her local trust's rapid response team repeatedly – sometimes twice a day – asking for help for her mother. "I was insisting that they needed to come out and check her," she said.

Betty died at home of pneumonia on May 15. Her family believes she would have survived if she had been admitted when she first went to hospital. Barts Health NHS Trust has since apologised to the family for Grove's treatment and launched an internal investigation.

Donna said: "I get that they did have enough on their plate. They had Covid . . . but it doesn't mean to say they can push these people aside and just let them go home to die."

Tragic delay

The first wave's death toll left tens of thousands of families across the country in mourning. But for many that sadness has turned to anger as they have learned more about how their loved ones died and question whether they could have been saved with better medical care.

The families who spoke to this newspaper have great sympathy with NHS staff who worked night and day risking their own lives while isolating themselves away from their own families. More than 600 health service staff have themselves died from Covid-19. A mental health crisis is now feared within the NHS because of the emotional strain of being forced into making so many harrowing life and death decisions.

Instead the focus of the relatives has fallen on the government whose late lockdown allowed so many to become infected. More than 2,000 families have formed the Covid-19 Bereaved Families for Justice UK group and in the summer they wrote to the prime minister and the health secretary demanding an immediate statutory inquiry into their handling of the pandemic. They asked to meet Johnson and Hancock to put their questions in person. Both requests have been refused by the government's lawyers.

Elkan Abrahamson, the human rights lawyer representing the group, said the families are driven by a desire to prevent more unnecessary deaths during this second wave of the pandemic. But, he added, the government's legal department had "clearly been told to ferociously fight any attempt to elicit the truth about the first wave".

The government's response

In response to this article, a statement for the Department of Heath said: "From the outset we have done everything possible to protect the public and save lives.

"Patients will always receive the best possible care from the NHS and the claim that intensive care beds were rationed or that patients were prevented from receiving necessary care is false. Doctors make decisions on who will benefit from care every day, as part of normal clinical decision-making.

"Since the beginning of this pandemic we have prioritised testing for health and care workers and continuously supplied PPE to the frontline, delivering over 4.2 billion items to date. We have been doing everything we can to protect care home residents including regular testing and ring-fencing over £1.1 billion to prevent infections within and between care settings."

Professor Stephen Powis, NHS national medical director, also issued a statement saying that the health service "cared for more than 110,000 severely ill hospitalised Covid patients during the first wave of the pandemic" and older patients had "disproportionately received NHS care – over two thirds of our Covid inpatients were aged over 65."

He said: "The NHS repeatedly instructed staff that no patient who could benefit from treatment should be denied it and, thanks to people following Government guidance, even at the height of the pandemic there was no shortage of ventilators and intensive care.

"We know that some patients were reluctant to seek help, which is why right from the start of the pandemic the NHS has urged anyone who is worried about their own symptoms or those of a loved one to come forward for help."

Insight: George Arbuthnott, Jonathan Calvert, Shanti Das, Andrew Gregory and George Greenwood

REVEALED: SEVEN-YEAR CORONAVIRUS TRAIL FROM MINE DEATHS TO A WUHAN LAB

———•———

30 June 2021

IN THE MONSOON season of August 2012 a small team of scientists travelled to southwest China to investigate a new and mysteriously lethal illness. After driving through terraced tea plantations, they reached their destination: an abandoned copper mine where – in white hazmat suits and respirator masks – they ventured into the darkness.

Instantly, they were struck by the stench. Overhead, bats roosted. Underfoot, rats and shrews scurried through thick layers of their droppings. It was a breeding ground for mutated micro-organisms and pathogens deadly to human beings. There was a reason to take extra care. Weeks earlier, six men who had entered the mine had been struck down by an illness that caused an uncontrollable pneumonia. Three of them died.

Today, as deaths from the Covid-19 pandemic exceed half a million and economies totter, the bats' repellent lair has taken on global significance.

Evidence seen by *The Sunday Times* suggests that a virus found in its depths – part of a faecal sample that was frozen and sent to a Chinese laboratory for analysis and storage – is the closest known match to the virus that causes Covid-19.

It came from one of the last droppings collected in the year-long quest, during which the six researchers sent hundreds of samples back to their home city of Wuhan. There, experts on bat viruses were trying to identify the source of the Sars – severe acute respiratory syndrome – pandemic 10 years earlier.

The virus was a huge discovery. It was a "new strain" of a Sars-type coronavirus that, surprisingly, received only a passing mention in an academic paper. The six sick men were not referred to at all.

What happened to the virus in the years between its discovery and the eruption of Covid-19? Why was its existence tucked away in obscure records, and its link to three deaths not mentioned?

Nobody can deny the bravery of the scientists who risked their lives by harvesting the highly infectious virus. But did their courageous detective work lead inadvertently to a global disaster?

ONE: Where flowers bloom all year – the first victims of a new virus

Kunming, the capital of Yunnan province in southwest China, is known as "the city of eternal spring" because its unique climate encourages flowers to bloom all year. The sprawling high-rise buildings of the First Affiliated Hospital tower over the ancient city.

On Tuesday, April 24, 2012, a 45-year-old man with the surname of Guo was admitted to the hospital's intensive care unit suffering from severe pneumonia.

The next day a 42-year-old man with the surname Lv was taken to the hospital with the same life-threatening symptoms, and by Thursday three more cases – Zhou, 63, Liu, 46, and Li, 32 – had joined him in intensive care. A sixth man called Wu, 30, was taken into intensive care the following Wednesday.

All the men were linked. They had been given the task of clearing out piles of bat faeces in an abandoned copper mine in the hills south of the town of Tongguan in the Mojiang region. Some had worked for two weeks before falling ill, and others just a few days.

The illness confounded the doctors. The men had raging fevers of above 39°C, coughs and aching limbs. All but one had severe difficulty in breathing.

After the first two men died, the remaining four underwent a barrage of tests for haemorrhagic fever, dengue fever, Japanese encephalitis and influenza, but they all came back negative. They were also tested for Sars, the outbreak that had erupted in southern China in 2002, but that also proved negative.

The doctors sought the opinion of Professor Zhong Nanshan, a British-educated respiratory specialist and a former president of

China's medical association, who had spearheaded his country's efforts to combat Sars. Aware the men might be suffering from another Sars-related coronavirus, he advised the doctors to test them for antibodies.

The Wuhan Institute of Virology (WIV), a renowned centre of coronavirus expertise, was called in to test the four survivors. These produced a remarkable finding: while none had tested positive for Sars, all four had antibodies against another, unknown, Sars-like coronavirus.

Furthermore, two patients who recovered and went home showed greater levels of antibodies than two still in hospital, one of whom later died.

Researchers in China have been unable to find any news reports of this new Sars-like coronavirus and the three deaths. There appears to have been a media blackout. It is, however, possible to piece together what happened in the Kunming hospital from a master's thesis by a young medic called Li Xu. His supervisor was Professor Qian Chuanyun, who worked in the emergency department that treated the men. Other vital details, including the results of the antibody tests, were found in a PhD paper by a student of the director of the Chinese Centre for Disease Control and Prevention.

Li's thesis was unable to say what exactly killed the three miners, but indicated that the most likely cause was a Sars-like coronavirus from a bat.

"This makes the research of the bats in the mine where the six miners worked and later suffered from severe pneumonia caused by an unknown virus a significant research topic," Li concluded.

That research was already under way – led by the Wuhan virologist who became known as "Bat Woman" – and it adds to the mystery.

TWO: The Bat Woman heralded as a hero in China

For historians of the Chinese Communist Party, Wuhan is where the 72-year-old Mao Tse-tung took a symbolic swim in the Yangtze River in 1966 before launching the Cultural Revolution. For generations born since that disastrous era, the modern industrial city is the crossroads of China's high-speed rail network and was the centre of the Covid-19 pandemic.

For science, however, Wuhan is the centre for research into the coronavirus in bats. Shi Zhengli, nicknamed "Bat Woman" by her colleagues, is heralded as a hero in China and in scientific communities across the world.

But the bats in Yunnan are 1,000 miles from her laboratory, and one of the most extraordinary coincidences of the Covid-19 pandemic is that ground zero happened to be in Wuhan, the world centre for the study and storage of the types of coronavirus the city's own scientists believe caused the outbreak.

Coronaviruses are a group of pathogens that sometimes have the potential to leap species from animals to humans and appear to have a crown – or corona – of spikes when viewed under a microscope.

Before Covid-19, six types of coronavirus were known to infect humans but mostly they caused mild respiratory symptoms such as the common cold.

The first outbreak of Sars – now known as Sars-Cov-1 to distinguish it from Sars-Cov-2, the virus that causes Covid-19 – is one of the deadly exceptions. It emerged in Guangdong, southern China, in November 2002 and infected 8,096 people in 29 countries. It caused severe pneumonia in some and killed 774 people before petering out eight months later.

A race began to find out how a coronavirus had mutated into something so deadly and jumped from animals to humans. The initial prime suspects were masked palm civet cats, a delicacy in some parts of China. But suspicion shifted to bats, which had also been linked to other deadly viruses such as rabies. Perhaps they were the primary source and civets were just intermediaries that they infected.

Shi and her team from the WIV began hunting among bat colonies in caves in southern China in 2004. In 2012 they were in the midst of a five-year research project centred on caves in remote mountains southwest of Kunming when the call came to investigate the incident in the copper mine about 200 miles away.

They were joined by local disease control experts when they descended into the mine that August with protective equipment and bat-catching nets.

Over the next year, the scientists took faecal samples from 276 bats. The samples were stored at minus 80°C in a special solution and dispatched to the Wuhan Institute, where molecular studies and analysis were conducted.

These showed that exactly half the bats carried coronaviruses and several were carrying more than one virus at a time – with the potential to cause a dangerous new mix of pathogens.

The results were reported in a scientific paper entitled "Coexistence of multiple coronaviruses in several bat colonies in an abandoned mineshaft", co-authored by Shi and her fellow scientists in 2016.

Notably, the paper makes no mention of why the study had been carried out: the miners, their pneumonia and the deaths of three of them.

The paper does state, however, that of the 152 genetic sequences of coronavirus found in the six species of bats in the mineshaft, two were of the type that had caused Sars. One is classified as a "new strain" of Sars and labelled RaBtCoV/4991. It was found in a *Rhinolophus affinis*, commonly known as a horseshoe bat. The towering significance of RaBtCoV/4991 would not be fully understood for seven years.

THREE: An ordinary coronavirus - the top security lab at the centre of Wuhan

A new facility was taking shape on the virology institute campus on the west side of the Yangtze in Wuhan. Built by a contractor for the People's Liberation Army under strict secrecy, a top-security laboratory for handling deadly human pathogens was unveiled in 2017.

There were 31 such laboratories in the world at the time but this was China's first. The new lab had been certified by the Chinese authorities as "biosafety level 4", or BSL-4, the highest. But it was raising eyebrows internationally.

Scientists and biosafety experts were concerned that the closed nature of the Chinese state and the emphasis on hierarchy would prove incompatible with running such a dangerous facility.

"Diversity of viewpoint, flat structures where everyone feels free to speak up and openness of information are important," Tim Trevan, a consultant in biosecurity, told the science magazine *Nature* when it opened.

Laboratory leaks are not uncommon. In the past, Ebola and the fatal bat disease Marburg, which kills nine out of 10 people infected, have escaped from BSL-4 laboratories in the US. American health authorities recorded 749 laboratory safety breaches in the six years to 2015. Indeed, several people were infected by Sars in 2004 after an accident at China's National Institute of Virology in Beijing.

The need for a secure facility in Wuhan was obvious, however. Shi and her team had already collected hundreds of samples of the coronavirus – including RaBtCoV/4991 – from their work on bats across Yunnan province, and they were running controversial experiments to find out how they might mutate to become more infectious to humans.

This "gain-of-function" work is described in papers released by the WIV between 2015 and 2017, scientists say. Shi's team combined snippets of different coronaviruses to see if they could be made more transmissible in what they called "virus infectivity experiments".

It was controversial because it had the potential to turn bat coronaviruses into human pathogens capable of causing a pandemic. In 2014 the US government issued a ban on funding any endeavour to make a virus more contagious.

Shi's team argued that gain-of-function work increased its understanding of how an ordinary coronavirus might one day transform into a killer such as Sars.

Others disagreed. "The debate is whether in fact you learn more by helping to develop vaccines or even drugs by replicating a more virulent virus than currently exists, versus not doing that," explained Deenan Pillay, professor of virology at University College London. "And I think the consensus became that the risk was too much."

In January 2018 the US embassy in Beijing took the unusual step of sending scientists with diplomatic status to Wuhan to find out what was going on in the institute's new biosafety laboratories. They met Shi and members of her team.

Details of the diplomats' findings have been found in US diplomatic cables that were leaked to *The Washington Post* and others. "Most importantly," states a cable from January 19, 2018, "the researchers also showed that various Sars-like coronaviruses can interact with ACE2, the human receptor identified for Sars-coronavirus. This finding strongly suggests that Sars-like coronaviruses from bats can be transmitted to humans to cause Sars-like diseases."

The Americans were evidently worried about safety. "During interactions with scientists at the WIV laboratory, they noted the new lab has a serious shortage of appropriately trained technicians and investigators needed to safely operate this high-containment laboratory," the cable added.

Shi was in a conference in Shanghai on Monday December 30, 2019, when she received a call to say there was a new coronavirus on the loose – and it had surfaced in Wuhan, of all places. Since her work had established that such viruses were most likely to originate in south China, she found the news puzzling and extremely worrying. "I wondered if [the local health authority] got it wrong," she told the *Scientific American* magazine in a rare interview this year. "I had never expected this kind of thing to happen in Wuhan, in central China."

One of her initial thoughts, as she prepared to return immediately to analyse the virus, was "Could they [the new coronaviruses] have come from our lab?" It was a natural anxiety, although she said she was later able to dismiss it after examining the lab's records.

FOUR: Patient Zero – when did Covid-19 really start?

The precise point at which Covid-19 erupted in Wuhan may never be known. Various theories have been discredited.

A study by Harvard University claimed the virus may have started in August 2019. It relied on satellite images in which the car parks of selected Wuhan hospitals looked busier. However, the study's detractors have pointed to discrepancies in the evidence.

There is also a theory – propagated by the Chinese media – that the virus may have been introduced into the country by foreign athletes competing in the Military World Games in Wuhan in October 2019. They included the French former world champion pentathlete Élodie Clouvel and the Italian Olympic gold medallist fencer Matteo Tagliariol, who were laid low by fever during the Games.

Few of the athletes have been tested to find out whether they carry antibodies to Covid-19, apart from the Swedish team. Melina Westerberg, a Swedish pentathlete, has revealed that while many of her teammates were sick during the Games, they tested negative. "It was just a coincidence," she said.

It is possible that the virus did start patchily at around the time of the Military World Games. Yu Chuanhua, an epidemiology professor at Wuhan University, has told Chinese media that one man was admitted to hospital on September 29 with Covid-19-like symptoms but it is impossible now to show whether he had the virus because he died. There were two more suspected early carriers of the virus from November 14 and 21 in the city's 47,000-strong database of cases, but they are unconfirmed.

Probably the first confirmed case was a 70-year-old man with Alzheimer's disease, whose family had told researchers from Wuhan Jinyintan Hospital that his symptoms had begun on December 1.

From that point it accelerated to about 60 identifiable cases by December 20, according to government research data reported in the *South China Morning Post*. However, it would not be until a week later that Dr Zhang Jixian, of the Hospital of Integrated Traditional Chinese and Western Medicine in Hubei province, became the first person to report a suspected outbreak to the provincial government.

By then it had already spread as far as Europe, probably via regular flights from Wuhan. The virus may have been in Italy as early as December 18. The country's National Institute of Health reported finding traces of Covid-19 in sewage water collected in Milan and Turin on that date.

It was certainly in France, as a man called Amirouche Hammar was admitted to Jean-Verdier hospital in Paris on December 27. He had unknown respiratory pneumonia and was coughing blood. His samples later revealed Covid-19. His wife, who had a slight cough, worked at a supermarket used by shoppers leaving Charles de Gaulle airport, where there were direct flights from Wuhan.

In Wuhan itself, the first cluster of cases included traders and shoppers at the Huanan seafood market, a maze of small trading stores opening onto crowded alleys in the centre of the city. Despite its name, the market also sold meat and vegetables, and there was an exotic wildlife section in the west of the market.

On January 1 the Huanan market was closed and scientists found 33 coronavirus samples, nearly all in the area of the market where wild animals were sold.

It seemed like an open and shut case. When the results were released later that month, the Chinese state news agency Xinhua reported: "The results suggest that the novel coronavirus outbreak is highly relevant to the trading of wild animals."

However, an early study published in *The Lancet* made clear that of the 41 patients who contracted Covid-19 in Wuhan only 27 had been "exposed" to the market. A third had no connection to the market, including the study's "patient zero", who fell ill on December 1.

Months later George Gao, the director of the Chinese Centre for Disease Control and Prevention, revealed that all the samples taken from animals at the market had tested negative for the virus and that those found had been from sewage or other environmental sources. The Chinese health authorities are now working on the theory that the market helped spread the disease but was not where it originated.

FIVE: Mapping the virus – China warns world of deadly new strain

On December 31, the day Shi returned to the WIV to begin work identifying the new coronavirus, the Chinese authorities decided it was time to tell the world there was potentially a problem.

The World Health Organisation (WHO) was notified that a number of people had been struck down with pneumonia but the cause was not stated. On the same day, the Wuhan health authority put out a bland public statement reporting 27 cases of flu-like infection and urged people to seek medical attention if they fell ill. Neither statement indicated that the new illness could be transmitted between humans or that the likely source was already known: a coronavirus.

By the second week in January, desperate scenes were unfolding at Wuhan hospitals. Hopelessly ill-prepared and ill-equipped staff were forced to make life-and-death calls about who they could treat. Within a few days, the lack of beds, equipment and staff made the decisions for them.

Shi's team managed to identify five cases of the coronavirus from samples taken from patients at Wuhan Jinyintan Hospital using a technique to amplify the virus's genetic material. The samples were sent to another lab, which completed the whole genomic sequence.

However, the sequence would not be passed to the WHO until January 12 and China would not admit there had been human-to-human transmission until January 20, despite sitting on evidence the virus had been passed to medics.

One of Shi's other urgent tasks was to check through her laboratory's records to see if any errors, particularly with disposal of hazardous materials, could have caused a leak from the premises.

She spoke of her relief to discover that the sequences for the new virus were not an exact match with the samples her team had brought back from the bat caves. "That really took a load off my mind," she told the *Scientific American*. "I had not slept a wink for days."

SIX: RaTG13 – from bat cave to lab

She then set about writing a paper describing the new coronavirus to the world for the first time. Published in *Nature* on February 3 and entitled "A pneumonia outbreak associated with a new coronavirus of probable bat origin", the document was groundbreaking.

It set out a full genomic description of the Covid-19 virus and revealed that the WIV had in storage the closest known relative of the virus, which it had taken from a bat. The sample was named RaTG13. According to the paper, it is a 96.2% match to the Covid-19 virus and they share a common lineage distinct from other Sars-type coronaviruses. The paper concludes that this close likeness "provides evidence" that Covid-19 "may have originated in bats".

In other words, RaTG13 was the biggest lead available as to the origin of Covid-19. It was therefore surprising that the paper gave only scant detail about the history of the virus sample, stating merely that it was taken from a *Rhinolophus affinis* bat in Yunnan province in 2013 – hence the "Ra" and the 13.

Inquiries have established, however, that RaTG13 is almost certainly the coronavirus discovered in the abandoned mine in 2013, which had been named RaBtCoV/4991 in the institute's earlier scientific paper. For some reason, Shi and her team appear to have renamed it.

The clearest evidence is in a database of bat viruses published by the Chinese Academy of Sciences – the parent body of the WIV – which lists RaTG13 and the mine sample as the same entity. It says it was discovered on July 24, 2013, as part of a collection of coronaviruses that were described in the 2016 paper on the abandoned mine.

In fact, researchers in India and Austria have compared the partial genome of the mine sample that was published in the 2016 paper and found it is a 100% match with the same sequence for RaTG13. The same partial sequence for the mine sample is a 98.7% match with the Covid-19 virus.

Peter Daszak, a close collaborator with the Wuhan Institute, who has worked with Shi's team hunting down viruses for 15 years, has confirmed to *The Sunday Times* that RaTG13 was the sample found in the mine. He said there was no significance in the renaming. "The conspiracy folks are saying there's something suspicious about the change in name, but the world has changed in six years – the coding system has changed," he said.

He recalled: "It was just one of the 16,000 bats we sampled. It was a faecal sample, we put it in a tube, put it in liquid nitrogen, took it back to the lab. We sequenced a short fragment."

In 2013 the Wuhan team had run the sample through a polymerase chain reaction process to amplify the amount of genetic material so it could be studied, Daszak said. But it did no more work on it until the Covid-19 outbreak because it had not been a close match to Sars.

Other scientists find the initial indifference about a new strain of the coronavirus hard to understand. Nikolai Petrovsky, professor of medicine at Flinders University in Adelaide, South Australia, said it was "simply not credible" that the WIV would have failed to carry out any further analysis on RaBtCoV/4991, especially as it had been linked to the deaths of three miners.

"If you really thought you had a novel virus that had caused an outbreak that killed humans then there is nothing you wouldn't do – given that was their whole reason for being [there] – to get to the bottom of that, even if that meant exhausting the sample and then going back to get more," he said.

"I would expect people to be as clear as they can be about the history of the isolates of their sequencing," said Professor Wendy Barclay, head of Imperial College London's infectious disease department and a member of the UK government's Sage advisory committee. "Most of us would have reported the entire history of the isolate, [back] to where all that came from, at the time."

According to Daszak, the mine sample had been stored in Wuhan for six years. Its scientists "went back to that sample in 2020, in early January or maybe even at the end of last year, I don't know. They tried to get full genome sequencing, which is important to find out the whole diversity of the viral genome."

However, after sequencing the full genome for RaTG13, the lab's sample of the virus disintegrated, he said. "I think they tried to culture it but they were unable to, so that sample, I think, has gone."

In recent weeks, academics are said to have written to *Nature* asking for the WIV to write an erratum clarifying the sample's provenance, but the Chinese lab has maintained a stony silence. A spokesman for *Nature* said: "Concerns relating to this paper have been brought to *Nature*'s attention and are being considered at the moment. We cannot comment further at this time."

SEVEN: Ski holidays – the contagion spread through Europe

The director of the WIV, Wang Yanyi, gave an interview in May in which she described suggestions that Covid-19 might have leaked from the lab as "pure fabrication". She said that the institute managed to sequence the genome of RaTG13 but had not been able to return it to a live virus. "Thus, there is no possibility of us leaking RaTG13," she said.

Shi's interview with the *Scientific American* mentions the discovery of a coronavirus that 96% matches the Covid-19 virus, and has a reference to the miners dying in a cave she investigated. However, the two things are not linked and Shi downplays the significance of the miners' deaths by claiming they succumbed to a fungus.

Experts consulted by this newspaper thought it was significant the men had tested positive for antibodies against Sars. Professor Martin Hibberd, a professor of emerging infectious diseases at the London School of Hygiene & Tropical Medicine, said the antibodies provided "a good clue" that the cause of death was "a proper coronavirus", which "most likely" was Sars-related.

"[RaTG13] is so similar to all the other Sars coronaviruses and so I'd imagine all of that family can cause similar disease, so it makes good sense to me that if the miners caught it they would end up with something that looks similar."

On January 23 Wuhan became the first city in the world to go into lockdown and it would later suffer nearly 4,000 deaths, according to official figures that some people believe are too low.

Britain's first official cases – a Chinese student studying in York and a relative – would not emerge for another week, but it is highly likely the virus was already in the country. There were 901 flights from China to the UK between December 1, when the first known patient fell ill, and January 24. Of those, 23 flights brought thousands of passengers directly from Wuhan to Heathrow.

There is also evidence that Britons were bringing back the virus from Europe. Professor Tim Spector, an epidemiologist at King's College London, who runs the Covid Symptom Study app, says he was contacted by up to 500 people who had returned to the UK between Christmas and January with symptoms.

Many were returning from ski resorts, notably in Austria. In April, 42% of residents in the town of Ischgl were found to have antibodies. "I was interested in the Austrian surveys done in Tyrol because I was quite struck by the stories of all the people that came back from Austrian ski holidays in January, predominantly, feeling ill. It was very convincing because a lot of the stories were the same from different people," he said.

EIGHT: The investigation – how did this happen?

The origin of Covid-19 is one of the most pressing questions facing humanity. Scientists worldwide are trying to understand how it evolved, which could help stop such a crisis happening again.

The suggestion that well-intentioned scientists may have introduced Covid-19 to their own city is vehemently denied by the WIV, and its work on the origin of the virus has become an X-rated topic in China. Its leadership has taken strict control of new studies and information about where the virus may have come from.

A directive from the education ministry's science and technology department in the spring stipulated that such work had to be read by a taskforce directly under the state council – comprising China's president, Xi Jinping, and top ministers – before it can be published.

The secrecy has only increased as the origin of Covid-19 has become politicised as a weapon of aggressive foreign policy. President Donald Trump has described the virus as a "kung flu" and has delighted in claiming it is a Chinese disease. Scientists are dismayed and fear China will retreat further into its shell.

Professor Richard Ebright, of Rutgers University's Waksman Institute of Microbiology in New Jersey, believes there is now less than a 50:50 chance China will allow a transparent investigation into the origin of the pandemic. "That's unfortunate," he said. "And that largely reflects the poor handling of the matter by the US president, who chose to push this in a way that made it unlikely that there could be an open investigation."

Over the next few days, WHO scientists will be allowed to fly into China to begin an investigation into the origins of the virus after two months of negotiations. Many experts such as Daszak believe the source of the virus will be found in a bat in the south of China.

"It didn't emerge in the market, it emerged somewhere else," said Daszak. He said the "best guess right now" is that the virus started within a "cluster" on the Chinese border that includes the area where RaTG13 was found and an area just south of the mineshaft, where another bat pathogen with a 93% likeness to Covid-19 was discovered recently.

As for how the virus travelled to Wuhan, Daszak said: "Fair assumption is that it spilt into animals in southern China and was then shipped in, via infected people, or animals associated with trade, to Wuhan."

But how could such an infectious virus avoid causing a single noticeable outbreak during the 1,000-mile journey from Yunnan to the city?

Hibberd said it was feasible the virus could have travelled in an animal such as a pangolin, which passed it to a human wildlife trader when it was being transported for sale in the market. "Maybe a young guy moves a pangolin and sold it on and may have had a mild infection but didn't have any disease," he said. "It's not impossible for that scenario to happen."

On the other hand, Hibberd believes it is possible the virus could have been brought back by one of the scientists, who were frequent travellers between the caves and Wuhan. "If you imagine these researchers who probably did this are students – who are probably quite young – it's entirely possible that a researcher might become infected through the study of bats."

The WIV was not the only body of scientists from the city delving into virus-laden caves. On December 10 last year a Chinese state media outlet published an extraordinary video lionising the bravery of a researcher called Tian Junhua, who is said to have caught 10,000 bats in studies for Wuhan's disease control centre.

Tian admitted that he knew little about bats when he first started visiting the caves eight years ago, and once had to isolate himself for 14 days after being showered with bat urine while wearing inadequate protection. On occasions bat blood spilt onto his hands but he says he has never been infected.

The young researcher aroused suspicion because one of the offices of the disease control centre is about 300 yards from the Huanan seafood market. He has refused to talk to reporters, but his friends have firmly denied that he was "patient zero".

The final and trickiest question for the WHO inspectors is whether the virus might have escaped from a laboratory in Wuhan. Is it possible, for example, that RaTG13 or a similar virus turned into Covid-19 and then leaked into the population after infecting one of the scientists at the Wuhan Institute?

This seriously divides the experts. The Australian virologist Edward Holmes has estimated that RaTG13 would take up to 50 years to evolve the extra 4% that would make it a 100% match with the Covid-19 virus. Hibberd is slightly less conservative and believes it might take less than 20 years to morph naturally into the virus driving the current pandemic.

But others say such arguments are based on the assumption the virus develops at a constant rate, along lines that have been monitored over the past six months. "That is not a valid assumption," says Ebright. "When a virus changes hosts and adapts to a new host the rate of evolutionary change is much higher. And so it is possible that RaTG13, particularly if it entered humans prior to November 2019, may have undergone adaptation in humans at a rate that would allow it to give rise to Sars-Cov-2. I think that is a distinct possibility."

Ebright believes an even more controversial theory should not be ruled out. "It also, of course, is a distinct possibility that work done in the laboratory on RaTG13 may have resulted in artificial in-laboratory adaptation that erased those three to five decades of evolutionary distance."

It is a view Hibberd does not believe is possible. "Sars-Cov-2 and RaTG13 are not the same virus and I don't think you can easily manipulate one into the other. It seems exceptionally difficult," he said.

Ebright alleges, however, that the type of work required to create Covid-19 from RaTG13 was "identical" to work the laboratory had done in the past. "The very same techniques, the very same experimental strategies using RaTG13 as the starting point, would yield a virus essentially identical to Sars-Cov-2."

The Sunday Times put a series of questions to the WIV. They included why it had failed for months to acknowledge the closest match to the Covid-19 virus was found in a mine where people had died from a coronavirus-like illness. The questions were met with silence.

Insight: George Arbuthnott, Jonathan Calvert and Philip Sherwell

INDEX

B

B-26 185
Bacchini, Michel 286–7, 292, 346
Bahaji, Said 251–2, 255, 256
Bahrain 330–1, 358
Balfour Paul, Hugh 87
Balkans 64, 268
Ball, Sir Joseph 27
Balniel, Lord 140
Bangladesh 333, 334
Bangoura, Aboubacar Bruno 321
Banks, Tony 226
Barclay, Wendy 473
Bari, Shahedal 458
Basnight, Arvin O. 182–4, 187
BBC 35, 386, 399, 415
Beckenbauer, Franz 340, 342
Beckett, Margaret 227–8
Beckham, David 308, 323
Beersheba 208–9
Begley, James 151
Beijing Olympics 2008 357, 359
Beirut 20, 23, 76, 83–8, 240, 250–1
Belgium 58, 282, 286
Belkhayat, Said 316
Bell, Trevor 201–2
Bellingham, Henry 221–2
Ben Gurion, David 210
Benjamin, Daniel 259
Benson, S. H. 41
Bentinck Street, London 31–2
Berger, Sandy 257–8, 261–2
Betts, B. H. 122
Bevin, Ernest 64
Bhamjee, Ismail 287, 292, 307, 344–6
Bhamjee, Naeem 307
Bhatt, Samir 422
Bhutan 333, 334
Bhutto, Murtaza 199
Bhutto, Zulfikar Ali 199
Bin al-Shibh, Ramzi 255
Bin Atash, Tawfiq (Khallad) 269
Bin Hammam, Aisha 305, 306, 309, 321, 324, 334
Bin Hammam, Mohamed 280, 294–8, 299–302, 303–7, 308–24, 325–7, 329–37, 339–43
Bin Laden, Osama 234, 236, 245–6, 250, 252–6, 257–63, 265–9, 271–3, 275–7
Bismarck (battleship) 39
Bitel, Nick 365
BKA (German federal police) 274–5

Black, Cofer 259, 263
Black, J. A. 128–9
Blackpool 226
Blake, George 86
Blake, Heidi 13
Blasiu, Augustin Peter 97–8
Blatter, Sepp 280, 285, 296, 298, 308–9, 312, 331, 340, 344
Blazer, Chuck 300, 345
Bletchley Park 38
Bloody Sunday massacre 1972 11, 133–67
Blunt, Anthony 24, 32, 36
Bodenstein, Ralph 250
Bodine 271–2
Boeing 747s 171, 172, 173, 177, 178
Bogside 136–9, 159, 166–7
Bolsheviks 34
Bolt, Usain 352
Bonn 103–4
Bonner, Mary 148
Boothroyd, Betty 228–9
Bosnia 243
Bosphorus 54–5
Boston 233, 235, 277
Boston Globe Spotlight 9–10
Boston marathon 365, 367
Botswana FA 297, 318
Boulami, Brahim 358
Boyes, Roland 224
Bradford council 459
Bradley, Father Denis 153, 156, 164
Bradley, Lt. N. Michael 145–8
Brazil 296, 322
Brewer, Sam Pope 30
Brexit 405–7, 409–11, 415, 420
Bridge, Michael 145, 146, 147
Brightman, Lord 228
Brisard, Jean-Charles 306
Britain 22, 43, 45, 50–1, 56–9, 63, 68, 75, 87, 114, 120, 123, 196, 200, 206, 210, 214–15, 217–29, 356, 359, 393, 474
see also England; United Kingdom
British Army 134, 136–8, 141–67
SAS 375, 376, 377–84, 385–90, 391–401
British Athletics 363
British Council 78
British Expeditionary Force (BEF) 30–1, 41
British Healthcare Trades Association (BHTA) 413–14
British Medical Association (BMA) 442
British Raj 21, 60

Muggeridge, Malcolm 43, 49, 54
Muinjo, John 297, 318, 320
Munich 256, 368
Munro, Sir Gordon 59
Murdoch empire 227
Muslim Brotherhood 239–40
Muslim fundamentalism 242–3
Muslims 242–3, 248, 250–2, 255, 266–7, 325
Musonye, Nicholas 324
Mutko, Vitaly 341
Myung-bak, Lee 333

N

NACODS 200
Nagasaki 211, 213
Nagbe, Eugene 320
Nagpaul, Chaand 442
Nairobi 254, 258
Namibian FA 318, 320
Nanshan, Zhong 464–5
Napley, David 126, 128
Nash, Alex 151
Nash, William 150–2
Nassau, Bahamas 315
Nasser, Gamal Abdel 238, 240
National Audit Office 459
National Health Service (NHS) 110, 120, 122, 124, 404, 406–7, 411, 413–14, 417–18, 421, 428, 430, 432, 435–7, 439–62
National Institute of Virology, Beijing 467
National Socialists 26
  see also Nazis
National Transportation Safety Board 178
National Union of Mineworkers (NUM) 196–7, 199–203
Nature (magazine) 467, 471, 473
Nazis 22, 25, 93, 119, 255
  see also National Socialists
Negev desert 207, 214
Neil, Andrew 11, 12
Neil, Ed 29, 30
Nepal 333, 334
Nervtag 410, 415, 434
Netherlands 286
New York 234–5, 271–2
New York marathon 365, 367
New Zealand 283, 290–1, 303, 305, 423

Newark 235, 277
Newell, Claire 13
Newlinds, John 111–12
News2 443–4
Newton, Shelby G. 190, 191–2
NHS see National Health Service
NHS England 413, 456
NHS Highland 447
NHS South West London 456
Nicholas, Tai 291
Nigeria 284, 288–9, 292, 307, 314, 320
Nightingale hospitals 417, 441, 451
Nike 367
Nile 237, 284
Nixon, Richard 185
NKVD 50–1
Nolan, Lord 218
Nolan Committee 12
Noon, Brian 457–8
Noon, Desley 457
Noon, Kerry 457
Noon, Maria 457
Noriega, Henry C. 190, 191, 192
Norman, Jesse 364
Normanbrook, Lord 84
Norris, Jim 152
North Atlantic Pact 62
North, Col. Oliver 245, 259, 263
Northern Alliance 253, 260
Northern Ireland Civil Rights Association (NICRA) 138
Northwick Park Hospital 442–3
Nowel, Dr 103, 106
Nsekera, Lydia 313
Nulsen, Ray 98
Nuremberg trials 91, 93

O

Oakes, Gordon 224
O'Brien, Winifred 156
Observer, The (newspaper) 7, 12, 70, 76, 83, 84
Oceania 303–5
Oceania Football Confederation (OFC) 283, 285, 290, 291, 295, 298, 303, 305
O'Donnell, Jimmy 160
O'Donnell, Paddy 153, 156
Office for National Statistics (ONS) 443–4, 457
Ogura, Junji 332, 335–7
O'Kane, John 153, 157, 158

Rus

from

ins

at the 'Th